THE
ROCK OF TRUTH

OR

Spiritualism
The Coming World Religion

BY
ARTHUR FINDLAY

"Truth, whether in or out of fashion, is the measure of Knowledge. Whatever is beside that, however authorised by consent, is nothing but ignorance or something worse."

Locke.

First and Second Impression 1933
Third and Fourth Impression 1934
Fifth and Sixth Impression 1935
Seventh Impression 1936
Eighth Impression 1937
Ninth Impression 1938
Tenth Impression 1939

Out of print during the Second World War because of a shortage of paper.

Eleventh Impression 1948
Twelfth and Thirteenth Impression 1949
Fourteenth and Fifteenth Impression 1955
Sixteenth and Seventeeth Impression 1959
Eighteenth Impression 1964
Nineteenth Impression 1965
Twentieth Impression 1968
Twenty-first Impression 1976
Twenty-second Impression 1986
Twenty-third Impression 1994

This Impression 1999

ISBN 0 902036 07 6

ARTHUR FINDLAY wrote some of the finest books on Spiritualism. Other books in the series are: On the Edge of the Etheric; The Unfolding Universe; The Torch of Knowledge; Where Two Worlds Meet; The Way of Life; Looking Back; The Psychic Stream; The Curse of Ignorance.

THE SPIRITUALISTS' NATIONAL UNION was left the copyright to all of Arthur Findlay's books, with the request to keep the titles in print. The SNU is the largest Spiritualist Church organisation in the UK and owns the Arthur Findlay College at Stansted Hall.

The SNU is based at
Redwoods, Stansted Hall, Stansted, Essex, CM24 8UD.
snu@snu.org.uk
http://www.snu.org.uk

This edition is produced by
SNU PUBLICATIONS

Printed in Great Britain by J. W. Arrowsmith Limited, Bristol

CONTENTS

PART 1

		PAGE
Introduction		V
Foreword		VI
The Author		IX
Chapter	I - The Truth	1
Chapter	II - The Old Religions	9
Chapter	III - The Christian Religion	28
Chapter	IV - What did Jesus really teach?	83
Chapter	V - Another Reformation needed	93
Chapter	VI - Reconstruction	104

PART II.

Chapter	VII - Spiritualism, and what it stands for	115
Chapter	VIII - The Philosophy of Spiritualism - Part I	144
Chapter	IX - The Philosophy of Spiritualism - Part II	158
Chapter	X - The Philosophy of Spiritualism - Part III	169
Chapter	XI - Weighed in the Balance	178
Chapter	XII - Life's Certainties	193
Epilogue		204

INTRODUCTION

The lay person confused by the rapid changes taking place within our western civilisation, and seeking clarification of reason and purpose behnd these events in both the spiritual and temporal sense, is commonly confronted by philosophies based on occurrences that took place thousands of years ago.

It is to those who cannot reconcile pronouncements of ancient times that are delivered mostly as religious rhetoric particularly in the light of present-day science, but who nevertheless understand that there is an underlying spiritual basis to life, that the author of this book, Arthur Findlay, addresses himself.

Over the years since its first imprint in 1934, *The Rock of Truth* has made sense to millions searching for that previously illusive commodity.

A scholarly, yet readable analysis of life's great mysteries, this book has led many to accept Arthur Findlay's own way of life, Spiritualism.

It was to further promote the scientific philosophy that he himself followed, that the author gave his own home, Stansted Hall, to the Spiritualists' National Union, as a seat of learning for the expansion of psychic faculties, the development of mediumship and as a place for spiritual renewal. It is known as the Arthur Findlay College.

This world renowned educational and research establishment stands as a tribute to one man's determination to find and give to others the Rock of Truth.

Eric Hatton, MSNU
President,
Spiritualists' National Union
1994

FOREWORD

THIS book can be considered as a continuation of *On the Edge of the Etheric*, and I hope to amplify the subjects herein considered in a third volume.

We are living in an age when old traditions are crumbling, when, in both politics and religion, beliefs for long held sacred are being carried away by an onrush of new ideas formed as the result of our ever increasing knowledge. Some regard the new era with fear and apprehension and cling firmly to the old traditional way of life and thought, whilst others, braver than the rest, put truth first and follow where it leads.

Our ignorant ancestors accepted what they were told by both king and priest, and pursued their placid lives as do children, but, with the coming of printing and the discovery of how to make paper, thoughts began to pass from one mind to another, to end eventually in the people of most civilised countries learning to read and write.

With education came thinking, and with thinking came wonderment, questions, doubts and fears. The old long-established religious and political order consequently began to crumble away, to be replaced by an intellectual philosophical agnosticism in religion, and a humanitarianism in politics which rightly gave more consideration to the rights of man than had ever been envisaged in the past.

Here we are concerned mostly with the religious aspect, the political side of life being reserved for a later volume. The Rock of Truth consequently envisages a new outlook on religion, and one which can be accepted by every thinking man and woman because it is based on reason, observation and experience.

Supernatural religion is passing away, never to return, the old creeds are too narrow and too cruel, they being based on an outlook on life which greater knowledge and a higher ethical sense have swept away. Natural religion is therefore replacing supernatural religion, and it is about this natural religion that the second part of this book is devoted. The first part reviews the old religions, particularly Christianity in the light of modern knowledge, and from this comparison the reader can better choose between the old and the new.

The old is certainly based on nature's revelation of man's destiny hereafter, but ignorance has burlesqued what is plain and simple, and woven it into mystical doctrines and creeds which are quite unrelated to the facts of life as we now know them. On the other hand, what we have now discovered to be true can be accepted without recourse to faith, and the comfort this new knowledge brings is much more satisfying because it is based on observation and experience.

Under the name of Spiritualism, nature's revelation is the only religion mankind requires, because it scientifically answers those questions which the old orthodox religions attempted but failed to fathom. Moreover, it gives positive proof of our continued existence after death, and, besides this, it provides an incentive to live righteous lives here on earth because we reap just what we sow. Here and now we are making our characters, which will determine whether or not we shall be good and wise inhabitants of the etheric world which will some day be our home.

Spiritualism explains life here and hereafter. It does not fall back on ancient tradition, it does not rest on faith, and all that it asserts can be proved and vouched for here and now. Everyone can prove what it asserts for himself or herself, under conditions to satisfy the most exacting critics. Spiritualism is the coming religion of mankind. It is the basis of all the religions of the past, which have been corrupted by the ignorance of the times in which they were born and through which they passed.

Incorrectly as the founders of the great religions of the past have been reported, owing to the lack of the means we now have of recording our observations, it is still possible, in some instances, to discern through the extraneous matter which has gathered around their teachings, that they were guided by supermundane intelligences working through the psychic power with which they were specially gifted.

As they were unique in their day and generation, much of what they said was misunderstood, misinterpreted and confused, both by their contemporaries and those who handed down their teachings by word of mouth from generation to generation. How much of their teachings which have survived can be accepted as reliable it is difficult to say, but fortunately we need not go back to ancient tradition, because we have today in our midst many who have this same psychic power, through which we can get into contact with the higher minds of the etheric world who are able and willing to guide us throughout our earthly existence.

Those great teachers of the past, of whose doings and sayings we have such a feeble record, were undoubtedly the forerunners of the gospel of Spiritualism, many of the principles of which they taught to an ignorant multitude. Unfortunately their message was passed on in a form which cannot now be accepted or appreciated by intelligent and thoughtful people.

As the result of the development of psychic gifts in recent times, we are acquiring a greater and better understanding of our place in the Universe, our origin and our destiny. The religious teachers of the past doubtless attempted to make this understood but failed, by reason of the ignorance of their times.

In consequence of the growth of knowledge and the achievements of science, we are now able to under-stand better the meaning of the profound truths which are coming through to us from the advanced minds in the etheric world, and these are being correctly recorded. For nearly a century the fundamental principles of Spiritualism have been repeated time and again through mediums in every part of the world.

It is the purpose of this book to help to make this knowledge, possessed by but a few, known throughout the whole world, because only by increased knowledge and wisdom can we rise to higher levels, attain increased happiness, and gain a real understanding of the reason for our existence here, and our destiny hereafter.

ARTHUR FINDLAY.

Stansted Hall, Essex.
May 1933.

THE AUTHOR

ARTHUR FINDLAY was born in Glasgow in 1883 and died in July, 1964. He came of a long line of ancestors who have been famous in Scottish history. He was a direct descendant of Allan Fitz Flaand, whose son Walter became first High Steward of Scotland in 1185, rounded the Stewart family and gave to Scotland its line of Stewart kings. In the fourteenth century one of Arthur Findlay's ancestors so distinguished himself at the Battle of Bannockburn in 1314 that he was given the barony and lordship of Kilmarnock, besides large tracts of land in Ayrshire. The following century, in the reign of James III, one of his ancestors became Lord Chancellor and Regent during the King's minority.

Ayrshire was Arthur Findlay's home county, and there his Presbyterian ancestors, in the seventeenth century, played a prominent part in their opposition to being forced to attend the Episcopalian Church, one being hanged in the Grass Market at Edinburgh in 1688, while another was imprisoned, awaiting the same fate, when William of Orange landed and he was pardoned.

Coming to more settled times we find Findlay's forbears, over the past two hundred years, prominently connected with the commercial and financial life of Glasgow and the west of Scotland. He was a Freeman of his native city and, during the First World War, he was awarded the Order of the British Empire for his organisation work in connection with the British Red Cross Society.

On leaving his preparatory school he went to Fettes College and then to Geneva University. At the age of twenty-five, on the death of his father, he became senior Stockbroking partner of one of the leading Stockbroking and Chartered Accountant firms in Glasgow. After a remarkably successful business career he retired from active business at the age of forty, when he bought the estate of Stansted Hall in Essex, where he and his wife resided until their deaths. As a Magistrate for Essex and Ayrshire, and Chairman of Administrative councils in these counties, he gave much of his time to county work.

Agriculture was one of his many interests, and the improvements he effected in methods of milk production are generally well known.

Arthur Findlay, however, is best known to the public through his books and addresses on History, Spiritualism, Mythology and Religion. When Chairman of Psychic Press Ltd., the proprietors of Psychic News, he took a prominent part in the furtherance of the knowledge of Spiritualism. He spoke in the largest halls of most of our great cities, in several of the capitals of Europe, and his books are read to an ever-increasing degree in almost every country throughout the world. He, moreover, took a prominent part in the Church of Scotland's enquiry into Spiritualism.

To bring light into dark places, to enlarge the vision and increase humanity's intellectual horizon, has been the aim of many pioneers of the past, and, in the realm of history and religion, Arthur Findlay ranks with the other torch bearers who have carried forward the light of knowledge.

PART I.
CHAPTER I.
THE TRUTH.

WHAT is the truth? has ever been the cry of mankind, but always in the past the answer seems to have eluded him. Only since we became intelligent enough to adopt precise methods of investigation, has it been possible to say, with greater certainty what the truth really is. To the ancients it seemed to be the truth that the sun circled round the earth, but we, with our greater knowledge, now know that this apparent motion is caused by the rotation of the earth on its own axis.

We may accept this explanation as a scientific fact, just as we can accept the fact that water always finds its own level. Truth today is therefore very different from truth as understood by the ancients, and the truth, as it appears to us today, may, and probably will, mean something far different to the generations yet unborn. Truth is but a gradual unfolding of some grand panorama, and, though we see now more than those who preceded us, yet it is still but a glimpse of the whole and no more.

Truth is eternal and unchangeable. We who are finite and subject to change can only appreciate it little by little. Truth is always the same, but as we change and advance mentally we can grasp it better. Until we are mentally developed, truth will not be fully comprehended, but, as we evolve, it slowly becomes clearer. Often in ignorance we mistake for truth what is error, and the history of man is the history of error gradually giving place to truth.

The following remarks, made by a well-known man, shortly before his passing on, make my meaning clear. "My life is ended, I have now written the last page. I have put my hand to the last word, my book of life is finished." Life, if we take his words literally, is but a narrow vale between two bleak eternities, one short span between the cradle and the grave. That remark no doubt represented the truth to him, but it does not represent the truth to a Spiritualist, because he knows that this life on earth is only the starting point of our conscious existence, and that our life continues in the etheric world, to which we shall all pass at death.

In the past, life after death was a question of faith, not a question of knowledge, and in this slough of ignorance atheism and agnosticism flourished. When knowledge is lacking faith sustains, but to know is better than to hope and trust.

To Spiritualists death is not a wall but a door; it is not the end of existence but the beginning of life in a new environment; it is not the closing of wings for ever, but the opening of pinions to fly.

Life and death to the orthodox are very different from life and death to Spiritualists, but the former have never had the wonderful opportunity we have been privileged to enjoy of getting in touch with those we knew on earth who, as we now know, continue to live in the etheric world, about and around this physical world of ours. One of the fundamental doctrines of Christianity teaches that the dead are consigned to the grave until the great Resurrection Day, when they will rise again in their physical bodies.[1] No wonder it was considered that the end of life would come at death!

The fact of death was accepted as it appeared. The appearance of death was taken as a reality, but much of what we accept in life is true is directly the opposite to what it really is. Appearances are deceptive and nothing is more so than death. When, therefore, we attend a funeral and hear from the lips of ignorance the orthodox funeral service, we come away with the thought in our mind that never again shall we see our friend, and never again shall we clasp his hand or hear his voice.

Here we are the victims of one of nature's many illusions. Science has proved that everything we see is quite different from what it seems to be. Consequently, when we remember that reality is so different from appearance, it will not seem so absurd to believe that Spiritualists have often spoken to friends who have passed into the etheric world, and not into their graves.

Astonishing as it may seem to be, it is nevertheless true that instances are on record of the so-called dead person returning and conversing with someone on earth, at exactly the same time as his or her physical body was being lowered into the grave. This makes clear that the personality is something apart from the physical body, and that what happens to the latter is only of passing interest to the one who has died.

---

1 This statement may be disputed by some, but nevertheless it is true. According to Cruden, one of the greatest authorities on the Christian Faith and whose *Concordance* is in nearly every clergyman's study:- "The belief in the general resurrection of the dead, which will come to pass at the end of the world, and which will be followed by an immortality, either of happiness or misery, is a principal article of the Christian Religion, and is very expressly taught both in the Old and New Testaments."

Many instances are on record of the dead person being seen as an etheric being at his or her own funeral, which makes absurd the orthodox belief that we sleep in our graves until the Resurrection.

Before the year 1543, everything was taken as it appeared to be. There existed a great mental calm which was then broken by the famous Polish astronomer Copernicus. In that year he announced his belief in the rotation of the planets round the sun. This apparently absurd idea was, however, accepted by another sane and rational man, the astronomer Kepler, one of the founders of modern Astronomy who propounded what are now known as his three laws. His contemporary, Galileo, asked the priests of his time to look through his telescope and see for themselves the wonders of the universe, but they would not do so. The telescope, they said, was the invention of the devil because what it revealed was contrary to the Holy Scriptures. Galileo was consequently made to recant under the threat of imprisonment and torture.

This time in history is known as the Renaissance, or re-birth, when Leonardo da Vinci, that brilliant all-round man of science, engineer, anatomist, botanist, geologist, sculptor, painter, architect and musician, also used his great mind to help in breaking down the arrogance and ignorance of his times. During the same period, noted for its pioneers of modern science, Giordano Bruno, one of the most genial of men, suffered death at the stake in Rome after seven years' imprisonment. He was tried, convicted and imprisoned in a dungeon. He was offered his liberty if he would accept the Scriptures as God-inspired, but he refused.

After seven years' imprisonment he was taken to the place of execution, draped in a robe on which was painted hideous devils. He was chained to the stake, and around his body were piled faggots. The priests then lit them to the glory of God, and in the name of Jesus Christ, and thus perished one of the noblest and grandest men who ever trod this earth. He was the first martyr to science, who met his death without thought of reward or punishment, his only crime being that he helped to lay the foundations of our modern science of Astronomy. He has rightly been called the Morning Star of the Renaissance because he never varied in his opinions, which neither imprisonment nor torture could induce him to modify.

From that time onwards life was somewhat easier for those who put knowledge before faith, but nevertheless many suffered torture, banishment, imprisonment and death. Then came the discoveries made in the 17th century by Sir Isaac Newton, who revealed that the universe is governed by law and not by the caprices of the gods. From this time onwards the supernatural gave place to the natural, to be crowned in 1859 by Charles Darwin's great book Origin of Species. This showed that life on earth was not a spontaneous creation, and that man, instead of having fallen from a higher order, was the outcome of a slow but continuous evolution from a lower to a higher state of existence. From that time onwards Darwin was denounced from every pulpit in Christendom, and the greater the ignorance of the parson the more devout a Christian he was considered to be.

That, however, was not all, because ancient orthodox tradition was to receive still another shattering blow which was to discredit it entirely in the minds of all thinking people. In the year 1848 there occurred mysterious rappings in the presence of two young girls, of the name of Fox, in the little town of Hydesville in New York State, U.S.A. The Fox family consisted of John David Fox, the father, who was a farmer, his wife, and two daughters Margaretta, aged fifteen, and Catherine who was twelve years old. In this quiet little place, in the month of March, rapping noises commenced in their house, to become so insistent and loud that the family could obtain no sleep.

The parents at first thought that the children were responsible, but it was not long before that was disproved. They, like their parents, were just as terrified until Catherine called out "Mr. Splitfoot, do as I do", clapping her hands meantime. For every clap a rap was heard, and then Margaretta said "Count after me", when one rap was given for one, two raps for two, and so on. Then Mrs. Fox asked how many children she had, and she got the right number of raps. Next she asked the age of each child, and this was correctly rapped out.

Soon it became evident that there was an intelligence working behind the raps, and, when this was discovered, the invisible person was told to rap once for A, twice for B and so on down the alphabet. By this means messages began to come through, and the communicator stated that he had been murdered five years previously in the house and his body buried in the cellar. He also gave his name, stating that he was a wandering pedlar and that the previous occupier of the house, named Bell, had murdered him. All this was unknown to the

Fox family at the time but was found afterwards to be true, the remains of the body being discovered in the cellar.

That is how modern Spiritualism began, and, arising from this simple occurrence, we are now receiving profound teaching from some of the inhabitants of the etheric world. Very many thousands have received comfort and consolation through the converse they have had with those who have passed on to this world of finer substance. Nevertheless only a comparatively small proportion of the human race realises that communication between the two worlds has been opened up, and only a small number has been privileged to receive instruction and guidance from those more developed and experienced beings who have accepted the task of educating the people of earth in the things concerning our hereafter.

Just as we are deceived by the apparent movement of the sun, so are we misled when we regard space as being empty. Those of us, who have been in close touch with the etheric world, know that what seems to be empty space is but a different order of substance surrounding and interpenetrating this physical world, and that the universe consists of etheric vibrations. We all know that the sky is not a dome, that the earth goes round the sun, that the earth is not flat and that it revolves on its own axis. Few, however, know that the physical body is not the real body, and that we have an etheric duplicate which holds the physical body together.

Besides this, the etheric body is the real body, and, governed by mind, it continues to exist after: leaving the physical body behind it at death. Only Spiritualists know that the physical world is only a very small part of the real world, that the etheric world forms much the greater part, and that the physical universe is but a fraction of the real universe. Only when we die shall we begin to gain experience of the greater world, and then the physical to us will cease to count.

Everything, as I say, is different from what it appears to be to us physical creatures, but it may well be asked, why is it that we are only now discovering these greater truths of reality? The answer is because our ancestors looked on mediumship as coming from the devil. We are the products of ages of ignorance, and some of the most barbaric ignorance is to be found in what many people of this country still call "The Word of God", commonly known as the Bible. This book is in places the product of savages. It approves and encourages the most barbaric cruelties. In the book of Exodus there is a text "Thou shalt not suffer a witch to live", and this command ruled Europe for fifteen hundred years. In Geneva the Protestants burned 500 witches at the stake within three months. In the diocese of Como in Northern Italy 1,000 were burned in one year, and in Germany it is calculated that over 100,000 suffered this fate, the last being burned in 1739, but the persecution continued in Switzerland until 1780, and in Belgium till a later date.

In England, within two hundred years, 30,000 so-called witches were burned to death, and these witches are what we today call mediums. Witch-burning also took place in what is now called the United States, rounded by the Puritans who could not get liberty in England to worship as they pleased. Such was the bigotry of those days, that whenever the victims obtained power they in turn made others suffer. This text "Thou shalt not suffer a witch to live", was the cause of unimaginable misery and cruelty, and, as mediumship is a hereditary gift, mediums were almost extinguished.

In the year 1576, Bessie Dunlop, of Lyne in Ayrshire, was burnt as a witch because in her presence voices were heard which claimed to be those of people who had passed into the beyond. In other words she was a Direct Voice medium, of whom we have a number in our midst today, one of the most developed being John C. Sloan, to whom much reference is made in my book On the Edge of the Etheric. Many instances similar to the above could be given, but here we can only touch on the subject of witchcraft and pass on.

From the time of the Roman Emperor, Theodosius the Great, the first orthodox Christian ruler, the pages of Christian history are red with the blood of heretics and witches. In the year 381 Theodosius decreed that all who did not accept the Nicene Creed were to be considered as traitors to the State and liquidated, and, from that time onwards to last century, religious history is a tale of imprisonment, banishment and slaughter. Priests everywhere were appointed as informers, to become known as Inquisitors of the Faith. Heretics, Jews and witches, all in fact who did not conform to the orthodox teaching of the Church, were slaughtered, and the roll of victims between the time of Theodosius and last century numbers some 25,000,000 men, women and children. This is a truly astounding figure for an institution which claims to represent God on earth and a kindly humble Jew, called the Prince of Peace, whom it elevated to the second person in the God-head.

From 1712, when the burning of witches ceased in England, mediumship has developed, and is expanding at an increasing ratio everywhere. At its present rate of progress, in consequence of what is revealed through mediumship, the most advanced countries in the world will gradually and imperceptibly accept the basic principles of Spiritualism, and lead the rest of mankind to a more advanced outlook and improved way of life.

This book will attempt to tell the truth as the author sees it, because nothing is greater, nothing is of more importance, than to find truth amid the darkness and errors of life. This book will make a candid examination of the beliefs of the past and the present. It will attempt to make clear some of the past and present errors of humanity, and show how they can be avoided in the future. It will not be a popular book to many, and it will be attributed to the devil by some.

This, however, will be history just repeating itself, because everyone who has propounded something new, or told the unpalatable truth, has been linked with the devil, and, if the orthodox are right, this mythical individual has been responsible for all the knowledge we possess today. On the other hand an earthquake, an eruption, or a tornado is termed an act of God. The orthodox, with the aid of the devil and the Bible, have fought a losing battle throughout the centuries of Christendom. They have been driven from one defence to another, and, now that Spiritualism can give proof positive of a life to come, they fight it tooth and nail, ignoring the fact that Spiritualism is now giving knowledge in place of hope, and facts instead of meaningless words.

Throughout the ages, by countless efforts, the creature we now call man slowly developed a brain, changed four legs into two legs and two arms, and two feet into two hands. Into the darkness of his mind has penetrated some glimmering of reason. Through remembering his mistakes, he has advanced just in proportion as he has mingled his thoughts with his deeds, and put reason first and faith second.

Through countless ages he has groped, struggled, stumbled, and climbed towards the light. In the name of education, mistakes have been given him for instruction instead of facts. In the name of religion he has been given ignorant speculations as a divine revelation. With love he has been taught hatred, and, besides forgiveness, he has been taught revenge.

Nevertheless during the past hundred years Europe has been slowly entering a new age of thought. Almost unnoticed, the intellectual world has changed, and books could be written of what was once considered essential to man's salvation, and is now considered of no importance whatever. For sixteen centuries free speech and free thought in Europe were considered an insult to God. To express an honest opinion was considered a crime against the Almighty.

Today, however, we are living in different times. The orthodox are now looked upon by intelligent people as the ignorant, and those who think for themselves are now respected and honoured. Consequently the religion which will attract the intellectual, the honest and the good, must rest on a foundation of established facts, not on tradition, not on faith, and not on a so-called holy book or holy church.

Our outlook, our philosophy and way of life, must help to make men free, to make them honest, to make them kind and make them good. The religion of the future, by uniting our knowledge of this world with that of the next, by abolishing sects and dethroning false gods, will bring all humanity into one great family. Only Spiritualism can do this, because it is natural religion based on nature's laws. It is the religion of the future, because it rests on truth scientifically established.

CHAPTER II.

THE OLD RELIGIONS.

RELIGION and politics are the two principal factors which govern our lives. The one deals with the future, and the other with the present. We are thinking creatures, and besides the present we give thought to what is to come. Besides our bodily comforts we at times think of what is to happen to us when the hour strikes for us to enter a new environment. Our surroundings here, and what they are to be hereafter, occupy our thoughts almost entirely throughout our earthly life. Just as right thinking in politics and economics means comfort on earth, so right thinking as regards religion gives us an enlarged and correct view respecting our future.

A profound change is coming over the thoughts of all thinking people at the present time. It has been slow in coming, but all important changes in the world's history, which have become permanent, have been slow in appealing to the reason of mankind. The effects of evolution are permanent, but the effects of revolution seldom are. Nature makes all her changes slowly, but surely. Consequently this new orientation will, when absorbed, completely alter our outlook on life from every point of view, and give to mankind an entirely new idea of his origin and destiny. It is disclosing a new world, and in so doing is revealing in truer light the mistakes and failures of the past.

Into the frozen north man has gone. He has conquered the ice, the snow and the bitter cold. Into the jungles of the tropics he has found his way, and he has explored the seven seas; he has charted their depths, he knows every hidden rock. But there is another world to be explored, and this will engage his energies and his thoughts in the years to come, because into that world we shall all pass at death. The more we know about it, the more anxious we shall be to learn how best we can fit ourselves to enable us to enter it, not in ignorance as did our ancestors, but so adequately equipped mentally that we shall be able to accept our new environment calmly and naturally.

It is the purpose of this book, to give to its readers the very valuable information I have received from those who have spoken to me from the etheric world about and around us. Over a period of five years I have spoken on numerous occasions, for hours at a time, with those whom the world calls dead. Hundreds have spoken in their own voices, some of which have been recognised, and they have told me things which at first I found extremely difficult to understand or appreciate. Only as I came to understand better the laws governing the Universe, was I able to comprehend what was told me by those who once lived here on earth.

Those who read this book, who disbelieve in the possibility of communication between the two worlds, those who consider that what goes under the name of Spiritualism is either humbug or fraud, had better lay down this book at once because it is not for them. If they are anxious to learn more, and get to know something of the inter-communication which is progressively increasing between the two worlds, then there are many books full of evidence. on the subject, besides opportunities to acquire the personal experience.

Spiritualism, embracing as it does psychic phenomena, philosophy, biology and history, is a vast subject, one of the most comprehensive of all the sciences because it is all-embracing. It opens up a new world of thought, it enlarges the human outlook, it is closely concerned with the make-up of the human body, it was the cause of every world religion and it has had a profound effect on history down the ages. This being so, it is impossible for one book to encompass all there is to say about it, but in the years to come I shall do my best to cover this new knowledge by a series of books which I intend to publish. Meantime let us give some consideration to some introductory aspects of our subject.

The earlier chapters of this book give a rapid survey of the principal religions of the world, what we might term the old religions, and the later chapters give more detailed attention to the new religion. As the old is the ancestor of the new, so were ancient religions the forerunners of the new religion. The religious instinct in man is based on an inherent belief that this world does not constitute the sum of all his interests and activities. The feeling has generally existed in a vague way that the cemetery is not the end of life. Today, with our greater knowledge, we can understand better the reason for the instinct that life on this earth is only one stage in our career.

We know now that men and women are possessed of an etheric body, which is an exact duplicate of the physical body. We know that this etheric body is governed by mind, and that through the etheric body mind controls the physical body.

During one of my many talks with those who have passed on, I asked particulars about our etheric body, and this was the answer given in a clear, distinct voice, quite apart from the medium, and taken down in shorthand.

"I have a body which is a duplicate of what I had on earth, the same hands, arms, legs, and feet, and they move in the same way as yours do. This etheric body I had on earth interpenetrated the physical body. The etheric is the real body, and an exact duplicate of our earth body. At death we just emerge from our flesh covering and continue our life in the etheric world, functioning by means of the etheric body just as we functioned on earth in the physical body.

"This etheric body is just as substantial to us now as the physical body was to us when we lived on earth. We have the same sensations. When we touch an object we can feel it, when we look at something we can see it. Though our bodies are not material, yet they have form, feature, and expression. We move from place to place as you do, but much more quickly than you can. You bring your mind over here with you. You leave your physical brain on earth. Our mind here acts on our etheric brain, and through it on our etheric body, just as your physical brain acts on your physical body."

As to the reality of the world in which they live, the following is the answer I received in reply to my enquiry.

"Our world is not material but it is real for all that. It is tangible, composed of substance in a much higher state of vibration than the matter matter which makes up your world. We live in a real, tangible world, though the atoms composing it differ from the atoms which make your world. All in the same plane can see and touch the same things. If we look at a field it is a field to all who look at it. Everything is real to us. We can sit down together and enjoy each other's company just as you can on earth. We have books, and we can read them. We have the same feelings as you have. We can have a long walk in the country, and meet a friend whom we have not seen for a long time. We all smell the same aroma of our flowers as you do. We gather the flowers as you do. All is tangible, but in a higher degree of beauty than anything on earth."

Nothing could be clearer or more definite than that. The next world is a very real world to its inhabitants.

We now know that the universe is made up of substance, and what we sense, namely physical sub stance, is only etheric vibrations. In other words, the universe is made up of a gigantic scale of vibrations, which goes under the name of "substance". Physical substance can be seen and handled, but there is also etheric substance, no less real, which in our physical bodies we are unable to sense.

Our physical bodies are a trinity, made up of mind, etheric

substance and physical substance, but, owing to our having this etheric body, and because of the fact that the physical body is but a cloak or a covering, it can be understood how throughout the ages mankind has always had a vague instinct which enabled him to look on the physical world as a state of preparation for the world to come.

Ancient graves reveal the fact that primitive man believed in an after-life, and it is possible that he was aware of beings formed like himself, or ghosts as we call them, coming within his everyday experience. He consequently came to believe in another order of life about him, and with this belief came religion. Religion began with revelation, and the first man or woman to see an apparition gave birth to religion which, from that date onwards, grew into a great tree which threw off many branches. As mind developed he thought and wondered, and his imagination supplied what his reason could not fathom. Realising that there was another order of life about him, he turned to it for an answer to the riddle of existence. In our day we turn to science, or knowledge, to obtain the answer, but in those far-off days religion answered everything.

This being so, religion throughout history, and before history was recorded, has been one of the most powerful influences in moulding the characters and shaping the destinies of humanity. Why did plants grow? Why did the sun and moon move without apparent contact ? Why was there everywhere growth and decay? What caused the wind, the thunder and lightning? To answer these questions he turned to the other order of life for an explanation, until everything that happened which he could not understand was attributed to the gods, these unseen beings whom he saw at times and who made their presence felt in various mysterious ways. What we today call psychic phenomena brought religion into being, and to it can be traced every religious belief.

So a separate god became the cause of each phase of natural phenomena, and, as the gods were generally unseen, he worshipped what he believed was their creation. Consequently to primitive man the sun, the moon and the stars, thunder and lightning received his worship, and to each he gave a divine name. He was a child of nature and nature he worshipped, because to him nature represented the activities of the divine order which he believed controlled his small universe.

It was, therefore, natural that the sun was the first thing to be worshipped, and nothing could be more natural when we consider that it gives us light, warmth, comfort and growth.

For our food and raiment we must thank the sun. Consequently it came about that wonderful stories came to be told about the doings of the sun. How it was born in the morning and died at night. How darkness meant death and light symbolised life. So sun worship developed until it became a complicated system, and one of the foundations of the ritual and doctrine surrounding every world religion.

The fusion of the beliefs which followed from experiencing psychic phenomena, with those of nature worship formed the basis of every religion. Out of psychic phenomena developed Ancestor Worship, the result of clairvoyants and clairaudients seeing and conversing with the so-called dead, and this held the thoughts of mankind everyvhere throughout the inhabited world for many thousands of years. It, in combination with nature worship, was the first and only universal religion, and on this original catholic faith has been built all the world's religious systems and beliefs.

Years passed and mystical minds developed strange and wonderful beliefs, until the time came when what is called theology, or the knowledge of the gods, came into being. Theology represented the science of mankind until the 16th century of our era. It answered all his questions. To the gods everything was referred, and they were made responsible for all natural phenomena. Consequently, when we go back to the time of early man, we find reliance was placed on mediumship, on the one who in trance acted as the medium for the gods to communicate their wishes to mankind. This led to the formation of the priesthood who had charge of the holy place, or holy of holies, where the medium sat to deliver the divine communications. The partnership of priest and medium continued for a time, to break ultimately when the priest discovered that by magic and fraud he could deceive the people and make them think that he, and not the medium, was the oracle of the gods.

With the coming of priestcraft came sacrifice, because the priestly mind imagined that the gods are the etheric duplicate bodies of human beings. Then the people were cannibals, and they thought that the gods were likewise cannibals. So the priests became the purveyors to the gods, the temple the divine eating-house and the altar their table. On this holy table the victim was killed, the gods eating the etheric counterpart and the priests the flesh, the blood, representing life, becoming the sacred drink.

With developing mind came the sense of right and wrong.

Besides requiring the help of the gods to provide the necessities of life, it came to be believed that there were good and bad gods, those who helped and those who hindered mankind. The god who represented the sun was good, but the thunder was the voice of a bad god and the lightning his battleaxe. So the priests told the people that those who were good on earth would go after death to live with the good gods, while those who were evil would spend eternity with the bad gods.

Next developed the idea of original sin, and that death was the curse sent to mankind for his wickedness. Instead of keeping company with the gods in heaven, death was the end of everything because the gods would consume the etheric bodies or otherwise destroy them. Many priestly dogmas arose because the priests wished to keep the people ignorant, and in nearly every religion, as it developed, we find that the thirst for knowledge was regarded as the road to destruction.

Nevertheless there was a loophole, because the priests promised that some day the curse would be lifted. Out of this hope developed the Saviour-god religions, a slow and rather involved theological process. Here the evolution of the saviour-god is too long and complicated a subject to explain, but away back in ancient times we have found the origin of the idea which, thousands of years later, gave rise to the belief in the saviour-gods, to become widespread throughout the world.[1]

So we now arrive at the time when the belief in saviour-gods took the place, in some lands, of Ancestor Worship. To these saviour-gods great praise and adoration were given, and the stories hitherto told of the sun were told of them. Like the sun they, by their death, had conquered the serpent of night and risen again, but the drapings came later because of the fact that they were seen as apparitions after suffering death as a human priestly sacrifice.

On a rare occasion a sacrificed victim was seen after death as an etheric being. This was taken to mean that he had appeased the gods, broken the curse of death, and that the people after death would not be eaten by them when they arrived in their presence in their etheric bodies. The victim had conquered death, broken its curse and opened heaven to mankind. He had reconciled the gods towards frail humanity and,

---

[1] Since *The Rock of Truth* was written the author has published *The Psychic Stream* which traces the evolution of the saviour-god religions up to the time of the Christian era.

The Old Religions

because of this work of mercy through sacrifice, a humble victim was elevated to the rank of a divine being and called the Mediator, Saviour and Redeemer of the human race. Then a mystical religion, made up of doctrines and dogmas, developed, and the story was told of how the gods had told early man that some day a victim would come to earth to break the curse of death and open heaven to all believers.

The greatest honour our early ancestors could give to this glorified Christ, who had gone before to open up the way to heaven for mankind, was to surround him with all the esteem, love and devotion of which they were capable. He had broken the curse of death, removed for believers the taint of sin and established friendly relations between the gods and mankind. Because the sun rose again and caused day to follow night, so the Saviour was imagined as conquering the serpent of night. Consequently we find Krishna, the Hindu Christ, given all the attributes of the sun. The Ganges at his birth thrilled from its source to the sea, and all living things burst into life. He died a victim at night and, like the sun, rose (an etheric being) in the morning.

The halo, which is seen around some mediums, was transformed into a golden orb like the sun, and the saviour-gods were depicted with the sun behind their heads. Likewise they were in other ways associated with nature, being called The True Vine, The Bread of Life, The Fountain of Living Water and so on, but here only this brief outline can be given of the honour and glory which was accorded all the different saviour-gods who were believed to have come from heaven to earth to save mankind. The original human victim became a god-man and one of a trinity of gods in heaven, it being believed that God, like man, was of three parts, physical body, mind and etheric body, each part being deified to form this triune being.

So the Father-god sent his etheric counterpart (called the Holy Spirit) to earth, impregnated a virgin and endowed her child with his mind, or logos (reason) as the Greeks termed it. Thus came the godman to earth to die a victim for the sins of mankind, and rejoin the Father-god in heaven after death. All this irrational mysticism, and much more, was worked up by theological minds over ages of time, and draped round each priestly victim when seen after death, to become sacred tradition and be accepted as a divine revelation. Only by getting back to the original cause can the later effects be understood, because the human victim always came first, to be evolved into the glorified Christ, whereas what is called sacred history always puts the supernatural first and ignores the natural cause.

All the main beliefs associated with these Christs of the past are similar. As they were supposed to have come from heaven to earth, they required divine fathers and virgins for their mothers. Their births, it was believed, were announced by the position of the stars, and celestial music was heard when voices proclaimed that blessing had come on earth. Though Buddha was not a saviour-god, yet, when he was deified, the story was told that the celestial choir sang "This day is born for the good of men Buddha, and to dispel the darkness of ignorance, to give joy and peace to the world" just as we are told it sang something similar at the birth of Jesus. Tyrants, representing the devil, sought to kill some of the god-men when they were young, and the story of Buddha's birth, and what followed, is similar to the story told about Jesus.

Just as at their birth all was gladness, so at their death all was darkness and gloom. At the death of Prometheus the earth shook, and the whole frame of nature became convulsed, the rocks were rent, the graves opened, and the dead came out of them "when the saviour gave up the ghost". He then arose from the dead and ascended into heaven.

The time of the year now called December was allotted to some god-men as the month of their birth, their birthday being what we now call Christmas, when the days commence to lengthen. They were worshipped by wise men who brought them' gifts at their birth. They all met violent deaths, and rose again from the dead. The virgin birth of the Saviour came to be associated with the sun rising out of what seemed a flat earth, born from a single patent. This idea developed further, and mother earth was supposed to be fertilised by the rain and heat from heaven to produce offspring. This contact between heaven and earth came to be applied to the various vegetation gods, in relation to their virgin births. Later the idea came to be associated with god-men, and this belief is to be found in almost every part of the world.

All religions have as a basis for the stories about their gods the same thread running through them-miraculous birth, light coming to the world, then the descent into the darkness of the grave to rise again and give life to the world. Just as they were born when the heat of the sun began to strengthen, so, after death, they rose from the dead when Spring was turning into Summer, and the hitherto dead earth was beginning to give forth life.

The different seasons of the year had a story about the sun which came to be woven into the life of each god-man after his death, and Jesus was no exception. The story of the sun at midsummer, for instance, was that it was the feeder of the earth's multitude from a few loaves and fishes, which symbolised abundant food from a much smaller quantity of seed. Like the sun, the god-man rose steadily in strength and power, and likewise his power waned. Throughout this waxing and waning process, appropriate stories were recorded which were more or less similar for each godman. There was a story about the sun for every month in the year, which became interwoven with the lives of the god-men of the past, including Jesus. In all, the number of god-men known to religious history comes to thirty-four, and of these seventeen became saviours, around whose lives a story was told similar to the one told about Jesus.

Much labour has been expended by eminent scholars in tracing out the connection between all the world's religions and the rites connected with sun worship. The more diligent the search the clearer it becomes that all theological affirmations originated in psychic phenomena, and became symbolised in the apparent annual and daily journey of the sun through the sky. Day was the symbol of good, and night of evil. Each day of the week was dedicated to a planet or a star, which were considered to be gods. The months of the year were dedicated to the moon. Periods of years, centuries and ages were mapped out for incidents in the lives of the solar deities.

For thousands of years the ancients pursued their astronomical studies, during which they elaborated their various systems of solar worship. They mapped out an imaginary zone in the heavens, within which lie the paths of the sun, moon and the principal planets. It was divided into twelve signs, and marked by twelve constellations called the Zodiac. There was a feast to celebrate the entrance of the sun into each sign, and the ancients regarded the various heavenly bodies as visible expressions of divine intelligence. The twelve constellations were considered as the sun's bodyguard, which number was given to the god-man as the number of his disciples.

The heavens above, to the ancients, were a stage divided into various scenes of astronomical time. The heavenly bodies were the actors, and their movements were their performance during each act in a grand heavenly drama, which lasted into eternity, and was witnessed by the inhabitants of this globe, who were the audience, and the earth the auditorium.

Theology, with all its rites and mysteries, is astronomy as it appeared to those of long ago, and ecclesiasticism is the play composed of myths and legends wound round real or imaginary lives, to whom was attributed all that was ascribed to the sun. Consequently everywhere throughout the world the theologians draped round the god-men, who became arisen Christs, the mythical stories attributed to the sun, the planets and the stars.

The god-man was sometimes a healer, the doer of supernormal deeds, and was probably often a powerful medium. Some were reformers and attacked the priests, but whether they did so or not the priests, when they were able, arrested them and made them priestly victims. When, on rare occasions, one or more of the victim's disciples saw their master as an apparition after death, the stage was set for a new religion. The apparition was the seed from which all the theology later developed, because it was believed that the gods had spared this good man who had consequently opened the way to heaven for all believers.

As we have already read, each sacrificed priestly victim who was seen after death was deified, and had attributed to him the stories related about the sun, the name Mary, or something similar, being sometimes given to his virgin mother. This name comes from nature, as it is derived from the root word given to the sea from which sprang all life. The month of May, the beginning of Spring, has a similar origin. The god-man was also born in a stable, or something similar, this being the story associated with the sun in the zodiacal sign "Capricornus".

The Saviour-god's birth was foretold by a dream, and his virgin mother became pregnant because of her contact with a god. He was visited by wise men, who were guided to his birthplace by a star, they having read of his birth in the heavens. Shepherds also came and worshipped him, and angels were seen with him at his birth. He was of royal descent. He was preceded by a kinsman who prepared the way for his teaching. A tyrant sought to kill him and murdered many innocent children of similar age in his attempt, but the young child and his parents escaped to another country.

He astonished the wise men of his time by his learning at an early age, and he was tempted by the devil on a mountain. Miracles were numerous. He was transfigured, cured lepers, turned water into wine, and healed the sick. Ointment was poured on him by a woman, and he washed the feet of the outcasts. He had a triumphal procession riding on an ass. He incurred the anger of the people and had a farewell supper with his disciples, who numbered twelve. Then came the betrayal, the agony and the fear, the trial, the crown of thorns, the scourging and crucifixion, or something similar.

At the god's death the earth shook as the result of a great earthquake, and the dead rose from their graves. He descended into hades, rose again, was first met by sorrowing women and then ascended bodily into heaven, to resume his part with the other two gods making up the Trinity. Some day, it was believed, he would return to judge the earth and receive all believers into glory, he having taken the punishment for their sins.

Such is the story, with just a variation in the number of the details, of the sixteen saviour-gods known to history previous to the birth of Jesus. The beliefs surrounding each are given at considerable length in The Psychic Stream, a book devoted to the different religions which contributed to the beliefs now embraced under: the Christian religion. Here space is only available to refer to these ancient beliefs in a general way, because the purpose of this book is not so much a consideration of ancient beliefs as an attempt to show that natural religion, which Spiritualism is, can appeal to the reason of all mankind, whereas supernatural religion has to rely on faith.

The legends surrounding Krishna (the Sanskrit for Christ), the saviour-god of the Hindus, are in many important respects similar to what I have just written. He became incarnate, so we are told, a thousand years before the birth of Jesus, and the place to which he was taken, when a tyrant king sought to kill him, is exactly the same place, namely Mathura, which, in one of the early gospels, not included in the canon, was given as the place to which Joseph and Mary took Jesus.

His sayings and claims are similar to those of Jesus, and students of his life find 346 striking analogies between his sayings and doings and those of Jesus. Images of ancient Indian gods have been found, and on each there is a figure of a man nailed to a cross, with feet placed one over the other, pierced, the hands pierced, and also the side, and round each head is wound a band which may represent a crown of thorns.

Mithra, another saviour-god, had attributed to him much the same as Krishna and Jesus. He was worshipped in Persia four hundred years before the birth of Jesus. Osiris, the great Egyptian saviour-god, had similar miraculous events ascribed to him, and these legends go back thousands of years. In the ancient *Egyptian Book of the Dead,* one named Petra was the doorkeeper of heaven.

In China similar legends exist as are found in India, Persia, Babylonia and Egypt, and as came to surround Jesus. Many other examples could be given, such as the legends surrounding the lives of Pythagoras, Prometheus, Dionysus, Horus and many others, but it would just end in repetition, because all that is attributed to Jesus was attributed to the god-men who lived before the Christian era.

The Hebrew scriptures contain two different words for the creator, though in the Bible translation both words are translated God, or The Lord. In the first chapter of *Genesis* the Hebrew name for the creator is Elohim, a name which embraced several gods. El was the god of Sumer whence came Abraham from the city of Ur. El was the god of Abraham and a quite distinct creation from Yhvh, translated Jehovah, who was the god of Moses. The meaning of Yhvh is "Rain cloud", and it is probable that this was the name given to the spirit control of Moses. From what we read of Moses it is quite evident that he was a medium, and it is interesting to notice that in these far-off days, just as they do now, the controls of mediums took names associated with nature.

When Moses fled from Egypt to Midian, that vast silent wilderness whence rise five granite peaks, he was evidently, from time to time, entranced and controlled by this strong personality who became in after years the god of the Israelites. He was not the god of Abraham, as is made clear (Exodus iii, 15), but a new personality who controlled his medium Moses, and in the years to come was acknowledged by the children of Israel as their divine lord and ruler. According to *Genesis* the plural god-head, called Elohim, created the earth, not Jehovah, the reason for this being that the creation story came from the ancient Sumerians. Consequently the correct reading of the first verse of the first chapter Of *Genesis* is "In the beginning the gods created the heaven and the earth". Elohim occurs more than two thousand times in the Old Testament and in each case should have been translated "the gods". It was probably a trinitarian name, but after the return of the Jews from captivity in Babylon it was accepted as signifying one god only.

The modes of Egyptian worship were not unlike those instituted by Moses. The Ark of the Covenant of the Hebrews was copied from Egypt, and so also was the Passover, which was a copy of an Egyptian feast. It is thought that the rite of circumcision came from Egypt, and likewise the order of the

Jewish priesthood with its ornaments and dress, which were exact copies of Egyptian models. The Jewish fast days, their celebrations and musical instruments, can also be traced to Egypt.

Both Egypt and Babylon contributed largely to the religion of the Jews, whose scriptures are based on Cabala, or secret doctrines, handed down through the priesthood. Biblical prophecies are based mostly on astrology. The ten commandments, as we now know them, are to be found in the ancient sacred books of China, which are much older than the Bible. The Bible is a storehouse of some of the wisdom, folly and cruelty of the ancients, drawn from all the countries surrounding Judea and from as far away as India and China. Volumes only could contain the noble truths and gracious sentiment, combined with ignorance and cruelty, to be found in the scriptures of the Hindus, Egyptians, Persians and Babylonians. All ancient sacred books contain good and bad, wisdom and folly, and are the product of the times in which they were written.

The devil figures in all religions in one form or another. The one Christianity copied came from Paganism, and to it he was known as Pan the mountain Goat-god, with horns, hoofs and tail. He was god of the mountains, and the legend of Jesus being taken up a high mountain, to be tempted by the devil, is just the story borrowed from the Pagans of Pan taking Jupiter to a mountain-top and offering him the surrounding country.

All the forms, symbols and ceremonies of Christianity were borrowed from sources further back, and can be traced to forms and ceremonies connected with primitive worship. The Hindus, Egyptians, Greeks and Romans used holy water. Baptism is an ancient ceremony, infant baptism coming from the Romans, as did the confessing of sins to the priest.

The rite of the Eucharist, or Holy Communion, came from the Pagans, this sacred ceremony to the saviour-gods Dionysus and Mithra being celebrated on what they called "The Lord's Day" once a week in much the same way as happens today. From the ceremony surrounding Dionysus, the saviour-god of Tarsus, the Apostle Paul, or someone else, probably copied the story of the Last Supper, as told in the eleventh chapter of the first Epistle to the Corinthians from which it was copied by those who manufactured the Gospels.

The Pagans, moreover, had their Eucharistic feasts after the harvest, when the wheat and the wine had been gathered, and they gave thanks to Ceres, the goddess of the fields, and Dionysus, the god of the vine, saying "This is the flesh of the goddess", when eating cakes made from the wheat, and "This is the blood of our God", when drinking the wine. This was the outcome of a more primitive ceremony, when the body of the victim sacrificed was eaten, and the blood drunk. This victim was in some cases human, in others an animal, and the partakers of this celebration considered, just as Christians do today, that the victim received the punishment of their sins and that they were fortified by partaking of his body.

A design, similar to the cross, has been used as the symbol of life for thousands of years, and has been found on the graves of inhabitants of Italy long before the time of the Etruscans. In South America, on the ancient ruined temples, the cross is found and on it a bleeding victim. In Egypt the cross was a symbol of life for thousands of.years, and in an ancient sculpture on the wall of the temple at Luxor the annunciation to the virgin mother is depicted, the Egyptian holy spirit being shown as holding a cross before the face of the virgin mother.

In consequence of this she is pictured in the next scene as having given birth to a god-child, and being surrounded by figures in adoration. The cross was also the symbol of love and sacrifice in Greece, and likewise in India and Tibet. The origin of the cross as a symbol of life came doubtless from ancient fire worship, the fire-god being always represented by two crossed sticks. To the ancients fire represented life, and we can assume that the two crossed sticks became the symbol of life, because fire was produced through the friction caused by their being rubbed together.

The Trinity is not exclusively a Christian belief. In Egypt the Father, Son and Holy Ghost were Osiris, Isis and Horus who were worshipped for many centuries before the Christian era. Mithra was the second person in the Persian trinity, and Brahma, Vishnu and Siva make up the trinity of the Hindu religion of India. Just as we find the belief in a trinity of gods in pre-Christian religions, so likewise we also discover the belief that the saviour-god died for the sins of believers.

The early Jesuians, the followers of Jesus, believed, after he had died a victim to the priests, and had reappeared in his etheric body, that he could be none other than a god because all apparitions in those days were termed gods or messengers of the gods. Only as time went by, and as the result of Paul's teaching, did the belief prevail that Jesus had returned to earth after death because he had broken the curse of death and opened heaven to mankind. The same cause, namely the reappearance after death of a priestly sacrificed victim, had brought similar beliefs into being and produced earlier saviour-god religions.

Consequently we find that what Christians call the atonement was a wide-spread pre-Christian belief, and this was now copied and made part of what came to be called the Christian religion. The atonement was incorporated into this new religion, and made to refer to Jesus after Paul had elevated him to be the heavenly Christ. Then, and only then, did Christianity come into being, but it is clear from what Paul wrote to the Galatians that the disciples of Jesus did not accept Paul's doctrines. This being so, they should be known as Jesuians and not Christians. Jesus lived and died a Jew and never founded a new religion. But for the enthusiasm of Paul his disciples would have remained Jews. Moreover the organisation that became the Christian Church was a slow development extending over several centuries.

Sixteen pre-Christian sacrificed saviour-gods were all supposed to have died for the sins of the world[1] Their reappearance after sacrifice regularly brought about the same beliefs, namely that they had broken the curse of death and opened heaven to mankind. Consequently, through their suffering, salvation had been secured and each became known as Saviour, Mediator and Redeemer. When the belief became general that Jesus was a saviour-god he was given the title of Christ, a similar title being given to the previous saviour-gods.

It comes from the Greek, meaning the anointed one, because the victims before they were sacrificed, and offered up as burnt offerings, were covered with oil to make them more tasty dishes for the priests and worshippers to eat, it being then the prevailing belief that by eating the sacrificed body the virtue of the victim would be transferred to the communicant.

When these sacrificed victims came to be looked upon as god-men on earth and christs in heaven, they could not have been born as other men were. Consequently to each was attached a story of a god impregnating their mothers, which tale was likewise copied by the Christians and made to relate

---

[1] The following are the sixteen slain saviour-gods believed by their followers to have lived and died for the sins of the world, together with their countries of origin and approximate dates: Osiris (Egypt), 1700 B.C.; Bel (Babylon), 1200 B.C.; Atys (Phrygia), 1170 B.C.; Thammuz (Syria), 1160 B.C.; Dionysus (Greece), 1100 B.C., Krishna (India), 1000 B.C.; Hesus (Europe), 834 B.C.; Indra (Thibet), 725 B.C.; Bali (Asia), 725 B.C.; Iao (Nepaul), 622 B.C.; Alcestis (Pherae), 600 B.C.; Quexalcote (Mexico), 587 B.C.; Wittoba (Travancore), 552 B.C.; Prometheus (Greece), 547 B.C.; Quirinus (Rome), 506 B.C.; ,Mithra (Persia), 400 B.C.

to Jesus. It was at least a century after the birth of Jesus that the virgin birth was thought of. There is no mention of it in the Epistles, or any of the other earliest Christian writings, in fact his paternal ancestry to David is given in Matthew and Luke.

Both these family trees differ materially and are now looked upon as forgeries, but when they were compiled it was for the purpose of making the Jews believe that Jesus was descended from David. Many years afterwards, when the belief changed from regarding him as an earthly deliverer to that of a spiritual saviour, his mother's name was added, and this made ridiculous the entire record of his lineage because, if Joseph was not his father, why this effort to prove that Joseph was descended from David ?

Moreover, those parts of the Gospels which are the oldest and most nearly related to what was originally written, explicitly say that Joseph was the father of Jesus, and report Jesus as saying that he was not God. This being so, he cannot now be the second person in a trinity of gods, and his mother was not a virgin. Further, we find that the word translated "virgin" means "a young woman" in the original Hebrew. (*Isaiah* vii, 14.)

All religion can be traced back to psychic phenomena, which made early man realise that other beings, to most people invisible, likewise inhabited this planet. They were believed to be the creators, rulers and directors of all the powers of nature. Because they were invisible, stories were told about them in association with what was believed to be their handiwork; everything relating to the earth and the heavens.[1] The invisible gods, and visible nature, thus became intertwined, and gave birth to the ceremonials and beliefs which slowly evolved from this common origin.

Those who have followed the discoveries and researches of Professor Max Mailer, who did so much to raise the study of comparative religion to the rank of a science, can only come to

---

1 Some of the standard works on this subject are Frazer's *Golden Bough*; Grant Allen's *Evolution Of the Idea of God*; Robertson's *Pagan Christs* and *Christianity and Mythology*; Dupuis' *L'Origin de tousles Cultes*; and Bryant's *Eastern Antiquities*. A comprehensive review of Eastern religions will be found in *Asiatic Researches*, a monumental work of sixteen volumes, revised and added to by several authorities, especially by Sir William Jones, one of the most learned of Oriental scholars, and past president of the Asiatic Society. Refer also to *Child's Progress of Religious Ideas*; to Higgins' *Anacalypsis*, and to Gerald Massey's *The Beginnings* and *Ancient Egypt*.

the conclusion that religion is the result of a slow growth, that underlying all religions one finds a similar root, and that this basis is man's instinctive belief that there is a hereafter, and that there is some power in the universe guiding and controlling his destiny. From this root has sprung the tree whose branches have shot out in every direction, and be he Christian or Jew, Buddhist or Mohammedan, man's beliefs can be traced back to this one origin.

Just as languages are the result of the geographical distribution of races, so also are religions, and, in earlier times, religion and language generally went together. Owing to this isolation each race naturally thought that its own religion, and its own political system, were the best. Just as each race thought that other nations were its inferiors, so it thought that those who held different religious beliefs were wrong, and consequently were under the displeasure of its god or gods. No one can read the history of the Hebrew race, as recorded in the Bible, without realising how closely nationalism and religion were associated. The children of Abraham considered that they, and they only, worshipped the one and only true God.

Each religion of the past has been insistent on the fact that it is of divine origin, that its teachings must be observed by its followers, and that its records were sacred and divinely inspired. Incidentally, every one who did not accept its teachings was condemned, but those who were its true followers would be saved in the life to come. If we, therefore, had been born in Turkey we would have been the followers of Mohammed and believed in the inspiration of *The Koran*; that Mohammed visited heaven and talked with the angel Gabriel.

If, being born in Turkey, we had denied these beliefs and held the opinion that Christianity was the true faith, we would have been branded as infidels and, in the old days, put to death. We would have been told that the best and wisest had always believed in The Koran, that it was the best of books, and that to it, and to it alone, Turkey owed her greatness. We would have heard that millions had died, gladdened and helped by the passages from The Koran, and that mourners had been comforted by the thought of the departed partaking of the joys and delights of heaven.

In like manner, where Christianity prevailed, its adherents were instructed by the Church that it was the only true religion, and that only through it could the portals of heaven be entered. All religions have this belief in common, namely that there is only one way to heaven and that the only right way is the one defined by each particular revelation, all the others being of the devil. This is as true today as it was yesterday, and, in all probability, similar beliefs were held before history was ever recorded.

Into the dim and misty past, we peer through ages of history to the time before history began. In that vast cemetery, called the past, most of the early religions of man lie dead and forgotten. From our present-day knowledge we can realise how it was that they began and developed. The etheric beings who produced these ideas live on, but Olympus is silent and Venus is now but a graven image. No longer does Jehovah speak to his chosen people and Mount Sinai's thunders have long since ceased.

Many of the sacred temples of India are in ruins and the ancient religions of Peru and Mexico are forgotten. The Sacred Nile no longer harbours the wandering Isis searching for the dead Osiris. Memnon is no more. From the wild north we never hear the mighty Thor dashing the mountains to pieces, and with him has gone Odin, the giver of life and death. The Druids no longer dominate this fair land of ours, which once was theirs, and with them have gone all the gods brought here with Caesar's conquering legions, whose names are now borne by the planets of our solar system.

Religions, Like nations, have their periods of birth, growth and decay. What is orthodox in one age is rejected in contempt by the next. The gods have passed away like those who created them. Those worshipped today will receive no reverence tomorrow. Mithra in Persia, Zeus in Greece, Isis and Osiris in Egypt, and Jove in Rome have all been dethroned and others have been put in their place. What has happened in the past will happen in the future. The Christian religion will be no exception. Already Jehovah has lost the place he once held, and his cruel laws are no longer obeyed.

Many of the extravagant claims once made for Jesus by his zealous devotees have now been abandoned, and today amongst enlightened Christians his simple, unselfish life, his teachings of the fatherhood of God and the brotherhood of man, are put forward with emphasis. Amongst the more enlightened clergy these aspects of his life are stressed to the disregard of others.

Many have now come to a realisation of the fact that man must be his own saviour, and that the death of another cannot save him from his own misdeeds. As a man soweth so shall he reap. Man is his own saviour, and the most intelligent have now ceased to consider themselves miserable wretches, or believe that another has taken their punishment. Far nobler is it to enter the next world without a mortgage hanging like a millstone around one's neck, and have the satisfaction of knowing that the place one occupies has been reached by one's own effort, and not through the suffering and the death of one who lived nearly two thousand years before we were born. Such a belief makes believers intolerant and selfish, it does away with the urge to do better, and is quite contrary to the teachings of Jesus, as will be discovered when we come to Chapter IV.

Zeus   Isis   Osiris.

Mitnra

Jove

CHAPTER III.
THE CHRISTIAN RELIGION.
ITS ORIGIN.

THE Christian religion, it is generally believed, owes its origin to Jesus of Nazareth who, according to tradition, suffered on a cross at Calvary, near Jerusalem, having been sentenced to death by Pontius Pilate who was governor of Judea from A.D. 26 to 36. This belief has had a profound influence on world history. The tradition of the birth, life and death of Jesus is recorded in what is termed the New Testament, the record being in the form of four biographies written at different dates. The authors are unknown, but they go under the names of four men associated with early Christianity. No original document of the Gospels has survived, and no record exists of such documents ever having been seen.

Some authorities hold the view that the origin of Christianity can be traced back to the year 100 B.C., to one called Jesus Barabbas, who was handed over to the people at the time of the Passover as a sacrifice. Against this it must be remembered that Irenaeus, the early Church Father, stated that when he was a boy he met Polycarp, and that Polycarp spoke of his intercourse with John and others who had seen and heard the Lord. This is a chain of evidence going back from Irenaeus, through Polycarp and John, to Jesus, and is well worth remembering.

Without doubt the central figure of Christianity is shrouded in uncertainty, the reason being, as Gibbon says, that "The scanty and suspicious materials of ecclesiastical history seldom enable us to dispel the dark cloud that hangs over the first age of the Church." However, for the purpose of this book, what is natural is assumed to have happened, because, during the last half of the first century on to the year 120, there appeared a dozen independent documents, based solely on tradition, but all alike testifying to a certain Jesus, a Jew of Galilee, who was considered by a small section of his countrymen as the Messiah.

In consequence of this tradition, what are known as epistles, or letters, were written, and to these at a later date names were given. These are also included in what is called the New Testament. The books of the New Testament are not historical documents, no one knows who wrote them, nobody has reported ever having seen the original documents, and nobody knows when they were written. Various estimates have been made as to the dates of their origin, but nothing is known for certain.

One thing, however, is certain, that a profound mental change occurred in Palestine nineteen hundred years ago, and an acorn which was sown those many years ago has today spread into an oak tree of great magnitude. What did Jesus really teach? is the great question. We know what the Church says he taught, but the great difficulty is to know what he really did teach, as there is every reason to doubt that what the Church says he taught he ever taught at all.

Before, however, I touch on this question, and examine the origin of the records purporting to contain his teaching, let us consider what is now known regarding Christianity from sources apart from the New Testament.

As to the origin of Christianity, Saint Augustine wrote as follows:- "For the thing itself which is now called the Christian religion was known to the ancients, and was not wanting at any time from the beginning of the human race until the time that Christ came in the flesh, from whence the true religion that had existed previously began to be called Christian, and this in our day is the Christian religion, not as having been wanting in former times but as having in later times received the name."

Saint Augustine was one of the early Christian fathers, born in A.D.354, and his remarks will be better understood by the time this section of the chapter is read. This opinion of Saint Augustine was also the opinion of Eusebius, the father of ecclesiastical history, born in Palestine in A.D. 265, who says "Those ancient Therapeutae were Christians and their writings were our gospels and epistles," and "the religion published by Jesus Christ to all nations is neither new nor strange", expressing the view that what is called Christianity was borrowed from the Therapeutae, or Essenes, a view held also by other outstanding men of the early Christian Church.

These Therapeutæ were known under the name of Essenes, or healers, and they had their origin in Egypt. It was there that the Essenes principally dwelt for over two hundred years before the birth of Jesus. Their centre was Alexandria, the world's theological university, where the wisdom of the time was focused in those days, and where there was the greatest library of the ancient world.

These Essenes were taught the art of healing at the University of Alexandria, which had a special medical school, and along with this art of healing certain mystical rites were observed. Their belief in the immortality of the soul came from the influence of Greek philosophy. They were the custodians of the teaching followed for hundreds of years before the birth of Jesus, which came to be incorporated in the New Testament at a much later date. Alexandria should be looked on as the birthplace of Christianity, as there centred all the knowledge of the world's various religions, out of which developed what we today call Christianity.

According to Philo, the famous Jewish author, who lived at the time of Jesus, the Essenes were philosophers and ascetics as well as healers. They divested themselves of all worldly goods, and thus relieved themselves of all worldly cares. Their outlook on life can be summed up in the words "sell all that thou hast and give to the poor", and "lay not up treasures on earth, but rather in heaven where moth and rust do not corrupt". The teachings of Jesus and the teachings of the Essenes are remarkably alike, and the similarity of many of the sayings found in the Gospels to those of the Essenes is striking. The teachings of Jesus with regard to this world and the next can be traced to Essene sources.

What is known as the Sermon on the Mount can be traced to the same sources; in fact the sermon is just a stringing together of quotations from the Psalms, Proverbs and other Jewish literature, all of which were well known to this sect. As a community they were equal as far as worldly goods were concerned, and none exercised authority over the other, all rendering mutual service to the community. The Essenes strove to live lives of purity and holiness, sacrificing this world's pleasures for the happiness of the world to come. They lived a monastic life, which may account for nothing being known of Jesus till the years of his ministry.

At the time of the birth of Jesus the Jewish race was divided into Pharisees, Sadducees and Essenes, and most Jews belonged to one or other of these sects. Jesus constantly rebuked the Scribes and the Pharisees, but never the Essenes, the reason probably being that he was one of them. The Essenes practised what today we call psychic healing, and so did Jesus. This art he taught his disciples, but it was lost to the Christian Church which, preferring dogmas and creeds, has left its master's teaching to others.

Professor Dr. Ginsburg, the well-known Hebrew scholar, who, in 1870, was appointed one of the first members of the committee for the revision of the English Version of the Old Testament, contributed a comprehensive article on the relationship of Essenism to Christianity in *Kitto's Cyclopedia of*

Biblical Literature. Therein he shows that what Jesus is reported to have taught, the Essenes taught before him. The article is too long to quote, and I only refer to it in case some may be sufficiently interested to wish to study this question more deeply than it can be dealt with here. *The Encyclopedia Britannica,* under "The Essenes", also gives a detailed account of this sect, and there are various other authorities on the subject. Gibbon was of the opinion that early Christianity, before it became surrounded by the myths, legends, doctrines and ceremonials of other religions, was just a new name given to the teachings of Essenism.

Whence came this holy brotherhood? They can be traced first from Judea to Egypt and from Egypt to India. In other words the Essenes were in all probability the western offshoot of the followers of Buddha. That Spiritually Enlightened One, Prince Siddhartha Gautama, commonly known as Buddha, was probably the source whence sprang the teachings of the Essenes.

The origin of many of the ethical teachings of Christianity, therefore, do not date from one thousand nine hundred years ago, but from 560 B.C., when Gautama the Buddha was born. He died 480 B.C. Doubtless the teachings of Buddha can be traced back to an even earlier date, and there is little doubt that he was greatly influenced in what he taught by the teachings of Brahmanic philosophy in which he had been nurtured. According to tradition, Buddha (the Enlightened) was not born perfect; neither was Jesus. As Gautama obtained the name Buddha the Enlightened, so Jesus received the name Christ, the Anointed. Both grew to perfection and to wisdom through suffering. Each had a miraculous birth attributed to him. To both at their birth came wise men with rich gifts. Both were hailed at birth as the Saviours of the World, by an aged saint, who used similar words, the only difference being that Buddha was born in the garden of a tavern under a tree, and Jesus was born in a stable.

Just as there is a correspondence as regards the environment and associations surrounding the births, lives and teachings of these great religious teachers, so also there is a corresponding degradation of their teachings after their deaths. What Constantine did for Christianity at the Council of Nicaea in the year A.D. 325, King Asoka did for Buddhism. Both these potentates consolidated the simple teaching of these great men into creeds and dogmas. In both cases the words of the master were changed into doctrines, fixed and definite. Just as after the death of Jesus, differences of opinion sprang up amongst his followers, so, likewise, after the death of Buddha, differences occurred amongst his followers, and councils and conferences followed for the purpose of trying to bring all the followers into harmony.

Again, just as numerous gospels, reporting what Jesus said and did, were written, similarly numerous gospels were written narrating what Buddha did and said. These are known today under the name of Buddhist Suttas. As amongst early Christians there were Gnostics and Arians, so were there similar sects who took different views with regard to Buddha. Some called him divine and others took the view that he was human like themselves. Just as the Arians held the view that Jesus was human. and not God, or part of God, so the Gnostics, with their mystical speculations, paved the way for Jesus becoming accepted as a divine being. Paul's epistles are mostly Gnostic in character.

As Constantine made Christianity through adopting it as a state religion, so also Asoka, adopting it as a state religion, made Buddhism, the only difference being that Asoka was a great and wise ruler and Constantine an unscrupulous tyrant and murderer. He murdered his own wife, son and nephew.

Both religions, on entering under state control, began to entertain worldly aspirations. Then orthodoxy was born. Some four centuries after Buddha's death, about the year 88 B.C., the canon of his life and teaching was compiled just as was the Christian canon in the fourth century of our era. In the year A.D. 397, at the Council of Carthage, it was. decided what writings should be considered as suitable for the canon and what were to be rejected. It was then that the New Testament, more or less as we know it today, came into being. It was written on papyrus, without points and without commas.

Before that time there were no authorised gospels or epistles, and in consequence there was much diversity of opinion. The means adopted by the Council to decide what books were to be included in the New Testament, were so unworthy of an important assemblage that they are unbelievable in the present time. Much discussion centred on which of the numerous gospels were to be included, the two most influential men, Augustine and Jerome, failing to agree. The opinions of Augustine and Jerome carried great weight, but today could only be ridiculed by intelligent people.

The foregoing, however, refers to the adoption of the New Testament by the Church officially. Irenaeus, another Church father, at the end of the second century expressed his opinion that there should be only four gospels and not more, as there were four winds and there were four corners of the earth. By now it was considered that only the four gospels, *The Acts*, the thirteen epistles of Saint Paul, the first epistle of *Saint John*, and the Revelation of Saint John were authoritative. It was not, however, until the year 397, that what was called the canon was adopted officially, and from that date the crystallising process set in, when orthodox Christianity became firmly established.

As in the case of Buddhism, so also in the case of Christianity, after an interval of hundreds of years the fundamentals of the religion were in a state of flux, of doubt, and the subject of constant debate. The virgin birth, and all the other miraculous happenings which in course of time had gathered round the founders of these two religions, came to be focussed and centred in written documents authorised by the Church, under the protection of the State.

Many of the teachings of Buddha and Christ are similar in character, for instance the stories of the Prodigal Son, the Loaves and the Fishes, and the admonition as to the plucking out of the right eye if it gives offence, to mention only a few. Other incidents of a similar nature are common to both records, such as the story of Peter walking on the sea, and the woman at the well.[1] The Jewish Talmud contains parables which recall those of the Marriage Feast, the Labourers in the Vineyard, and the Pearl of Great Price.

What Christians call the Last Supper originated in an Essene custom, observed when taking leave of a brother about to depart on a journey, and this simple story is now surrounded by rites, ceremonies and beliefs taken from Mithraism and the worship of the Greek saviour-god Dionysus.

Many other Christian beliefs are common to both religions, such as justification by faith and purgatory, to mention only two. The Buddhists have their Madonna and Child; their priests, until recently, were celibates, and they have masses for the souls of the dead. The resemblance between the two religions is so obvious that early Catholic missionaries thought

---

1 Max Muller in Science of Religion remarks "Some of the Buddhist legends and parables sound as if taken from the New Testament, though we know that many of them existed before the beginning of the Christian era."

that the Buddhists had copied their religion from Christianity. These parallels could be multiplied considerably further, but let us now consider more closely the origin and development of Christianity itself.

The origin of the name "Christian" was the fact that oil was used in anointing kings and priests. The word "Christ" in Greek means the anointed one, and Jesus was ultimately given the additional name of Christ, the Anointed One, and finally it resolved into Jesus the Christ or Jesus Christ. Prior to this, however, Saul, now called Paul, had retired to Arabia to be imbued with the teachings of the older religions, and he returned to join the disciples full of the idea that Jesus was the longed-for Messiah awaited by the Jews.

The earliest trace we have of an account of the life of Jesus describes him only in human terms. The reconstructed Quelle document, a Greek translation of an earlier Aramaic document, which is quite as early as the early part of *Mark*, and is the farthest back we can get, makes no reference to the miraculous. The birth, death and resurrection legends are not referred to, only his simple teaching. This then is the best evidence we have of the real Jesus, a teacher and reformer, and, but for the idea evolved in the mind of Paul that he was the Messiah, he would never have been regarded as anything else.

Other Jewish messiahs have come and gone, but only those who study Jewish history know anything of them. Paul, however, decided that Jesus was to be made known to the Jews first and then to the Gentiles, and to gain converts amongst the latter his ideas changed to meet their beliefs. First of all he regarded Jesus as the Messiah of the Jews; then the idea developed that he was the world's crucified saviour. This is noticeable as only when Paul comes into contact with the Pagans does he preach the crucified and risen saviour, which, based on their mythology of suffering saviour-gods, they could understand, whereas a Jewish messiah meant nothing to them. The purport of his teachings, as witnessed by letters attributed to him, is that "as in Adam all die, so in Christ shall all be made alive".

The writings attributed to Paul are considered of earlier date than the Gospels, and to all who have studied the ancient religions of Egypt and Greece it becomes clearly noticeable how much the writer was influenced by the beliefs surrounding Osiris and Dionysus. The 15th Chapter of 1st *Corinthians*, on the arguments for the resurrection, might have been written by a worshipper of Osiris, as all the fulminations therein had been current for thousands of years in the land of the Nile. It is just the same old story, but in this case the god is Christ instead of Osiris.

Here we have the foundation of what is now termed the Christian faith, which was added to bit by bit as it absorbed something from each of the old religions. What we know today as the Christian beliefs did not owe their origin to Jesus, but in embryo to Paul, and his enthusiasm for the idea that Jesus was the longed-for Messiah of the Jews, and the Saviour of the human race. But Paul's views carried weight only amongst a certain section. Other leaders came on the scene who had entirely different conceptions as to the meaning of the mission of Jesus, and these opinions varied wherever Christians assembled.

According to the great biblical authority, the Reverend Dr. Davidson, it was not until one hundred and seventy years after the birth of Jesus that the collection of Christian documents assumed any form, and only from that time onwards were some considered of more authority than others. They were uncritically taken from tradition, and gradually elevated to the rank of divine documents, Dr. Davidson describing those early fathers who were responsible for their choice as "credulous and blundering, passionate and one-sided".

Ultimately, as previously said, these documents were formed into a canon at the Council of Carthage in A.D. 397. To the early Christians the Old Testament was the only book which was considered inspired, and the text often quoted, that all Scripture is given by the inspiration of God, referred to the Jewish Book of the Law, and had no reference to the New Testament, which, when this was written, did not exist and was not even thought of. The early Church fathers did not consider the books now contained in the New Testament as sacred documents and clothed with divine authority. To them the Old Testament was the Word of God, and only after the lapse of about two hundred years did certain writings rise in the estimation of Christians, and become considered as equal in value to those of the Old Testament.

We know that the people of Syria in the time of Jesus spoke the Aramaic language, but the earliest documents recording his deeds and sayings are known to have been written in Greek. No one knows when or how the Greek history of those occurrences was recorded. We do know, however, that four hundred years after the events recorded something resembling our present New Testament was collated into what is now called the Latin Vulgate, a translation from the Greek documents into Latin. This was made by Jerome who altered the copies of many previous copies to make them correspond with the Pagan beliefs which were now accepted under the name of Christianity.

The New Testament was brought together into one book at the close of the 4th century, and the two testaments were combined into one book in the 6th century. This book differed considerably from our present Bible, which came into being as late as 1611. Prior to this, numerous conferences were held to decide which books were inspired and which were not, and finality was reached only in the 17th century. Before this date, right back through the Christian era, nearly every book now forming part of the Bible was at one time or another looked upon by the Christian Church as spurious and not divinely inspired.

Were the divines at Westminster inspired to decide which books were inspired, and, if so, why were the priests composing the numerous previous Councils not also inspired? How is it that Christians had to wait until the 17th century before it could be decided what was true and what was not?

When all this is carefully considered, how foolish it is to wrangle over texts as if they were God-inspired! Did we fully realise this, how differences dividing various sects would dissolve! Had our ancestors never heard the word "inspiration", how much better it would have been for humanity! Many millions of lives would have been saved, and the Church would have come through the last sixteen hundred years with clean hands, innocent of bloodshed.

The New Testament as we know it today consists of books whose origin is unknown, and whose authors are unknown. They were chosen uncritically by ignorant men, steeped in superstition. What was merely tradition became elevated to the rank of sacred documents, word by word inspired by God, and Christians were exhorted to follow every divine mistake and pious contradiction. The earliest existing copies of the books now comprising the New Testament belong to the end of the 4th century, but they are only copies, and no one knows whether they are in any way like the original documents or not.

The Arians, a sect of the early Christians which maintained that God and Jesus were not the same, and that Jesus was subordinate to God, lost their amendment at the Council of Nicaea in A.D. 325, that most decisive event in the history of the Christian Church. Arius, the leader, was an Alexandrian presbyter of the Church, and, after weeks of arguing, the antidivines first carried the day, and then the pro-divines, when ultimately it was decided by a majority that Jesus was the Son of God and the second member of the Trinity.

To decide this great question there assembled at Nicaea 2,048 ignorant and superstitious Christian priests, and also representatives of Paganism.[1] Numerous resolutions were presented to Constantine, who presided, but he burned them all without reading them, "lest the contentions of the priests should become known to anyone". Out of this puerile assembly grew the Nicene Creed which officially added Jesus to the Pantheon of Incarnate slain god-men, thus increasing their number to seventeen.

The creed received royal assent, a royal command was issued that everyone must believe it, and that Christianity thus defined was to be the state religion of Rome for the future. The bishops who opposed it were cast out as heretics, and those who had been on the winning side were promoted and given places of authority under the holy name of "orthodox". Then persecution began, and Christianity entered on its long record of bloodshed which did not end until some 25,000,000 victims had been slaughtered.

Nicaea was the birthplace of Christianity and the grave of what we imagined Jesus taught. From 325 onwards to the present time Christianity has been a religion comprising the superstitions of previous religions, because what was believed to have happened to the earlier saviour-gods was made to centre around Jesus when Paul evolved him into the heavenly Christ after seeing his apparition.

To understand correctly how Christianity evolved out of the simple teachings of the Nazarene, one must keep in mind that, before Nicaea, Christianity was only a sect amongst numerous other sects, with no particular standing. When, however, the power of Rome came behind it the position immediately altered, and, as Constantine decreed that Christianity was to be the state religion of the future, then those who controlled its destinies were determined that it would not be inferior to rival sects and cults of its time. Consequently its teachings and

---

1 The history of the Council of Nicaea is given in The History of the Christian Church by Canon Robertson, and in The History of the Eastern Church by Dean Stanley.

ritual had to be up to the level of prevailing religions, and the more the miraculous was emphasised the more likely was the new religion to be accepted by the ignorant masses.

Following this we find that the Nicene Creed was substantially altered long after the Council of Nicaea, at some place unknown, at an unknown date, by some person or persons unknown, when the miraculous was further stressed, and on this unauthorised creed rests the beliefs of the Christian Church today. There is no need to consider the Apostles' Creed, as its origin is unknown. It has grown out of obscurity, and cannot be traced in its present form to an earlier date than the middle of the 8th century. All that is known for certain is that the apostles knew nothing of it, but it was given that name by the Church so as to increase its authority. The origin of the Athanasian Creed is likewise unknown, and it was given the name of this leading churchman to increase its prestige, but Athanasius was certainly not the author of it, as it was not brought to light for hundreds of years after his death. All that need be said of it is that it has caused great perplexity for centuries, and it is a document that every decent-minded Christian should be utterly ashamed to repeat, as so many do, on their special feast days.

The coming of Christianity under state control preserved it as a religion and as an organisation, and this event was the death knell of all the other Roman cults and sects. Had Constantine decided to retain Mithraism,[1] the then state religion, instead of putting Christianity in its place, the latter would have been obliterated and not Mithraism. The Emperor Julian, who followed Constantine, went back to Mithraism, but his short reign of less than two years, from 361 to 363, could not change what the strong mind of Constantine had decreed. Besides this, his defeat and death in battle in Persia, the home of Mithraism, was used by the Christians as an argument against the old and in favour of the new, and was looked upon as an omen that Christianity had divine approval. If this noble Pagan had been spared to reign some years longer the entire history of Europe would have been different.

---

[1] Mithraism is considered at great length, and all the authorities referred to, in J.M. Robertson's standard work *Pagan Christs*. Refer also to "Mithras" in *Encyclopædia Britannica*; Chapters 15 and 16 of Gibbon's *Decline and Fall of the Roman Empire*; *Les Mysteres de Mithra*, by Franz Cumont; *Mithraism and Christianity*, by Patterson; *Mithraism*, by Stuart Jones.

Under Jovian, the emperor who followed, the substitution of Christianity for Mithraism made further headway and we now find the old Pagan beliefs, such as Divine Sonship, the Virgin Birth, the Cross, Resurrection, Salvation, Baptism, the Trinity and the Eucharist, becoming generally accepted as the basis of Christianity. Christianity, from now onwards, contained all these, and many other, features which can be traced back to the religions of the east, but especially to Mithraism, which should be looked upon as the parent of the forms, ceremonials, rites and creeds of the new religion. Christianity absorbed Mithraism, and all it stood for, and consequently its chief rival in the Roman Empire disappeared.

Mithraism, the name given to the religion followed by those who worshipped the sun god Mithra, came to Europe from Persia. From Persia it spread through Europe, including Great Britain. In point of universality it was the most wide-spread religion in the western world in the early centuries of the Christian era. It made its appeal both to freemen and bondmen, and its monumental remains are scattered about in all the countries of Europe which then included the civilised world.

What, then, were the beliefs of this religion? These go back to a period long before the Christian era. Its followers worshipped the god Mithra, the Deity of Light and Truth created by, yet coequal with, the Supreme Deity. They believed in the Trinity - the Father, the Son and the Holy Ghost - Mithra being the Son. Mithra was styled "the most beloved by men", and to him were assigned very lofty ideals, he being also the Lamb slain for the sins of the world. They kept Sunday, the first day of the week, as their day of worship. Mithra was its Lord, and Sunday was known as "The Lord's Day". Their chief festivals were what we now call Christmas and Easter *(from Eostre, the goddess of Spring)*. Mithra was born at Christmas and died at Easter. At Easter the formalities representing the death of the deity were gone through, and what is now called Lent was observed.

What is now termed the Eucharist or the Lord's Supper, or the Holy Communion, was observed, the bread being eaten and the wine drunk in memory of Mithra. Baptism was practised, and a sign believed to be that of the cross was made on the forehead of the baptised. Mithra was the Logos, the Incarnate Word, and was sacrificed for sin. He was considered the Mediator and Saviour of all believers, conferring on them eternal life in heaven in return for their belief. The human soul, they believed, had been separated from God, and through this sacrifice attained reunion. Mithra is represented as the Lamb slain for the sins of the world.[1]

Only after successive pontifical decrees were the people as a whole made to accept Jesus as the world's Saviour instead of Mithra. Mithra was born in a cave, just as in the early Christian writings Jesus is reported as being born in a cave. Shepherds came to adore him and offer him gifts, his mother was a virgin, he was buried in a rock tomb, and when they looked for his body it could not be found. Mithra, after death, passed into hades and rose again from the dead, his followers believing that on the last day a general resurrection of the dead would take place when he would return to judge the world.

In view of this long series of signal parallels between Mithraism and Christianity, what other view can an intelligent individual take than that the doctrines, dogmas and ceremonials of Mithraism were added to the simple teachings of Jesus, when it is known that Mithraism is the older religion of the two? It first became known to the Romans in 70 B.C., but it was an established religion in Persia more than four hundred years before the Christian era. These two religions lived side by side for three centuries until Christianity, instead of Mithraism, became officially recognised by the State. Christianity, the new state religion, absorbed its rival and they became united under one name, Christianity. There is nothing mysterious about it, everything is natural, all that happened being the dropping of the god Mithra in favour of the god Christ, both being theological names which conveyed the same idea of saviour and mediator.

Thus, it is not surprising to find that the older religion supplied the Christians with not only many of their doctrines, symbols and rites, but their priests with the form of their vestments, and the Vatican Mount, the site of Mithraic worship, with the place for the principal church of Christendom, in which rests Saint Peter's chair, of probable Mithraic origin, and round its dome are graven words of Mithraic origin. From Mithraism Christians probably copied the placing of their churches facing the east, the direction of the rising sun, and also the numerous forms of terminology such as "The Good Shepherd", "The King of Glory", "The Light of the World", "The Lamb of God", "Lord and Father" and "Lord of all".

---

1 Unfortunately no Mithraic documents have survived, and what is known of Mithraism is derived from its monuments and the writings of the early Christian fathers.

By 377 we find Christianity sufficiently strong to suppress by force its former rival. In that year Mithraic worship was suppressed both in Rome and Alexandria. Still it was a formidable opponent, and only slowly did the people forsake the old and adopt the new. Though it was the old wine, yet it was being given to them in a new bottle. Even the Emperor at this date found he had to proceed warily against this esteemed Pagan religion. Once begun, however, the persecution continued, and from being the persecuted, Christians, from now onwards, became the persecutors, until they finally obliterated as a separate religion that which had contributed to their forms, ceremonies and beliefs.

It was not, however, until the year 527 that it was decided when Jesus was born, and various monks equipped with astrological learning were called in to decide this important point. Ultimately the Emperor decided that 25th December, the date of the birth of Mithra, be accepted as the date of the birth of Jesus. Up to the year 680 no thought had been given to the symbol of Jesus crucified on the cross. Prior to that date veneration was accorded to the Mithraic symbolic lamb, but from this time onwards it was ordained that in place of the lamb the figure of a man attached to a cross should be substituted.

Our greatest authorities on comparative religion concur with Augustine and Eusebius in their belief that what is called Christianity was borrowed from contemporary or ancient religions, and that it is just a new name for much older beliefs. Robertson in his book *Christianity and Mythology* remarks as follows:- "Christianity we find to be wholly manufactured from pre-existent material within historic times."[1] Sir James Frazer takes the same view, and states in *The Golden Bough*, that monumental work of eight volumes, as follows:- "In respect both of doctrines and of rites the cult of Mithra appears to have presented many points of resemblance to Christianity. Taken all together the coincidences of the Christian with the

---

[1] Mr. Robertson and those who think with him, such as Dr. Drews and Professor W.B. Smith, consider that because of the numerous legends and myths surrounding the person of Jesus, he was a purely mythical character, and never lived on earth. This seems to me to be overstepping the bounds of reason, as for every effect there must always be a cause. Myths can gather round an individual and teaching be attributed to him, but we cannot imagine this happening to one who never lived. Mr. F.C. Conybeare, in *The Historical Christ*, puts in a few words what I have attempted to do throughout these pages: "The critical method tries to disengage in the traditions of Jesus the true from the false, fact from myth, and to show how in the pagan society (which, as it were, lifted Jesus up out of his Jewish cradle) these myths inevitably gathered round his figure as mists thicken round a mountain crest."

heathen festivals are too close and too numerous to be accidental. They mark the compromise which the Church in its hour of triumph was compelled to make with its vanquished and yet still dangerous rivals."

In the past all who studied Christianity in a logical and rational way were looked on by Christians as subverters of the truth. It is therefore interesting to notice the change which is taking place amongst enlightened Christians, who are being forced by the evidence to face the truth. Canon Streeter, in his book *The Buddha and the Christ*, published in 1932, quotes in support of his argument the following saying of Newman:- "A great portion of what is generally received as Christian truth is in its rudiments, or separate parts, to be found in heathen philosophies and religions ."

I find also in *Mythic Christs and the True*, by the Rev. W. St. Clair Tisdall, M.A., D.D., that only in three instances does he consider that there is no parallel between Mithraism and Christianity. In all the other numerous instances he admits a parallel. The exceptions he takes refer to the belief of the Mithraists that Mithra was born of a virgin, that he was buried in a rock tomb and rose from the dead. In making these exceptions he omits to consider some of the most conclusive evidence in their favour; but this is by the way as everything else he fully admits.

As to the story of the virgin birth, death and resurrection of Jesus, the Christian story was doubtless taken from one of the numerous legends of deified men current at the time, and it would be incorrect to claim that these Christian incidents were solely taken from Mithraism. The evidence is all in favour of their origin being found elsewhere.

According to Mackey's *Lexicon of Freemasonry*, freemasons taught the doctrines of the crucifixion, atonement and resurrection long before the Christian era. Saint Justin, one of the early Christian fathers, argued in favour of the virgin birth, the crucifixion, resurrection and ascension of Jesus, because Christians claimed no more than the Pagans did for their saviours.

Many who have studied the question believe that the origin of the crucifixion of saviour god-men at Easter came from the crossing by the sun over the equinoctial line at the commencement of Spring, as, with its increased heat, vegetation flourished and the people were saved from starvation. The chief Pagan festivals were held at what we now call Christmas and Easter, the first when the sun enters the Winter solstice and the days begin to lengthen, and the other when it reaches the plane of the equator and the days are of equal length. The god-man was believed to have been born on the day the sun commences to return to give heat and life to the earth, just as it was believed that he died, rose again, and ascended into heaven, which was symbolical of the death of Winter, the return of life with Spring, and the ascent of the sun into the heavens which culminates at Midsummer.

The virgin birth legend was attached to so many outstanding men and gods that it was just as common to attribute a miraculous birth to a great man in those days as it was in the Christian era for a king to claim that he ruled by divine right, which claim was the rudiment of the belief in a supernatural birth. To attribute to an outstanding man a supernatural birth was the greatest honour those who followed him could think of bestowing on his memory. As those great ones had supernatural births conferred on them, likewise they had attributed to them in many instances supernatural deaths; and so we find, as Vivian Phelips says in *The Churches and Modern Thought*, that "of all the old world legends the death and resurrection of a virgin-born, or in some way divinely-born, Saviour was the most widespread".

As to the death and resurrection of Jesus, I think that there is no difficulty in discovering that the story originated in Babylon, and that it is just a copy, with elaborations, of the story of the trial, death and resurrection of the god Bel, to which has been added the details of the death, and what accompanied it, related of the god Prometheus.

The account of the death of the Greek god Prometheus, more than five hundred years before Christ, records how he descended to earth for the sake of elevating humanity, and after a short time on' earth he was tried and sentenced to death. He was chained to a rock on Mount Caucasus, and through his death the gates of heaven were opened to all believers. Seneca, the famous Roman historian, and other writers, record this story. At the death of Prometheus the earth shook and the whole frame of nature became convulsed, the rocks were rent, the graves opened, and the dead came out of them "when the Saviour gave up the ghost". He then rose from the dead and ascended into heaven. The story of this god is similar to that recorded of Jesus, and "it is doubtful whether there is to be found in the whole range of Greek literature deeper pathos than that of the divine woe of the god Prometheus crucified on the Scythian Crags for his love to mortals", says *The New*

American Cyclopedia. Ovid, the Roman poet, put in verse the story of the healing-god Æsculapius, whose virgin birth, life and death follow much on the same lines as the story of Jesus.

The sacrifice of a saviour-god was quite a common belief in ancient religions and took similar forms, all for the purpose of appeasing a deity. At the time of the birth and growth of the Christian religion, the form in vogue attributed to the god-man the desire to take the world's sins and thus redeem humanity. He became the sacrifice in place of humanity, and thus appeased the Almighty. The legend of the death of Prometheus is only one of many, and the account of the death of the Babylonian god Bel, known to the Jews as Baal, is just another. The Egyptian god Osiris, and the Greek god Dionysus, were believed to have had experiences similar to those told about Jesus. Dionysus was termed "The only Begotten", "The Born Again" and "The Saviour", but they all received epithets similar to those later bestowed on Jesus.

From the translation of a tablet discovered in Babylonia, it is evident that their god Bel was believed to have had experiences similar to those at a later date attributed to Jesus. This tablet, of Babylonian origin, produced hundreds of years before the Christian era (some believe two thousand years), giving the record of the Babylonian Passion drama, when placed alongside of the chief events recorded in the Christian drama, is remarkably similar, so much so that I shall now record what it reveals, and give alongside the corresponding events of the Christian story.

BABYLONIAN LEGEND	CHRISTIAN LEGEND
Bel is taken prisoner.	Jesus is taken prisoner.
Bel is tried in the Hall of Justice	Jesus is tried in the Hall of Pilate
Bel is smitten.	Jesus is scourged.
Bel is led away to the Mount.	Jesus is led away to Golgotha.
With Bel are taken two malefactors, one of whom is released.	With Jesus two malefactors are led away; another, Barabbas, is released.
After Bel has gone to the Mount the city breaks out into tumult.	At the death of Jesus the veil of the Temple is rent: from the graves come forth the dead, and enter the city.
Bel's clothes are carried away.	Jesus's robe is divided among the soldiers.
Bel goes down into the Mount and and disappears from life.	Jesus from the grave goes down into the realm of the dead.
A weeping woman seeks him at the gate of burial.	Mary Magdalene came weeping to the tomb to seek Jesus.
Bel is brought back to life.	Jesus rises from the grave alive.

As this discovery is of comparatively recent date, and has consequently received little publicity, I called on the Curator of the Babylonian section of the British Museum to obtain confirmation of the existence of this tablet and its correct translation. I was told that the particulars I have given can be correctly considered as "a list of parallel instances (which was drawn up by the late Professor Zimmern) found both in the story of the god Bel and of the Christ. Zimmern deduced the incidents of the story of Bel from ritual texts which seem to describe a primitive kind of religious play". This confirmation, as I have given it, was received by me in writing and I have it now beside me as I write.

Each event recorded on the tablet is supposed to have been the name given to each act of the drama, and it is not unreasonable to believe that this Babylonian programme was the basis round which the gospel writers wound the story about Jesus, each, as we know, differing as to details, but similar throughout. These Passion dramas were quite common in the east prior to the Christian era, and the one favoured by the Jews, some authorities think, had as the suffering god-man one called Jesus Barabbas, Barabbas meaning "The Son of the Father".

A careful study of the gospel legends of the great Christian drama, had led some authorities to believe that the story relating to Jesus of Nazareth was written from the chief events of a Passion play, and this Babylonian discovery proves that the Christian story did not originate in Palestine. 'This discovery certainly lends added weight to this explanation of the origin of the great Christian drama, especially as there is hardly a detail of the agony, trial, crucifixion, resurrection and ascension, as told about Jesus, that was not told about gods who preceded him.

Those gods were believed to rise from the dead at the time of the year we call Easter, at the Spring Equinox, when the dead of Winter has passed. They went through similar experiences before and after their deaths as are reported as happening to Jesus, and, in those days of old, when only the priests could read or write, the people were kept in memory of it all by means of this Passion drama. These Passion dramas were continued by Christianity, and we find them recorded in the early days of this religion.

The special interest to us of the Babylonian account is that we have at last discovered the actual programme of the drama, which confirms the conclusion previously reached by men who have given the subject a life study, that the gospel story is just the legend of what was told in drama of other suffering saviour-gods. At each act, prior to the drama being enacted, a priest is believed to have either read or told the assembled throng what was about to occur and its meaning.

In the popular pre-Christian religions of Greece, Egypt, Asia and, as we have seen, of Babylon, the dramatic representation of the principal episodes in the lives of the suffering gods were regularly enacted. Herodotus tells us that this took place in Egypt, the god being Osiris. Likewise we find the same dramatic representation in connection with the gods Adonis, Attis, Mithra and Dionysus. The mythological explanation is doubtless the same, the annual death and resurrection of vegetation which was closely connected with the waning and the waxing of the sun. Thus we find these beliefs translated into annual festivals in connection with the worship of both Vegetation gods and Sun gods.

The various myths attributed to other gods evidently slowly came to centre round Jesus, and these were added to the early Christian writings. This also seems to have happened with the Passion dramas connected with other gods, which also were made to have reference to Jesus. A careful reading of the gospel narratives, with this in mind, will perhaps make clear much that was previously difficult to understand.

Take each episode of the climax of the life of Jesus, especially as related in Matthew and Mark, and it will be realised that the narrative could easily have had as its basis this Passion play centred round the god Bel. The theatrical character of the gospel story can be traced out in each event, and, if anyone is sufficiently interested, this whole subject will be found carefully reasoned out by John M. Robertson, who was a well-known authority on Shakespearean drama, in *Pagan Christs*, where much space and thought is devoted to each event recorded in the gospels.

When he wrote this book the Babylonian tablet, to which have just referred, had not been discovered. This discovery was all that was necessary to establish the reasonableness of Robertson's argument, taken as it was from what we know occurred in other religions, as, with the actual programme of the Babylonian Passion play now before us, the probable source has been discovered of the Christian story.

Thus we find that a supposed event, the belief in which has had an immeasurable influence on countless millions of lives, rests on natural phenomena, namely the annual decrease and increase of the power of the. sun, and the consequent death and re-birth of vegetation each year. This was translated into the death and resurrection of god-men. The legends surrounding these events were dramatised in various countries by different religions, and copied by Christians in the 1st or 2nd century of our era, so as to bring their religion up to the same level in regard to the life, death and resurrection of its Saviour, as was claimed by rival cults of that age with regard to their saviours.

The foregoing explains why nothing was recorded in the archives of Rome about what the Gospels tell us happened to Jesus, and why all the Roman historians of the time failed to record it. Gibbon could never understand why men of the high intellectual level of Seneca, Pliny, Tacitus, Plutarch, Epictetus, and many others, could obtain no sane or sensible statement from the Christians of the 1st century with regard to their religion. If all that the Gospels report as happened to Jesus is true, is it not extraordinary that those great thinkers and writers could never obtain this information from the Christians of their time? What a wonderful story it would have been, what a sensation it would have caused, and yet their writings ignore it all!

Is it not also remarkable that, in spite of the marvellous works reported as being performed by Jesus, the Jews during his life considered him only a blasphemer, as one who wished to upset the beliefs of the people in the orthodox religion of his day? It is quite contrary to all reason that they should have considered him only as such if the gospel stories are true.

Even among savages, one who was believed to have the power to bring the dead back to life would never have been made to suffer and to die. Surely it is more rational to accept the account of Jesus as given in the Jewish Talmud as the more probable story. *The Talmud*, containing the traditional laws of the Jews, and dating back to the 2nd century, gives a very different story about Jesus from what is contained in the Gospels. There the only reference made to him is the statement that he was arrested for blasphemy, was tried in the Jewish court, condemned, stoned, and then hanged on a tree, which, by the way, agrees with what we are told in *Acts* xiii, 29, as to how he died.

This is a much more probable story than the gospel legends, filled with marvellous and miraculous occurrences, which no contemporary of Jesus considered worthy to record. Let us all, as sensible individuals, forget the mistakes of our early training, and believe that Jesus was born in a natural way, lived a natural life and died a martyr's death for his convictions. Let us relegate the miraculous in the Christian story to its right place - with that of the mythologies surrounding the lives of other gods. We now know that this is where it should be placed, and that, as regards the final drama, as recorded in Christian mythology, of the life of the Christian god, it is but a version in words of an earlier Passion play incorporated into Christianity. This display was enacted annually throughout the east for centuries before Christianity was thought of, to satisfy the human longing for further knowledge with regard to the hereafter, a yearning which all those early religions show was just as strong then as it is today.

The study of Religion proves beyond the shadow of doubt that mankind, in ignorance of his future, yet instinctively feeling that he persisted after death, has been immeasurably helped by the beliefs and ceremonies of religion. They have acted as a crutch to him throughout his earthly pilgrimage. True, he has been exploited by priests and religious organisations, who have kept him ignorant and taken advantage of his craving for further knowledge. On the whole, however, they have helped to make life easier for him, as, without their aid, life would have been unintelligible.

Round the inherent instinct of all men and women that they have immortal souls, and that there is a greater power in the universe than themselves, have been coiled superstitions which in various ways make up the world's different religions. In ignorance man has practised cruelties in his attempt to placate what he considered was a wrathful deity. He has imagined the necessity for a mediator between himself and God, and these mediators throughout the ages have taken different forms, and been surrounded by different ceremonies, but still the same golden thread runs through it all - the instinctive belief that humanity is destined for something more than this world has to give. In mankind's evolution, as he slowly developed in intelligence, he has suffered much through ignorance because of this. one ruling passion, this fervent desire for further knowledge of the mysteries of life and death.

The profound thinkers of the golden age of Greece and Rome developed a philosophy for which the world was not prepared. They appeared like an oasis in a desert of ignorance. Their high and pure thoughts could not be appreciated by the rest of mankind, as it was not yet ready for them. Humanity still required a saviour, a god-man, forms, ceremonials and creeds, and so Christianity developed quite naturally out of other religions, and took the place it was fitted for as the need for it was there. Mental development has continued, however, and some of us now foresee a more rational religion based on the only revelation received from heaven, which proves that the afterlife is a reality, and that we are undoubtedly etheric beings.

Now that this positive proof has come, so will go slowly from the minds of mankind the belief in crucified saviours, in god-men and all that appertains to them, whatever may be the cult to which they belong. The drapings only will go, but the great essentials, which are necessary to satisfy humanity, are becoming more apparent than ever. Naturally, amongst the uneducated, opposition is determined because the unthinking always believe that what is must always be.

The Egyptians always boasted that for ten thousand years the hand of man had never been allowed to touch one of the sacred monuments in their temples. Orthodoxy in Egypt, just as in Christendom, had ruled that God's revelation, as given by his authorised priests, was final and complete. As Egypt changed so Christendom will change, but we need not fear the change as a bright and glorious dawn is succeeding the world's night of ignorance.

Just as the discoveries in Babylonia and Egypt are proving to us that Christianity is not a revealed religion, but simply a new name given to the forms, ceremonies and beliefs of the ancient world, so there is opening out before us a wealth of beauty and thought contained in the new revelation coming to earth from the etheric world. Mankind finds that he is not alone on his journey to some unknown destination, that he is now in contact with those who have made the change called death, and that they are now coming back to help him and guide him on his onward course. With this increased knowledge he can throw away the crutch of orthodoxy, and step out relieved from this now unnecessary encumbrance. To us the future is bright instead of being dark, and what was a great and awful mystery has now become clear as the result of our increased knowledge.

In our coming freedom from the superstitions of the past, we must thank not only those who have helped in opening up the way for communication with the etheric world, and thus setting our minds at rest with regard to our future. There are others besides who have also helped, by increasing our knowledge of the past, and making us understand more clearly that what we thought was a divine revelation is but a continuation of the superstitious beliefs of earlier religions. Just as the discovery of the use of steam revolutionised our industrial life, so did the discovery of how to read the Babylonian and Egyptian languages revolutionise our religious outlook. These two latter discoveries must be looked back upon as amongst the great events of history, and they have been the means of making us understand the Bible in a way that we never could have done had these discoveries not been made.

Sir Henry Rawlinson was responsible for the decipherment of the old Babylonian language which was forgotten. In 1835 he took from the Behistun Rock, near Babylon, a copy of what turned out to be a decree of King Darius written in Babylonian, Scythian and Persian. He made paper casts of this inscription, and it was possible, owing to the fact that the Persian was known, to translate the Babylonian and the Scythian. In consequence of this discovery, the numerous Babylonian tablets since found have been translated, and much of what is contained in the Old and New Testaments can now be traced to Babylon.

The stories of Adam and Eve, the Flood, the Tower of Babel, and other events, were all current in Babylonia long before a book of our Bible was written. They were copied there by the Jews when in captivity. The story of Moses being hidden in the bulrushes may also have been taken from Babylon, as we have discovered a similar story relating to Sargon, an early king of Babylon, the river in his case being the Euphrates. Sargon, after death, was looked on as a god, was accredited with a virgin birth, and most of the miraculous wonders ascribed to all the great men of the past were likewise attributed to him.

Just as we have learned much of Babylonian history from the discovery of how to read their cuneiform writing, so have we discovered much of Egyptian history through learning how to read Egyptian hieroglyphics. This came about through the discovery of what is called the Rossettastone, found at the mouth of the Nile near Rossetta, when Napoleon invaded Egypt in 1798. It contains a decree in honour of Ptolemy and is written in Hieroglyphic, Demotic and Greek. As the Greek was known the others could be translated. This discovery throws much light on many of the stories in the Bible, because Egypt greatly influenced the political and religious history of the Jews.

Likewise both countries contributed much to the origin of Christianity. This religion was not born from one single parent, but from many. Its rites, symbols, ceremonials, teachings, doctrines and legends were all derived from countries surrounding Palestine, and the religion of each helped to make

Christianity what it became in the 4th century. What is called Christianity was then a reservoir into which flowed many of the beliefs of all the old-world religions.

The reason the best was accepted, and the worst discarded, was because those who were responsible for its growth lived at a time when that part of the world, in which the religion grew up, had reached a high state of culture. Consequently the best was adopted from contemporary religions and much that was crude was rejected. Superstition was accepted because it was a superstitious age, but the higher moral tone of Christianity is undoubtedly due to the fact that it was cradled and nurtured in Greece and developed to manhood in Rome. The first century of its life was a time of greater wisdom, and then lived more men of eminence than the world had previously known. Unfortunately their pure and noble philosophy was rejected, their pleas for education ignored, and Christianity carried on the old Pagan superstition, to become eventually so powerful that it blotted out by massacre and exile the knowledge and wisdom of the philosophers.

Pagan literature is known only to the few, and from childhood upwards we are taught that all we have and are today is the result of Christianity. This is quite wrong. Cicero, Plutarch, Marcus Aurelius and Seneca, to mention only four great Pagans, teach a higher moral philosophy, containing higher aspirations of virtue, toleration and humanity, than does any religion before or after their time. We ignore the source whence sprang the high level of culture of these times, and in ignorance attribute to Christianity what really came from Pagan philosophy.

Unfortunately, when Christianity obliterated the old religions of Rome and Greece it also submerged their philosophy, the place of which was taken by creeds and dogmas, so much so that to believe in the Trinity and other Church dogmas was the test of a good Christian, and not his life. The teaching of the great Pagan writers and thinkers was buried under the dogmas of the Church, and in consequence Europe entered the dark ages. It emerged from them only when the Pagan teachings were relearned in the 16th century. What is called "Our Christian Civilisation" is therefore due to the great classical thinkers who lived between 600 B.C. and A.D. 200.

When Christianity triumphed under Constantine, the civilised world received a setback from which it did not recover for 1,3oo years. As Farrer, that thoughtful classical authority, says in his book *Paganism and Christianity*, "There is indeed no fact more patent in history than that with the triumph of Christianity under Constantine the older and finer spirit of charity died out of the world, and gave place to an intolerance and bigotry which were its extreme antithesis, and which only in recent years have come to be mitigated."

What a mental and moral gulf there is between non-Christian men such as Seneca, Plato:. Marcus Aurelius, or Plutarch, and Athanasius, Ambrose, Augustine and Jerome, to mention only four of the earlier Christian Fathers, with their warped and narrow minds, writing always with the object of compressing the human mind into their narrow creeds and dogmas. What a contrast there is between the high and noble humanitarian aspirations expressed by the Pagans, and the creeds and dogmas of the Christian Church!

It is utterly false to say that the idea of the brotherhood of man originated in the teaching of Christianity. It was one of the dominant ideas of Pagan philosophy before Christianity was thought of. Marcus Aurelius rises from the common conception of the political community, to that of the wider community of humanity, with a breadth of mind that at no time has belonged to the Church. He, and others like him, envisaged mankind in one common brotherhood, each working for the good of humanity.

It was a primary tenet of the higher Pagan faith that every man, inasmuch as he shared the spirit of God, should consider himself as a Son of God, and that it therefore behoved him to conduct himself in a manner befitting such a relationship, and to regard all his fellow men as brethren by virtue of their belonging to the same family as himself. What a contrast between the sublime writings and thoughts of the great Pagans, and the cruelties, wars, persecutions, and numberless horrors, which were the outcome of Christianity, as the result of its followers' belief that it was the only true religion, and that all must believe in it or everlastingly perish.

The general idea held by most people, that Christianity was responsible for raising the moral and spiritual level of the Roman world is a pious illusion for which there is not a particle of evidence. By the 6th century we find all the schools of philosophy closed, all education and learning banned, all the worst of Paganism continuing, the best obliterated, and Europe in a night of intense darkness which lasted for more than a thousand years. Daylight came only when people became intelligent enough to doubt the Christian story, and the claims of the Christian religion, and from that date the less they have

The Christian Religion 53

been believed the better and happier has become Christendom.

Much of the teaching attributed to Jesus is considered by many to be peculiar to him and him only, and it is supposed that he was the first to teach love, gentleness, the love and fatherhood of God, and all the other virtues. This is quite wrong, though this false way of regarding his teaching is encouraged by the Church, which claims that he originated all these injunctions. I cannot count the number of sermons I have heard upholding this falsehood.

Long before the time of Jesus there were teachers who taught everything that is attributed to him, and there is nothing of value ascribed to him that was not said before his time. "Return good for evil and overcome anger with love", and "he that would cherish me let him go and cherish his sick comrade", were sayings attributed to Buddha. "Do unto others as you would that they should do unto you" was said by Confucius. "Whenever thou art in doubt as to whether an action is good or bad, abstain from it" was said by Zoroaster a thousand years before Jesus.

"One who is injured ought not to return the injury, for on no account can it be right to do an injustice, and it is not right to return an injury or to do any evil to any man, however much we may have suffered from him" was said by Socrates four hundred and fifty years before Jesus. "Let us not listen to those who think that we ought to be angry with our enemies, and who believe this to be great and manly. Nothing is more praiseworthy, nothing so clearly shows a great and noble soul, as clemency and readiness to forgive" was said by Cicero seventy years before Jesus. "If a man strike thee and in striking thee drop his staff, pick it up and hand it to him again" was ascribed to Krishna centuries before Jesus was born.

Similar teachings could be quoted from numerous sources in great numbers, attributed to men who lived hundreds of years before Jesus was born. The immortality of the soul was taught by the Hindus, Egyptians, Greeks and Romans, and many others. It is one of the earliest beliefs and is found in every religion.

What is termed "The Lord's Prayer" originated in Babylon, the tablet, on which is written a prayer resembling it, being discovered in 1882. It is one of the oldest Jewish prayers, repeated for long by them in the Chaldaic language, they having learned it in Babylon during their captivity. Likewise all the high ethical teachings attributed to Jesus can be found in many pre-Christian writings, such as the Bhagavad Gita, the sacred book of India, and in the writings of Seneca, Ovid, Aristotle, Epictetus, Plato and many others.

As Thomas Whittaker, in his able work The Origins of Christianity, truly remarks, "It is a remarkable fact that Christianity, said to have been revealed, has had to recur for every serious effort to find in the universe the manifestations of a rational and moral order, to thinkers who never pretended to have obtained what they might offer in this direction by anything but the exercise of their own reason."

Those who have made a study of the origin of Christian literature are of the opinion that the various events and sayings recorded in the Gospels can all be traced to earlier origins than the events to which they refer. The four gospels are therefore the result of the collation of ancient stories and traditions prevalent in the east at the time they were written.

From a careful study of the four gospel narratives, from the knowledge we now possess of the religious beliefs prevalent in the east one thousand nine hundred years ago, and from what we now know of the history of the Roman Empire at that time, it is possible to follow up a quite natural event right through its various developments.

I would divide these into four stages, thus:- *First Stage:* Natural birth of Jesus some years prior to 4 B.C., as Herod died in that year. In his youth he worked with his father. He was religiously inclined, and either joined the Essene Brotherhood or studied their beliefs, living with them probably until he was about thirty years of age. He then went out as a teacher and healer, going from place to place over a period of less than two years.

His strong psychic power made him able to heal the sick. He was perhaps clairvoyant and clairaudient, and so could speak with some authority of the etheric world, which to him at times might become a reality. He attracted followers by the realistic way in which he could present his views, and his ethical teaching made him revered by all who knew him. Maybe he was controlled at times by higher intelligences in the etheric world, and, when so influenced, was able to impress the people by his gift of speech.

He incurred the anger of the authorities by his outspoken remarks on the orthodox Church and priests of his day. This led to his martyrdom, as it has led to the martyrdom of many reformers both before and after him. Quite possibly he was seen after his death by some of his followers. Owing to our present-day knowledge of psychic matters what seemed miraculous in those days, namely his healing power, his other psychic gifts, and his being seen in his etheric body after death, can now be related to natural laws. What seemed unique then is today recognised as of more 0r: less common occurrence.

Second Stage: Paul comes on the scene, believes he has had a vision of Jesus, also a message, and, with his strong personality, confirms the disheartened band of Jews in the belief that Jesus was the Messiah foretold by the prophets. As it was believed that the world was about to come to an end, nothing of the doings or sayings of Jesus was put in writing, and, as time went on, these were handed down from father to son, with the tendency always to exaggerate and to emphasise the miraculous. Paul went about preaching this message of hope, and, as the adherents of this new sect grew, he wrote them letters.

The fall of Jerusalem in A.D. 70 helped to consolidate the new cult, as many in despair, because of the break-up of Judaism, joined the new sect, being encouraged by its belief that the Messiah would soon reincarnate to restore his kingdom. The incubation period of the new sect dates most likely from this date until the end of the first century.

Either just before or just after the fall of Jerusalem there began to appear, perhaps in Antioch, a short narrative of this much-talked-of Jesus, giving a description of his simple life, sayings and doings, and incorporating material borrowed from Essene sources. Other narratives followed, each tending to emphasise the miraculous. A diary now called the *Acts of the Apostles* also appears, relating what is claimed to be the deeds of some of his principal followers.

The new sect gradually becomes known by the Greek name of Christian, and Jesus to many has definitely become the Messiah, or Christ, who had fulfilled all the prophecies of old. Slowly the belief changed from regarding Jesus as an earthly deliverer to that of a spiritual mediator. Thus this doctrine, attributed to Paul, took root, and the way was prepared/'or what was to become orthodox Christianity in the 4th century.

Third Stage: The new sect gets so strong that its leaders become ambitious, imbued by the desire to succeed to the theocratic powers of the Jewish hierarchy and found a world religion. Other sects with whom they are in contact claim their founders to be divine, as having had miraculous births, and that miraculous events had occurred at their deaths. Gradually what was attributed to other religious founders, or deities, was attributed to Jesus, so much so that by the 2nd century after his death he was looked upon by some as divine, but by others as a teacher only.

Numerous writings are by this time in existence, some emphasising this divine aspect, others entirely ignoring it, and everyone differing as regards facts. Moreover, it is considered by some that many of the doctrines attributed to Paul are of a much later date than his time, and that to him, as to Jesus, was attributed sayings and doings, so as to give the authority of his name to the doctrines of the Church of the time.

Fourth Stage: The last stage comes when this sect attracts the attention of Imperial Rome, and Constantine decrees that it is to become the state religion of the future, thus displacing Mithraism which had been the State religion of Rome for the previous two hundred years. From the time of the Council of Nicaea (325) onwards the consolidation of Christianity into an organised religion is rapid. As it had become the new State religion. then it must not be inferior to its rival Mithraism which it had superseded. Four gospels, in which the miraculous is emphasised, are chosen out of the many, and then and later further miraculous incidents are added.

Biblical scholars can now easily trace how the early records have been added to, and how what were originally simple records of a simple life became augmented with miraculous events. Thus, a life which was in every way human became embellished for the purpose of making it appear divine.

Some of the various letters which were attributed to the apostles also came to rank as divine documents along with the four gospels, but they, like the Gospels, had been, or were, altered from time to time to suit the growing belief in the miraculous.

This sect had now become a strong organisation, and, in taking the place of the old Mithraic religion, it incorporated into its dogmas, doctrines and ceremonies the mystic beliefs and rites of the older religion, but, as the gospels and epistles had been written prior to this absorption, these added beliefs and ceremonials were absent in the gospels and epistles of that time. This omission was so obvious to the Church authorities that interpolations and additions were made from time to time, and these are well known to all New Testament scholars.

For instance, the only reference to the Trinity in the Bible occurs in the First Epistle of St. John, fifth chapter, seventh verse. This reference is not found in any Greek manuscript, as the Doctrine of the Trinity was not part of the Church's teaching until it was incorporated into Christianity at the Council of

Nicaea. Consequently this verse is now omitted from the Revised Version of the Bible which was published in 1881.

In the Revised Version of the New Testament there is no reference whatever to the Trinity, and the Church has not a scrap of authority for claiming that Jesus is part of God, and that they, together with the Holy Ghost, make up one God. The intelligent leaders of the Church today know tiffs, but in spite of the fact that they have not a particle of evidence to produce to justify the preaching of this doctrine, they continue Sunday after Sunday deluding the people and making them think that they have divine authority for this assertion. Never a Sunday passes but the clergy, of the Anglican and Roman Churches especially, repeat at various times throughout the service the phrase in one form or another, "In the Name of God the Father, God the Son, and God the Holy Ghost."

If they are in the least intelligent they must know full well that this fundamental doctrine of Christianity, on which the whole edifice of superstition is built, has no justification whatever, and that the doctrine of the Trinity is an ancient belief, which can be traced back for thousands of years into the dim and misty past. Many other instances could be given of what is now part of Christianity, but was quite unknown as such to the original writers of the Gospels; but this is all that space permits.[1]

As the Bible has played, and still plays, such a large part in Protestant Christianity, this chapter would not be complete without some consideration of its origin, and how it has come to us in its present form. This being so, I shall now give a short history of what Christians call

THE HOLY BIBLE

I have calculated that during my life I have listened to at least two thousand sermons, but I do not remember hearing a parson on any occasion ever refer to the origin of the Christian religion. Neither can I remember ever hearing a parson tell of the origin of the Holy Bible. Our religious teachers ignore

---

[1] Anyone wishing to pursue this subject further should read *Christianity in the Light of Modern Knowledge*, especially the able contribution by Dr. Gilbert Murray (Professor of Greek at Oxford University), which shows clearly how Christianity developed out of the beliefs of the superstitious and ignorant cults that abounded in the countries surrounding Palestine 1,900 years ago, all having their suffering Saviour-gods and beliefs similar to what gathered round the simple teachings of Jesus, this medley of different beliefs becoming known as Christianity.

origins for the very obvious reason that when we begin to look into the question of the origin of Christianity, or the origin of the books of the Bible, we find that the Church's claims for these have no foundation whatever.

As I could get no information on this question from our official religious teachers, I have studied the subject for over thirty years, and have found that the claims and assertions they make for Christianity have no basis and are quite untrue. It might here be said by some: "Why worry about an old book, or why worry about what the parson says? No intelligent person today takes a parson seriously." This is to some extent true, but at the same time there are many people who still look on the Bible as their sheet anchor and as their guide to another life, even as they still look on the parson as their one and only source of information as to the after-life. Besides this, there are still many people who attend church regularly, who go through the service and accept it without question or doubt. The Church has its hold over the people of today solely because the average individual accepts what is him, told and does not think for himself.

On the other hand there are a large number, and an increasing number, who are so dissatisfied with the Church and its teachings that they have ceased to attend divine service, preferring to believe nothing rather than something which outrages their reason. An increasing number are now attending Spiritualist services, which appeal more strongly to their reason and conscience.

In the old days everyone went regularly to church, and accepted the words of the parson as if he were a divinely inspired authority on how we should live in this world, and what we must do to reach the next. Today, however, this is not so, and few intelligent people would think of making the parson their confidant with regard to their religious beliefs, for the simple reason that the thinking man and woman realises that he is just a cog in a wheel, that he has been taught certain theological maxims, which he has accepted without thinking, and that his business is to try to keep the old beliefs alive as long as possible, and discourage any intelligent enquiry into their foundations.

Except for the very few who make a stand for truth, the standard of intellectual honesty amongst the clergy is by no means high. They seem quite content to jog along, and follow their daily routine, without the consciousness that their responsibility is a great one and that their first duty is to tell the truth, no matter whether they offend the more ignorant members of their congregation or not.

Hundreds of thousands of men and women have wasted their lives studying the Bible, trying to make all its contradictions harmonise, trying to find out what exactly was God's scheme of salvation, a subject on which so many disagreed. They have wasted their time trying to explain its cruelties, abominations and absurdities, trying to justify every crime, trying to turn a God of vengeance and injustice into a God of love. All this time has been wasted on documents of no historical value. If, instead, they had spent their time in an intelligent way trying to discover the origin of the books of the Bible, who wrote them, and when and why they were written, it would have been more to their advantage.

If they had made a study of the history of the times in which the various documents were written, they would have discovered that these manuscripts, as a foundation for religious faith, do not deserve any serious consideration, and that it would have been much better to spend their time studying the Book of Nature, the real Bible, or the works of the great thinkers and philosophers of the past.

To very many, the Bible and the Christian faith are a continual stumbling-block to their acceptance of Spiritualism, the name now given to this very old but much misunderstood revelation. They are tied to the tradition of the past, and quote texts from some ancient Biblical book as if that settled everything. Many also believe that all that can be known of this life and the next is already known, that it has been revealed to us only in the Holy Scriptures, and that nothing beyond this revelation has ever been given to mankind. They hold the view that revelation stopped when the writer of the book of *Revelation* finished the last word. They believe that God has been silent from that time onwards, and that *The Holy Bible* contains everything man needs to know, and ought to know, with regard to his life here and hereafter.

Though some who read *The Rock of Truth* are sufficiently enlightened to realise that even to discuss the unreliability of the Holy Scriptures is a waste of time, as it is so self-evident, yet there are doubtless many who have never given the matter a thought and have always accepted what they have been told. Consequently this attitude of mind makes them unreceptive to the communications which are coming through to this earth from the etheric world, to which we shall all pass in time. Without, therefore, wishing to weary anyone by the recital of what is so obvious to many, let us consider something of the origin and history of what the clergy each Sunday refer to either as "The Word of God" or "The Holy Scriptures". Each Protestant church has in it a Bible, and for this reason alone it is not out of place to consider something more about this book than is ever told to congregations from the pulpit.

The Bible is made up of two sections, one the Old Testament and the other the New Testament. The origin of these two sections is very different, and it was not until the 6th century that they were brought together. It was not until the year A.D. 405 that Jerome translated the Old Testament from the Hebrew into Latin, and this book, as we know it today, was not even then accepted among the Jews. Since that date certain books were added and certain books were omitted, but no one can say on what basis, or by what authority, the books in the Old Testament as we now know it were retained. However, Jerome made a start by translating the writings now known as the Old Testament, but it was not until the 9th century of the Christian era that we find the Bible in the shape and form approximating our present Bible, though it contained a number of books omitted at the Reformation. But let us go back to the beginning.

After two hundred years of exile, a tribe, as ignorant and creel as savages, and just escaped from bondage under the rulers of Egypt, found its way into what is now called Palestine under a leader called Moses. They were poor and wretched, without any education and knowledge of the arts, but with some of the mystical knowledge derived from their time in the Land of the Nile. Their leader Moses, who we are told had been raised in the family of Pharaoh, was doubtless more learned than the others, as he had received as much education as it was possible to give anyone in those ignorant times.

Moses was a great leader, and unfortunately died before his people settled in what they called the Promised Land. He was followed by Joshua, and gradually this wandering tribe conquered and took possession of what is today known as Palestine, a name derived from the Philistines who were its former inhabitants. After a time kings began to reign over them, but it is all a very chequered story. One after another of the kings did evil in the sight of the Lord, and the bad kings were succeeded sometimes by good and sometimes by worse. The surrounding tribes were continually pressing in on them, and wars, famines and pestilences were frequent occurrences, but the climax came when this people was at last conquered by

King Nebuchadnezzar of Babylon, in 586 B.C., who took them into captivity and subjected them to many indignities.

At last, after many vicissitudes, they regained their land about seventy-four years later, and their history is now obtained from the writings of various men who went under the name of prophets or seers. It is a very incomplete history, in which there are many gaps, and the last the Old Testament has to tell of them relates to the events that took place about the year 397 before the birth of Jesus. They were conquered later by the Romans in 63 B.C. and kept in bondage, their miseries being relieved only by their belief that the longed-for Messiah would come on earth and become the nation's leader in driving out the hated conquerors. The New Testament, recording the birth, life and death of Jesus, and the letters about him attributed to some of his followers, besides a record of some of their doings after his death, complete the Bible story.

The Children of Israel made certain laws and recorded the outstanding events of their history, this legal code and narrative being called the Book of the Law which was kept in the Holy of Holies of the Temple. The time, however, came when the Temple was burned, and with it the Book of the Law. Then there arose, on the return of the Jews from captivity in Babylon, Esdras, who believed that he had instructions from God to rewrite the Book of the Law. All this is told in the book of Esdras, which, at the time of the writing of the text "All scripture is given by inspiration of God", was part of the Jewish scripture. So what he says should have as much weight as anything else in the Scriptures. Esdras had just returned from captivity in Babylon, and he was well aware of the Babylonian stories of the creation of the earth and heaven, of the Tower of Babel, and of Noah, the ark and the flood. He was also aware of their laws, and he set out to write a new Book of the Law on the basis of all the knowledge he had acquired in Babylonia. Thus it does not astonish us to find that the Babylonian accounts of the events mentioned, and the Biblical accounts, correspond. with one another, and that many of the Jewish laws correspond with those of Babylonia.

For instance, the Sabbath, known in Babylonia as Sabatu, was the Babylonian day of rest which occurred on every seventh day, and this was incorporated into the Jewish law. The only reason the Sabbath was held sacred was because the Babylonians believed that their God ended the work of creating the earth on the seventh day, and rested on that day. Because of this Babylonian superstition, which Christian countries received through the Jews, all true Christians cease from labour, not on the Sabbath the last day of the week, but on the day following, namely on Sunday the first day of the week, considering it a holy day, and many laws were made making it an offence to live a sensible and rational life on that day. Fortunately, the miserable Sabbath which some of us remember has passed into oblivion, but it is unlikely that those who experienced it will ever forget

We find nothing about the Sabbath in those books of the Bible known as *Judges, Joshua, Samuel, Kings,* or *Chronicles*, nor in *Job, Esther, Song of Solomon,* or *Ecclesiastes*, but only in the earlier books of the Bible written by Esdras after his return from Babylon, and in the later prophetical books. What Esdras wrote was probably written on the skins of beasts and placed in the Temple.

The Jews were again conquered by the Romans under Titus in the year A.D. 70, the Temple was destroyed, and, at the request of Josephus, the Jewish Book of the Law was sent to the Emperor Vespasian at Rome and it has never been seen since.

There was, however, what was claimed to be a translation of it into Greek, called the Septuagint, made by seventy scribes, but it was a translation of the Law only, the other books following later. These were all burned in the Bruchium library forty-seven years before the Christian era. The only other so-called copy, known as the Samaritan Roll, is considered of no value. Have we today a true copy of the old Book of the Law? No, it is certain we have not, and nobody knows how many variations from the original there are in our Old Testament.

The oldest Hebrew manuscript in existence was written in the xoth century of the Christian era, and the oldest Greek copy was made in the 5th century. Even if the original was inspired by God, no one knows how much has been added to or omitted from our present Old Testament, and how much represents the script of the original writers. No one knows anything about the original, all that is known being that there is no basis whatever to found the belief that our Old Testament truly represents the original. Certainly there is no justification whatever to call this doubtful copy of very many copies "The Word of God", as is continually being done by our clergy, who would never do so if they set the truth before their own self-interests.

Many chapters in the Old Testament are incomplete, and parts of the different books are written in practically the same words. Neither do *Leviticus* and *Numbers* agree as to facts or teaching. Nothing is said about the after-life. Wherein, then, lies the inspiration? Why attribute the Bible to God, with all its falsehoods, cruelties and crude teaching? To do so is blasphemy, and this blasphemy is uttered every Sunday from thousands of lips speaking from Christian pulpits, by those who claim to be the divinely appointed leaders of the people in all things appertaining to their souls.

What is termed today *The Holy Bible* is a compilation of certain of the books known as the Book of the Law, with others added for some unknown reason, and to these again were added certain documents chosen at the Council of Carthage. The bringing of the Jewish Book of the Law and the Christian documents together in the 6th century of the Christian era was the beginning of what became known as the Bible[1] which in original Greek means Book. The Jewish book became known under the name of the Old Testament, and the Christian under the name of the New Testament. This book has been looked upon since the Reformation as holy and inspired by God, as word-for-word true, as man's only guide to heaven, and his only way to salvation. During the time before the Reformation it was never read by the people, and known only to the priests and monks. In fact the people knew little about its contents. The Church, and the priests only, were looked on with awe and reverence by the ignorant masses.

Between the years 1517 and 1545 some, however, were intelligent enough to throw over the so-called Infallible Church, and strike out for themselves. They went under the name of Protestants, not because they protested against the practices of the corrupt Church, but because they protested against the orthodox Catholics being allowed to worship in the German states which had adopted Lutheran Christianity. Those who became Protestants no longer venerated a Church, and instead they worshipped *The Holy Bible*. Claims of so fantastic a nature were made for this book that it is difficult, in these more enlightened days, to understand how ever they could have been believed.

The invention of printing helped to circulate the Bible. It came to be read more and more, and, as it was the only book known by the masses, it is hardly to be wondered that the claims made for it were believed by the people of those

---

[1] The word "Bible" comes from Byblus on the coast of Syria, where the first book was produced.

ignorant times. Every word in it was accepted, every word in it was believed to have been given direct from God to man, and the awful crime of blasphemy was invoked to prevent the authenticity of this book being too closely enquired into. Anyone who doubted its authority was cast into prison and tortured.

So time went on. Gradually, as people became more and more intelligent, it came to be realized that the book contained mistakes and mis-statements, and, as the people became more civilised, they began to realise that many of its passages must have been written by depraved and cruel men. The more the Bible has been studied in an intelligent and unbiased way, the more has it become apparent that the book is a collection of documents written at various times by different people who were just a little more intelligent than their contemporaries.

No one knows who wrote any of the books of the Bible, no one knows when or how they were written, no one is reported as ever having seen or heard of anybody who had seen an original of any of the books of the Bible. We know, however, that the many existing copies differ greatly from one another, as the transcribers added what they thought should be put in, and left out what they thought should be omitted. The numerous interpolations in the New Testament were put in by scribes at a time when it was not considered inspired, and thus the most outrageous liberties were taken for several hundreds of years. We are, therefore, on safe ground in saying that not one of the books of the Bible remains today in its original form.

From out of this welter of confusion and ignorance has grown the Bible, and it was not until the time when printing was invented that it began to take concrete shape and form. Since the time when the Authorised Version of James 1st of England was produced little alteration has taken place, as much care was exercised in preserving the text, but, before that date, it is well known that every possible liberty was taken with its contents by monkish scribes.

As time went on it became evident that the Authorised Version was far from correct. Consequently in 1881 a new Revised Version was produced, and those responsible for this new version stated that they had discovered 36,191 mistakes in the old version. We now know that if a new version were published today, the alterations that would have to be made would be equally Striking. The Revised Version should have been the death blow to the Church's claim for the infallibility of the

Bible, but this was not so, and it has the support of many foolish people who quote texts to prove their theories. These people read it without thinking.

When they open their Bible they close their reason, yet, if they will consult the *Encyclopedia Biblica,* they will find that the article in it dealing with the Resurrection points out that in the various gospel stories of this event there are twenty-two contradictions of a most serious character. Why should anyone be asked to believe in an event recorded in such a way, and why does the Church, on this evidence, claim the Resurrection of Jesus to be the fundamental truth of Christianity?

This is of necessity a very brief record of the history of what Christians call God's chosen people, and of the life and teaching of Jesus and his disciples. From this mass of contradiction, born in an ignorant past, what is called the Christian faith has developed. It is still claimed that we are a Christian people and indebted to Christianity for all the progress we have made, but there is still a vast difference of opinion as to what Christianity really is. This has been discussed and fought over for many centuries, and numerous sects have arisen owing to the many differences of opinion. It is difficult to find out exactly what every different sect believes, but, generally speaking, they are in agreement more or less as regards the following tenets:-

That there is a personal God who created the earth and the stars; that he created man and woman who were tempted by the devil, and in consequence fell from the high state in which he had created them. Mankind became more and more wicked, until God's patience became exhausted, and he drowned every living person with the exception of eight people.

Afterwards he selected from their descendants Abraham, and through him the Jewish people. He gave these people laws and tried to govern them and make them good. He wrought numerous miracles, he inspired men to write the Bible, and in the fullness of time, it having been found impossible to reform mankind, God came upon the earth as a child born of the Virgin Mary. He lived in Palestine where he preached for about two years. He went from place to place teaching and preaching, occasionally raising the dead, curing the blind and the halt, and healing the diseased. Ultimately he was crucified, because God had told the Jews that they were to kill anyone who claimed to be God. Consequently God was killed as a result of his own laws, and, in crucifying Jesus, the Jews only did what God told them to do.

Christians agree, however, that, as a result of God being thus crucified, he took away the sins of all who had faith in him; that he was raised from the dead, ascending bodily into heaven where he is now making intercession for all who believe in him; that he will forgive the sins of believers, and that those who do not believe in him will be consigned to torment. Further, that this God is really three Gods and that Jesus is one of the three; three Gods, yet he is only one; and so the mystery of the Trinity has to be added to the other Christian beliefs already noted.

Lastly, there are two sacraments, one of baptism for all young children, although nothing is said about this in the Old or New Testament, in which only adult baptism is taught, and that of the last supper, or what is commonly called Holy Communion, a service of commemoration of the death of Jesus. Some hold that the bread and wine at this ceremony are turned into his body and blood, and others believe that this doctrine is blasphemy, though Jesus himself is reported to be the originator of the idea.

This is roughly a synopsis of the Christian religion, and I cannot be far wrong, as the bishops of the Church of England only a few years ago emphasised by a resolution that Christianity was contained in the creeds and doctrines of the Church. I have been told, however, that few today believe in the Adam and Eve story, and that it is accepted that we are the products of a slow and continuous evolution.

If this be so, then the foundation stone of the entire Christian fabric is removed. Paul, Christians believe, said quite clearly, "As in Adam all die so in Christ shall all be made alive." If you do away with Adam you must do away with Jesus as a saviour, and so it comes about that Jesus by many is now regarded merely as an example, one to follow, though there are still many millions who cling to the old orthodox view, because they see that to give up Adam means the abandoning of Jesus as their saviour.

What I am trying to show is that there is no basis whatever for the creeds and dogmas of the Church. They are all man-made things, and must perish with other man-made things. There is nothing divine about them, there is not a spark of divine inspiration in one single text or creed or in one single dogma of the Christian Church. Doubtless these fictions have acted as crutches in the past to many weary souls who have found much comfort and consolation in the teachings of the Church, but against that it must be admitted that they have been the cause of numberless crimes and barbarities. The history of the Christian Church is stained with the blood of 25,000,000 victims who have fallen to the intolerance of those who claimed to be orthodox in their faith.

I readily admit that a vast multitude has received comfort from the Christian religion. The name of Jesus has given consolation to countless people, and the Bible has been a source of strength to untold numbers. Millions have entered the valley of the shadow of death with his name on their lips, to their strength and comfort. His gospel has been carried to the ends of the earth by men and women who have sacrificed much to spread his teaching. What, however, is true of Christianity is true also of other faiths, but this in no way alters the fact that all the comfort and self-sacrifice Christianity has occasioned has no historic basis.

A child receives comfort from a fanciful story, and our ancestors had mostly childish minds, but, as we grow more intelligent, the comfort orthodox religion brings must decrease until it ultimately disappears altogether.

THE CONSEQUENCES OF FAITH.

The foregoing is a brief history of the foundation on which the Church has built its edifice of creeds and dogmas. We shall now consider what the consequences have been. After Constantine adopted Christianity as the State religion of the Roman Empire, much of the Mithraic worship was incorporated into the Church's ritual. Anyone visiting St. Peter's in Rome, or any other Roman Catholic church, and taking along with him Lord Lytton's *Last Day of Pompeii,* in which there is given an interesting description of what took place in pre-Christian days in a Roman temple, will find many similarities between the Christian ritual and that observed by the Pagans of Rome.

The Christian Church, backed by the authority of Imperial Rome, grew and flourished. When the Popes, Christian emperors and then later the converted Christian kings went out to conquer, the conquered nations were butchered into acceptance of the new religion, and this went on until the 12th century, when Christianity had complete control over the greater part of Europe. This was the time now known as the Dark Ages, when everyone in Europe thought only about churches, altars and relics, besides their ordinary occupations, husbandry and fighting.

Europe, after the fall of the Roman Empire, was submerged

in a sea of barbarism, and due acknowledgment must be given to the work of the early monks who kept themselves apart from the turbulence of the times. What civilisation there was in those days, and it was very slight, could be found in the monasteries throughout Europe. Monastic life, in all parts of the world, had this advantage in those days, that the monasteries were holy ground, and those inside them were safe from devastation.

The Christian Church took its idea of monastic life from Buddhism, and in the early days the copying and illuminating of the Scriptures took up much of the monks' time. They were just a little more intelligent than their neighbours, and, until they became corrupt, they did what healing and teaching they could. It is difficult to imagine the ignorance of those days, or the depth to which men's minds had fallen from the height reached at the zenith of the greatness of Rome and Greece. Barbarism was rife everywhere and Christendom mentally was in the darkness of a night of dense superstition.

To relieve this monotony a ripple came over the stagnant waste with the advent of Mohammed in 622, and five centuries later by the various attempts to free the Holy Land from the Turks. Europe rose as a man to free Palestine from the Infidel, but after two hundred years the Christians were driven out and nothing was achieved by this fruitless enterprise.

The history of the Crusades is the story of cruelty, treachery and misery. Whichever side obtained the upper hand, the consequences were the same. From a Christian point of view, it is one of the blackest periods in this religion's history, it being just one continuous round of massacre, breaking of faith and treachery from beginning to end. Crosses and hymn-singing, priests and prayers, treachery, butchery and cruelty, all combined, is the story of the Crusades in brief, and they are only one of many similar episodes in the history of the Christian Church.

Christianity, for two hundred years, turned Europe into a madhouse, and this insane desire to free the Holy Land from the Infidel caused untold misery, suffering and loss. Had it been confined to adults only it would have been bad enough, but the Church conceived the insane idea that failure was caused because the Crusaders were not innocent enough. Consequently it encouraged the wicked idea of sending out children to fight the Infidel, and 50,000 boys and girls of tender age were gathered together and dispatched to the Holy Land. Few, if any, survived to return. They were captured in the countries through which they passed, died of disease, were starved or made slaves, and so ended another of the many tragedies of this long night of superstition.

Again stagnation followed, but, in spite of the grip the Church had, men's minds were slowly developing and wondering, and this process culminated in what is known in history as the Reformation of the 16th century. The cause of this great event was the breakup of the Eastern Empire[1] when the Turks captured Constantinople in 1453. Much literature found its way to Venice and elsewhere from Constantinople before its capture, and, in consequence, the Latin and Greek classics, which had been banned by the Church, were again read. It is inconceivable, in our more enlightened days, but it is true nevertheless, that when the Church was supreme all learning, apart from the knowledge of the Scriptures, was looked upon as heresy and sin. This period of awakening is termed the Renaissance or New Birth.

If, indeed, printing had not been discovered, it is doubtful if the Reformation would then have occurred. Printing was invented in 1450. Martin Luther was born in 1483. Until printing was invented, individual thoughts could not be passed on from one to another, and the stagnant pool of orthodoxy remained untroubled. The invention of printing stuck a dagger into the heart of Christendom, and from that day onwards Europe and the world have gradually freed themselves from the curse of priest-craft.

In the century previous to the Reformation, Wycliffe, Huss and others had sounded a warning note that all was not right in the Christian Church. Then followed Luther, who took up the cause in Germany, Ziska in Bohemia, and Zwingli who espoused it in Switzerland. The adherents of the new reform movement became numerous. Much was made by the reformers of the wholesale selling of indulgences by papal agents, and when Luther attacked these iniquities he found willing followers. After much controversy the reformers boldly propounded the principles of the reformed Christian religion, and from that time onwards the struggle grew fast and furious.

---

1 After the fall of the Roman Empire the Pope in Rome became the sovereign power in the west. What remained of the Empire in the east was ruled by emperors from Constantinople, and is known as the Eastern Empire

Hitherto no Bible had been read by anyone except the priests and monks, the people being unable to read or write. Following the invention of printing came the capacity to read and write, and consequently the reformers claimed that the Scriptures should become public property, and not remain only the possession of the Church. The reformers also rejected the doctrine of transubstantiation, the adoration of the Virgin and the saints, and the leadership of the Pope. Luther's excommunication naturally followed, but, as the people began to read and think, the Reformation spread. Ultimately the greater part of Germany, Switzerland, the Netherlands, Scandinavia, England and Scotland were won over to the new teaching.

Living as we do today in a more enlightened world, we do not perhaps fully realise how ignorant were our ancestors before printing was invented, and it is difficult for us to gauge how much the dawn of a new day meant to the world after a night of intense darkness. Luther's whole religious outlook was changed when he got a copy of the Bible and read it through. "I tormented myself to death," he said, "to make my peace with God," and there and then in his monastery he dedicated himself to the task of showing the world the errors of the Church, and what he thought was the only true way to salvation according to the Scriptures.

The reformers were, however, men steeped in ignorance and superstition. Calvin committed murder for the advancement of his trinitarian opinions, and Luther believed Christ's body was present in the holy sacrament, his coarse vehemence being always used against the mental freedom of his opponents. John Knox was only in favour of religious toleration when he was in the minority, and when he obtained the upper hand religious freedom was abolished.

From the discovery of printing also dates the advance of science. Prior to this event everyone took everything just as it appeared. Nothing was known of medicine, astronomy, biology or geology, and the writings of the wise Greek and Roman philosophers and doctors had long been forgotten. Orthodoxy had almost completely obliterated man's reasoning powers, but, as the spark of intelligence burned anew, thoughtful people began to question the divine origin of the religion that had entailed such awful consequences.

The few began to compare Christianity with other religions, and came to the conclusion that the difference between them was negligible. They also wondered why men had to be inspired in order to teach that God instructed his chosen people to make slaves of the people who lived amongst them, whilst Epictetus, a heathen, who was not inspired, could write:-

"Will you remember that your servants are by nature your brothers, the children of God. In saying that you have bought them you look down on the earth and into the pit. It is not the law of the gods."

They also wondered how Cicero, a Pagan, seventy years before Jesus, who had never heard of the Christian scheme of salvation, could write, "They who say that we should love our fellow citizens but not foreigners, destroy the universal brotherhood of mankind, and thus benevolence and justice would perish for ever." Zeno, the founder of the Stoics, endorsed this sentiment in similar words.

A comparison of the teachings of the inspired Bible with those of the Pagan writers, who were not inspired, brought to light the fact that the uninspired teachers were definitely superior to the inspired, which latter the Christian Church, with its warped mentality, still prefers. Why could Cicero, uninspired, write the following: "They whose minds scorn the limitations of the body, are honoured with the frequent appearance of the spirits. Their voices have been often heard, and they have appeared in forms so visible that he who doubts it must be partly bereft of reason"? Yet the writer of Ecclesiastes required to be inspired by the creator of heaven and earth to write the following: "For the living know that they shall die, but the dead know not anything, neither have they any reward, for the memory of them is forgotten."

Why was it necessary to inspire someone to record that Jehovah ordered a Hebrew general to make war, and then gave him the following instructions: "When the Lord thy God shall deliver them before thee, thou shalt smite them and utterly destroy them. Thou shalt make no covenant with them nor show mercy unto them"? And yet Epicures, called a heathen by Christians, could so far surpass his creator in magnanimity that he could say, "Live with thine inferiors as thou wouldst have thy superiors live with thee."

According to Christians, God is reported in the Bible as saying: "I will heap misfortune upon them. I will spend mine arrows upon them. They shall be burned with hunger and devoured with burning heat and with bitter destruction. I will also send the teeth of beasts upon them, with the poison of serpents of the dust. The sword without and the terror within shall destroy both the young man and the virgin, the suckling also, and the man with grey hairs." This, according to Christians, is the morality of their God; whereas Seneca, who was a Pagan, wrote as follows: "The wise man will not pardon every crime that should be punished, but he will accomplish in a nobler way all that is sought in pardoning. He will spare some and watch over some because of their youth, and others on account of their ignorance. His clemency will not fall short of justice, but will fulfil it perfectly."

Again we read that the God whom Christians worship said: "Let his children be fatherless and his wife a widow, let his children be continually vagabonds and beg; let them seek their bread also out of the desolate places. Let the extortioner catch all that he hath, and let the stranger spoil his labour. Let there be none to extend mercy upon him; neither let there be any to favour his fatherless children." And yet Marcus Aurelius, the noblest of the Pagans, who lived as he taught, and gave the world one of the finest examples of the possibilities within humanity, wrote: "I have formed the ideal of a state, in which there is the same law for all, and equal rights and equal liberty of speech established, an empire where nothing is honoured so much as the freedom of the citizen."

Jehovah to his servant Moses gave the command: "Thou shalt have no other gods before me. Thou shalt not bow down to them nor serve them, for I the Lord thy God am a jealous God visiting the iniquities of the fathers upon the children unto the third and fourth generation of them that hate me." The words attributed to the God Brahma by the Hindus showed their God in a much more favourable light as, unlike Jehovah, not fearing competition, he said: "I am the same to all mankind. They who honestly serve other gods involuntarily serve me. I am he who partaketh of all worship, and I am the reward of all worshippers."

All impartial students of the past can come to no other conclusion than that the belief in the inspiration of The Holy Bible, though it has given strength and help to millions, has nevertheless been one of the greatest hindrances to the progress of humanity. This being so, is it not strange that this book is still called "Holy" and "The Word of God" in any civilized place of worship? We can now understand why every battleship when launched receives the blessing of the Church, and is dedicated to God!

Consequently, need we be surprised that history records that amongst professing Christians are to be found some of the greatest blackguards of the past? How could it be otherwise, when they conceived a tyrant in heaven who, they believed, issued instructions to mankind which would disgrace the most brutal savage?

However, the sayings of the great and the good of other lands and of other faiths, men who did not worship a tyrant, brought light to Europe after a dark night of Christianity, during which time the wonderful literature of Greece and Rome lay buried for centuries under the debris of orthodoxy.

It was also found that other non-Christian nations, looked upon as heathen, knew more than Christians did; that in China the astronomers, two thousand four hundred and forty-nine years before Christ, had calculated eclipses, and knew something of the movements of the planets; that in Babylon, five hundred years before Christ, the annual movements of the sun and moon were calculated to within ten seconds of accuracy for the entire year, whereas Christians burned and tortured their astronomers. Thinking people wondered why the authors of *Kings* and *Chronicles* were regarded as inspired while Gibbon, uninspired, could write unaided *The Decline and Fall of the Roman Empire*. Why was the story in the book of *Joshua*, about the sun standing still, inspired, when the Babylonians were not, though for three hundred and sixty years they made astronomical calculations, the longest ever made by man, our Greenwich observations going back only one hundred and eighty one years?

Intelligent people also found that the so-called heathen, the Greeks and Romans, had hospitals and medical services which were obliterated by the coming of Christianity, its teaching being that by prayer the devils causing the disease could be removed. The oldest treatise on surgery was written in Egypt five thousand years ago, and four thousand years ago the Egyptians were writing mathematical treatises of astonishing penetration. So people at last became tired of building cathedrals, and thought the time had come to turn the huts and hovels of the people into decent dwelling-houses.

The thinking people after the Reformation also began to realise that learning had been almost entirely lost, and that if the people had been educated, if they had known more of the literature of Greece and Rome, had studied the science of Aristotle, the ethics of Pythagoras, the philosophy of Plato, and the moralising of Zeno, Epictetus and Epicurus, and had heard less of the teachings of Christianity, Europe would have been a better, happier and more prosperous place.

During the night of Christianity, Europe produced no literature. For a thousand years the minds of men were paralysed by this superstition, and only slowly after the Reformation was the lamp of learning re-lit by the ancient literature of Greece and Rome. The wisdom of these two nations was the basis on which Europe built up her science, literature[1] wisdom and knowledge. The light of Reason, which Christianity extinguished, was re-lit by the writings of men who were not "inspired" or "called" or "saved", and had never heard of the Christian God. The Moslems were the friends and protectors of Science when Christians were burning its pioneers, and it is to the Arabs that we are indebted for laying the foundations of modern science.

This wider outlook not only created a great change in the thoughts of the people from a religious but also from a scientific point of view, and we now see two groups emerging. One, discarding the teachings of the old orthodox Church, held to the Bible as the anchor of their new religion, and the other, comprising men of science, who felt their way forward by appealing to the thought and reason of mankind. By observation and experience they led the thinking section of the people towards a new line of thought and action. The narrow way of the Church, they argued, had led Europe into a wilderness, and they advocated the broad way now being taken, with its borders enriched by all the glories which art, refinement and science could give.

Those leaders of science had to suffer, and suffer cruelly. The early years of the Reformation had given the old Church a cruel blow, yet it was by no means paralysed. We find that Copernicus felt safe in publishing his discoveries, with regard to the planetary system, only on his death bed, and dedicating it to the Pope. Galileo, under the fear of the Inquisition, had publicly to renounce on his knees that the earth moved round the sun, and it was not until the beginning of the nineteenth century that the Church of Rome admitted its error. Spinoza was cut off from all intercourse with his contemporaries, and the anathema which was placed upon him in the name of God stated that he was execrated and cast out of the community. The anathema is too long to quote, but his only crime was that he used the sacred gift of reason, which everyone is given, and by its exercise came to the conclusion that the Bible contained errors and contradictions.

1 Paganism and Christianity, by Farrer, makes clear that we are indebted to the great Pagan philosophers and teachers for our laws, our code of morals, and our ideals, in fact for our present civilisation. Similar views are expressed bit Professor Gilbert Murray in Christianity in the Light of Modern Knowledge.

The so-called divinely appointed Church of Christ 'did not even know the shape of the earth. It thought that diseases were caused by devils. It was not the Church that demonstrated that the earth was round, but Magellan, who left Spain on 10th August 1519, and kept sailing until his ship reached Seville on 7th September, 1522. Bruno, one of the greatest of men, taught the plurality of worlds at a time when the Church believed in a flat earth with its centre at Jerusalem. In those days the Church thought that this earth was the only world in the universe, and that the sun and planets circled the earth. In 1609 Kepler published his book *The Motions of the Planet Mars,* in which he mathematically expressed the relation of distance, mass and motion. He was one of the greatest of scientists, and his three laws were the foundation of the science of Astronomy.

Then followed Newton, Herschell and Laplace, when the astronomy of Joshua faded further into insignificance. Then men began to examine the Locks and strata of the earth, to find that instead of the earth being a few thousand years old, it is hundreds of millions of years old. On the basis of the known rate of the disintegration of the metal uranium into lead, experts can calculate how long these two metals have been in contact, and their calculations prove that the requisite period for uranium to turn into lead is from 340 million to 1,700 million years, according to the nature of the ore.

The Church, since the Council of Carthage, has rested its supreme authority on the statements of Holy Scripture. It based all its knowledge of astronomy, biology and healing on the writings of an ignorant age, and what was the result? It plunged Europe into a night of darkest ignorance, and only when its autocratic power was somewhat overthrown at the Reformation, and men, by slow degrees, were allowed to reason, think and calculate, did Europe make progress and become prosperous.

However there still remained obstacles to progress, because many of the religious reformers were just as cruel and ignorant as the Church they had left, the result being that for two centuries after the Reformation there is one long story of torture, slaughter and misery. All who dared to think for themselves, or thought differently from the reformed Church, were imprisoned, exiled, or put to torture and death. Though Servetus was the first to discover the pulmonary circulation of the blood, yet, because he had unorthodox opinions about the Trinity, he was cruelly murdered by the Protestants. He was the first

Protestant to be burned by Protestants.

The Inquisition was not confined to what is now called the Roman Catholic Church. The Inquisition, and all its accompanying tortures by thumb-screws, racks and other fiendish devices, was just as formidable, and just as fierce, in Protestant Edinburgh and Protestant London as it was in Roman Catholic Spain. Torture inflicted by one sect of so-called reformed Christians on some other sect did not cease in Britain until the landing of William of Orange in 1689, when all those awaiting torture or the scaffold for their religious beliefs were liberated from prison. Imprisonment for unbelief, however, continued until the middle of the 19th century.

Torture, moreover, continued for many years longer in France and throughout Europe, the most appalling cruelties being recorded. Voltaire, who is contemptuously and inaccurately called an atheist by narrow-minded Protestants, abolished torture in France and helped many sufferers. His writings, which exposed the infamies of the Church of his time, did much to break its power in France. He died an old man in 1778, after having lived a life of great vigour and usefulness. All the ridiculous stories of his misery at his death have now been proved to be lies spread by the Church.

I have so far described the conditions in Europe, but the Protestants in America, whither they had gone to obtain religious freedom from the Protestants in England, were just as bigoted and cruel as their co-religionists. Thomas Paine, for instance, one of the founders of the United States of America, who all his life fought for freedom and liberty, and abhorred slavery, was denounced from every Christian pulpit. His crime was that he wrote *The Age of Reason.* He simply took the ground that it is a contradiction to call anything a revelation from God that does not come to us direct. The revelation must be personal, not made to someone else.

He also showed that the so-called prophecies of the Old Testament had nothing whatever to do with Jesus, and that the Old Testament was too barbarous to be the work of an infinitely benevolent God. He did not think there was any evidence that Jesus was God; in other words he was a Unitarian. From the date of the publication of *The Age of Reason* his doom was sealed. He was denounced, deserted, ostracised, shunned, maligned and cursed. He could not safely appear in the streets, and he was treated as a leper. Under the very flag of liberty he had helped to fly his rights were forfeited. He helped to give liberty to more than three million of his fellow citizens, and they denied him his own.

From the moment of his death Protestants started manufacturing the horrors that were alleged to have attended his deathbed, how his bedroom was filled with devils rattling chains, and so on. The truth is that he died in peace, but what he experienced many others suffered from the cruelty and bigotry of Protestantism, and it is well to remember that all the cruelty of the past was not confined to what is now called the Roman Catholic Church, as all Protestant children are taught.

In addition to the suffering and sorrow caused to humanity by the intolerant Church, both Catholic and Protestant, one other crime must be laid to its charge, and that is one from which we are only gradually recovering. The text in *Exodus* already referred to, "Thou shalt not suffer a witch to live," was responsible for the awful crime of witch-burning, and in consequence many thousands of super-sensitive people, called mediums, were almost exterminated.

According to one account I have read, a woman was burned as a witch in Scotland in June 1676, the following notice about it revealing what went on throughout Christendom for five hundred years: "Nae preaching here this Lord's day, the Minister being at Gortachy burning a witch." The Church today can only tell lies about mediums to congregations still steeped in ignorance of the subject, owing to the worship of *The Holy Bible*. If it had been otherwise, and these gifted individuals had been allowed to live, and if people had been intelligent enough to understand them properly, how different would have been the history of Europe!

The gross materialism of the Church and of Science would never have developed, and, instead of science working on purely materialistic lines, it would have realised better man's true position in the universe. Neither theology nor science has yet the correct knowledge of the meaning of our existence and destiny. Theology has searched amongst ancient documents, thinking that from them the riddle of existence could be unravelled. Science, on its part, has ignored the psychic nature of man and looked on him merely as a material creation. Certainly the neglect of psychic science has been a tremendous loss to humanity.

Since 1712, when the last witch was burned in England, mediumship has developed and revealed to us another world about and around us. It has also demonstrated that we are possessed of an etheric body, the exact duplicate of our physical body, that mind is substance which controls the physical body through the etheric body, and that about and around us there is an etheric world to which we shall all pass at death, irrespective of our theological beliefs. Through mediumship Spiritualists have also learned that the material universe is not the whole universe, but only a small part of the universe. What suffering and misery would have been saved to humanity, if this text about killing witches had never been written and mediumship had not been misunderstood!

Moreover the Reverend Jonathan Edwards, and other Protestant divines, if hell had never been invented, would not have tortured the people by teaching that: "The view of the misery of the damned will double the ardour of the love and gratitude of the saints in Heaven." Here is an extract from another theologian's sermon: "The God that holds you over the pit of hell, much in the same way that one holds a spider or some loathsome insect, abhors you and is dreadfully provoked." I shall only quote one more: "The world will probably be convened into a great lake of fire in which the wicked shall be tossed to and fro. Their vitals shall for ever be full of a glowing melting fire, enough to heat the very rocks and elements for ever and ever without any end at all."

These are a few specimens of Protestant preaching, and, if imagination does not reach the same height today, it is because the Bible is taken less seriously in consequence of the advance in scientific knowledge and the teachings of Spiritualism. Protestantism is just as cruel a creed as Roman Catholicism. The two who did as much as any to promote their acceptance and growth were murderers. Constantine killed his own kith and kin, and Calvin murdered Servetus because he disagreed with him. All branches of the Christian Church were tyrannical when they had the power, giving no mercy to anyone. That is the consequence of an "inspired" Church and an "inspired" book. Whenever men think that they, and they only, have divine authority, cruelty and intolerance follow.

Everything advocated in the Bible was considered as coming from God. From every Christian pulpit slavery was upheld because the Bible taught it. The pulpit was the rostrum at which bondage was advocated, and only as the idea of the Bible's divine authorship was abandoned did England cease to support the slave trade, but the Church continued to advocate slavery, to its lasting shame, until the 19th century. Parsons, and others, held stock in slave ships and slave-trading concerns, and justified this by quoting Bible texts. Wilberforce and Clarkson, who dedicated their lives to the abolition of slavery, were denounced from every pulpit in the country, and on them the Christian Church poured contempt and hatred for advocating a course contrary to the will of God.

Just as the belief in inspiration faded, so did the social status of women improve. The Bible looks on woman as the slave of man, and advocates her humiliation. The Bible considers woman to be the property of man. She is, it says, as much below her husband as he is below Christ, whatever that may mean. Nothing is to be found within its covers of a civilised home, with the wife having the same rights and privileges as her husband. She has even to ask forgiveness for bearing children, and take "a sin offering unto the door of the tabernacle, unto the Priest".

Had our ancestors been in closer touch with the etheric world during the Christian era, they would not have quoted Biblical texts to support intolerance of other people's beliefs, or persecuted Spiritualists who, in the early days, were stoned and mobbed going to and from their meetings. Christians would not have everywhere persecuted the Jews because they had crucified Jesus, and so saved the Christians from hell. Clergymen would never have condemned chloroform in childbirth by quoting the story of the fall of man, nor would they have denounced evolution and every contribution to the advance of knowledge made by science.

How different indeed would much of the world have been had the Bible never been considered inspired, and how much happier Christendom will be when all come to look on it as they do other books, admiring its beauties, but ignoring its mistakes and falsities. In view of past mistakes, and the crimes and atrocities it has committed in the name of its founder, the Church today should be humble and penitent instead of arrogant and reactionary.

I look back and see the coiled serpents of superstition awaiting their prey. I see them seize all who try to use the sacred gift of reason. I see gorgeous temples reared amidst degradation and filth, and money spent on sacred edifices instead of on the housing of mankind. I see altars red with the blood of human beings, and the cross of Christ turned into a sword.

I look forward and see a world freed from priestcraft, when everyone possesses the right to express the opinions his reason dictates, without being condemned from the pulpit by those who think they have a divine revelation handed down to them, either through an inspired Church or through an inspired

Book. I see the fear of death removed, and communication between this world of ours and the etheric world, surrounding us, free and untrammelled. Then mediums will be looked upon as sacred instruments, and not denounced by ignorant clerics as they are today. Just as man has developed in other directions and acquired knowledge by experience, so will this knowledge come to him in time, to the great increase of his happiness and well-being.

If Jesus is God, or part of God, as the Christian Church claims, and as Christians say each Sunday they believe, why did he not tell the world something new, something that had never been told before? Why did he not look into the future and say:"In my name, if I do not warn you, crimes, horrors and iniquities will be committed. The hungry flames will torture thousands at the stake. This must never be. That horrible text in Exodus about burning witches must be ascribed to ignorance, and be ignored. My followers must never persecute those who differ from them, as God's holy gift of reason cannot be extinguished. No thumb-screws, racks or scaffolds must be used in my name, and no one must be imprisoned because they are unable to understand the Trinity, or reconcile the contradictions of the Scriptures. No one who disbelieves in the atonement will be punished in hell, and believers in creeds and dogmas will not be the only occupants of heaven."

If Jesus is God he must have known of all the religious wars that would be waged in his name, and the cruelty and the misery which would follow his life on earth. Why did he not warn his followers not to shed blood, to torture and imprison in his name? Why did he leave his disciples with the idea that the world would soon come to an end? Why did he not say which books of the Old Testament were inspired and which of the New Testament would be inspired, instead of leaving it to the Westminster divines to find out, thus allowing Christendom to remain in ignorance of this vital matter for sixteen hundred years?

Why did he distinctly say that he was not God, and that there is only one God, when all the time he was one of three gods? Why did he continually refer to himself as "a human being", which is what has been translated as "Son of Man"? Why did he not explain that what would be translated "Son of God" meant nothing more in the original Aramaic than Servant of God? Why did he never mention the Trinity, if he is one of the three Christian gods ? Why did he give this world no details of the after-life ?

Why did he not say whether Roman Catholicism, Anglicanism, Presbyterianism or Methodism was the way in which he preferred to be worshipped ? Why did he not say that though everything written about him would be traced to earlier religions, yet he only is God, and that all who had preceded him or would follow him, as religious teachers, were impostors? Why did he never mention Christianity, and that it would become the only true religion?

If Jesus is God, the creator of the universe, why did he not tell his followers that this earth is but a speck in immensity, that it is round and not flat, and also something about Astronomy, Geology, Medicine, and the other sciences and arts? Why did he not himself write what he wished us to believe, and not leave his words to be tossed about for centuries in a sea of ignorant superstition, to be the cause of sects and divisions in his Church? Why did he say nothing in favour of education, or whether Evolution or the Adam and Eve story is true?

If Jesus was God he still is God; if God consists of three parts, he is one of them. Christians say, at least once every Sunday, that they believe this. If this be so, then Jesus must have known all the past, and the present, and the future. To him all wisdom, all knowledge, must have been like an open book, and yet he went to his death without telling the world one single fact it did not know before.

Why? Because he was a man and did not know.

Consequently, Christian doctrines, based as they are on error, must give place to a new natural religion based on truth and in conformity with nature's laws. Just as Christianity is the product of preceding religions, which it absorbed, so in time it will inevitably be displaced by Spiritualism, and, as each year passes, the resistance to the unavoidable will decrease until it eventually ceases altogether.

In concluding this chapter I should like to quote from the contribution made by the Rev. James H. Baxter, Professor: of Ecclesiastical History at St. Andrew's University, to that monumental work *Christianity in the Light of Modern Knowledge*. His words are as follows :-

"Upon the popular interpretation and practice of Christianity, the effect of its establishment as the State religion had been profound. If Paganism had been destroyed, it was less through annihilation than through absorption. Almost all that was Pagan was carried over to survive under a Christian name.

Deprived of demi-gods and heroes, men easily, and half unconsciously, invested a local martyr (Jesus) with their attributes, and labelled the local statue with his name, transferring to him the cult and mythology associated with the Pagan deity. Before this century (Fourth) was over the martyr-cult was universal, and a beginning had been made of that interposition of a deified human being between God and man which, on the one hand, had been the consequence of Arianism, and was on the other the origin of so much that is typical of medieval piety and practice. Pagan festivals were adopted and re-named, and Christmas Day, the ancient festival of the sun, was transformed into the birthday of Jesus."

That Christianity was just a new name given to old religious beliefs, rites and ceremonials there is not the least doubt. The reason people continue to believe the old dogmas and creeds is because they were taught them in childhood as true, and have never taken the trouble to investigate the subject for themselves. With mental development the light is now breaking through, and we are now finding that the new knowledge gives us infinitely greater satisfaction than the old beliefs, as it not only satisfies all human longings and desires but, more important still, it is based on truth scientifically established.

CHAPTER IV.

WHAT DID JESUS REALLY TEACH?

IN the foregoing chapter I have given an account of the origin of Christianity and its sacred books, its teachings, and the consequences of these teachings. The Christian Church has no historical basis for the claims it makes with regard to Jesus. These claims are all based on tradition, on stories which passed from one to another, and no one can possibly say whether, as they are now recorded in print, they are in any way like the original statements.

Besides having no historic basis, the claims made by Christians for Jesus are now found to have been made by other religions about their saviours long before the Christian era. Consequently the uniqueness of Jesus has disappeared, and we must now accept the fact that, as portrayed to us, he is only one of many similar legendary crucified saviour god-men whose worshippers believed had died for the sins of the world.

In the introduction to his book *The Jesus of History,* T.R. Glover states that, "The gospels are not properly biographies; they consist of collections of reminiscences, memories and fragments that have survived for years, and sometimes the fragment is little more than a phrase. The gospels are almost avowedly not first hand," and yet, on this flimsy basis, his book advances the most extravagant and absurd claims about Jesus for which there is not a scrap of evidence. This acknowledged pro-Christian book is typical of all Christian literature, but fortunately the people are beginning to find out that they have been deceived by their Christian leaders. For truth and honesty they are now turning to those men who have been termed "Agnostics", "Infidels", "Rationalists" and "Free-thinkers", all terms of reproach in the old days, because they viewed Christianity in a rational way. This chapter will therefore deal with facts, not with fancies; it will keep strictly to the truth, and not try to mislead people into believing something for which there is no evidence.

If we read about an everyday event, an earthquake, for instance, and were told that this event had occurred nineteen hundred years ago, and then discovered that the story had been handed down by word of mouth for forty years or so, to be ultimately recorded in writing. Then we found out that this recording was done by someone who was extremely ignorant of the art, that in those days accurate thinking and writing were not considered important, and that the original had been lost.

However, copies of the original had been made, and lost, but copies of the copies existed, though all the copies in existence differed from each other. Would we be inclined to believe that the details so recorded were in any way reliable?

In this case we are not asked to believe something which we know is a common occurrence, but, on this so-called "evidence", we are asked to believe that something happened that had never happened before and has never happened since. That God the creator of this immense universe came on earth, was born in an unnatural way, raised the dead, and did other wondrous things, without the people of the time believing in them or in him. He was crucified because he was accused of claiming to be God and of having political ambitions, and after death he appeared again in his earthly body to his disciples, ascending afterwards bodily into heaven. If such events were reported as happening today no one would believe them.

We are told, further, that marvellous occurrences took place at his death - earthquakes, the day turned into night, the dead coming out of their graves and walking about Jerusalem. This all happened, though Pliny (who died in A.D. 79, and recorded every earthquake within the knowledge of his time) never mentioned this particular event. We are not told what the dead had to say about having to come back to earth, if they were glad or sorry to be back, or what the other world was like. Was no one sufficiently interested to ask them? If it had been true, we would surely have heard something direct about the other world on this famous occasion. Besides that, we are told that God, by coming to earth, took upon himself the sins of those who believed this, and much more impossible nonsense, and that these would be saved, to live for ever in a fantastic heaven, while those who did not believe would suffer eternal torment in hell.

That is briefly what the churches have preached since A.D. 325, though some of the more enlightened leaders tell us today that this is not now their teaching. Why is this so? What has happened to make the Church change its teaching? And if the Church has changed its beliefs why does it not publicly say so, and withdraw all the books and documents it has published, and is still publishing, supporting this teaching? Until the Church does this publicly it must be accepted that Christian teaching is still substantially the same today as it has been since the Council of Nicaea decided what Christianity was.

I must, therefore, accept the Nicene Creed, the Athanasian Creed, the Thirty-Nine Articles of the Church of England, the

Confession of Faith of the Church of Scotland, and the Shorter and Longer Catechisms, and all the assertions they contain, as representing Protestant Christianity. Roman Catholicism still stands by the old creeds and never wavers, so its position is never in doubt. If these documents do not represent true Christianity, what does ? What is true Christianity, and whence comes the authority for modern Christianity about which everyone has a different opinion?

It is indeed fortunate that enlightened people today do not give a thought to these documents or assertions. They are relegated to a bygone age. The Church today, they realise, has nothing of any value on which to base its claims, and it is supported only by people who have always accepted what it has taught and never reasoned for themselves. Consequently it is only a matter of time for the change to come, because more and more people are now thinking for themselves. Moreover, the Church must ultimately adopt Spiritualism and all Spiritualism stands for. If it does not do so all its authority and influence will go, and it will become the byword of the generations still unborn.

There is no historical evidence that Jesus ever lived.[1] Philo, Tacitus, Pliny, Suetonius, Epictetus and Plutarch, all 1st-century historians of the highest standing, make no mention of him, except that three of them allude to the traditions current about him as promulgated by the Christians of their times. Celsus, the Roman philosopher of the 2nd century, wrote a treatise to prove that there was not a historical fact to show that the claims of the Christians regarding Jesus were justified. There is no historical reference to him anywhere except in what is now believed to be a forgery. The only important piece of evidence we have outside Christian literature is contained in a passage by the Jewish historian Josephus, who wrote in the last decade of the 1st century. This passage will be found in the eighteenth book of the *Antiquities of Josephus*. It runs as follows:-

"Now about this time came Jesus, a wise man, if indeed one may call him a man, for he was a doer of wonderful works, a teacher of such men as receive what is true with pleasure, and he attracted many Jews and many of the Greeks; this was the Christ. And when on the accusation of the principal men

---

[1] Historical and traditional evidence must not be confused. The evidence on which the life of Jesus rests is entirely traditional.

among us Pilate had condemned him to the cross, they did not desist who had formerly loved him (for he appeared to them on the third day alive again, the divine prophets having foretold both this and a myriad other wonderful things about him), and even now the race of those called Christians after him has not died out."

Is this passage accepted by historians and critics as genuine? No, with very few exceptions, they believe that it is an interpolation. It is out of its setting, as immediately following is an indecent tale of Roman society. Origen, the early Christian father, states that Josephus did not believe Jesus to be the Christ. Origen and the early fathers, moreover, were unaware of this passage. Josephus was a Jew, not a Christian, and never became a Christian. Consequently the passage referred to is inappropriate as coming from anyone who was not a Christian. Gibbon, the historian, distinctly states that there is no doubt that it is an interpolation added in the 4th century.

However, for the sake of argument, let us admit that it is genuine, and that Josephus did write it, and that it is a fair representation of the case. What then do we find? Nothing extraordinary, nothing certainly on which to build the creeds and dogmas of the Christian Church. He referred to Jesus as the Christ, which means the Anointed One, but this term was given to other outstanding religious teachers. He also referred to him appearing to his disciples the third day alive again, but this is not extraordinary, as apparitions were as common in those days as they are in our day. We therefore do not require to subvert our reason to accept this account of Jesus. Whether it is genuine or not is of no importance; if it is, it is the only statement there is respecting Jesus of any value.

Let us now consider, from the unreliable evidence we have before us,[1] from the contradictions of the gospel narratives, and their many obvious mistakes, what it is possible that Jesus really taught, and I think I can show from three of the gospels that what he is reported as having taught was just what we might expect from a religious teacher of his day. In none of the four gospels does he claim to be founding a new religion. He was born a Jew, lived a Jew, and died a Jew, as we have already remarked.

---

[1] Professor Harnack (called "one of the greatest living experts in this branch of scholarship" by the Christian Evidence Society) in his book *What is Christianity?* states that he believes the gospels are only credible in their outlines

Taking, first of all, the first three gospels as a basis for this discussion, let us go through them one by one. The gospel which is attributed to Matthew, tells us that our being saved depends on how we live. According to the gospels, Matthew was a disciple of Jesus and constantly with him for the two years of his ministry. Nothing is to be found here to justify the Church's creeds or doctrines. Briefly, Matthew tells us that Jesus taught that heaven would be attained by those who were poor in spirit, merciful, pure in heart, peacemakers, persecuted for righteousness' sake, and kept the ten commandments; also by those who forgave their enemies, who judged not, but who received righteous men and did the will of God.

According to Matthew, Jesus also taught that every man shall be rewarded according to his works, and that we must become as little children. That we are to sell all that we have and give to the poor; that we should forsake brethren, sisters, father, mother, wife and children for his sake; and, lastly, that we should honour our father and mother, feed the hungry and give drink to the thirsty, shelter to the stranger, clothe the naked, comfort the sick, and visit the prisoner in prison.

Again I read in the same book, "And behold one came and said unto him, 'Good master, what good thing shall I do that I may have eternal life?'" Now here was a chance really to find the truth. Here was an enquiry direct from man to God, so the Church Says, a direct question, the answer to which everyone of us wants to know. "What good thing shall I do that I may have eternal life?" What did Jesus reply? He did not say that his enquirer must believe that he is the second person in the Trinity. He did not say he must be baptised. He did not say that he must believe the Bible to be the inspired word of God. He did not say he must repeat something and believe something. No! Jesus simply stated, "Thou shalt do no murder, Thou shalt not commit adultery, Thou shalt not steal, Thou shalt not bear false witness, Honour thy father and mother, and Thou shalt love thy neighbour as thyself." What right has the Church to add conditions to salvation which Jesus did not think necessary? Why add to, or take away from, this direct answer to a direct question?

I now pass on to the gospel attributed to Mark. This document is considered by all students of the subject to be the nearest to the truth concerning the life and sayings of Jesus. It is the least legendary or miraculous of the gospels. Jesus is depicted as a good man, and the virgin birth, and the other miraculous stories about him, are noticeable by their absence.

My friend F.C. Burkitt, Professor of Divinity at Cambridge, published in 1932 *Jesus Christ, an Historical Outline*, it being an attempt to form a reasonable view of Jesus, his life and teachings. It should be read by those interested in pursuing the subject further. He regards the gospel of *Mark* as the oldest gospel, remarking, "I regard the framework of the Gospel of Mark as based on much the same authority as the contents, that is to say, reminiscences more or less faithful," and again, "Matthew and Luke on the other hand do preserve singly fragments of genuine tradition." On this "more or less faithful" story are built up, in his opinion, the gospels of *Matthew* and *Luke*, and that is all we have to go on in considering what is contained in the first three gospels.

I find that in this gospel of *Mark* there are also conditions stated regarding salvation which are similar to those given in *Matthew,* with one exception, and this occurs in a passage reading from the ninth verse to the end of the last chapter. It does not invalidate the argument, however, as this passage is now known to be an interpolation. It is not in the oldest manuscripts, and particular attention is drawn to this fact in the Revised Version of the Bible. It enables one to see how valueless the gospels are, as this is only one of one hundred interpolations which are easily recognised, occurring as they do in later versions, and not in the earlier versions.

The words in all these interpolations are quite out of their setting, and have no reference to what is being reported. One of the best examples of an interpolation is the remark attributed to Jesus that Simon Barjona would henceforth be known as "Peter, and upon this rock I will build my Church". This simple fisherman knew only Aramaic, the language Jesus and his contemporaries spoke. This language contains no word for church and it is most unlikely that Simon would receive a Greek name meaning a stone. This word-play could only be understood by one knowing Greek, and must have been inserted centuries later when a copy was being made by some zealous scribe whose enthusiasm for the Church was greater than his honesty.

Another blatant forgery is the story of the woman taken in adultery, which is a late addition and is not in the oldest known codices. This fact is clearly marked in the Revised Version, but it in itself is enough to cast discredit on the entire Bible. This, and many other instances, make clear that the book is just a patchwork of stories which have no veridical value, and are probably nearly all fictitious.

These interpolations and alterations to the original text started at an early date, and are known to have gone on up to the 17th century. To show how unreliable is the entire Bible, mention need only be made of the complaint expressed by Dionysius of Corinth in the year A.D. 170, who exposed the falsification of his own writings, but consoled himself with the fact that the same is done to the Scriptures of the Lord.

Passing on to the gospel of *Luke,* I find the same teaching, namely good works, good thoughts, injunctions to forgive our enemies, as, just as we forgive, so shall we be forgiven. In a few words, Jesus preached a gospel of love and service to our fellow men, and love to God, our Father in Heaven.

Lastly, we come to Saint John's gospel, and here we find the basis of the Church's teaching. Here we find that belief is everything, and that our reaching heaven depends on our beliefs and not on our deeds. This seems rather extraordinary. Here we have four records reputed to contain the sayings of Jesus. In three of them we are told that Jesus taught good works, good living, and kindness of heart, and never a word about belief. Why was it that Matthew, Mark and Luke never heard anything about salvation by faith?

How was it that they forgot to record that Jesus said, "For God so loved the world that he gave his only begotten son, that whosoever believeth in him should not perish, but have everlasting lie"? If these four records are inspired by God, why is this, and many other similar statements, omitted from three of them, and only recorded in one of them? If belief is essential to salvation it should at least have been the other way about, in fact it should have been recorded in them all.

However, reducing it to a question of mathematics, we have three to one against belief, and one to three in favour of belief, and the average good man, when he reaches heaven, if he is confronted by the question on the Day of Judgment, will have a very good case when he stands up to justify his claim to be allowed to enter heaven. He can tell the Judge of all the Earth that in the four gospels he finds that three of them stated that how he lived on earth determined his admission to heaven, and only one stated that it was a question of believing something he found impossible to believe. Can anyone imagine a righteous judge on earth condemning such a man? Certainly not, and no intelligent individual can imagine God doing so. We must not impute to the Almighty a justice inferior to our own.

Now, it may be asked, why is there this extraordinary difference between the gospel of *Saint John* and the other three gospels? The reason is readily apparent to those who have studied the origin of the gospels. The gospel of *Saint John* was not written until a later date than the first three gospels. It was written not earlier than the 2nd century, at a time when a small section of the Church had come to believe that beliefs were necessary to salvation. The document can be described as an afterthought, because "The contents of the Gospel of John do not seem to the present writer historical at all," and "I greatly doubt whether we can distinguish often in that gospel what is derived from tradition and what is derived from imagination." This is the view expressed by Professor Burkitt in his book already referred to.

I have already shown that a large section of the early Christian Church did not believe that creeds were necessary to salvation, or that Jesus was the son of God. There were quite a number of sects in the early Christian Church, and the gospel of *Saint John* represents the opinion which gradually developed, namely that one had to believe something to be a Christian. An early Christian looked on Jesus as a teacher and doer of good deeds, whereas this opinion gradually changed until it was evenly divided, some continuing to hold the original Christian view, and others the opinion that belief was necessary for salvation.

Thus we find that at the Council of Nicaea the two opinions were boldly expressed, and only by a majority vote did those who held that belief was necessary win their point. From that time onwards to hold a certain belief was necessary to be a Christian, but it was certainly not the teaching of Jesus, and it was not accepted by his early followers.

Paul is reputed to be the originator of the idea that to believe something was necessary to be a Christian, that Jesus took the sins of the world, and that we are justified by faith in him. What Paul wrote, or believed, we can only surmise, as the epistles attributed to him have no historical value; they are unsigned, no one knows when they were written; and the same can be said of the epistles attributed to the other disciples. Those who have carefully studied the previous chapter can quite reasonably believe that many doctrines now believed were later additions to the original.

None of the epistles attributed to Paul ever refers to, or quotes from, the gospels, probably because they were written at an earlier date. Assuming it was Paul who wrote them, it must be remembered that he never knew Jesus, and could not have been acquainted with his teaching as were his contemporary followers. The writer of the epistles attributed to him based his opinions on the Book of the Law, and was thus imbued with the idea that Jesus was the longed-for Messiah mentioned therein - a belief which was purely a personal one. As the origin of those epistles is unknown, no known person having seen the original documents, this opinion may be interesting but is of no value.

Those who have studied the question consider that the first three gospels represent the teaching of Jesus more accurately than does Saint John's gospel or the epistles. Nothing, it must be remembered, was put in writing for years after the death of Jesus, the reason being, as Dr. Moffatt says in his introduction to his *New Translation of the New Testament,* that there was no impulse to do so, as they were all awaiting the new age at any moment. So why should they write anything? When this great event did not materialise, according to Dr. J.A. McClymont in his *New Testament and its Writers,* "a considerable modification of the oral gospel would naturally take place, during the long period that elapsed before it was committed to writing".

What then is the answer to the question, What did Jesus really teach? The copies of the many previous copies of the original synoptic gospels, certainly lend the greatest weight towards the belief that Jesus taught that how we lived here would determine our place in the hereafter. He taught a very simple religion: belief in the Fatherhood of God; the Brotherhood of Man; belief in the after-life; that, as we lived here, we should live there, and that as we were forgiving and kind here, so would we receive forgiveness and kindness there.

Putting aside all the accretions which have surrounded this simple teaching, one can believe that Jesus, by means of his psychic gifts, was in close touch with a higher order of existence, and that he saw that this life on earth was a preparation for a better and a greater life hereafter. He went about doing good, trying to heal the sick with his psychic power, teaching forgiveness, love, charitableness, and preaching against the errors of his own day. He was a reformer in his own time, a man we must respect and admire. He was murdered by the orthodox of his day, who hated his outspoken criticism of their beliefs and actions. All who have the love of humanity at heart cannot but admire this unselfish and humane man, who went about doing good, but do not let us forget that many, both before and after him, have lived similar lives and sacrificed them for their fellow men.

His teaching was based on the basic principles which had

been accepted by all the great teachers who had preceded him, and only in Spiritualism do we find those great fundamental principles emphasised and the accretions ignored. I submit that Spiritualism is the only natural religion for the present and the future, just as it has been the only natural religion of the past. Just as today it is accepted only by the few who really know the truth, so in the past has it been accepted by the few who likewise knew the truth, because they, like the Spiritualists of today, were in close contact, and held communication, with the higher intelligences of the etheric world.

Round the basic truths of Spiritualism mankind, in ignorance, has coiled superstitions which in different forms have become embodied in the world's past and present religions. It is the duty of Spiritualists to uncoil the false from the true, and reveal the truth, which orthodoxy everywhere has hidden in a black robe of superstition and ignorance. When Spiritualists succeed in educating the world to recognise the truth, then men and women of all nations will have a common knowledge of the great facts of existence, all religious differences, now so evident, will disappear, and mankind everywhere will worship in one cathedral whose dome is the firmament, and whose true and only priests are the interpreters of nature.

CHAPTER V.

ANOTHER REFORMATION NEEDED.

FOUR centuries ago what is known as the Reformation occurred in the Christian Church. This organisation had become so corrupt, and so out of touch with the times, that it was split in two, some preferring to remain within the old Church and others deciding that a new Christian Church was needed. Under the leadership of Martin Luther, what is known as Protestant Christianity carved for itself a new Christianity, discarding some of the old Christianity hitherto thought essential, and adopting new interpretations of some of the old beliefs. Though the creeds were retained, a number of dogmas were changed.

The people in pre-Reformation times worshipped and adored the Church, believing it to be a divine institution, the Pope was regarded as the divine representative of God on earth, and the priests were believed to be endowed with divine authority. The priests claimed the power to forgive sin and punish wickedness, and so things went on until the Reformation. All that the people had to do was to go to Church regularly, repeat the Latin prayers, participate in the celebration of Mass, little thought being given to what it all meant. They were told that if they did so they would live in bliss in the life to come, and that if they did not do so they would suffer eternal damnation. This mental state of accepting everything the Church teaches still continues to exist amongst the ignorant people of today, both Catholic and Protestant.

The Protestant Church, which came into being at the Reformation, claimed that every one had the right to think for himself, but that, if any thought differently from what their leaders said was true, they would be damned eternally. The Protestant leaders, now that printing and reading had come into being, took the Bible as their guide, discarding the Pope and his divine authority. The Bible, however, was a very different book at the Reformation from what it is today. It contained many books that the reformers omitted, and there were many different versions in existence. Gradually it became realised that if the Bible was to be the standard of the new Church, a version of it must be produced which was standardised, and so, in the year 1611, what is now called the Authorised Version of the Bible was produced.

Following this, an assembly, called the Westminster Divines, met in London in 1643 and produced what is known as the Westminster Confession of Faith. This was rejected in England but accepted in Scotland. The Confession of Faith extends to thirty-nine chapters, ranging over the most abstruse topics of theology, and along with it are printed the Longer and Shorter Catechisms, also adopted by the Church of Scotland. The Confession of Faith, rejected in England, meant that the Church of England still relied on the Thirty Nine Articles, for whose production Cranmer was chiefly responsible. It took from 1536 to 1571 to settle these Articles. They were first ten in number, then rose to forty-two, and were finally settled at thirty-nine. The other Protestant countries in Europe also adopted various definitions of their reformed faith, and thus we find a repetition, in the years immediately following the Reformation, of what took place at Nicaea. The Christian religion was again recast.

The Protestant Church today still retains, repeats, and says it believes, the creed of Nicaea, formulated in A.D. 325, and the creed of Athanasius, formulated and accepted early in the 9th century. Besides this it bases its beliefs on those documents which were accepted as divinely inspired after the Reformation. The Roman Catholic Church still retains the beliefs and doctrines it has always held. There is, therefore, this feud between Roman Catholicism and Protestantism. The former is rounded entirely on the findings of the Councils in the early days of Christianity, while the other is established on the findings of these Councils, supplemented by the findings of the Councils of Divines which met together from time to time following the Reformation.

The Church of Rome, which claims to be the expounder of true Christianity, is at variance in some vital points with Protestant Christianity, because the Roman Catholic Church still advocates and preaches the views expressed in the 4th century, whereas the Protestant Church preaches and believes the views expressed in the 16th and 17th centuries. The Protestant Church claims that it is right and bases this claim on the Holy Scriptures, and the Roman Catholic Church asserts that it is right and bases this assertion on the beliefs as they had developed in the 4th century.

As education advanced, some thinking people began, with increasing frequency, to enquire as to the basic facts the Church as a whole had for its teachings. The intelligent person now wants to know why certain doctrines are being preached, and what foundation there is for those doctrines being claimed as divinely inspired and true. They want to know why in the

20th century, we must accept the findings of the Council of Nicaea, or the Council of Westminster, or the opinions of Cranmer. They want to know the why and wherefore of these fundamental doctrines. The more we enquire into the reason, the more we find to convince us that there is no real basis whatever for these doctrines, which were promulgated by zealous churchmen with little learning but a vast amount of credulity.

We find also that the Protestant Church, basing its doctrines on the Bible, has based them on sand instead of on a rock. Moreover, this was shifting sand, and, with the collapse of its foundation, a profound change has been brought about in the outlook of all thinking people on the question of what must be considered the fundamentals of belief. The Westminster Divines pronounced the Holy Bible divinely inspired word for word, that it contained no mistakes, no contradictions, and that it was a complete and final record of God's dealing with man and of God's plan of salvation. They asserted that the Bible contained a scheme which required to be believed in, and that this scheme ensured the believer's happiness hereafter, and the unbeliever's damnation.

They believed also that God's revelation to man ended with the last word of the last chapter of the book of *Revelation,* and that from that time onwards God had been silent. This still remains the orthodox belief held by the Protestant Church, whether it be Church of England, Presbyterian or Methodist. Officially, the beliefs expounded in the 16th and 17th centuries are the beliefs of our Church today, and consequently the book of Common Prayer is read word for word as it was read hundreds of years ago, and the Bible is read word for word as it was read hundreds of years ago.

The reader commences the reading of the Bible by saying, "Here beginneth the Word of God," and ends his reading by again quoting God as the author of what he has read. Every petition and prayer is ostensibly to the same God that the Jews still worship, and concludes with the name of Jesus Christ, no petition being considered valid without this ending. The Bible is still considered officially a holy book, sacred and verbally true. Its stories are preached on as if they were true, and its scheme of salvation is still propounded as the only way of man's salvation. No parson ever preaches from any other book than the Bible, as the opinion of the Church still is that it, and it only, has been divinely inspired.

In the Anglican Church all these antiquated formulae and

expressions of opinion are repeated Sunday after Sunday, and presumably the people who do repeat them believe them. If they do not they are very dishonest. If they do they are extremely credulous.

Officially, the Church has never changed its views, and still retains the same antiquated ideas about many of the fundamental and most important things of life. It would be easy to criticise and make light of many of the expressions in the Prayer Book, in connection with the baptism, marriage, confirmation and the morning and evening services. It would be also easy to criticise the funeral service, and show how out of date are many of the expressions of opinion. How foolish, for instance, it is to believe that what the Church calls "the dead" sleep in their graves until some future time called the Resurrection, when the bodies are to be reanimated and rise again from the grave. It would be easy to say how unworthy it is to repeat glibly the many horrible expressions of cruelty and lust in the Psalms. It would not be difficult to show the cruelty and absurdity of the Athanasian Creed, and the stupidity of the Nicene Creed. In fact it would be easy to criticise and pull to pieces the entire Prayer Book, but to do this would require a chapter instead of a page.

Presumably, those who regular/y attend Church believe all they say they believe, as if they do not they are making wilful utterances of what they know to be false, and this wickedness must react on their characters. At some future date, when they recognise more clearly the necessity for honest thinking in building up their characters, they will regret subverting their reason to common custom and usage. This criticism can also be extended to what is called the Free Churches, and the Church of Scotland, as though the people do not repeat these absurdities, they yet listen to them being uttered by the parson.

Fortunately, however, there are people who are honest enough to refuse to repeat what they do not believe, and consequently they stay away from church.

Because of this attitude of the Church, never to change with the changing times, the attendance at public worship is gradually getting smaller, and the pews are gradually emptying. Various devices are adopted by ingenious parsons to try to fill their churches, but they are only temporarily effective, because, as the novelty passes off, the church is nearly empty again. The truth of the matter is that an ever greater number of people today believe that truth comes before usage and custom. They object to their reason being debased every time they enter a church. Those who feel like this are steadily increasing in number, and the progress of Spiritualism is making the decline in church attendance all the more marked.

Last century the people, rather than believe nothing, subverted their reason, thinking that in doing so they were pleasing the Almighty. Today, however the position is different. In every large centre there are quite a number of Spiritualist churches, and in the smaller centres there is at least one. The Spiritualists are buying up churches from impoverished orthodox communities, and the number of Spiritualist churches is increasing yearly, as the people, through Spiritualism, are finding their longings and aspirations satisfied. They are discovering in it a religion that satisfies their reason and their conscience, a religion that helps them through life arid comforts them at death, a religion that makes clearer to them their origin and their destiny.

The foregoing is a brief statement of facts, and I challenge anyone to refute them. So the time has come to ask seriously, What is the Christian Church going to do about it? Is it for ever going to remain tied to the theologians of the past? Will it never be able to evolve a religion that will satisfy the intellect of the average intelligent member of the community? Are its priests going to continue to pander to the ignorant, and, when these have become educated, are they going to continue to preach the old doctrines and dogmas to empty pews? Do they think that the hand of time is standing still, and that what they consider heresy today is not going to become the orthodoxy of tomorrow? Do they think that history will fail to repeat itself, as it has repeated itself in the past, for the heterodoxy of one age has always become the orthodoxy of the next. The mind of man never remains for long stationary. *Semper idem* is a very dangerous policy.

I am not prepared to prophesy what the Christian Church intends to do, as the mentality of the clergy has always puzzled me, and I would not be so bold as to try to unravel such a tangled skein. I shall, however, say this. If the Church does not move with the times, and does not discard all its old dogmas and doctrines, and accept Spiritualism, then within a few generations it will be discredited and abandoned. A new Church will have taken its place, and that Church will be guided, not by the theories and formulae of dead theologians, but by some of the great minds who have survived death, and are today guiding the Spiritualist Church on its road to victory. No man can stem the ocean's tide, and no Church can stop the rising tide of Spiritualism, because the waves of the etheric world are breaking with increasing force on the shores of this world of ours.

There are, therefore, two courses open to the Christian Church to follow. One is to ignore all psychic phenomena, and continue to look upon them as fraud, or as the work of the devil. The other course is to accept what men and women of honour and intelligence have to say, men and women of our own time, who claim, and rightly claim, that what they affirm is not their theories, but teaching which has come from those who once lived here and have been appointed to guide the lives of those on earth.

If Christians prefer to go back nineteen hundred years, and accept as true what is reported to have been said by people in those far-off years, handed down in writings of more than doubtful value, then there is nothing more to be said. If they prefer to believe what someone is reported to have said about something, which is recorded in a copy of many age-old doubtful copies going back some nineteen hundred years, and disbelieve the hundreds of thousands of people of the present day, in our own country, who have experienced the validity of this new revelation, then again there is nothing more to be said.

In Great Britain alone there are nearly 1,500 Spiritualist churches, and at least three million Spiritualists, people of honesty and intelligence, many of whom claim to have communicated with those who have passed on, and in consequence cannot do otherwise than consider the old dogmas and doctrines to be the product of an ignorant age. The number of Spiritualists throughout the world amounts to many millions, and is increasing everywhere.

The choice is difficult for the clergy to make, because they have kept their congregations so long in ignorance, and in most cases they are as ignorant as their congregations, but the choice some day will have to be made, and that day is looming nearer and nearer.

Spiritualists have never tortured or persecuted those who differed from them. They have always upheld the freedom of thought and avoided doing harm to anyone. Instead, therefore, of parsons holding Spiritualists up to ridicule and scorn, calling them deluded people, the victims of the devil and his followers, the clergy should remember the terrible history of their own institution, the crimes it has committed in the name of religion and its 25 million innocent victims.

Of course, all I have written with regard to the origin of Christianity and the Bible should be well known to every intelligent individual. Is it not all recorded in many standard books, whose findings have never been disproved, and also by various leading professors of Biblical history who likewise have never been proved wrong? This being so, would it not be more correct to say that the clergy and not the Spiritualists are under a delusion? It is the Spiritualists who are at pains to prove all things, and whose beliefs, based on present-day evidence which is incontestable, are founded on truth, whereas the clergy rely on very doubtful tradition and ancient superstition for their beliefs, and cannot bring forward any historical evidence for their assertions.

It would be well for the clergy to cease from branding Spiritualists as "The servants of the devil" when they have no authority whatever for expressing such an opinion. Just as most of the clergy in this country made fools of themselves and their congregations by denouncing evolution, so they are likewise making themselves and their congregations look ridiculous by their latest attempt to mislead the people.
Here are quotations taken from four recent sermons which are typical examples of many. The first is:-

"Spiritualism affords the devil and his angels the opportunity to drag men down to perdition." The next is:-

"Spiritualism is a perfectly devised instrument of the devil. A conspicuous feature of this cult is the absence of God." And this, in spite of the fact that the first principle of Spiritualism is the Fatherhood of God. The third is :-

"Spiritualism breaks God's laws and is the work of the devil."

Consider the bigotry of these self-appointed interpreters of God's purpose towards men! It is calculated that there are 100,000 seances held in Great Britain every week, and in practically every case prayer is offered to God, and protection is asked against the forces of evil. Approaching the unseen in this spirit of reverence protects us from all danger, as, with minds of high purpose, our etheric friends can keep away all evil influence. This preaching against Spiritualism takes place Sunday after Sunday up and down the country, and I could fill very many pages with similar extracts, but, as they all run on the same line, I shall quote but one more.

"Spiritualists are a deluded people, seduced into belief in a lie, and the victims of the evil one."

I withhold the names of these four representatives of the

Protestant Church as some day they will regret their folly, and I do not wish to brand them for life.

These pronouncements, however, are samples of the preaching delivered from Christian pulpits throughout the country by the clergy, whose mission in life is to keep the people believing the Church's doctrines at all costs, and, by throwing dust in the people's eyes, by fair means or foul, to prevent them from knowing the truth. They quote various Biblical texts to support their theory, but do not tell their congregations that there is no historical foundation or basis for any of those texts quoted, and that there is no evidence of divine inspiration for one of them. It is they, and their fellow Christians, who are believers in a lie, not Spiritualists, who can adduce scientific reasons for the beliefs they hold, and, moreover, can prove to anyone wishing to have the proof that all they assert is true.

Unlike Spiritualist newspapers, which will publish articles and advertisements of books for and against Spiritualism, most Church newspapers will not publish any advertisements of books on Spiritualism, and only articles against Spiritualism. They remind me of a boy who has blown up a soap bubble, and who protects it from every breath of wind in case it bursts. If the Church doctrines were founded on a solid basis of truth there would be no need for any fear, as truth can always protect itself. The clergy today are either misrepresenting Spiritualism or, by means of the Christian Press, exerting themselves to keep the people from knowing about it. The more they vituperate and lie the nearer is coming the collapse of the whole edifice of creeds, dogmas and superstition.

The clergy add nothing to the sum of human knowledge, they produce nothing, and take the first tenth of all the produce of the land for work similar to what is done in Spiritualist churches voluntarily and wholeheartedly.[1] The people, in their ignorance, pay heavily to be taught error, whereas, when they become sufficiently intelligent, they will find that revelation will come to them from the higher intelligences of the etheric world.

The clergy officiate at marriages, which can be done equally well by the Registrar, they can sprinkle water on infants,

---

[1] Spiritualist churches and Sunday schools are all run by voluntary effort though the clairvoyant at the church service usually gets a small fee. Funeral services are conducted voluntarily, and so also are all the social services connected with each church. Those in trouble or sickness are helped and cared for by voluntary helpers. Most churches have healing circles at which all help is voluntary.

perform before the altar, and pronounce meaningless words at the grave-side, and many millions of pounds are spent annually to keep this class in comfort while thousands of would-be producers are in poverty. They flourish on ignorance, and where the people are most ignorant priests are most numerous. They excel in the art of devising reasons why the people should never think for themselves, and they have been the greatest obstacle to progress recorded in history. They keep the people in ignorance and then take credit for comforting them in trouble, sickness, old age and bereavement, whereas, if the people were encouraged and helped to think for themselves, their ministrations would not be required.

Those of us who are known to have been in touch with the etheric world are daily in receipt of a large correspondence from people in trouble, people in sorrow and people who are losing all hope. Those people have lost faith and belief in the old religion, and they turn to us for guidance and for comfort. Those who are paid to do this work have failed the people, and this is becoming more and more generally recognised. *If the Church leaders could see the correspondence which comes into my house every day from people who have been kept from suicide, who have been kept from the asylum, and who have regained hope and received comfort as the result of the help, satisfaction and guidance Spiritualism has been able to give them, they would realise how lamentably the Church has neglected its opportunity, and how disastrously it is failing in its duty.*[1]

It would be difficult to count the number of people who have told me of the help Spiritualism has given them in the darkest hour of their sorrow. This testimony is poured out on all hands. Just the other day a woman spoke to me after I had addressed a large audience in the Birmingham City Hall. She told me she had recently lost her husband.

The vicar had called, and the only consolation he could offer her was to suggest that she should attend Holy Communion. "How will this satisfy me that my husband still lives?" she

---

[1] The following is an extract from a letter from a clergyman who is one of the London Missionary Society's missionaries on an island in the Pacific. He is devoting his life there to work amongst the lepers: "I am most happy and overjoyed with *On the Edge of The Etheric*. This is the Gospel. All goodness is worth while in a way I never understood before." I give this extract to show that self-sacrifice will not cease when Spiritualism takes the place of Christianity.

asked him. To which he answered, "We have the blessed hope of everlasting life through Jesus Christ our Lord." She replied: "Whatever is the good of hope? I want help from someone who knows, not from someone who hopes only." Thus he left her, and she told me that what I had told her that night in my address was the first real comfort she had experienced since her husband's passing. I put her in touch with a good medium, and great was her delight in heating her husband speak to her, and prove without doubt that he still lived, and that they would meet again.[1]

In this country alone, many millions of pounds are spent annually by the community to maintain the clergy and their churches, for the purpose of preserving ancient and worn-out creeds and dogmas. These clerics are securely entrenched in their positions, as the majority of them are entitled to emoluments which it is very difficult for the people to divert into other channels. In the Church of England the people have no say as to who is to be their parson. He is appointed by a patron who may have no interest in the congregation, but he owns the living as an investment. These livings are bought and sold, and the people accept tiffs system like sheep as they do everything else in connection with the Church. In Scotland this scandal was swept away ninety years ago.

Our religious leaders feel they are safe and comfortable, and they think that all they have to do is to continue as their predecessors did and repeat the same worn-out formula. But it will not do. Immediately prior to the Reformation the same complacency was exhibited by the priests of what we now call the Church of Rome. Then men arose and led the people into a new and different line of thought. What happened then is happening today, slowly and surely, and gradually the Church is becoming alarmed at the number of desertions among its adherents.

[1] I arranged that this lady should go quite anonymously and no one would know who she was. She travelled many miles to sit with the medium, so she was consequently a stranger to him. The following are some extracts from her long letter reporting to me the results obtained:-

"You asked me to let you know the result of my sitting. I cannot express my gratitude for all your kindness to me. It is beyond words. I had a most successful sitting. Many friends spoke to me by the direct voice. My husband spoke to me, using his pet name for me, and giving his own name correctly. It was all most convincing. I managed to arrange a second sitting and this was as good as the first. I have been truly comforted and convinced"

This is only one of many hundreds of similar letters I have received from people who have obtained conviction and comfort as the result of the contact made with the etheric world through mediumship.

Those who are sufficiently interested to enquire further will discover the reason. Spiritualist services are attracting ever larger congregations, and everywhere, throughout London and in the provincial towns, meetings, both large and small, are held, the largest halls available being often packed to capacity when a well-known medium is giving clairvoyant and clairaudient messages to the audience from the platform. The people are desperately anxious to find out more about the after-life, and only the influence of the Church prevents the B.B.C. from broadcasting a Spiritualist service.

There are some Spiritualists who believe that the Church will adopt Spiritualism, lock, stock and barrel, and discard in one fell swoop all its dogmas and doctrines. Others think that Spiritualism will permeate the teaching of the churches slowly, just as the belief in evolution did. Personally I believe in the leavening process as the one likely to happen, and that it will come about by necessity, not by the wish of the clergy, but because truth must prevail.

An interesting episode in Church history, relating to mediums being banished from taking part in church services, will be found in my book on the origin of the Christian faith, entitled *The Psychic Stream*. Up to the 4th century, mediums took the leading part in the service, but, as the power of the priests increased, the medium was banished, because he, or she, overshadowed the priest. For the same reason today the priesthood will not take second place to the medium.

Historians of the future will have the same old story to tell, namely the Church, which claims to be divinely inspired, being led into the way of truth but never leading; always reactionary, and only accepting something better when forced to do so. If truth only had been the watchword of the Church, and if we had heard less of divine authority, how differently religion would be looked upon today! Fortunately, at long last, the people are now differentiating between Religion and Superstition. What goes under the name of Christianity is superstition; true religion is something very different.

CHAPTER VI.

RECONSTRUCTION.

THE reason why I have given so much space to the consideration of the Christian religion, is because so many earnest and devout people find that their belief in Christianity makes it impossible for them to accept the teachings of Spiritualism. The last thing I wish to do is to unsettle anyone's beliefs regarding the great fundamental issues of life and death. If I thought I was doing this, I would be the first to regret it. Some of those who have read this book thus far may think that I have tried to destroy all that they hold most dear. If they will read to the end of the book, they will realise that I have only pulled down for the purpose of building up.

History shows us that in the past the majority of the people have generally been opposed to change of any kind, either in politics or in religion. Both political and religious reformers have had to suffer from the criticism and enmity of those who believed that what is, must always be. In earlier times those who wished to change the political or religious views of the people had to suffer imprisonment and often torture. However, in our day and generation, all that need be expected by would-be reformers is criticism and perhaps abuse.

At the risk of repetition, I wish to make my position quite clear, so that there may be no misunderstanding. Christianity, it will be admitted by everybody, originated in an age of intense ignorance. It was born at a time when hardly anyone could read or write, and even those who could write had very poor material to work upon. At that time paper was unknown, and anything that was written was written on papyrus, manufactured from reeds and rushes. Accuracy of speech or thought was hardly known. Facts had not the value then that they.have now, and greatly exaggerated stories were told and circulated about events, especially when those events were of an unusual character. Anything unusual, or not understood, was considered to be the direct act of God or the gods.

It is only within the last three centuries that we have come to realise that the universe is governed by law and order, and that every event is but one incident in an unbroken chain of cause and effect. The workings of nature in years gone by were not in the least understood. Nineteen hundred years ago nothing whatever was known by the masses about Astronomy, Biology, Chemistry, Physics, the art of healing or any of the other sciences. In Palestine, at the time of the birth of Jesus, the people were more ignorant and more uncivilised than are the American negroes of today. They were poor, ignorant and superstitious.

From this well of ignorance, the majority in Europe and America draw all their information with regard to their religious beliefs. In the old days they drank long and deep, but, as they advanced in intelligence, the draughts became lighter and less frequent. What, then, is the position today with regard to this source of knowledge? Simply this: a large section of the Christian community still hold to the old beliefs, but in a much more feeble way than of yore, while there is a large and increasing section to whom the claims of Christianity make no appeal. Though they may be nominally Christians, they are absolutely indifferent to the whole subject. In other words, orthodox religion makes no appeal to them. They hold the view that their duty in life is to do the best they can, and, if there is another life after death, they will take the consequences of what they have done. A much smaller section have no religion whatever, and are strongly anti-Christian, because of the false claims made by Christianity, believing that all religion is superstition which should be avoided by every sensible-thinking man and woman.

Lastly, we come to the increasing body of people called Spiritualists, who hold the view that the basis of all religion is the same, and that what is called religion officially is nothing more than superstition. They believe that we are destined for something better and greater than this world, but that owing to ignorance man has invented beliefs and ideas which, though originating in his religious instinct, have little to do with true religion. Religion and Superstition are two different things. Superstition is that which has accumulated round religion. Religion is a central truth in man's life, which has always been and always will be. One might say that superstitions come and go but religion goes on for ever.

Now superstition and religion are often mixed up and confused. People think, for instance, that they are religious if they go to church; if they attend Holy Communion; if they cease from doing certain things on holy days; if they read the Bible; if they repeat prayers, and if they believe certain words and certain documents to be inspired by God. Less civilised people believe in offering up sacrifices, or beating tom-toms, or worshipping images. Those outward forms and ceremonies have, however, nothing whatever to do with real religion. They are the draperies, the superstition which surrounds it.

Real religion does not consist in believing that God, the maker of this immense universe, which no human mind is capable of fathoming, came down to earth and lived for two years wandering about Palestine. Neither is it religion to consider a certain book is holy and inspired by God. It is not religion to repeat certain words after a parson, or to partake of Holy Communion, whether you consider that what you eat and drink is part of God, or the service is only one of remembrance. These things are only the clothes that have been put on to religion; religion is the something underneath the outward drapery.

Doubtless all those beliefs, ceremonies and ideas, which have accompanied religion, were needful until the time came when we could realise better our true position in the universe. We are all the product of our times, and, if our ancestors evolved a creed, it was done to keep them in mind of something very important. If they sacrificed human beings, or animals, it was also done for an object, the purpose being to pass on to God or the gods their etheric bodies which the worshippers believed were relished in heaven. Then it was believed that these unseen powers would multiply the crops and make life more pleasant on earth. We have advanced beyond sacrifice, and we shall, likewise, evolve beyond creeds and dogmas, holy shows that everywhere creeds, dogmas, holy books and holy churches have retarded the mental development of the race, though they have given great comfort and help to many.

We have now arrived at a stage in our evolution, when intelligent people find full satisfaction for the religious instinct in the knowledge we now possess, without having recourse to the past. We now know, from the definite and verifiable information we receive from the etheric world, that we are here for a purpose, that our life on earth is only a preparation for a life in a better place, and that place is the etheric world which surrounds us and interpenetrates this earth.

We now can converse with those who have passed on, whom Christians call dead. In the etheric world it is not those who believed in a particular creed who are the happiest, and those on earth who think such a belief is necessary are mistaken. We now find that as we live here so shall we live there. If we live up to our highest ideals nothing more is expected from us. There is no necessity to attend church, to read the Bible, to repeat creeds or prayers, in order to reach this other world, because it is as natural for us to pass into the etheric world as it is for us to enter this world.

Our birth took place with no effort on our part. Our reaching the etheric world will take place likewise with no effort on our part. If we prefer to live a debased life on earth, if we prefer to be cruel rather than kind, if we prefer to think of ourselves only and never of others, then we shall mix with those of a similar kind in the etheric world. It is all a question of desire. If we desire something different, something better, if we give our thoughts on this earth to the development of our characters, and try to mould them so that they get better instead of worse, then in the other world we shall find ourselves in the company of those who have the same ideals and aspirations, people of all races and religions.

It is a well-known fact that often those who make much profession lead the most selfish lives, and that those who make little profession lead the most unselfish lives. Sin is selfishness. The more unselfish we are the less sinful we are, and the more selfish we are the more sinful we are. I have spoken to those in the etheric world who held strong dogmatic beliefs on earth, and I find that they are not so happy as others, who have also passed on, who lived good, unselfish lives on earth, ignoring entirely creeds and dogmas. Dogmas and creeds make for selfishness. The dogmatists and doctrinaires have no better a place than those who gave little thought to these matters, those decent men and women who lived their lives to the best of their ability, unselfishly and for the good of others. If the former continue to retain their views, they sink to a lower state of intelligence and mix with those of similar mentality.

We do not think it is necessary, on going a journey to another country, to commit ourselves to certain beliefs before we shall be allowed to enter it; nor before starting on the journey that lies death. There is nothing mysterious if we were all intelligent enough, we could save the expense of keeping holy men to repeat creeds and go through various acts of devotion, in the belief that by so doing our position at death will be better than it would be otherwise.

I have never forgotten a message which came through at a seance from one speaking from the etheric world to which he had passed at death. It was as follows: "God never meant religion to be a mystery. It is man who has made it so. His handiwork is plain enough for all to understand, and religion was never meant to be in any way different. What should be simple has been made obscure. You have but to do your best - no one can do better, and the future will gradually unfold before you and your duty be made clear."

This is surely easy for everyone to follow, and what a gain it will be to mankind when all realise that they have been making difficulties where no difficulties exist. They have been adding to life's burdens by making themselves believe a certain book was holy, or a certain church was holy, or a certain act was holy, or a certain belief was holy and pleasing in the sight of God.

Intelligent people must realise that Infinite Intelligence is absolutely indifferent as to whether we believe the Bible to be inspired by God, or that God became man and dwelt with us or did not; that Infinite Intelligence cares nothing for the repetition of creeds, or the repeating of prayers, or the counting of beads. All these man-made attempts to placate the Almighty originate in the fear of the unknown. They are the result of ignorance, and will survive only so long as man is ignorant of his true position in the universe.

What then is man's true position in this illimitable universe, which mental .development is unfolding to us just in accordance with our capacity to comprehend? As this book proceeds ! hope to be able to go more deeply into this question, but first let us consider it in as simple words as possible. Why are we here and what is our destiny? These questions have been answered so differently in the past, that even with our increased knowledge one hesitates to be dogmatic, and, were it not for the knowledge I have obtained from the etheric world, I should hesitate to answer them. First of all let me repeat what was said by one who has joined the great majority and knows more than we do. His words were as follows:-

"You are just as much an etheric being now as you will ever be. You are just as much in the etheric world now as you will ever be, only you do not appreciate the fact in consequence of your having a physical body attuned to physical surroundings. The etheric world is about and around you, and, at death, when you discard your physical body, you are in the etheric world without having to travel any distance to get there.

"You became immortal at your birth, and you are just as immortal now as you will ever be. Your physical body covers your etheric body, and you cannot appreciate your etheric body because it is made up of substance at a higher rate of vibration than your physical eyes can see. When you die you will appreciate the etheric body, and cease to appreciate your physical body.

"Your new body grows more and more refined as time passes, and you will rise to higher and higher planes of consciousness. You will see more, and you will see further. You will hear more, and you will hear more clearly. Any deformities you have will be corrected here. If you have lost a leg or arm you will have it here, as it was only the physical arm or leg you lost.

"Your understanding will be enlarged, and you will be more conscious of the beauties of your surroundings than you are in the physical body. Your scope of usefulness will be extended beyond the limit of your present imagination.

"You will not have to trouble about money, about earning a livelihood, about eating or about clothes, or about a house to live in, as your mind will be in so much greater control of your surroundings that it will be able to mould those surroundings to meet your desires.

"There will be no more pain or sorrow or regret, no more grieving over separation after your loved ones from the earth have joined you. You will cease to regret the errors of the past through rectifying past mistakes. You will then enter on a life of eternal progress and everlasting blessedness."

From the foregoing it will be seen how futile it is to give much thought on earth to those things which many people consider of such paramount importance, such as titles, as you drop them when you enter the etheric world.

As this book proceeds, our correct outlook on life will become clearer, but before I close this chapter I wish to revert to the subject I discussed at the commencement, namely the reason why I have in previous chapters given so much consideration to the Christian faith. The reason, I repeat, is because the Christian faith is the great stumbling-block to the acceptance of Spiritualism in Christian countries. Christians quote Biblical texts to show that God does not mean us to converse with the dead. They quote texts written by ignorant people in an age of ignorance, who burned witches and perpetrated other ghastly cruelties, while they omit to obey the instructions given in the texts which follow and precede those texts relating to conversing with the departed.

Some people take the trouble to try to explain that those texts relating to witchcraft refer to necromancy, which has nothing whatever to do with Spiritualism, but, personally, I do not think it is worth while to trouble oneself as to whether those texts do refer to necromancy or to communication with the departed. To me they are of no value whatever. They are not God-inspired, and there is no more reason why they should be taken as rules for our lives in the 20th century than should the instructions contained in the code of Hammurabi, King of Babylon, one of the best and most comprehensive legal codes produced by the ancients, and greatly superior to the teachings of the Old Testament. Hammurabi lived in the 16th century B.C., long before a book of the Old Testament was written.

Again it is said that it cannot be right to converse with the departed, because those who speak to us say they are happy and in a better world, though many of those who do communicate are known not to have been Christian people on earth. Christians say this proves that it is the devil, or his angels, who assume those personalities in order to deceive us, and subvert our belief in Jesus as the saviour of mankind. They argue that, in this surreptitious manner, the servants of the devil will make it all the more certain that a larger consignment of the human race will find its way to hell than would otherwise have been the case. This is a very ingenious proposition, but I do not believe it. Neither do I believe, for the reasons previously given in this book, that God came to earth and had any scheme of salvation through the death of himself on the cross.

One further objection that Christians have to Spiritualism, is that we are calling back the dead and that this is contrary to God's Holy Word. This can be easily answered, because it is absolute/y untrue. No one on earth calls back the dead. It is our friends on the other side who come back of their own accord, because they wish us to know that they are alive and happy, and because they are anxious to he/p to rid mankind of all the superstitions which surround religion.

They realise how much we are handicapped by our ignorance, how much time we waste in forms and ceremonies, and how much we suffer through trying to believe impossible dogmas and doctrines. They want to tell us how simple a matter it all is, and that we have to believe nothing unnatural; that all we have to do is to try to live good and upright lives. They are specially anxious to let us know that they are alive, because Christianity teaches that the dead lie in their graves until some future resurrection day. Until the advent of Spiritualism this was everywhere believed. I am now told that this idea is not held generally, and probably it is not, though the Church burial service and hymns still repeat this orthodox belief. Spiritualism has played its part in educating the people on the subject.

It is because I believe that Spiritualism is being handicapped and thwarted by orthodox Christians, through ignorance, that I have tried to show that there is no basis for the beliefs of Christianity. Christians, greatly as they err, certainly take life seriously, and are the very people who should be Spiritualists, because they, like Spiritualists, take the view that life on earth is more than it really seems to be. Christians, through their ignorance, and through their attachment to a holy Church and a holy book, which they think are divinely inspired, are obstructing the spread of a great revelation which is slowly but surely coming to enlighten the earth.

Through their ignorance they are preventing a natural development of those faculties inherent in every man and woman, which may be described as the psychic gift. Little do they realise what disappointment they are causing their friends and relatives in the etheric world, who wish to come back and communicate with them, but get no chance to do so because few Christians will attend seances.

We are still very ignorant of many things, and the public Press is just a reflection of the public mind. In the old days crowds gathered from all directions to see a witch burned; anything for a change from the monotony of life. The mentality of the people today has only changed to a degree, and, instead of paying priests to burn witches, the public buys newspapers which "expose" mediums. Of course newspapers would not do so if their readers did not approve, just as the clergy would not have burned witches if they had not received the support of their congregations.

The point I wish to emphasise is that medium-hunting is still the sport of the public, through the Press. Every newspaper investigation is undertaken for the purpose of providing news, and, up to the present, the so-called medium exposures have assisted the circulation of the newspaper concerned. Gradually, however, our newspapers are finding out that the public are thinking for themselves, and realising that there is much more than trickery and humbug in Spiritualism. They are finding also that medium-hunting does not appeal to the public in the way it did some years ago. However, so long as the people are ignorant enough to like this milder form of "witchburning", so long will it be provided for them.

Can we expect the masses to be otherwise than ignorant when they are encouraged, as they are from nearly every pulpit in Christendom, to look on mediums as frauds? Every leading parson who denounces Spiritualism and mediums is reported in the newspapers, though within the last few years there has been a much fairer tendency observable, and several newspapers have given prominent announcement to the successful results achieved in this field of investigation by men of science.

When a medium is dishonest he or she is quickly exposed by Spiritualists themselves, not as a stunt but as an act of discipline. Just because here and there a pseudo-medium is exposed by Spiritualists, it does not follow that every medium is a fraud; far from it. Until now, however, it has benefited the Press and the Church to "expose" mediums, and so long as it does so this will go on. It is in the hands of the public to stop it, and until they do so they will continue to get a one-sided view of Spiritualism, to their great loss. Mediumship is so new to the general public that the great host of reliable honest mediums are quite unknown except to those who make it their business to have contact with them. The next step is the withdrawal from the statute book of the Witchcraft Act, enacted by those who burned witches, thinking they were possessed of devils.[1]

Spiritualism will come into its own in time, and Spiritualists must do all in their power to illumine the darkened minds of those who guide the destinies of both Church and State. Anyone who attends the large Spiritualist meetings which are being held all over the country, must be impressed by the enormous crowds who gather there. Wherever Spiritualist meetings are held, the largest halls available are packed. I have spoken in most of the leading cities in Great Britain, and there was seldom a vacant seat. I do this work as a duty, accepting neither fee nor travelling expenses, because the public are clamouring for the truth which only Spiritualism can give.

One of the most impressive sights I have ever witnessed was in the Royal Albert Hall, London. It was a gathering of some six thousand people interested in Spiritualism. I was the chairman of the meeting, and I thought that this occasion might be used to show the rest of the world that large numbers of people claimed to have had communication from those called dead. So I took this opportunity to ask everyone in the audience, who was satisfied that he or she had had communication with departed friends, to stand up. Almost the entire audience rose immediately.

Here was testimony enough to satisfy the enquirer about his destiny, without his having to rely on ancient creeds, or the

---

[1] Parliament repealed the Witchcraft Act in 1951.

opinion of Jesus, Paul, Socrates or Cicero. They, and many outstanding men of the past, believed in communication being established between the two worlds, but why rely on the past when hundreds of thousands of responsible people today can testify to having had these psychic experiences which produced the necessary evidence to make them accept the fact of survival?

This belief is not confined to some individuals who lived long ago, and it is held today by a greater number of people than ever before in historical times. The Christian belief about what happens after death is so vague and unsatisfactory that it is difficult to understand. The orthodox opinion is that the dead lie in their graves until the Resurrection Day, when they return to their old bodies and are then judged for the sins and wickedness they committed on earth. This belief came from Egypt.

The ancient Egyptians embalmed their dead because they believed that the physical bodies would be re-animated by the soul on its return to earth at the end of the world, when the dead would all rise in their resuscitated physical bodies. Paul obtained his views of the resurrection from the opinions which had prevailed in Egypt thousands of years before Jesus. The Egyptian view was accepted by the Pauline school of thought and adopted by the Church, as the priests did not know any better. It was the best they could arrive at with their limited knowledge, but now, with our greater knowledge, we know that this view of death is a travesty of the truth.

Spiritualism provides the greatest support mankind has ever received to justify, the religious instinct within him. It has, moreover, corroborated our instinct that this life is a preparation for something better. When the world adopts Spiritualism, and all that Spiritualism stands for, a new and brighter era will have been entered by the human family who will by then have come to realise that as we sow here, so do we reap both here and hereafter.

Had Spiritualism been allowed to develop naturally, and had our ancestors not been so ignorant as to kill off all the mediums, it is reasonable to believe that our philosophical and ethical outlook today would be better than it now is. If we went back to the doings of our ancestors, and tried through physical means or legislation to obliterate mediumship, the world would sink into a state of gross materialism, and humanity would again be wandering in the wilderness of ignorance.

Let each one of us be frank with ourselves and think as

rational individuals, and let us realise that we have been too long harnessed to the dogmas of dead theologians, who gave to their fellow men only what they thought was the truth. Let us remember that these men were human like ourselves and, being more ignorant, they were more liable to error. They knew nothing of the sciences, and they knew nothing of communication with the etheric world.

Let us in future, when reading the Bible, read it as we would any other book, admire its beauties and delight in its stories, realising that it is a human production like any other book. Its cruelties and lack of culture we pass by as the work of cruel and ignorant men, but never let us attribute its follies and barbarous laws to the creator of the universe. Man makes God in his own image, and in the Bible we find many aspects of God envisaged by men in all stages of mental development. Consequently, let us not make the mistake made by our ancestors of attributing everything in the Bible to the creator of heaven and earth and calling it the Word of God. The Christian Church, as it is today, is similar to what the Jewish Church was like in the days of Jesus. If he were on earth today he would call the Christian Church a whited sepulchre, sheltering the dead bones of the past. He would direct our thoughts forward to the life to come and not to the worship of the dead past, and he would call the priests of Christendom blind leaders of the blind.

We, in the 20th century, with our vastly increased knowledge, must not be enslaved by the theories and doctrines of the past. We must think for ourselves on the basis of modern knowledge. We must put aside all the dogmas and creeds which have been considered so essential, but which our present-day greater knowledge reveals to be so unessential. We must not close our minds to reason when we open a Bible or enter a church. If we follow these principles, it will be possible for all of us, with open minds, to consider without prejudice the revelation which is coming through to our world, and which goes under the name of Spiritualism.

Now that I have cleared the ground I can begin to construct a new edifice. Consequently the next chapter will be a consideration of what Spiritualism is, and what it stands for.

PART II.

CHAPTER VII.

SPIRITUALISM, AND WHAT IT STANDS FOR.

SPIRITUALISM is not the faith of a sect or a cult; it does not rest on tradition, nor on writings, ancient or modern. It has no ecclesiastical organisation claiming to interpret God's purpose towards mankind. It has no forms and ceremonies, pomp or circumstance. What Spiritualism stands for is a fact, of the same nature as the fact that we exist. It is the only revelation that has ever come to man from a higher level of intelligence than exists on earth. It does not depend on the sayings or teachings of a past age, nor on inspired writings. It rests fundamentally on the fact that communication takes place between the inhabitants of this world and the inhabitants of the etheric world. This is a scientifically established fact, and, once it is accepted, what follows is natural.

Under the required conditions - that is, in the presence of a medium - voices quite apart from those of the sitters or the medium speak and can be recognised. These voices claim to be the voices of those who once lived here on earth, who retain their earth memories, and claim relationship where it exists. They converse on subjects which concerned them and their friends while they lived on earth. They tell us that they have survived death, that death is only an incident in life, and that it brings about only a change of appreciation of the conditions of life, because of the discarding of the physical body. They tell us that they each have an etheric body, the exact duplicate of the physical body, and that this etheric duplicate was the real body on earth, which acted as the framework of the physical body. They also state that they are living in a real tangible world, interpenetrating and surrounding our earth, composed of substance too fine for us in our physical bodies to sense and appreciate.

Once this fact of communication between those who once lived on earth and ourselves is accepted, everything that was relegated to the region of faith emerges into the full day of knowledge. Knowledge takes the place of faith, and consequently errors and conjectures are discarded.

We can converse freely with our friends in the etheric world, and with others whom we have never known on earth, people belonging to all religions and races. Though their environment is changed, the means of communication by word of mouth is still unaltered. They tell us that they live under better and happier conditions than those they knew on earth, and none has ever expressed the wish to come back to live on earth. This fact at once disposes of the creeds and dogmas' of all religions, as we find that entrance to the etheric world does not necessitate any passport.

Those who have passed on from this world to the etheric world, and who come back and speak to us, tell us that they are living together happily in companionship with those who had different beliefs on earth, and even with those who had no beliefs whatever. When asked questions on the subject of religious belief, they tell us that earth beliefs count for nothing with them, and that these are soon forgotten after we leave the earth. This is not surprising to intelligent people. Why should God wait until we die to punish us? Could he not do so here just as easily? Moreover, people of divergent opinions live happily together on earth, so why should they not do so in heaven?

Our etheric friends tell us that they can now comprehend things more clearly, and have a better understanding of the problems of existence than they had on earth. They tell us that they are instructed and guided by higher intelligences than their own, and that these greater and wiser people were once men and women like ourselves who lived on earth, but, having lived so much longer, and being so much more experienced than are our friends, their guidance and help are of the greatest value to all wishing to gain further knowledge and wisdom.

Here on earth we are limited in our ideas, and in all that appertains to sight, hearing and the other senses. We may be likened to the Caddis worm living at the bottom of a pond, which, when the day comes for its liberation, sheds its sheath and becomes the Caddis fly, with all the expansion of faculties which such a change of condition implies. It can now sense something of the beauties of earth, which hitherto had been denied to it. So with our friends who have passed on. They have a wider vision and a greater knowledge, and they use the opportunities afforded them of conversing with us on earth to tell us something about their world, which has the effect of increasing our understanding, and making us realise more clearly the relationship of each created thing to the universe, of which both worlds are a part.

Just in so far as our capacity to understand increases, are we given information from those in the etheric world, who have made it their duty to increase our understanding. The ordinary individual, attending a seance for the first time, will doubtless get in touch with some friend or relative who will, without difficulty, give him ample proof that he still lives. This satisfies the great majority of enquirers, but only to those who wish to get beyond ordinary conversation is deeper knowledge imparted.

A high dignitary of the Church of England recently publicly expressed the view that only trivial remarks are ever made at seances. He had never been to a seance, but this is what he thought was the case. If he had gone to one and received trivial remarks, as he called them, from friends of his on the other side who were anxious to prove their existence in another world, the reason for them being trivial would have been because his mind was entirely limited to earth conditions.

I remember on one occasion he was my guest along with Sir Oliver Lodge. They both sat alone together for a considerable time, but never a word passed between them on the subject of psychic phenomena. Though I gave this churchman every opportunity to discuss this question with Sir Oliver, who was a recognised authority on the subject, yet he always sheered away from it and changed the conversation. Only those who keep an open mind, who have put prejudice aside and are willing to learn, discover many things to be true that the intolerant and narrow-minded pass aside as impossible.

The basic teachings of Spiritualism come from the minds of those who, though they have passed through death, yet endeavour to guide and help mankind on earth. The basis of their teaching is very simple, so elementary that the simplest of us can understand it: The basis of Spiritualism is contained in what is called the Seven Principles of Spiritualism, which are accepted by Spiritualists in every part of the globe, not as an act of faith, but because the same teachings are given from the etheric world to all who make contact with it, no matter where they be.

Those who call themselves Spiritualists believe that it can be accepted as true that:-

(1) The universe is governed by Mind, commonly called God. That all we have sensed, do sense, or will sense, is but Mind expressing itself in some form or another.

(2) The existence and identity of the individual continues after the change called death.

(3) Communication, under suitable conditions, takes place between us here on earth and the inhabitants of the etheric world, into which we shall all pass at death.

On these three fundamental principles, which Spiritualists believe can be reasonably accepted, the following logical deductions are naturally drawn from the information which comes to us from those who have passed on to this larger life.

(4) That our ethical conduct should be guided by the golden rule, given first to the world by the great Confucius, "Whatsoever you would that others would do to you, do it also unto them."
(5) That each individual is his own saviour, and that he cannot look to someone else to bear his sins and suffer for his mistakes.
(6) That each individual reaps as he sows, and that he makes his happiness or unhappiness just as he harmonises with his surroundings. That he gravitates naturally to the place in the etheric world in harmony with his desires, as there desires can be gratified more easily than here on earth.
(7) And finally, that the path of progress is never closed, and that there is no known end to the advancement of the individual.

The foregoing are the Seven Principles of Spiritualism, which are based on the evidence obtained and received through mediumship. They can be accepted by the intelligent Christian or Jew, Mohammedan or Buddhist, Hindu or Confucianist. These Seven Principles contain all the religious instruction required by the average man or woman. They act as a guide to our conduct on earth, they give the necessary urge for improving our conduct and strengthening our character, they give us something to live for, and they give the basis for an understanding of man's origin and destiny. No 'one need ever fear getting old, as age is only an earth condition. Lastly, they give comfort in sorrow, especially in the sorrow occasioned by parting as a result of death.

Besides this, when these principles are accepted, and all the creeds, dogmas and ceremonials which surround orthodox religion everywhere have faded away, mankind will be knit together by one common belief, as would always have been the case but for ignorance. There is no darkness like ignorance, and Spiritualism is filling the world with intellectual light.

When, by the acceptance and practice of these principles, mankind is bound together by this common link, the human race should become as one family, and thus will be brought about the brotherhood of man, so longed for by the great minds of the past. When everyone realises his origin and his destiny, and is convinced that his conduct here will determine his place hereafter, wars will cease, and our social conditions will improve beyond anything we can possibly imagine. The time wasted trying to placate the Almighty will be used for more useful purposes, and man will at last have become a rational being.

Some, doubtless, though glad to have the scientific support Spiritualism gives to their faith, still feel the need of a personal Saviour or the performing of some ceremonial. They have been imbued with this idea since childhood, and nothing will change them. They have certain fixed ideas, and nothing will alter them. This being so, their faith satisfies them and they are happy. So be it; but the number of people holding these views is slowly dwindling, and what satisfies them does not satisfy the average thinking man and woman, especially the young. If Spiritualism had not come along to take the place of the old dying faith, many of our younger generation would have become materialists, denying everything outside the physical universe.

With the increase of knowledge, and in the absence of any proof for the claims the Church makes for what it calls the supernatural, all belief in anything above or beyond us would have vanished. In what a different position religion would be in Russia today, if the Orthodox Church had not kept the people in such abysmal ignorance! If there were a Spiritualist church in every centre in Russia, as there is in Great Britain, religion would not be cast aside, and contemptuously called the dope used in the past to keep the people from aspiring to improve their social conditions.

With this brief introduction, let us now consider the Seven Principles of Spiritualism in greater detail.

THE FATHERHOOD OF GOD.

I have adopted this sub-title for convenience' sake. In the past the Fatherhood of God has been accepted in a very narrow sense. The Jews believed that Jehovah was their special protector, and that there was no other God but Jehovah. He was like themselves, only more powerful, but just as cruel and passionate. This peculiar and isolated view of the Deity brought them into conflict with all the surrounding nations and made them bigoted and oppressive. But their beliefs were not unique.

Every other nation had its own God who was its special protector, and Christians have always believed that Jesus the Christ is their own special God, making intercession for them in heaven. Whatever Christians have done or do, has been, or is, done in the name of this particular God, but besides him there are two other gods of equal importance. Jesus, however, is the God who specially interests himself in the doings of the Christian people. To Spiritualists the doctrine of the Trinity is such an absurdity that they cannot understand how any sane and rational person can believe it. However, so it is.

Christians believe that there are three gods, but that these three gods are only one God. I must leave it at that and not waste time on this mathematical puzzle. The only Trinity that Spiritualists understand is the Trinity of mind, etheric body and physical body. Here we have a three-in-one entity so Long as we are on earth, but in the etheric world it becomes a two-in-one. We are a trinity, but a very different trinity from that of the theological conception of the Godhead. This, probably, is the origin of the theological idea of a three-in-one God, but only Spiritualists understand its true meaning, because they are told from the other world that the universe is made up of mind, etheric substance and physical matter.

To Spiritualists, Mind, or the directing force of the universe, constitutes God, and the all-embracing nature of this directing Mind is covered by the words "The Fatherhood of God". We are all part of this directing and creating Mind, and through mind we are related to the guiding intelligence of the universe. All members of the human race, whether here or in the etheric world, are brothers joined together by this common link. We therefore believe that Mind, or God, has never had, and never will have, any particular cult on which is bestowed a special blessing.

Those who claim this special privilege do so through ignorance and conceit.

Though all the gods of the past, made in the image of man, must perish, yet man made under the direction of Mind, or God, remains, and God in man will reign eternally.

Next to the Fatherhood of God comes

THE BROTHERHOOD OF MAN.

One follows the other naturally. /f we are all part of God, we are all one family. The history of man contains much about slavery, brutality and injustice. This has all happened because of ignorance. Someone a little stronger, a little more clever than the rest, enslaved his fellows for his own selfish ends. Man has been the sport and prey of kings and priests. Through fear of starvation he has been forced to cringe at the foot of the tyrant, and through fear of the unknown he has supported churches and priests. He has carried on his back the officials of Church and State, who have profited by his ignorance. However, education is gradually making mankind realise that he is not here to be down-trodden by over-lords. Equal education gives everyone equal opportunity, but those with more developed minds will always take the lead.

The ignorance amongst the masses is still pitiful, and what it must have been some hundreds of years ago can only be imagined. Man, by developing his mind, will free himself from his past miseries, and raise himself in self-respect and independence.

> Then let us pray that come it may,
> As come it will for a' that,
> That sense and worth o'er a' the earth
> May bear the gree and a' that!
> For a' that, and a' that,
> It's coming yet, for a' that,
> That man to man, the world o'er,
> Shall brothers be, for a' that!

Such was the wish of Robert Burns one hundred and forty years ago, and only gradually do we see those prophetic lines being realised. Only last century Britain freed herself from the curse of the slave trade, as also did the United States, but still today there are five million slaves in Asia and Africa, and only the combined pressure of the civilised nations will ultimately bring this evil to an end.

Let each one of us, within the limits of the possible, take intelligent thought for the future. Let each one of us, where possible, rescue the fallen and help the helpless. Let us distribute words of kindness, cheerfulness and encouragement. By doing all the good we can, by binding up the wounds of our fellow creatures, we are bringing nearer the great day when the brotherhood of man shall become a reality and not a platitude. To do all the good we can is to be righteous in the real sense of the word, to do all the good we can is to be a saint, irrespective of theological beliefs. To put the star of hope in the midnight of despair, to help those in need of help, and to succour those who suffer, is true holiness. This is the ideology of the future. This is what Spiritualists mean by the brotherhood of man.

Just in proportion as we cease to be the slaves of our conditions shall we advance. Just as we place a greater value on our rights does our position improve, and just as we value more highly the rights due to ourselves shall we increasingly recognise the rights of others. Just as we come to realise that this life is the preparation for a better one, so shall we cease to try to grab all we can for ourselves and work instead for the common good. When we are prepared to give to all what we claim for ourselves, then we shall be truly civilized and the world will be fit to live in.

As it is today, every individual to a lesser extent, and every nation to a greater extent, think only of their own needs first, and the needs of others last, whereas, if all would work together for the common good of the world, poverty would fade away. The enormous sums spent in self-preservation, and promoting superstition at home and abroad, would then be used to add to the wealth of the world, instead of being spent in keeping the people in ignorance, or for destruction, and the preparation for the destruction of what the labour of humanity has put together. If the world could rid itself entirely of its Napoleons of war, and encourage instead its inventors of instruments of cultivation, production and distribution, and, if this policy were pursued for the next fifty years, the hours of labour would be halved, our pleasures would be doubled, and the joy of living correspondingly intensified.

Only within the last two hundred years .has man applied his intelligence to making the forces of nature work for him to an extensive degree, with the result that our country now supports a larger population, and every one is working shorter hours. As we get machines and the forces of nature to do our work, in like proportion will our toil lessen. In 1750 the population of the United Kingdom was about ten millions, in 1932 about forty-nine millions. Today, with the aid of machinery, it is estimated that we are producing in many industries on the average one hundred times what was produced in 1750, and the consequence is that we are supporting five times the population. The working day has been reduced from sixteen to eight hours, and the standard of living is vastly higher than it was then, owing to the higher wages earned for less work.

The majority today have luxuries denied to kings and nobles three hundred years ago. Solomon had hundreds of wives, but no carpets. His great temple was lit by rushes, if it was lit at all. Today many of the humblest dwellings are lit by electric light. The working man in the newer houses being built for him today has more comforts and luxuries than had Queen Elizabeth. In her day there were no steel pins, no stoves, no cooking ranges, no baths, no carpets, no telephones, no quick travel, few books, no newspapers, no cinemas, and no wireless to entertain the people day and night with music and song. We live longer and our national health is better now than it was then.

Whom have we to thank? Inventors and discoverors first, and then all who have used intelligent thought in their work. It has all been achieved by the combination of intelligence, education, industry and labour. Watt, Descartes, Fulton, Stephenson, Kepler, Crompton, Franklin, Kelvin, Faraday, Marconi, Edison, and numerous others such as Lister and Pasteur, are the men we should thank for all we have and are today, and like minds will make us what we shall be in the future.

Slowly but surely has man evolved; first the protoplasm, then the fish, then the mammal, all these branching off and forming various species, until man emerges above them all. Why? Because his brain has been the receptacle of a mind capable of more creative thought than the rest. His development in the past has been slow, but steady and sure, and each time he has advanced he has done so by giving a little more consideration than formerly to his brother men. Truly it is more blessed to give than to receive, and, by reason of his capacity for giving, man has advanced beyond the beast. Gradually, as he advanced, he became capable of understanding better the feelings of his neighbours. First of all the family gathered together, then the tribe, and lastly the nation came into being.

We have still to take the next step, when all the nations of the world will be bound together in one human family. This will come about naturally through mental development. In the past, man lived at first only for himself, then for his family, then for his tribe, and then for his country. At the beginning of last century Thomas Paine declared that the world was his country, and, when we all come to believe that, there will be realised the brotherhood of man and the unity of the human race.

Spiritualism is developing in every country in the world. Communications are coming from the etheric world to every country in the world. This common link may slowly bind humanity together. It is only a matter of time until there is an international language-one is already nearly perfected - and then nations will understand each other better. Wireless has already done more to unify the world than any other invention. If we could understand one another telepathically, as they do in the etheric world, there would be less need of a language, as the mental images behind speech are the same in all cases.

It is only within the last few years that we have really applied concentrated thought to our conditions. For thousands of years social conditions remained much on the same level; mankind remained stationary. Conditions three hundred years ago were very similar to those of three thousand years ago. With the increase in knowledge, resulting from scientific enquiry, we are now gradually getting more and more control over the forces of nature. We are gradually getting more for less work, and it is not difficult to imagine that within the next hundred years, if the present rate of progress continues, the work of each one of us for a few hours a day will produce all our desires and requirements.

The more we reduce the hours of labour the greater will become the scope of our advancement in knowledge, and I can see the time coming when mankind will have such command over his surroundings that our whole economic system will be changed. Our needs, in consequence of the application of machinery to our requirements, will be met by the minimum of effort. We shall get the forces of nature, right down to the enormous energy within the atom, to work for us under intelligent direction and with the expenditure of very much less manual labour. Gradually the superiority of mind over matter is asserting itself and becoming increasingly evident, and some day we shall be able to mould physical matter into the shapes and conditions we require by the minimum of exertion, thus bringing our conditions on earth more in line with those prevailing in the etheric world, where creative thought can make conditions in a way not yet understood on earth.

These thoughts may help us to understand what our etheric friends mean by saying that they are in advance of the earth, and that what we now have they have enjoyed for long. We follow a long way behind them, but fortunately we shall continue to follow. We are learning to take control of our surroundings, as they have known how to do for ages. That is why scientists and philosophers in the etheric world are greatly in advance of those on earth, who mistakenly consider that all knowledge pertains to this world.

I could tell of many other ways in which we are following behind the etheric world, but I shall mention only one more, namely that the Kingdom of the Mind on earth is receiving more respect today than ever before. What one is, mentally and morally, now receives more consideration than does our social position at birth, whereas in the days of old the reverse was the case. Slowly mind on earth is coming to be recognised as king, and to have all things subservient to it.

Before I leave the subject of the brotherhood of man, let me impress on everyone the truth that all life continues after death. Life is indestructible, and needless pain and suffering to any creature has been too common in the past. As, however, we come to realise that all creatures are endowed with mind and can suffer like ourselves, and that all life continues beyond death, so shall we give more serious consideration to the alleviation of needless pain and suffering.

It is unmanly and unwomanly, to say the least of it, to chase a fox or a stag to its death. It is a cruel deed first to stop up most of the "earths", so that the fox can find little refuge, and then to hunt the animal for miles, ultimately to dig it out alive when it gets to earth and throw it to the hounds. This is called "sport" in Christian Britain, and never does the Church raise its voice in protest against cruelty which its founder, were he on earth today, would, we imagine, be the first to condemn. These "blood sports" are relics of barbarism, and I hope to live long enough on earth to see public opinion sufficiently enlightened to stop all needless suffering which is caused to give pleasure to those who always put their own feelings, and selfish pleasures, first, and the agony of the animal last. Such pastimes are degrading to the character of anyone who takes part in them, and, just as other cruelties are passing away, as mankind develops mentally, so also will pass all forms of barbarity to the lower creatures.

As to the future, this we can read only from our knowledge of the past. In the past, just as man has combined his thought with his labour has he advanced, and improved his social conditions. Likewise in the future, in proportion as he continues to apply his mind to his surroundings will his conditions improve, and, just as he develops mentally, so will life become easier. To the same extent as he thinks more of others will his own happiness increase, and the greater will become the harmony of the entire human family.

CONTINUED EXISTENCE AND COMMUNICATION.

The belief in another world has existed from time immemorial, and, as has already been shown, this belief is the result of man's psychic structure. It can be traced back for thousands of years, and found to be held by people of all degrees of culture right down to the savage.

If we were but mechanical creatures, and our thoughts and actions were produced only by some chemical reaction, is it imaginable that we would have devoted the time and the trouble that we have done to giving thought to another environment? The past, however, has relied on instinct translated into hope and faith. Today we are in a new era, and knowledge can now take the place of faith. It is no longer a subject for hope that our friends, whom we call dead, are still living. It is easily proved that they live, by anyone who cares to take the necessary trouble. True, the number of good mediums is limited, and some enquirers try in vain to make contact with their friends through those who are undeveloped, because they have not the time, not the opportunity, to get in touch through a really fully-developed medium.

However, the next best thing to acquiring knowledge by personal experience is to learn from the experience of others. I, personally, in common with most others, have never carried through the necessary scientific experiments to prove many things that I, and others, accept as part of our everyday knowledge. We accept them as true, because they are told us by men of repute, who have spent their lives investigating and examining the laws of nature. So the time will come when most people will accept without question what is told them by those who have experimented, and found by these experiments that survival is a fact.

Up to the present we have been handicapped in accepting this fact, owing to the prejudice resulting from our religious upbringing, and the materialistic outlook of science. Christians consider that they, and they only, know, or can know, anything about the after-life. Consequently those who believe that continued existence can be proved without the aid of Christianity are deceived, and are accepting a belief contrary to the will of God. Fortunately this prejudice is passing.

All the discoveries of science are tending in the direction which Spiritualists have been led to expect from their communications with the other side. Though science has made no pronouncement on the subject, yet the number of Spiritualists among scientists is steadily increasing, and I could mention the names of some of our leading men of science who are attending seances regularly and gaining knowledge thereby. One of our most outstanding physicists does so, but prefers to keep the matter secret, as he does not wish it to be known because it is not yet orthodox to do so. His mental outlook is consequently widening, and he is gaining new knowledge which his more orthodox brethren are still lacking.

This is a question of mental development. It is so difficult to discover reality, wrapped up as it is in appearances. Because of our early scientific and religious training, it is very difficult to believe that it is possible for another world to exist about and around us, especially so because this knowledge is quite beyond our everyday sense perceptions. Not everyone has had the objective proof that Spiritualists have received. It is hard to accept the fact that we have an etheric body which continues animated after death, carrying with it our mind, containing our memories and our character.

The fact of continued existence is one of the fundamentals of Spiritualism, and is accepted in consequence of the communications Spiritualists receive from the other side. This knowledge that we survive is, moreover, amplified and supported in other ways, such as by materialisations, apparitions and psychic photography, all of which confirm the assertions of clairvoyants that in appearance the inhabitants of the etheric world are like unto ourselves.

In the past, few have believed that communication was possible until they personally experienced it. When they did experience it the belief was easy. Consider, however, the population in this country and the relatively small number of fully-developed mediums in whose presence reliable communication takes place, and it will then be realised how impossible it is for everyone to get personal satisfaction. If the number of mediums was multiplied a hundred times there would not be sufficient to meet the demand. Meantime, until they do increase, those who have not been privileged to hold converse with the other world should accept what is told them by those who have, just as they accept the statements of other scientific investigators.

Is it not strange that the clergy, and Christian people generally, will believe Biblical stories of psychic phenomena, and will not accept what present-day writers tell them on the subject? Spiritualists are shocked at the want of enquiry, and the want of thoroughness in the average Christian towards his beliefs. He accepts psychic stories if they are in the Bible, never enquiring as to their authorship, never investigating their origin, or questioning whether or not they are correctly recorded. In the earlier part of this book I try to show how unsatisfactory is the evidence for all Biblical records, and yet today Christians are bold enough to stand up and call Spiritualists credulous people, to jeer at them and make them out to be a deluded cult, when all the time it is they who lay themselves open to these charges. Intelligent Spiritualists accept nothing coming from the other side that has not been absolutely proved by every possible method.

Take, for instance, the Bible story of Samuel. He heard a voice and reported to Eli what this voice said. Other instances are the story of the Transfiguration, and the one about Peter in trance. Here we have reports of three psychic occurrences, but they are only three of many mentioned in the Bible, which Christians accept as true. There is no documentary proof that they are true, but at least this much can be said, that events similar to those reported in the Bible are occurring in this country every day.

They are not strange occurrences to Spiritualists, who are quite accustomed to them. Samuel, Spiritualists would say, was a clairaudient medium just as Mrs. Annie Johnson and Mrs. Estelle Roberts are today, to mention only two of a large number. As to the story of the Transfiguration, Spiritualists have experienced the phenomenon referred to in this instance on many occasions, and the most wonderful on record are the materialisations recorded by Sir William Crookes, one of our greatest scientists. He published in 1874 the results of his experiments, which lasted over many years, in a book entitled

Researches in the Phenomena of Spiritualism.

The story of Peter in trance, and his vision, is an example of a very common occurrence with Spiritualists when in the presence of trance mediums, in fact it is one of the commonest of all the phenomena of Spiritualism. There are more trance mediums in this country, and throughout the world, than any other class of medium.

The trance descriptions of the etheric world, as given by Mrs. Hadden, one of the most developed trance and direct-voice mediums of our time, are far more wonderful and graphic than anything recorded in the New Testament as the result of Peter's trance. All this is happening in Edinburgh today, and being privately recorded by a group of well-known Edinburgh journalists, while among those who regularly attend are some of the leading medical men in the city.

Most of the Edinburgh clergy know what is going on, but, with the exception of the Rev. Dr. Norman Maclean, and two or three others, no parson in Edinburgh has yet referred to Spiritualism except to condemn it. Some must be impressed by what is taking place, as quite a number of them regularly attend this lady's seances, and at the moment there is a waiting list of clergy who will be welcomed whenever there is room available. They are given every opportunity to learn the truth, and this group gladly gives the Church every opportunity to retrieve its past mistakes, and learn what Spiritualists have known for the past ninety years.

However, when Sunday comes, these same parsons preach about Peter and his experiences, or other so-called miracles, to dwindling congregations, though those stories are thousands of years old, but they remain silent as to what is going on in their own city at the present time. The clergy are ready to criticise Dr. Maclean, and Spiritualists generally, but, as he says in his lucid book, Death Cannot Sever, recently published, which every Christian should read, they prefer to continue to sit at the feet of 17th-century theologians, as if those men had given the last word on everything relating to our existence and destiny.

The best that can be said about the Scottish Church, in its attitude towards psychic phenomena, is that the leaders of the Church took some trouble ten years ago to investigate the subject, but for all the good that came of it they might as well have done nothing. I was one of those who conducted the enquiry, and I did my best to educate the clergy who comprised the chief part of the committee. They obtained marvellous evidence in my presence of the truth of the claims of Spiritualism, but it was evident throughout that they did not wish to face the truth. It is not in their interests that the truth should be known, and they have refused ever since to open up the question again, though it has twice been raised at the General Assembly.

The attitude of the Church of England is just the same. Dr. Temple, when Archbishop of York, stated, "I am quite convinced that direct evidence of survival is not either attainable or desirable." His views on this subject are clearly set forth in the 3rd February, 1933, issue of *Light*. It is well to note carefully this remarkable sentence from a Christian Archbishop. He considers first that direct evidence of survival is not attainable, and yet survival is one of the best-proved facts of science. Next comes his opinion that evidence of survival is not desirable. This is typical of the clerical mind, and shows how superstition has rotted away the whole spiritual basis of the religion as taught by Jesus. What is called his Church is nothing more than an organisation for the purpose of keeping alive borrowed Pagan beliefs, superstitions, ceremonies, rites and practices, which have been handed down from past ages of ignorance for thousands of years.

The Church is so prejudiced, so averse to relinquish its hold over the people, and let them realise it is not the custodian of a special revelation from God, which it has always claimed to be, that this new revelation is coming to the people through the people against the united opposition of all the Christian churches. At my large meeting in the Usher Hall in Edinburgh in October 1932, though all the Church of Scotland clergy in Edinburgh were asked to come on the platform none accepted, and Dr. Norman Maclean, who acted as my Chairman, received no support from his brother clergy in his brave stand for the truth. Owing to this official opposition, only slowly will the truth permeate the Presbyterian mind. On the other hand, in England, the so-called Church of England enquiry has ended in nothing! No report has been published, doubtless because the leaders find they cannot condemn the truth, but nevertheless are afraid to admit it.[1]

---

[1] Since the foregoing was written the committee appointed by the Church of England to enquire into Spiritualism has handed its report to the Archbishop of Canterbury. This it did in 1938 but it was never published. The editor of *Psychic News* then heard that a majority report favourable to Spiritualism had been presented and that the minority report was noncommittal. In November 1947 Psychic News secured a copy of this majority report favourable to Spiritualism and immediately published it.

My old friend Dr. John Lamond of Greenside Parish Church, Edinburgh, always believed that Spiritualism would take root in Scottish churches and spread there from throughout the whole country. He based his views on the fact that, narrow and rigid as are the Scottish clergy, at least they are not tied to a liturgy like many of their brothers in England. Whether he was right or not the future only can show, but it is certainly remarkable that three of the most prominent clergy in Edinburgh have been brave and honest enough to declare publicly their belief in Spiritualism, and that the old theology is dead.

I know no other city in Great Britain where Spiritualism is more actively discussed, and where it receives more thoughtful consideration, than in the capital of Scotland. This is doubtless due to the fact that the leading newspapers of the city are strongly pro-Spiritualist, in consequence of the knowledge those who administer them have gained at the seances just referred to with Mrs. Hadden.

All honour also to Dr. Lamond for the brave stand he took on the side of the truth some fifteen years ago, when he was a voice crying in the wilderness! He will go down to history as one of the pioneers amongst the clergy, who saw where the Church was heading, and did his utmost to divert it from its error into the channels of truth.

Clairaudience and clairvoyance, which are so frequently reported in the Bible, are common occurrences at the present time, and anyone who attends a Spiritualist meeting, when good clairaudience and clairvoyance take place, cannot doubt the fact that some people have the gift of hearing and seeing more than the ordinary individual, with his limited capacity for hearing and seeing.

I have been present in large halls on many occasions, when Mrs. Estelle Roberts, Mrs. Helen Hughes, Mrs. Annie Johnson or Mrs. Helen Spiers, to mention only four of our best-known clairvoyants, gave clairvoyant descriptions or clairaudient messages. From. forty to fifty correct names and messages, on each occasion, are usually given to the people in the audience, from their friends in the other world.

I have often heard the most minute details of their/ire and appearance on earth, passed on by the medium, the percentage of mistakes being less than two per cent. The 98 per cent. correct descriptions absolutely rule chance out as an explanation, and fraud is equally impossible because these ladies arrive at the meeting just before it commences. On many occasions I have known them to arrive by train, ha/f an hour or so before the meeting commenced, and go direct from the station to the meeting.

They go from town to town throughout Great Britain, and I have been present at meetings when the clairvoyante had just arrived in the town on the first occasion in her life. Mrs. Estelle Roberts, for instance, who took part at the meeting I addressed in the St. Andrew's Hall in Glasgow, in May 1932, arrived in that city just before the meeting, and it was the first time she had been in Scotland in her life.

She gets only a small fee, and her expenses, so it is obvious that she could not afford to pay people to make enquiries beforehand, or to have her own accomplices scattered throughout the audience. Such a suggestion, which is sometimes seriously made, can be ruled out as absurd, because it would require an organisation and a considerable amount of money to maintain. I have personal proof, however, of the genuineness of our recognised clairvoyants, as many of my own personal friends have received intimate communications through them, which have been correct to the minutest detail.

One is surprised at the number of people who have this gift. The other day a friend of mine attended a funeral. As the coffin was being lowered someone took a photograph of the mourners, and, when the plate was developed, the photograph of the man whose body was being buried appeared standing beside his wife. This was shown to the clergyman who officiated and he replied, "Yes, I saw him standing there just as the photograph depicts it." My friend then said, "Well, you should tell your congregation that from the pulpit." To which he replied, "I would not dare; my Bishop would object." Yet this same parson will preach about the disciples walking to Emmaus in company with an etheric man, whom they saw and spoke to, but he dare not say that he himself has seen one. Could anything exemplify better the present hopelessly illogical position of the Christian Church?

We have, therefore, the extraordinary position to recognise, that Christian people will accept as true occurrences recorded by tradition as happening thousands of years ago, but that they will not accept what is recorded by men and women of standing and repute at the present day. In my book, *On the Edge of the Etheric,* I refer at some length to notable men of the past fifty years who have vouched for all that Spiritualism stands for. I have recorded there some of the experiences I myself have had, but, though more extensively and carefully recorded than are the experiences of most Spiritualists, they are exactly similar to what hundreds of thousands of sane and sensible people have experienced who are living in our country at the present time.

It is impossible to imagine that the thousands of people who have recorded their experiences are deluded or fraudulent. Their word on other matters is accepted, so why should their word on this question not also be accepted? They have had the experience, and those who have not should accept what they say. If Christians will not accept what their contemporaries tell, they are most illogical in accepting what is in the Bible. In other words, if Spiritualism is a fraud and a delusion, so also are the psychic stories in the Bible, the only difference being that Spiritualists affirm that their statements can be proved by anyone who likes to take the trouble to do so, whereas the Biblical stories cannot be verified by investigation.

Whether the details of the Biblical stories are correct or not, at least Spiritualists can accept them as possible of explanation without having to resort to the belief in miracles, or something contrary to nature, as Christians have to do in order to believe them. Spiritualists do not believe in miracles, or in the supernatural, or in anything contrary to nature. They believe in law and order in the universe, and they never talk about supernatural events or miraculous occurrences. When they refer to something occurring beyond our limited sense perceptions they refer to it as supernormal. No miracle, or supernatural occurrence, has ever taken place in the history of the universe, so far as our knowledge extends.

In my book, *On the Edge of the Etheric,* I have devoted a great amount of space to records of conversations I had, over a period of five years, with friends of mine who have passed on to the etheric world. I do not propose in this book to go into those details again. All I will say is that I have careful records of thirty-nine seances, and the possibility of fraud or delusion cannot be imagined owing to the precautions taken. In the reviews of the above mentioned book, which number nearly one hundred, little or no criticism was ever made on this point, and it was generally accepted that I had obtained genuine supernormal phenomena.

Voices quite apart from the medium spoke to me, or to friends of mine I took with me, and some of these voices were recognised. I was given two hundred and eighty-two facts which I recorded in writing at the time and which I afterwards verified, but, besides these, I have had numerous others unrecorded. One hundred and eighty of these I class as A1, as it was impossible for the medium, or anybody else, to know anything whatever about the facts which were given to me. To ascertain what possibility there was that these communications were guess-work on the part of the medium, an eminent mathematician computed that the chances against this were thirty billions to one. One hundred I class as A2, because the facts given could be traced to reference books or newspapers, though I do not believe for one moment that the medium resorted to this method of obtaining the information. One item of information given to me I could not trace, and the other was slightly inaccurate, but if it had been given in a slightly different way it would have been correct.

After five years' careful investigation of psychic phenomena, through the mediumship of Mr. John C. Sloan of Glasgow, I was completely convinced that the voices which spoke to me were the voices of those they claimed to be, and that neither fraud nor delusion could account for them. I have already shown in *On the Edge of the Etheric* the care I took to prevent fraud or delusion, and how, slowly but surely, I was convinced against my will that 1 was in contact with those who once lived here on earth, who, after passing through the change called death, continued to inhabit another world around and about us.

Hundreds of different voices 1 have heard, of different tone and strength, some loud enough to be heard two hundred yards away, others soft, and some recognised. Of all the discoveries of man this is surely the greatest, and, if it could be obtained regularly by means of an instrument, and thus become generally known, it would be accepted as such by everyone. Unfortunately, only a comparatively small number have experienced this phenomenon, and, because of its novelty, only slowly are people coming to believe in its possibility.

These very careful experiments, which I carried out, ended in 1925, but since then I have carefully and critically examined the experiences of hundreds of other people, and what they have told me, and what they concluded from these experiences, agrees to the minutest detail with my own experiences and the deductions I drew from them. Since 1 published *On the Edge of the Etheric,* I have been in receipt daily of a large correspondence from all parts of the world. I have not received a single hostile or critical letter, but many letters tell me how greatly my book has helped and comforted the writers. Others ask how they also may obtain similar experiences.

Other letters, again, are from people who have had experiences like myself, and though the letters come from all parts of the world - Brazil, the Argentine, the United States, Canada, Australia, New Zealand, South Africa, India, and most of the countries of Europe - yet they all tell of similar experiences with Direct Voice mediums. They also confirm what has been told to me about the conditions in the other world, and show further that the explanation I received of the methods adopted for communicating with us has also been given to them. I have such a mass of information in those letters, that extracts from them would make up a book somewhat similar in size to this one.

The evidence I myself have had from all parts of the world, that survival and communication is a fact, would be enough in itself to prove the claims of Spiritualism, even if no other proof existed. If, however, you multiply by one million my experiences, we would be nowhere near the end of the sum total of the evidence for survival and communication which has accumulated during the last eighty-four years. Is it conceivable that what Spiritualism stands for can be fraud and delusion when all this is carefully considered?

I shall now refer to only three incidents to show how strong is the case for survival. The first is one of many which was given to me by Mr. Edward C. Randall, one of the leading lawyers in Buffalo, with whom I stayed when I was in America ten years ago. We still correspond with each other, and interchange any new information we obtain. During twenty years, he told me, he has had sittings in his own house with Mrs. Emily French, one of the world's most gifted Direct Voice mediums, when shorthand records were taken of what took place on over seven hundred occasions. Mrs. French, for some years, stayed in his house so as to be under his direct supervision. In a letter received from him in February 1933 he states that the recorded sittings now number over one thousand.

Thousands of different voices spoke to him, clear and distinct, every one different and easily recognised. The most profound problems were clear/y discussed, and from hostile unbelief he was led on and educated in what I might term Universal Science. Some day this greater knowledge will work in partnership with physical science, when our scientists are wise enough to study those profound questions as students taught by etheric world scientists. Our scientists must some day humble themselves sufficiently to realise that their ingenuity alone cannot solve the riddle of the universe, and that to do so they must learn many things of which they are quite ignorant from those who inhabit the world of finer matter about and around us.

Mr. Randall and I spent many hours discussing the information we have been privileged to receive, and then we told each other some of our own personal experiences, of friends coming back and proving their identity. I shall long remember one of the most evidential cases that has ever been brought to my attention, because it rules out entirely the absurd theory, held by some, that unless the information is unknown to everybody, it is of no value. Consequently, as it would be impossible to verify, they say, survival cannot be proved. Those who hold this theory are very limited in number, as well as in their knowledge of the evidence which has come through, but what Mr. Randall told me is a sample which excludes every known normal explanation, and leaves only the Spiritualistic explanation to account for it.

One morning, at ten o'clock, the Brown Building in Buffalo, which was under repair, collapsed, and the few people working there were all buried under the debris. No one knew who they were, or how many there were, and this was not known until some days after, when the bodies were recovered and identified. On the day the building collapsed, however, when Mr. Randall was sitting with Mrs. French, one of those killed spoke to him and told him that four people had been in the building at the time of the collapse, and that he, the speaker, was one of them. He then gave their full names as follows: William P. Straub, George Metz, Michael Schurzke, a Pole, and Jennie M. Griffin, a woman. This was proved to be correct several days later, when the bodies were recovered.

Now, when this was told to Mr. Randall, no one on earth knew who had been killed, only the people themselves, and the men and women who were looking after them in the etheric world. No one on earth knew, and, this being so, that much-abused explanation, telepathy, will not fit in here. I could give similar experiences of my own, to prove that the Spiritualists' explanation is the only one to fit all the facts, but, as I have already given some of my experiences in my previous book, I shall not deal further with this question of evidence beyond mentioning two more very evidential cases which have occurred within recent months, the first being the experience of Lady Caillard.

She is the widow of Sir Vincent Caillard, who was a director of Vickers and the Southern Railway, and who died in 1930. She has published her experiences in pamphlet form, but this is briefly what she told me. She first became interested when attending a Spiritualist meeting, as then her husband was described to her by a clairvoyante as standing beside her. She then attended a seance, and her husband sent through messages by means of the Reflectograph, an earth instrument operated by the etheric personality communicating. Her sister-in-law at the same time had a message from her husband.

The following day Lady Caillard attended another seance. She told me she heard her husband's voice, calling her by a name which only he used, and which was known only to themselves. Next he said, "I am coming to show myself to you if I can." Then he appeared standing before her and was easily recognised. He held out his hand and shook his wife's with a firm grasp. He then took her hand in his two hands and pressed it to his lips. Then conversation followed and he promised to come back again on the anniversary of his passing, which he did, and she told me, "I saw him just as he was in life."

All present saw Sir Vincent, and these numbered ten people. "There was no doubt about him being my husband," she told me, "and he was seen by everyone." He told his wife many things which no one but he could have known. She touched him, stroked his hair, and kissed him. He put his arm round her neck and drew her head on to his shoulder. The medium, I might remark, was a woman.

I mention this case because we have here everything one could desire, not only the voice but the bodily form. What more evidence could we have to satisfy our reason that we are speaking to someone who once lived on earth? None. To know people on earth, we recognise their voices and we see their bodily appearance, just as Lady Caillard heard, saw and recognised her husband.

The only difference is that our earth friends can remain with us, and be seen and heard wherever we go; but our etheric friends can be seen and heard only in the presence of a medium, who gives off ectoplasm which enables them to materialise for a brief period. How this all happens is fully explained in *On the Edge of the Etheric*, and I have not the space here to go again into the details.

Briefly, the medium supplies a substance called ectoplasm, which the Etherians mix with a substance of their own. This they call psychoplasm, and the combination of these two substances produces a substance called teleplasm, with which they cover their vocal organs, etc., and thus so slow down their vibrations that they can vibrate our atmosphere. It will be noted that I use the word "Etherian" instead of Spirit people. They prefer this designation, and I hope in time it will be used generally, and the word "Spirit" dropped, because they are not spirits as we understand the word, but solid men and women like ourselves.

The last experience I shall give occurred when I was in Belfast in September 1932. I went there to give two addresses, one in the Ulster Hall, the largest hall in Belfast, accommodating over two thousand people. The hall was packed. My chairman was Colonel Sharman Crawford, D.L., Deputy Governor of Northern Ireland, and, in his opening remarks, he said, "I know that my deceased son is standing beside me." After my address, at the close of the meeting, a man from the audience came to speak to me. He described a man in etheric life standing beside me when I spoke. He gave me a very careful description of his appearance, describing him from head to foot. Also, he said, the man was killed near the war period on a motor-cycle, and came tonight dressed just as he was when killed, in military motor-cyclist's uniform. My informant could not get his name, but said he must be a friend of mine or someone I knew. I denied all such knowledge, and he seemed disappointed. I thanked him, and told him that if I remembered who this man was I would let him know.

On my way home I told my hostess what had been told me, and she at once said, "That was Colonel Sharman Crawford's son; I knew him quite well." This was confirmed the next day by the Colonel, and it so impressed him that he allowed it to be reported in all the Belfast newspapers. I learned afterwards that the clairvoyant was well known for his gift. He evidently saw the soldier standing between me and my chairman, and thought he was a friend of mine, whereas it just confirmed Colonel Sharman Crawford's own clairvoyance that his son was with him. Here were two independent testimonies given to me about someone I did not know, but recognised by someone else. All were honest people connected with the event, and it will be seen that no one had anything to gain by falsehood or misrepresentation.

No, Spiritualists are not a "deluded people", but very much the reverse. They are sane and practical, thorough and critical, and, if a medium is found to be fraudulent, it is Spiritualists who expose the medium, not non-Spiritualists. It has been said, and never contradicted, that no non-Spiritualist has ever exposed a medium. Some so-called exposures by non-Spiritualists have taken place, but it has been found afterwards that the medium has been tricked, or that the exposure was false. I do not necessarily concur with these statements, because I have no proof to support them; but what I wish to emphasise is this, that Spiritualists will never tolerate fraud, and, if ever a medium is proved to be fraudulent, that medium's day is past, and he sinks into oblivion. His name is published in all the Spiritualist journals, and he is discredited for the rest of his life.

I shall not deal further with this question of intercommunication between the two worlds, because I have no more space to do so, and it is not the purpose of this book to give detailed consideration to the evidence Spiritualists have of survival after death. There are hundreds of books on the subject, and there are numerous standard books by men and women of repute whose accuracy is undoubted. I must leave it at that, but should the reader wish to pursue the matter further he will find some of these books regularly advertised in the psychic newspapers.

The Fifth Principle of Spiritualism is known under the heading of

PERSONAL RESPONSIBILITY.

It is easy to be wicked if you are not to be held responsible for your misdeeds. It is not difficult to defraud your neighbour, if you feel that all you have to do is to ask forgiveness and believe that Jesus took your sins away and suffered for them two thousand years ago. The possibility of transferring your sins to some other person, or creature, is a very old delusion. Most of us know the Old Testament story of the paschal lamb, which was killed as a sin offering. The Arabs had a similar custom, and the belief in a sacrificed saviour is to be found in many of the world's religions.

This belief was general throughout the east at the time of the early Christians, and gradually the idea developed that Jesus took the place of the paschal lamb, that his crucifixion was a punishment for the sins of the world, and made all believers safe for eternity.

This doctrine is one of the most pernicious that has ever been preached. It has been the cause of more crime in Christendom than any other of the teachings of Christianity. The idea that any individual, or deity, suffered for us, and that, no matter what we do, we can solely by faith be absolved from our sins and shortcomings, is too ludicrous to require much consideration. It was born in ignorance and flourished in ignorance, and those who still preach it today are as stupid as those who preceded them.

Fortunately this belief is dying a natural death, and is being hastened to its grave by the teachings of Spiritualism. We know now, from what we are told by those who have preceded us into the etheric world, that each one of us has to bear the consequences of his own sins and shortcomings, and that as we sow, so shall we reap. If we live selfish, evil lives we shall reap our reward, not only here but hereafter, until we change. The idea of a fixed place for the unbelievers is a myth. We create our own heaven and our own hell. The selfish and wicked are perhaps miserable in this world, and they may be more miserable in the next, though not necessarily. The good and the unselfish in this world may be happy here, and may be happier hereafter. We know now the reason and how simple it all is.

Our mind conditions our surroundings here to a certain extent, but to a much greater degree in the etheric world. If our mind here is self-centred, making us selfish, if it cares nothing for the feelings of others and only for itself, it will create an isolated condition for itself in the etheric world. Through the power of mind we mould our surroundings to a much greater extent there than here, and, as we think, so we are. It is not difficult to imagine a wicked individual here surrounding himself with equally wicked fellow beings. In the etheric world like draws to like to an even greater extent than here, and consequently evil-doers congregate together.

Just as it is with the wicked, so it is with the good, but there is no great gulf fixed between the two, as the next world is not only a place but a condition. Those who make for themselves evil conditions have always the power of changing them by their thoughts, of thus improving their conditions, and ultimately having harmonious relations with the good. There we get into closer harmony with our desires than we can here. Many a bad individual on earth can cloak his wickedness by his wealth and bluff, but not so there. Our character there is more transparent, whereas here it is not so.

All men and women who have passed from this world to the next have found their level. They may have been kings or queens, princes or lords, looked up to and honoured on earth because of their worldly position, but there, character only determines their position. There they live in a world of finer matter which is more easily influenced by mind, and naturally they gravitate to the surroundings which their minds can best influence. It would be quite impossible there, where only minds in tune harmonise together, for the wicked and the good to live together. They naturally repel each other. It is all very similar to the conditions on earth. There, as here, "birds of a feather flock together", but, as character is more transparent there than here, one is summed up at once without mistake.

Each one of us is responsible for his own actions and thoughts. Our mental make-up determines our condition hereafter, and no one need be deluded by the idea that belief in some vicarious atonement is going to alter the position each mind determines for itself.

This being so, the Sixth Principle of Spiritualism can be easily understood.

COMPENSATION AND RETRIBUTION HEREAFTER.

Each one of us will receive compensation or suffer retribution both here and hereafer for all good or evil done on earth. Each one of us will receive his reward, as effect follows cause there, just as it does here. We shall not appear before a judge at some judgment seat on some judgment day. Every day we are passing a sentence on ourselves. As we live here, so shall we live there, because here on earth we are making our future conditions. It is character that counts, not beliefs.

Thus it will be seen how all the inequalities of life are straightened out. Wealth and position, so highly valued here, count for nothing there; only character. Money, and working for money, is unknown there, because as our thoughts are so are our surroundings. Those who have trodden the difficult and straitened path of poverty on earth will not receive happiness in heaven because they were poor on earth, but they will enter into conditions in accordance with the development of their minds and characters here. Many of the best people on earth are the poorest in worldly goods, and some of the worst are the richest. Nature gives no thought to poverty or wealth, as it considers only the mental calibre of each individual.

Those who have not been educated on earth will be taught and instructed in the next world, and, if their minds respond to the teaching, they will advance. All obtain this teaching who are willing to receive it, and the worst can in time become the best if the desire to do so exists, but, if the aspiration is not there, progress does not take place.

Creeds and dogmas stifle the mind. They make for selfishness, they give the believers in them a sense of superiority, and this reacts on their conditions hereafter. Many of the worst people the world has ever known were the greatest believers in creeds and dogmas. Constantine presided at the Council of Nicaea; Torquemada, the Christian prior, ruled over the Inquisition in Spain; Cortez converted Mexico, and Pizarro Peru, to Christianity by the slaughter of thousands by the basest treachery and callous brutality.

The knowledge that Spiritualists possess, that as we develop mentally here so shall our conditions be hereafter, is a great stimulus for everyone to live justly and unselfishly. To put it briefly, all unrighteousness can be described by the word "selfishness", and the more selfish we are the less righteous we are. Selfish and unselfish people are to be found in all degrees of life, and each one of us is consequently making our future habitation in the etheric world.

The last principle of Spiritualism is

CONTINUED PROGRESS.

Every human being has a path of continuous progression in front of him, and it is for him to take it or leave it. In the next world he cannot live his best by hanging about this earth and never getting away from earthly things. Loved ones on earth often keep him in close touch with earth conditions, but sooner or later everyone must lose their interest in earth and take up the new life in a natural way. We can, however, still forget about the earth and yet make no progress, if we confine our thoughts solely to ourselves.

If we wish to acquire wisdom and knowledge for the purpose of helping others, and, if we become less selfish, the path is opened to us, and, as we increase in wisdom and character, we draw nearer to perfection. In the etheric world there are different phases of development, and, as we progress, we pass from one to another. The only difference between death in the etheric world and death in this world is that here we leave a body behind us to be buried. There, however, as we progress, we appreciate more advanced stages of environment, just as our mind and body become capable of responding to the vibrations of ever more intense frequency. Progress is dependent on desire, and as the mind develops the etheric body responds to these vibrations. This is a faculty possessed by the etheric body, but not by the physical body.

Here on earth we have this condition of desire exemplified. I know a man who went out to Japan, for a holiday, and spent his time there wandering about the docks of Yokohama, watching the ships being loaded and unloaded. This he did for a fortnight and then returned home. He never saw any of the beauties of the country; he never studied the inhabitants and the living conditions of that interesting race. He consequently came home as ignorant as he was when he left this country. Mentally he was incapable of appreciating something above and beyond what was his daily occupation, that of a stevedore. So it can be understood how in the etheric world our mind conditions our environment, and only if we have the desire for increased knowledge, and the desire for something better, shall we attain it.

It does not necessarily follow that undeveloped people are wicked - far from it - but they make the conditions for which they are mentally fitted. Their backward state need not last for ever, as the time can come when increased knowledge, and better surroundings, are desired, and when the desire comes it is gratified. For all of us, therefore, there is a path of progress laid out, and we have but to follow it. If the desire is there the path will be taken, but, if not, then, until the desire comes, our development is arrested, and for a time we neglect the way that is ours as part of our inheritance.

CHAPTER VIII.
THE PHILOSOPHY OF SPIRITUALISM.
PART I.

THE foregoing chapter, dealing with the Seven Principles of Spiritualism, makes it clear that Spiritualism is a practical, sane and sensible religion, suitable for the sane and practical man and woman of the present day. There is no emotionalism nor sentiment about it. The intelligent Spiritualist believes in proving all things and believing only what he has proved. What he cannot prove he leaves aside until knowledge increases sufficiently to make what is doubtful more explicit.

Christians, on the contrary, believe much without any evidence whatever; they think faith such a virtue that they believe everything a holy book or a holy church prescribes, no matter how fantastic. Personally I have never seen any virtue in faith devoid of rational thought. Being practical by nature, I have always looked on the realm of faith as the borderland of ignorance. Fortunately we are now living in the days of the decay of faith, and entering the age of reason and knowledge.

Spiritualism is the only satisfactory religion for this new age which we are now entering. It holds that it is the duty of every man and woman to investigate questions of religion for themselves, accepting nothing without first weighing up all the evidence. No man, in whose brain burns the torch of reason, need fear to investigate and to think on these great problems, which in the past have been relegated to a select few to ponder over. To get someone else, or some organisation, to think for us is mental indolence. We must think out these deeper problems of life for ourselves.

Intelligent Spiritualists, owing to the knowledge they have received from the advanced minds in the etheric world, have now a philosophy which can harmonise all human knowledge into one complete whole. To the thoughtful Spiritualist, religion and science are one. Scientific fact is the foundation for his knowledge, combined with the information given to him from minds wiser than earth minds, about the unsensed universe around us. We cannot complete the picture until we include the study of this unsensed universe, and this we can only do by making use of the contact mediumship establishes between the sensed and unsensed.

The difference between scientific Spiritualists, and other scientists, is that the former make use of this connecting link, and in consequence gain in knowledge, while those who ignore it deprive themselves of the entire range of available knowledge. Spiritualists, by making use of all the knowledge available, have built up a philosophy which is the most complete, and therefore the most advanced, in the world today. They have a larger, and a more comprehensive, outlook on the universe, and can consequently understand and comprehend it better.

To show, however, how greatly we are in the minority, and how few comprehend the Spiritualist philosophy, I cannot do better than include here a copy of a letter I sent to the Editor of *The Times* on 20th May, 1932, during a time when some of our leading orthodox scientists and philosophers were trying to explain the universe on a purely physical basis. The letter I wrote to the editor is as follows:-

The Editor,
The Times, London.　　　　　20th May, 1932

Dear Sir, - Your columns have recently contained letters of paramount importance to scientific thought, two on the reality of psychic phenomena as witnessed at the National Laboratory for Psychical Research, and the more recent ones on the attempt to grasp space and the universe.

I believe that it is quite impossible to understand, or even to get a working hypothesis of the universe from a purely physical standpoint. Those who try to do so are attempting to explain the infinite by our limited sense organs, which is quite impossible.

The material world is a transitory and passing world, and so also is the material universe, and matter, as we see it, is the least important thing in the universe, though to us to-day it seems to be the most important.

Psychic science, however, is opening to us a new universe, a universe of etheric substance, governed by mind, and only when orthodox science condescends to examine this new universe revealed to us through mediumship, can it possibly hope to get a true perspective of the universe as a whole.

A physical, or material, explanation of the universe is impossible, because the physicist is looking at, and considering only the physical universe, whereas the real universe is the etheric, and physical matter is but the result of a minute quantity of vibrations compared with those which constitute space, where the real universe exists.

Space is the real universe. We think it is empty but it contains life and growth, a real objective world to its inhabitants.

This I have learned after fifteen years of experimenting and studying of psychic science. What I have found, others, such as Crookes, Wallace, Lodge, Barrett, Flammarion, Richet and Lombroso have likewise found. Orthodox science, however, will never be able to approach to a true explanation of the universe until it accepts the means nature has put before it, namely through mediumship. Then it will learn things, now ignored and misunderstood, from intelligences in the etheric world who look on us as children groping for something we shall never find without their aid.

Those of us who have had the privilege of being taught by intelligences greater than those of this earth, find little interest in a physical explanation of the universe, because we have been taught to look on the universe as a gigantic scale of vibrations, or waves of motion, of which the physical represents only the equivalent of what an inch is to a mile. We are also taught that the realm of mind is the real universe, and that our individual minds are conditioned by the vibrations of our surroundings. As mind is indestructible, and never dies, our appreciation of the universe changes as mind responds to finer and finer vibrations.

How can anyone possibly explain the physical universe, when we now know that after death the physical ceases to exist for us, and we then appreciate the more frequent vibrations of etheric substance? The physical is only important to us during our earth life, but it cannot possibly represent the universe, now that we know that our earth life is only an infinitesimal part of our existence. Matter without mind is unthinkable, and consequently mind must be behind everything, and only in terms of mind can the universe be explained.

Yours faithfully,
J. ARTHUR FINDLAY.

Knowing the conservative attitude of our great national newspaper, and realising how alien the contents of my letter are to the official scientific mind and to orthodox thought, I was not surprised to have this letter returned to me with a polite intimation that the editor did not see his way to publish it. I comforted myself, however, by recalling that if *The Times* had been published in the days of Copernicus, and he had sent it a communication to the effect that the earth revolved round the sun, and not the sun round the earth, he would have had his communication treated by the editor of that day in a similar way.

Spiritualism, and its philosophy, are so new that it is hardly to be expected that our great national daily paper, which rather contemptuously ignores the subject, would make an exception in my case. The columns of The Times are reserved for official and orthodox Christianity and physical Science. To these two subjects it gives ample space, and the sayings and doings of the official leaders of Science and Christianity get prominent notice and support in its columns. To those who know the truth about the origin and history of Christianity, and the basis of sand on which it is rounded, this seems extraordinary. Spiritualism asks nothing from humanity contrary to reason. It puts reason first, as the magnetic north for each one of us to steer by. If we try to keep to our course, guided by reason, we may go astray, but not so far astray as if we put something else in the place of this paramount gift.

All the knowledge we possess, all the present comfort and happiness of humanity, is the result of man putting reason first, and just as he has put reason first and faith last has he progressed and improved his well-being. All the instruction and guidance we get from the other world is for the purpose of helping us to use our reason aright, but never for encouraging us to lean on external guidance and not think for ourselves. We are here in this world for the purpose of developing our characters, and Spiritualism is not going to weaken them. Quite the reverse.

The primary object our friends have in communicating with us is to let us realise that they are still alive and happy. The second object is to let us know that we too will continue to exist with them in this etheric world about and around this earth of ours. These are the two primary objects of the communication which they have opened up between the two worlds, but, in addition, they are glad to avail themselves of the opportunity to guide and help us, from their added experience, to increase in knowledge, and to live better and more rational lives than we have lived in the past. They see the world steeped in ignorance from which they are anxious to set it free.

This is as far as the average Spiritualist gets. He is quite satisfied when he has learned about his own destiny, and knows what has become of his friends. Automatically, old creeds and dogmas give place to a more rational outlook on life, and he accepts the Seven Principles of Spiritualism as a natural sequence. The average individual, whether he be Christian or Spiritualist, has no great philosophic bent. The majority have too much to do, even if they had the capacity to probe into the mysteries of existence or the riddle of the universe. All the same there is no doubt that the average level of intelligence amongst Spiritualists is considerably higher than amongst Christians, and some have travelled far on that difficult and endless road, commonly called philosophy.

It is this side of the question I now wish to consider at some length, as the philosophy of Spiritualism is the most advanced philosophy in the world today. This is not to be wondered at in view of the fact that Spiritualists, whose minds run in this direction, have been greatly helped and guided by the higher intelligences with whom they have been in touch.

After having had proof in abundance that life continues, that those who spoke were those whom they said they were, I decided that the only way to get down to the deeper problems of existence was to have private sittings, and to this proposal Mr. John C. Sloan, the medium, kindly consented. Then it was possible to delve deeper than I could do at ordinary seances, where everyone was anxious to talk to friends and relatives. I had by then reached the stage where I wanted to get beyond those recently passed over, and make contact with much more highly-developed and experienced minds.

My wish was granted, and at the first private sitting I had with Sloan, my stenographer being the only other person present, a greatly elevated mental atmosphere became quickly noticeable. No attempt was made to prove identity; that I had already proved to my entire satisfaction. I was not particularly anxious to know who spoke to me, but I was very anxious to know about many things that I could only learn from those on the other side who had given deep thought and consideration to them.

What follows from now onwards I put in my own words. It is the combination of my knowledge of physical science and the information I have received from the etheric world. I shall make what I have to tell as simple as possible, because much of what I have to say is new. Consequently, it must be difficult for the average individual, without any psychic experience, to comprehend.

Though I had the privilege of having these conversations with those in the other world, of a greater knowledge than that possessed by anyone on earth, yet it took me many years before I could sort out all the information I received, and bring it within the range of my comprehension. Much I was told I could not understand, and only gradually has enlightenment come to me.

In my conversations I went far beyond the knowledge of the medium, who is a working man in Glasgow, highly respected by his employers, but not one who has given thought to the philosophic side of life. He has suffered all his life from poor eyesight, and he told me more than once that he has seldom if ever read a book in his life. I have been in his house on many occasions and I have never once seen a book in it, and only once a newspaper. He started work at a very early age, and he has never had time to give thought to anything but his ordinary daily work. All his life he has refused to take any payment in return for his mediumistic services.

He was born a medium, and has been aware of his supernormal gifts all his life. In his presence, as I have proved on many occasions, voices speak which are the voices of intelligences quite apart from the medium's own vocal organs and mind. They are the voices of men and women, who once lived on earth, speaking from the etheric world, who have materialised their vocal organs by taking what is called ectoplasm from the medium. I have had my ear close to his mouth on many occasions, when one or more voices were speaking at the same time, several yards away from the medium, and there was not a sound coming from it.

The medium is in deep trance while this takes place, and he knows nothing of what has occurred when he comes out of the trance at the end of the seance. After the seance I have told him some of the things I have been told, but he could not understand them, and has remarked that they were quite beyond his capacity to comprehend. He is a good workman but not a student, and his range of knowledge is limited to what one might expect from the environment in which he has lived. He is a decent, upright, honest British working man, but his being a medium does not mean that he knows more than his associates; rather the contrary, because he never hears what takes place at a seance.

I have already accentuated the fact that appearances in this world are very different from reality, the outstanding example being the way we are deceived as to the movement of the sun. This is one instance of many, but it is a good one. Now I come to another deception of nature. Matter, which appears to us to be solid, is nothing of the kind. Can anyone imagine a more real or solid thing than a ton of iron? If anything is solid, iron appears to be so. It certainly fulfils to us in every degree the definition of the word solid. It is heavy to lift, and it is hard to the touch. Physicists, however, would not call it solid.

In our everyday life the sun appears to go round the earth, but astronomers would say that this deception is caused by our living on a globe which turns on its own axis, and thus gives us the impression of the sun going round the earth. So with iron. We have the appearance of solidity, but physicists tell us that matter is an open net-work of electrons and protons, and that the distance between these electrons and protons is immense in relation to each other.

Just as we have had to recast our views on Astronomy, when using our reasoning faculties, so likewise we have had to readjust our opinions about physical matter. Matter, which looks so solid, is, in reality, not solid at all. Of what then does matter consist? Matter is composed of atoms and these atoms are in turn composed of electrons and protons. The electrons condition the substance and the protons condition the weight. According to the number of protons, so is the weight, and according to the number of electrons, so is the substance. Thus iron, which is very heavy, has more protons than wood, which is lighter. Iron is iron because it has a certain number of electrons and protons in each atom, and wood is wood because it has a different number. In iron, for instance, there are always twenty-six planetary electrons in each atom, and so everything that has twenty-six planetary electrons appears to us as iron.

The centre of each atom is known as the nucleus, and this nucleus commands the same position in the atom as the sun does in our solar system. Just as the planets revolve round the sun, so the electrons and protons revolve round this centre. The distance these electrons and protons are apart from one another and the nucleus, is relatively about the same distance as the planets are from each other and from the sun.

Consequently it will be appreciated that the protons and electrons occupy a very small space in the atom, and it is in consequence of the speed at which they revolve that we get the impression that matter is solid. If we consider an atom as something the size of a village church, then a pin-head would represent the relative size of one of the electrons of which it is composed. The electrons are what we see and the protons are what makes a substance feel heavy, but what they move in we cannot see. They move in what is termed "ether", which is a word scientists use for this space.

What, then, are electrons and protons? They are electric charges, the proton being the positive and the electron being the negative. The atom is thus composed of two charges of electricity, positive and negative. Now we come down one step further and ask what is an electric charge? Physicists describe an electric charge under the name of "wavicle". It is not a thing which can be pegged down, so to speak, and examined. It is a vibration of the ether or a wave of motion. Therefore, when we get down to the constitution of matter, we find that it is composed of certain units called atoms, which units are composed of ether vibrations. In other words, physical matter is just ether vibrations and nothing more.

When we look at a house, what takes place to make us realise that we are seeing a house? Now, before I can answer this question, I must give some consideration to the person looking at a house. It will readily be granted that if no one were looking at the house, the house would not be seen by anyone. There must be two units, so to speak, to complete the picture. You must have the house and the person looking at it. Now, what are we? That is the great question which, before I go any further, I shall try to solve.

The universe, I believe, is composed of a gigantic scale of vibrations. Those which we appreciate on earth are only a small range of vibrations between two fixed points, namely between 34,000 and 64,000 waves to the inch, or from 400 to 750 billion waves to the second. That is the section of the universe which appeals to us, the one which makes up to us the physical world. Now the physical world is only a very limited scale of vibrations compared with all the other vibrations in the universe.

We have recently discovered how to produce another range of vibrations which we are able to tune into, as the result of the various devices which go to make up our wireless set. We have learned how to make these vibrations and convert them into sound, but before we knew how to do so they had not existed, though the medium through which they reach us has always existed. Without this ether we should be blind and frozen, as it carries to us the radiation of the sun.

The universe is one gigantic scale of vibrations, and I cannot repeat this too often, because until that fact is assimilated thoroughly the universe will never be understood. Official science recognises solely the physical universe, and only within the last forty years has it discovered that the physical universe is made up of these etheric vibrations. That is about as far as orthodox science has reached today, but those of us who have taken the opportunities afforded to get into conversation with the scientists in the etheric world are able to build on this in a way that no orthodox scientist can.

Science admits only what the physical senses and its instruments respond to, and nothing more, but outside of this there is a vast universe made up of more frequent vibrations on the one hand, and grosset or less frequent vibrations on the other. That is what Spiritualists know, and that is why they advise scientists not to ignore the seance room, because, until they cease doing so, they will continue to think of the universe as a "vast purposeless machine".

That other vibrations exist is well known by scientists, but only certain ranges, one the X-rays, which are waves of greater frequency than those which constitute physical matter, and the lesser frequency waves called dark heat waves and long electric waves. These are proved to our senses by instruments, but there are vast spaces still unknown to physical science. There is a big gap between the most frequent physical vibrations and the X-ray vibrations.

The vibrations of the etheric world, l am told by my informants there, commence just above those of the physical world. We have confirmation of this through the knowledge obtained from psychic photography and clairvoyance, and from the fact that etheric beings, called ghosts, have been seen from time to time through the ages. Thus their lowest vibrations must be just about touching our normal physical range of sight. The chart on page 153 makes this clear, and shows how limited are our sense perceptions. Only the black portion represents the physical world. This is all we sense of the innumerable etheric waves making up the universe.

We are told from the etheric world of this vast range of vibrations, and, knowing what we do of physical vibrations, we can appreciate how and where the two worlds meet. We have now no difficulty in relating physical matter to etheric matter. Physical matter is made up of vibrations within two fixed points. Etheric matter is made up of vibrations just beyond 64,000 waves to the inch. The etheric world is just a continuation of the vibrations beyond what our senses can perceive. We cannot sense beyond the physical range, so long as we inhabit the physical body. Clairaudient and clairvoyant mediums can do so to a limited extent, but they are exceptional, due to their etheric ears and eyes being less heavily coated by physical matter than those of normal people. How far beyond the physical range of vibrations the etheric world goes we do not know.

VISIBLE AND INVISIBLE VIBRATIONS

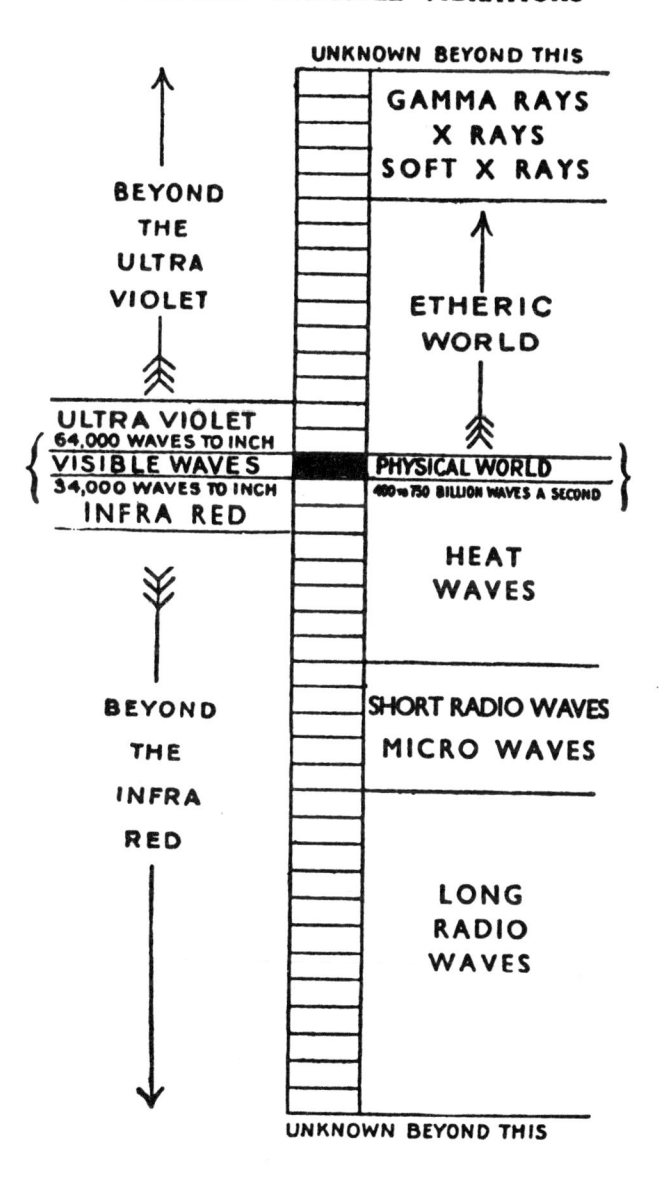

UNKNOWN BEYOND THIS

GAMMA RAYS
X RAYS
SOFT X RAYS

BEYOND THE ULTRA VIOLET

ETHERIC WORLD

ULTRA VIOLET
64,000 WAVES TO INCH
VISIBLE WAVES — PHYSICAL WORLD
34,000 WAVES TO INCH — 400 to 750 BILLION WAVES A SECOND
INFRA RED

HEAT WAVES

BEYOND THE INFRA RED

SHORT RADIO WAVES
MICRO WAVES

LONG RADIO WAVES

UNKNOWN BEYOND THIS

We are, however, told that a point is reached when the vibrations get so rapid that we reach the range of mind. Mind must be termed substance, just as physical and etheric matter go under the name of substance, but substance is just vibration, the rate of vibration conditioning the substance. We must use the word substance for the cause which produces the effect those vibrations have on our consciousness. Consciousness is the effect of substance acting on substance, or vibrations on vibrations.

Mind is composed of such fine vibrations that it has the faculty, when in contact with physical matter, of being moulded into the likeness of physical things. In the physical world it has also the power of moulding physical matter, through acting on it by means of our hands and feet. When, after death, it is in contact with the finer vibrations of the etheric world, it can mould etheric substance more easily than it can mould physical matter on earth. This mind substance is the creative power in the universe, and is called the Universal Mind. Its frequency of vibrations is so rapid that it is highly plastic. This plastic substance, this mind in each of us, makes images, as I shall explain, to which we give the name of "thought", and the more connected and varied these images are so is the thought more intelligent. The Universal Mind is the thinking substance of the universe, and it is for ever seeking expression. We appreciate it on earth only when in contact with physical matter, and in the etheric world it is appreciated when in contact with etheric substance.

What makes the electrons and protons revolve in an orderly way within the atom? Each atom must contain a minute proportion of this thinking substance. All matter contains this thinking substance, this Mind, as without it motion would cease, and without motion there would be no universe. Mind is at the back of all physical substance, and whether it be a stone or a human being, each is controlled by mind of a different degree.

When mind reaches a certain degree of creative strength it gathers round it etheric matter, and with this combination it can enter into contact with physical matter and promote growth. Then we appreciate life. Every cell of our body, every cell of every growing living thing, is controlled by mind in harmonious direct contact with the governing mind of that body. We are made up of this thinking substance. Life in the physical world is mind in combination with etheric and physical substance. That combination makes what we call a living thing different from what we term a dead thing, though in reality there is nothing dead in the universe. All is in motion, or all is motion, but only motion and growth which we appreciate receive the term "life".

Each one of us is endowed with mind just as every living thing is, but the human being is endowed with mind of a finer degree than any other living thing on earth. Each one of us has our share of this mind substance, and its interaction with physical matter is evidently for the purpose of training the mind in mental image-making.

Mind must be something super-physical because it does not decay; it remains permanent. If it decayed like all physical matter, then thought would decay also. We are continually renewing our physical covering, including our brain matter, but our thoughts and memories remain perfect right back to childhood. Mind, therefore, is something apart from the physical, only working in partnership with the physical brain during earth life. Death means that the partnership is severed, though we on earth see only the physical effect of this separation, the lifeless physical body. This is just another of nature's deceptions, as reality is far different from appearance.

Mind has the peculiar faculty of forming, or moulding itself into, the images and movements of its surroundings. These it can reproduce at will, and, through the medium of physical matter, cause change and movement here on earth. In the etheric world it has the power of moulding etheric matter in a more direct fashion, and, by thought, surrounding etheric matter can be changed into the forms which the mind imagines. Earth, then, is the mining-ground for mind which has become individualised. Here it is trained in image-making through contact with earth's grosser surroundings, and, as it develops, it takes more and more control over its surroundings. When it ceases to function through physical matter it takes ever greater control of its surroundings in the etheric world, until ultimately we become just as we think.

The individual mind of each of us, our ego or our self, is therefore trained in creative thought through contact with earth, which training conditions our surroundings here and hereafter. The mind does not die but continues developing, and, with its increasing command over its surroundings, both time and space become of less and less account. Ultimately they cease to exist. My mind is "me" and your mind is "you". Mind has been in existence for all eternity, though not so individualised as now. When it starts its earth experience it enters on a road which enables it to mould its surroundings more and more as it thinks. Our minds will ultimately be in control of our surroundings, and, as we think, so shall we be.

This, I believe, is our destiny, and our first step towards reaching this control over our surroundings, over time and space, is our time on earth, and it is to achieve this end that we, individualised minds, pass through our earth experiences. Children who die still-born, or as infants, are brought back to earth by etheric nurses to be trained in image-making through contact with the grosset physical vibrations.

We now can understand what we mean by saying that we see something. What happens is really this. *When we look at a house we see something composed of different substances. Each substance contains a different number of electrons and protons. The wood has so many, the glass has so many, and the bricks have so many. These electrons agitate the surrounding ether in accordance with their frequency. The substance that has one electron agitates the ether in a different way from the substance that has a hundred.

This affects our mind by the following process. Light, comprising the entire range of vibrations of physical matter, strikes the house, and its vibrations are thrown back to us in accordance with the vibrations of each substance. These we term colour. These vibrations agitate the atoms composing our physical eye and, by means of our nerves, they are transformed into vibrations of our physical brain and thence to our etheric brain, which is an exact duplicate of our physical brain. Through the etheric brain they mould our mind, that plastic substance which is located in the top forepart of our head.

The mind, in consequence, builds itself into the image of a house, and what we say we see and appreciate is our mind-image of the house. The mind is never at rest, always in action, always building itself into images, always creating new images, and, as these images are, so are we. Our existence is made up of the images which the mind constructs. Likewise our mind gets the impression of solidity through our nerves by the same means. When we stand up, sit, or lie down, we are continually being bombarded upwards and supported by a great multitude of vibrations delivered by the atoms making up the substances on which we .rest.

It is, however, incorrect to say that here, or the hereafter, is an illusion. That word gives an entirely wrong impression of life. Life is real here and hereafter. Our surroundings here and hereafter are real, because all matter substance acts on mind substance, and without substance there would be neither mind nor matter. This world is consequently real and so will the next world be, because reality is this mind image-making, and wherever you have this you have reality. It is impossible to imagine mind without something to act upon, or this something acted on without mind to image it, or appreciate it, and fashion it.

Hence, wherever mind is individualised, it will image and then create, fashion and mould its surroundings, and so, in the etheric world, its inhabitants create houses, clothes and everything else that the mind creates on earth. So also the mind that forms the images of trees, flowers and grass on earth, through physical matter, likewise after death forms them through our duplicate etheric eyes, because the vibrations of etheric trees, etc., appeal to mind there, just as here. All, and much more, that exists on earth exists also on the etheric world. Consequently life there to its inhabitants is very similar to life here, but to those capable of appreciating its beauty it is more beautiful than the earth, because of the finer vibrations of the etheric world.

Mind has initiative of its own, and can build up images for itself without influence from without. Once it has learned to make an image it can make it again, and here we have the constructive capacity of mind, because mind, working always through the etheric brain on to the physical brain, can build physical matter as it conceives. All our bodily parts are built up as conceived by our mind. Every bodily movement, sensed or unsensed, is first imaged by the mind. The mind first thinks every heartbeat and every movement of the body, and, when the physical body cannot respond, then follows the separation called death, because when mind cannot function it leaves its physical instrument, taking with it the duplicate etheric body. Thus we see that mind is the most potent influence in every living thing, in the world and in the universe; in fact it is the ultimate reality, all else being its servant.

CHAPTER IX.
THE PHILOSOPHY OF SPIRITUALISM.
PART II.

I WISH now to go back to the beginning of all life, and trace its action and interaction with physical matter from the humble protoplasm, through the worm stage, on to the fish stage, through the reptiles and the marsupials to the apes, and then on to man. I wish to trace briefly the evolution of mind in its association with physical matter.

Evolution is but a word to comprise the long, long story of mind expressing itself through physical matter. Mind can act on physical matter only through etheric substance. The vibrations of mind are at too great a frequency for it to be able to obtain direct contact with physical matter. Mind therefore works through the etheric duplicate brain, and this etheric counterpart contacts physical matter. If we go back to the simplest protoplasm we find mind in the humblest form acting on physical matter. Protoplasm is the physical basis for life, and in its lowest form, such as the protozoa, it propagates by dividing itself into two perfect cells.

If we think carefully of this marvellous act, we come to the logical conclusion that life is propagated by part of the original trinity coming away and forming a new individual unit. As the original unit must have been guided by mind, it is evident that part of the mind which guided the original must have distributed itself between the two. Here we have a simple illustration of the propagation of the species. In humble life sub-division causes propagation, but, as life develops, it requires the sub-division of male and female to produce offspring, but the method is the same.

At some time far back in history, when this world of ours cooled sufficiently to enable mind through etheric substance to make contact with physical matter, a humble speck of physical matter was gathered round a humble speck of etheric substance. This humble speck of etheric substance was governed by mind substance, and this trinity originated life on earth in the earliest forms by sub-division. Life was propagated until the waters of the world, before the Palaeozoic Age, swarmed with protozoa. Once contact was made with physical matter mind became better able to express itself, and it conceived all sorts of forms and shapes. Just as it conceived them, so it built them up. Physical matter seems to be like a garden, in which mind is capable of growing and developing.

Propagation gradually assumed more complicated methods, but still the principle was the same, the parents passing down to the offspring a part of their own trinity - mind, etheric body and physical body. Again and again the old story was repeated, of life, growth, propagation, and then decay through mind and etheric substance parting from the physical. Mind could only remain in contact with the physical for a limited time. It was not a permanent habitation. The etheric duplicate could only retain contact with the physical for a short time, because physical matter is always in a state of decomposition, and evidently the etheric body could renew and control this material for only a limited time. Our physical body is being continually renewed, but the etheric structure is of a more permanent character. Consequently it survives the physical body.

The time, therefore, comes when the renewal of the physical body cannot be continued, and what we call death then follows. Death, however, is death only to the physical which has been temporarily animated by mind capable of creative thought. The life-giving mind still persists, controlling the etheric duplicate.

How long after death this combination of mind and the etheric duplicate body continued, apart from physical matter in the days of primitive life, no one can say. This, however, we do know, that a time came when the combination did continue, when mind was strong enough to retain its individuality and persist in the etheric world as an individual unit. Before this time the individual etheric unit was probably not sufficiently strong to stand alone, and its mind merged into the mass Mind of the Universe, to manifest itself again at some later period in some other physical form. Mind is only recognised by us through the physical, and, had we not the guidance and knowledge obtained through Spiritualism, we should be at a loss to understand what life really is, and what it means.

The time, however, came, after a long period of evolutionary effort, when man arrived on the scene, a thinking being, but, had we not the evidence of psychic phenomena, we could not account for his existence or know his destiny. Except for this evidence there is little to make us believe other than that he is a thinking being because of some chemical reaction taking place within his brain, and that when death comes the reaction ceases and his consciousness becomes extinguished. The fact that this is not so accounts for the religious instinct in man, and we know through the evidence obtained from Spiritualism that this instinct has a real meaning behind it.

Just as the original protoplasm was not merely a physical creation, so likewise we are not a physical creation. We are a mental creation. We belong to a higher substance than physical matter, and physical matter is just like a diver's suit. It is very useful for the diver when on the bed of the ocean, just as our physical body is very useful to us when in contact with the grosset vibrations of the earth. Just as the diver is not at home on the sea bottom, so are we not at home on the earth's surface. Otherwise we would not spend so much of our time in giving thought to what follows death. It is because instinctively we know that we are only temporary inhabitants here, that we have reached out to obtain knowledge of our hereafter.

Animals have not this instinctive feeling, because their minds are not sufficiently developed to retain their individuality permanently as man does. They retain their individuality for a time only, and then, with memories dissipating like a dream, their minds return to the mass Mind of the Universe. They have not the power to continue image-making. Animals, therefore, have only a temporary individuality which persists for a short time in the etheric world, but affection on the part of an etheric man or woman for an animal can retain that animal's individuality for a longer period than is possible if no human affection exists. This affection seems to stimulate the mind of the animal, but it is only a temporary stimulation, because ultimately the animal mind must return to the mass Mind. To put it briefly, creatures guided by instinct only, retain their individuality after death for a period, but, with man, guided by intelligent thought, the personality persists.

Human beings persist, though the lower types of human mind, more akin to the animal mind than the human, doubtless follow the line prescribed for animal life. Only the mind capable of continuing its image-making, retains its memories of the past and its individuality. When humanity reached this stage who can tell, but the time did come far back in history when the individual persisted after death and did not return to the mass mind.

It is Mind that makes us what we are. It seems to remember all the experiences it has had in the previous forms of life, because prior to birth each one of us goes through the different shapes and forms of more primitive lives. In the first four weeks after conception, there is little appreciable difference between the embryos of a man, of a dog and of a tortoise. The ultimate difference is due to the fact that we went on developing before birth to the man stage. A still-born child, an infant, or a child, continues its development in the etheric world until it becomes a man or woman.

Mind is the constructive thinking substance of the universe. It fashions all the flora and the fauna, and, in the most advanced of us, it seems to be so refined that it has become closely related to the directive power of the Universe, and is thus attracted to it like a magnet. We can thus understand what it means when we are told, by our friends on the other side, that as our mind develops we reach finer and finer planes of consciousness, where the mind has more and more direct bearing on its surroundings, and can mould, and be moulded by, its surroundings in a way unimaginable here.

Our destiny seems to be that we ultimately become as we think, when mind has such complete control of its surroundings that to think is to be; always, however, retaining our individuality. Just as the sea is composed of individual atoms, so our individuality and personality persist when we reach the ocean of full control and understanding, which is to become in full affinity with the Divinity, the all-directing power of the universe.

The universe is only limited by the limitations of mind, but, as it is impossible to imagine a region where mind cannot penetrate, the logical conclusion is that the universe is without limit. Limit is related to physical distance and time. In the region where mind is supreme, and in complete control, nothing is limited and there the universe will be comprehensible.

The universe, as I have previously said, is just one gigantic scale of vibrations. The finer ranges I term mind, which has the capacity of directing the other vibrations into the ways and shapes it conceives. This substance that mind acts upon I term matter. Mind is the positive, matter the negative, and these two substances, Mind and Matter, make up the .universe. Matter without mind is impossible to imagine, just as it is impossible to imagine mind without matter. Mind and matter are co-related; they are always found together. Mind cannot be acted upon by nothing, and without mind it is impossible to imagine matter.

Mind and matter are the two substances of which the universe is composed. Mind is that subtle substance which directs matter, and is the cause of matter because all matter has mind behind it, causing the vibrations which we call matter. They are twin brothers, inseparable. Mind directs the moving tons and electrons, but it is crude mind and cannot be compared with the mind which appreciates that such things exist. Mind is present in a tree; it is also present in the animal, but it is mind of a different degree. In the former it directs the growth of the tree, and what nourishment it is to absorb, and what it is to reject. In the latter it does all this and more; it appreciates the tree as well. The tree cannot appreciate the animal, but the animal can appreciate the tree. Plant life, therefore, does not make mental images as animals do, and thus does not survive death. Only mental image-makers do. Mind in the animal appreciates the tree according to its development; the appreciation of a dog is different from that of a bird. To the savage the tree means less than to the botanist.

Mind is of two degrees, one directing growth and the other capable of appreciation and intelligent thought. The first is called the sub-conscious and the other the conscious mind. Mind in a stone directs the whirling electrons and protons. Mind in an architect fashions the stone to its own design. The mind of the architect has therefore two qualities:the sub-conscious sustaining the functions of his body, and the conscious capable of creative thought. Mind can therefore be divided into four categories on earth: the lowest as found in a stone; then the mind of plant life; next the mind of animal life; and lastly the mind of man capable of creative thought, which makes all things subservient to him.

Mind, in different degrees, therefore controls the universe. It is the cause of the vibrations of the universe, and matter is the effect. In its higher degrees it can control and fashion matter, its less intelligent brother, and, as it reaches states of still finer matter, so does its control increase.

Matter is the effect of mind. Mind, this all-powerful cause energising the universe, causes motion, and that motion is matter. Matter, therefore, can be termed mind in motion, and the effect on us of this motion is what we term "matter". Mind is the universe, and all that we see and sense is the effect of the action of this energising thinking substance. We are therefore part of a universe of motion or vibration, the entire universe being motion and only motion. The slower motion, namely matter, inter-acts with the faster motion, namely mind; but all is mind varying in degrees of motion.

What we call physical matter, as I have previously, explained, is just this motion at a certain fixed rate or vibration. Mind in contact with the physical can only appreciate a certain fixed scale of motion. Etheric matter, which we do not sense, is matter at another fixed rate of vibration, and as this rate of motion varies so etheric matter varies in its relation to mind. The mind, as it travels onwards through death from phase to phase, appreciates increased frequencies of vibration, just as the sheath that covers it becomes more refined. At death, the heaviest sheath is cast aside, and mind appreciates a more frequent range of vibrations. This constitutes the first stage of its journey in the etheric world, but, as our etheric body gets more and more refined, it becomes fitted for a finer environment, when it experiences the realms of finer matter which are part of that world. On earth, however, we leave a body behind us, but in the etheric world our etheric body gets more and more refined in itself, and consequently it becomes fitted for a finer environment.

Everywhere throughout the universe we find these two states of motion existing, and, as the variation of motion is, so is the thought. Thought is the effect of these two motions. Their combination constitutes our consciousness, and consciousness consists of the mental images which are constantly being formed by our mind, because of the continual bombardment of minute vibrations on our sense organs. These pass through our physical brain which transmits them through our etheric brain on to the mind.

Therefore it follows that the different combinations of thought make up the individual's existence. Here in the physical world, mind, plus physical matter, make us what we are, and is the explanation of our consciousness. In a further stage mind, plus etheric matter, make us what we are, and, in a stage still further on, when the combination changes again, we shall be as is the combination, until we reach the stage when surrounding matter is so refined that it can be moulded into whatever shapes the mind conceives.

Then, and then only, shall we be able to comprehend the universe. Boundaries and limits, which to us here on earth are such an insuperable difficulty in our arriving at an understanding of the universe, will by then have disappeared, because limits are associated with matter but not with mind. Our present difficulties in grasping the universe arise through our mind being in association with physical matter, which is limited in its vibrations, and by attempting to explain the universe from a physical or limited angle. When we reach the region of mind, which is the universe, the all and in all, our difficulties will disappear. All we need to do now is to accept the fact of Infinite Mind, and that the Universe must be viewed from that angle and not from our finite or physical angle. Then the rest is easy.

In some far-off stage of our career, if we have the desire, we can become one with Infinity or Divinity, but, until that stage is reached, the universe will always remain a problem. The way to make it cease being a problem is, in imagination, to enter this region of pure thought and look on the universe now as we shall look on it then. Only when mind is fully developed can it comprehend all, but, in imagination, some of us can envisage a timeless, spaceless, limitless universe where mind is all and in all.

Beyond this we cannot go even in imagination. We have now reached the stage of pure thought, and have become as gods, with our surroundings at our complete control. We need not dwell too long in this region, as the illimitable time between us and it is so great. What is more important are the practical conclusions we can draw from this better understanding of mind.

As the universe is motion, and the planets and stars which we sense here on earth are just motion, at the same fixed frequency as our physical world, it is likewise conceivable that the sun and each planet have within and surrounding them etheric worlds also, and that the etheric sun gives light to the various etheric worlds. In a book which I hope to publish as a sequel to this one, this question will receive greater consideration than I here have space for.

The sun is the centre of our planetary system and round it are moving spheres. The sun itself is moving round another centre, and that centre may be moving round another, and so on. Where lies the fixed centre, if there be one, no one knows. There is doubtless an explanation of this seeming infinity of physical matter, but always remember that all physical appearances are different from reality, and consequently the explanation may be simple enough to understand when we are sufficiently developed mentally to realise the reality behind the appearance.

To take our own earth to begin with, by a slowing down of vibrations it has reached a stage to which we give the name "physical", but that is not our entire world. To physical people, yes; but theirs is a very limited outlook. In the slowing down of vibrations and the forming of the earth, can we not imagine how it all happened? Imagine a world at one time vastly larger than our globe as we know it. Imagine this whirling mass of fine substance, let us say ten thousand times the size of our earth. As it cooled the centre vibrated less frequently than the outer circumference, and so the cooling process went on, a hard material centre forming what we now call the earth. All around this core are various degrees of substances which we cannot sense, but still they exist and are as much a part of our world as we are.

The earth is the centre of the world, but the greater part of the world extends far out into space, and is quite unsensed by us physical beings. Heaven is no fantastic realm, as it has been painted to us in the legends of the past. It is an astronomical locality, and, this being so, I would suggest that in future it receives the name ETHERIA, instead of the name Spirit World, or Etheric World, which names have been used in the past to denote the super-physical world.

It is not in some far-off region in space, but is part of our world and goes round the sun along with this earth. Just as our earth turns on its axis, so the etheric world turns along with us. It is all part of one whole. The earth is like the stone in a peach and Etheria is like the fruit surrounding it. Just like the stone, so the earth is the life-giving seed to Etheria. Another good simile is that of an onion, which, made up of different skins, makes one connected whole.

The complete world is made up of a fixed scale of vibrations, and only a small range of these affects our senses. As time goes on we shah go up the rungs of the ladder, leaving the physical for the first plane beyond the earth, and so on, always appreciating the surroundings in tune with our etheric body; but, though we shall appreciate only one range of vibrations normally, yet, by thought, we shall be able to lower our vibrations and come back and appreciate the lower ranges through which we have passed.

To begin with, far back in history, mind could only enter into contact with physical matter in a crude state, but gradually the physical was able to accommodate mind of higher and higher quality, or, in other words, of finer vibration. It is logical to believe that we shall return to the range of vibrations from which our mind originally came, just as the beings below us will reach the range from which their mind came. It seems as if part of the universal mind reached down to the physical and, in each individual, is returning whence it came, like to like. Thus can be understood the saying, "We are all the sons of God, we come from God and we return to God." So also can be understood the reason for all the rites, ceremonies and symbols of all religions.

So the action and reaction goes on, mind embedding itself for

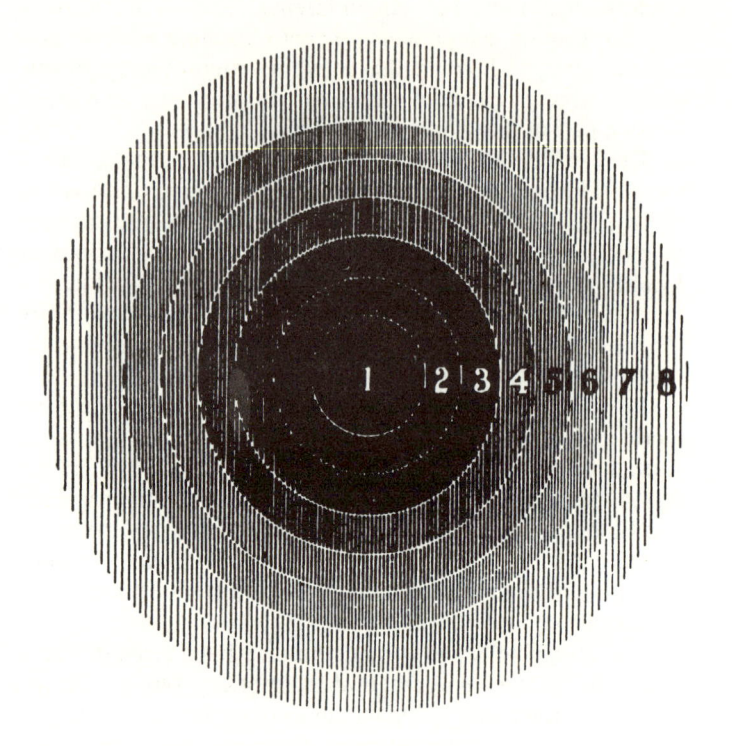

The above diagram has been prepared for the purpose of indicating as clearly as possible the real world. No. 1 represents the Earth, and Nos. 2 to 8 represent the various etheric worlds, each of which has a surface. They interpenetrate each other, but the distance of each surface from the other, which is represented in the above chart as being equal, must not be taken so literally, as the distances vary between the respective surfaces. It must also be understood that the etheric worlds extend to great distances into space, and that their relation in size to the earth is proportionately much greater than is here shown.

However, this is the best representation that can be made, and the reader must imagine each of the eight worlds interpenetrating each other and yet forming one complete whole. This can be more easily imagined when it is kept in mind that each sphere is made up of atoms vibrating at different frequencies. There is nothing known to physics to prevent waves of different frequencies being simultaneously present in the ether.

The earth is reflecting vibrations from 34,000 to 64,000 waves to the inch, which range represents the limit of vibrations we physical beings can appreciate. Each sphere has a range of vibrations of its own, which can be appreciated only by those attuned to its vibrations, and each range follows the other in frequency. Thus the highest earth vibrations just touch the lowest vibrations of No. 2, and so on.

There is nothing in science to contradict in any way the above conception of this greater world; in fact it can be said that the latest theories of physical science leave a place open for the etheric world, and it is only a matter of time before it is accorded its proper place by orthodox science.

a time in the physical and then leaving it, taking with it the etheric body, which it has shaped and which has been encased by a physical garment. This latter returns to the physical earth, to produce at some later date the habitation of other minds. Thus can be seen the true meaning of the resurrection of the dead body.

The physical bodies, as we know them, in the shape and form in which mind constructed them, are not re-animated at some future date by the return of mind to its former habitation. The particles, however, which composed the body, in one form or another may be re-animated by other minds, and again give physical form to a living creature. This comes about through plants which give food to animal life. This food replaces the wastage of the physical bodies of all animal life, and what was once an animated physical body dies to return to form a part of other physical bodies. In this, and this way only, can we accept the physical resurrection of the dead body. The framework, the etheric body, which held the physical together, however, passes from it at death, never to return.

This action and reaction goes on day by day, and each one of us is awaiting our turn to go through the same metamorphosis as has been gone through by all that lived on earth before us. This interplay of the two states of motion, to which we give the names mind and matter, has taken place on earth since the first protoplasm developed in some stagnant pool. It has gone on by slow degrees until the mind became sufficiently developed to act independently apart from the physical, and, through the etheric, become at death an etheric human being with a seemingly endless career before him. With this etheric body the individual is able to develop in a methodical way, though the body may change in shape and form as it reaches higher stages of development. Mind and the etheric body are inseparable; to imagine mind without a body is unthinkable. Immediately after death it reaches the level of vibrations to which the mind can respond through the etheric brain. It reaches its plane of thought, which is just as real and tangible to it in this new state as it was in the physical.

Doubtless this individualisation of mind came slowly, and it was long before the individuality could be maintained, but the time came when it could, and then it was that the etheric world was man's real home. Then step by step, as the mind became more and more developed, so the etheric world became inhabited, and we are now told of seven distinct planes of habitation, real and tangible. Each succeeding plane is more beautiful, and each in turn is inhabited by minds more and more advanced in proportion as the surrounding matter is more refined.

The place we reach immediately following the earth plane is of finer substance than physical matter, but of grosset substance than the plane beyond it, and so on, each plane being composed of finer and finer substance. As the mind develops, so it automatically rises to the place to which it becomes attuned. Our mind must reach a state of harmony with its surroundings, or otherwise there is no happiness, and, as in the etheric world we can harmonise ourselves with our surroundings more easily than on earth, so we reach the plane of our desire quite naturally. Consequently the etheric world, to all of a happy and contented disposition, can be a happier and more contented world to live in than is the physical world. As the mind is, so is our happiness or unhappiness.

Mind always responds to the vibrations to which it is fitted, from the physical to the etheric and from the etheric to the super-etheric. We are told that there are eight known planes comprising the greater world, if we include this earth's surface, and that there is even a region beyond it, quite apart from this world, which we shall eventually enter. Then this world will cease to be for us, and we shall cease to move with it. However, when we get thus far, all earth memories will have faded, and consequently there are none to return to tell us.

Wherever life is, all is natural, and so life on the next plane of thought is a natural and rational one. Just as mind is attuned to conditions on earth, so it will become adjusted to similar conditions in the etheric. It is the same mind, the factor common to both worlds, and it attunes itself to the vibrations to which it responds. Nature makes all changes slowly, and death is no exception. It is little noticed by some. Many pass on and hardly realise at first that a change has occurred, because the mind at once attunes itself to the new conditions, and these conditions, to begin with, are very like those to which we are accustomed in our earth surroundings.

Many, however, cannot get away from earth conditions, because their minds are so conservative, and in such cases as they were on earth so they are there. Do we not know many people who never want to change, and are always satisfied with their present conditions ? Only the mind that is prompted by the urge for something new, and something better, advances to higher realms. All the same I am told that to all, sooner or later, comes this urge or impulse, and with it the desire for something better. Then progress commences.

CHAPTER X.
THE PHILOSOPHY OF SPIRITUALISM.
PART III.

I HAVE been at some trouble to find out the different experiences which different types of mind have had after the change called death. Immediately surrounding the earth there is the lowest etheric plane of all, where life continues for a time for those of fixed earth ideas. Those with crude religious beliefs, definitely fixed, attend the religious services on earth to which their minds have been accustomed. Those of low morals attend the debased places of the earth. Those with drunken habits frequent our public houses. Conditions are decided by desire.

The man absorbed in business, or politics, maintains for a time after death his interest in these, attending at the office, or the factory, or political meetings, and showing no desire to rise above the earth plane. I have come across those who for years have been wandering about the earth's surface, interested only in earth's affairs, and some quite unaware that they have left the earth for ever. They could not understand how it was that they could go from room to room in their own houses, see everything that was going on, and yet not be heard or appreciated.

These persons are sometimes seen and heard, and are the cause of hauntings or ghosts; but they are exceptional. They are bound to earth by very definite ties of memory, such as a murder, or on account of something forgotten which affects their friends on earth, or some deed which is regretted. Those with something on their conscience may hang about this earth for many years, but to them time is very different, and what to us seems a long time is not necessarily so to them. Gradually the earth memory fades, and they rise to higher planes of consciousness to mix with others who (though they still retain their earth memories and may return to earth from time to time) realise the change that has taken place, and live a natural life in the new world to which they have become accustomed.

It is not those people who haunt the earth that come to seances, but they are at times brought to seances for the purpose of awakening them to a realisation of their new surroundings. Such seances are called "rescue circles", and are being held all over the civilised world. They are for the purpose of awakening an urge, or desire, for something better in those people who have never been able to untie their minds from earth, and reach the surface of their new abode. The old term Hades doubtless was meant for this interland between the two surfaces, where roam undeveloped souls. Etheric missionaries, however, are always at work trying to enlighten them, to raise them by thought to their proper place, and, with the desire for something better, they leave our earth's surface and reach the one above quite naturally. These helpers often find this impossible to do, and make use of us on earth to help them, because we are able to influence those backward people in a way they cannot do.

At the ordinary seances we meet again those who have passed on to their proper plane, and come back to tell their friends that they still live and are happy. The majority find their new level and take up the new life quite naturally. They realise the change that has taken place without much delay.

The mind plays a much larger part in the etheric world than it does here, and so it can attune itself to the surroundings for which it is fitted in a way it cannot do on earth. We all know people who are out of harmony with their surroundings on earth. That does not need to happen there. Here on earth we are meeting the good and the bad, the intelligent and the ignorant, though we may have nothing in common with those we meet. There, those of the same type of thought meet and live together. There the power of mind is so much more in evidence, that like draws to like in a far greater degree than here. Here our work and everyday occupations bring us in contact with minds of all types, but there minds of like development congregate together.

Harmony of thought is the magnet which draws like to like, but all the same, within certain limits of development, all kinds live on the same surface there as here, and communities having similar ideas and ideals live together. The best earth example I think of is a university or public school, where all live together with a common interest, but at different stages of development.

Recently I obtained some further valuable marion, by means of the Direct Voice, with reference to the exact situations of the various planes surrounding the earth, and the conditions in each. The replies I obtained to my questions are in complete agreement with the replies I received eight years ago when John C. Sloan was the medium. The medium in this instance was a London lady of independent means and she gives her services only to a few friends. She prefers that her name should not be mentioned. However, the same phenomena occurred as took place through Sloan's mediumship. I was anxious to have further information on this subject of location, and the replies I received will now be read as an important addition to the many answers to my various questions which I gave in *On the Edge of the Etheric.*

1. *Question.* - Do the planes on which you tell us you live, exist above the surface of the earth?

Reply - These planes move with the earth and form part of its orbit. The first plane is a kind of Clearing Station where the different nations live together. Family Life is most important, and the members await relatives of their generation to go on together to the next plane. So far as the first plane is concerned, it does exist above the surface of the earth, but it also is in connection with the earth plane.

2. *Question* - What is the distance of the first plane from the earth's surface, and the distance of the other planes which extend out into space?

Reply - The first plane is quite close to the earth. There is a distance between each plane, but distance does not mean quite the same thing on this side as it does to you on earth.

3. *Question* - If you live on a surface beyond the earth's surface, how do you get back to earth?

Reply - We lower our vibrations and pass through our surface. We then adjust our vibrations to those of your earth. It is easier to get through some places than others, as they have been regularly used, and can be called throughways or highways from our plane to your earth.

4. *Question* - How do you lower your vibrations?

Reply - By mental effort. It is easy for those in a higher plane to go to the lower, but those in the lower cannot go to those in the higher. Those coming from higher planes bring with them their atmospheric or rather their etheric vibrations.

5. *Question* - Do all people who die on earth live on the same surface, just as we live together on the surface of the earth?

Reply - The general answer is "Yes"; but it must be remembered that there are earth-bound souls who do not arrive at the first plane without assistance, and in some cases for a very considerable time, so far as time is reckoned on the earth. There are special places for children to be brought up in, as well as healing stations for those who come over, and other healing stations for those living on the first plane. But the word "place" does not quite signify the same thing as is meant by it on the earth plane.

6. Question - Does our surface appear to you as the bed of the ocean appears to us? Namely, you are above us and can get down to us?

Reply - It is true that the etheric planes are above and around the earth, but the first plane is close to the earth. The reference to the bed of the ocean can only be accepted as a simile. We have nothing quite corresponding to your earth vision of the ocean bed which we can give as an illustration of what your surface looks like when you are coming to us from earth.

7. Question - Has what is equivalent to our earth's surface in your world, got trees and houses?

Reply - Trees, houses, hills and vales exist on every plane from the physical plane upwards. When we have lowered our vibrations down to the physical plane we experience what exists on your earth's surface. The flowers and trees are brighter on our hills than they are in the vales; it is a matter of light.

8. Question - Are your vibrations similar to ours but faster? Are they of the same nature, but just above our capacity to sense?

Reply - The vibrations are faster and finer. This applies to each plane; that is, the higher the faster and finer the vibrations.

These replies should be read in conjunction with the replies given in my previous book. It is evident that the etheric world is part of our world, that it extends out into space, that each sphere has a surface which is somewhat similar to our surface. Each surface and sphere can be penetrated by what they term lowering their vibrations by thought, which explains how it is they can get back to earth, just as the reverse method explains how those who die reach the surface of the plane which is to be their home. Further, etheric substance, of which it is composed, is as free to its inhabitants as our air is to us, and, as it can be moulded by thought into the shapes required, without manual work as here, so life is easier, and there are no such things as working for money, or master and servant, all being free to live just as they choose.

The etheric world is different to every type of mind. To those of high and noble thought it appears different from what it does to those of low intelligence. All in the same plane can sense the same things, but these appear different according to the mental development. Everything is natural and responds to the vibrations of the various types of mind.

We hear of some having brighter clothes than others, the reason being that they are living in surroundings of finer matter, and consequently their garments affect the clairvoyant as being of a different quality from that of those living in grosser surroundings. The effect the finer surroundings have on the clairvoyant causes the clairvoyant to appreciate them as radiant light, whereas those living in low surroundings impress the clairvoyant as being of a darker nature. It is all a question of vibration. Dark objects vibrate more slowly than bright objects

These various planes are actual localities surrounding this world, but it is difficult for those in Etheria to convey any definite ideas of distance. In that world to think oneself from place to place is to accomplish the journey almost at the speed of thought. Consequently what would be called distance to us becomes no distance, so to speak, to them. However, these localities extend far above the earth's surface. Each sphere has a surface, called a plane, and above the surface of the first sphere is the surface of the second sphere. Those on the surfaces of the spheres below can look through the surfaces above them, just as we on earth are looking through all those surfaces and do not know it.

Each succeeding sphere is composed of finer substance, and consequently the surface that is of finer substance than the one below cannot be seen by those on the lower surface. As development proceeds, those who progress become more and more attuned to the finer substance beyond and above them, and so parting takes place there as here. Call it death if you like, but there is no body to bury, and those who pass to a higher plane can come back to their friends at will. By lowering the vibrations of their etheric bodies by thought, they come through their own surface from plane to plane right back to earth, but they cannot rise above the surface to which they are mentally and bodily fitted.

Those inhabiting Etheria are in advance of us here on earth, as this inter-travel between the various planes is a common occurrence and part of their lives. Likewise, the return of our friends from Etheria is assuming greater and greater proportions, just as the number of our mediums increases. In time it is reasonable to assume that, as we develop psychically, our appreciation of the presence of those called dead will become a more frequent occurrence.

Instead of being ignored on their return to earth, our friends will come back to be greeted by all, and then death will have lost its sting. Remember always that this earth of ours is a very small part of our real world, of which we are the inhabitants. Our earth, composed of matter called physical, contains only a small proportion of the substance which makes up our world. If we consider the whole world as composed of substance at different rates of vibration, then we might say that a small part has slowed down sufficiently to become physical. The remainder forms part of the world revolving with us, but it is unsensed by us physical beings.

Did the physical first give life to the unsensed, or did the unsensed give life to the physical? Did the physical propagate life in the etheric or the etheric life in the physical? Life is something apart from the physical, as the physical alone would be devoid of life. A dead tree has lost something a live tree possesses. When mind reaches a stage to cause movement, which can be appreciated, we call the object capable of movement animated, or living, and the cause of this we term life. The word includes mind the motive, and the etheric counterpart the mechanism.

This, then, is life, and, as life includes mind and the etheric structure, it pertains to the etheric and must have come from the etheric. Life can exist in the etheric apart from the physical, but not in the physical apart from the etheric. The physical, therefore, has been impregnated, and is still being impregnated, by this invisible inter-action with the etheric.

From the etheric has all life come, and to it will it return. The physical, however, gives individuality to life, but what constitutes life must have been in existence before the physical ever was. We think of life only in conjunction with the physical, but in this we are wrong. Life may have existed before the physical was formed, but of its nature we can only guess. What we believe is that the physical gives to life the individuality it has today and had in the past, and life, after passing through the physical, retains individuality for a length of time according to the mental development. Other types of life exist in Etheria which differ from those of this world, and presumably they came into being through interaction between the planes on which they exist and the planes above them. But all physical life came from the etheric, just as all etheric life has come from a higher source. The planes nearer the earth, therefore, are more like this earth than those farther away, as their vibratory conditions more closely resemble earth conditions.

And now in conclusion. From the information I have been

given from Etheria, we now realise that the earth is but a small part of the real world; and that this real world is composed of various spheres at different rates of vibration. We also now realise that mind is the governing power in the universe, but only when it is in conjunction with the physical can we appreciate it. Mind, however, never acts directly on the physical, but through the etheric counterpart on to the physical. The etheric duplicate is first conceived by the mind, and just as it grows it attaches to it physical matter.

The time comes to every individualised life when physical matter cannot be retained, and the etheric counterpart, governed by mind, returns to the etheric environment. We subconsciously will our own death. This interaction of mind with the physical has been proceeding on earth since the first protoplasm moved on its own initiative. Up through the various stages of evolution on earth, finer and finer mind substance was able to manifest through the physical, and consequently all life has developed. It has propagated itself through part of this trinity, mind, etheric matter and physical matter, detaching itself and forming offspring.

Mind has developed itself through coming in contact with the physical. For a time it was not strong enough to retain its individuality and its memories sufficiently long to become an etheric being, and consequently mind returned to the Universal Mind to again enter the physical, each time becoming stronger and more individualised. Then the time came when the first individual unit was able to retain his memory and identity, as his mind images were sufficiently strong to last in the etheric. Thus man became an etheric being, but not immortal. Only as mind developed did the stage come when his mind remained indefinitely individualised in the etheric. Then the etheric was his real home, and the physical only the starting point in his career.

If we now follow man in the stages onwards, we find that this individualised mind harmonises with its surroundings, and consequently reaches conditions to which it is attuned. Mind is capable of development, and consequently it can rise to finer and finer surroundings. This it does by obtaining greater and greater power over its etheric body, which it can attune to its surroundings by the power of thought. As mind gets into finer surroundings it can act with greater ease on surrounding substance, because that finer substance is more akin to mind. The mind behind it is more easily reached, because all substance is animated and guided by mind. Just as each of us can influence other minds on earth, so the time will come when we can likewise influence our surroundings.

Gradually the individual appreciates surroundings of ever finer or more frequent vibrations, and, as he does so, he gets more and more control of his surroundings, until ultimately his thoughts so condition these that he is as he thinks. Thus he reaches the region of pure thought, and that is man's destiny as far as I can tell. Call it reality if you will, but all is reality to us in every stage upwards. The reality of one stage ceases to be so at the next, which in turn becomes real, and so we go on from one reality to another, looking back on the previous stage as but an inferior expression of the one reached.

No finite being, at our stage of consciousness, can comprehend more than this state of pure thought. A picture, the painting of which will last throughout eternity, cannot be grasped when the preliminary sketches are first being pencilled in.

After we have reached this stage of pure thought, will each individualised mind not reincarnate? So some think, but to me it is inconceivable that mind, when it reaches that stage, will ever think of returning to earth. It has reached a stage of strength and virility, and its earth memories are forgotten. becomes separated from this whirling mass of physical and etheric matter, and all other stages have been passed and forgotten. To return would be retrogression, and we have no evidence that this is nature's plan. It sounds simple and believable only to those who have never thought out how we obtain our individual minds and become individual beings.

These come from our parents, and the sex is determined by the mind which takes control in the first instance when the two germs meet. So the one who believes that he or she is the reincarnation of some individual who once lived on earth, must explain how this separate individual mind took the place of the combined minds of his or her parents at conception. It is caused by a misunderstanding of the facts, and sprang from minds which could conceive a virgin impregnated by a god, an old belief with no scientific authority behind it.

The re-incarnation of a strong individualised mind is impossible to imagine, though the weaker undeveloped minds may possibly return to the mass mind just as may happen to the minds of animals, but I have nothing to support even this suggestion.

These views receive the support of my informants in the etheric world, who say that they know of no one who has incarnated again on earth. They have with them those who lived on earth thousands of years ago, and those not with them have gone on to higher planes.

It is reasonable to imagine the universe as a whole, as one great developing thought, or a series of myriad small thoughts, connected into one harmonious whole. As we know by experience that developing thought never goes back, but only changes, so we must assume that thought is continually evolving to higher heights of expression. There seems no end to mind, and, this being so, there is no end to thought, and no end to life.

To try to explain the universe from only a physical standpoint, is, therefore, a shortsighted localised effort. To us some day the physical will be the least important thing in our lives, and, this being so, why adopt this parochial outlook, as some of our noted scientists are still trying to do? When some day they realise that the universe is Mind, and that the physical is but an expression of this mind, our science will be revolutionised, our healing will be revolutionised, and our social conditions will be revolutionised.

We shall come then to realise that our time on earth is for the purpose of developing creative thought, and consequently the development of mind and character will be the object before every intelligent individual.

> "Two men looked out through prison bars—
> One saw mud, the other stars."

Could two lines better express the power of mind over our surroundings? As it is here, so will it be hereafter. Some minds are only sufficiently developed to see mud, but others to comprehend something of the majesty of the universe.

CHAPTER XI.

WEIGHED IN THE BALANCE.

ABOUT 2500 years ago a Chaldean king gave a great feast to a thousand of his lords, .so we are told in an ancient record. This king, Belshazzar by name, commanded that the golden and silver vessels, taken from the temple at Jerusalem, be brought and Used at the feast. In the same hour came the fingers of a man's hand and wrote on the wall, much to the discomfiture of the king, his princes, his wives and his concubines. They saw the writing but they could not understand its meaning, so Daniel was called that he might interpret it, which he did.'

And this is the writing that was written: MENE MENE TEKEL UPHARSIN, which he translated into meaning:

"God has numbered thy kingdom and finished it. Thou art weighed in the balance and found wanting. Thy kingdom is divided and given to the Medes and Persians."

That night the king was slain, and Darius the Mede took his kingdom. This is an ancient story, but its lesson is as evident today as it was of yore. Nature never stands still. Change is a law of Nature. Kingdoms and beliefs come and go, and nothing remains permanent in the universe. "Change and decay in all around" is as true today as it will be tomorrow, and as it was yesterday.

An individual, or a community of individuals, be they a nation, a political party, or a Church, if they do not change with the times, are bound by immutable law to perish. Each one of us, each community, is constantly being weighed in nature's balance, and a record taken. If we are found wanting, our kingdom is finished. Life pursuing life and in turn pursued by life, the fittest only surviving. Thus we are today what we are. This mental urge has raised the humble protoplasm, and made of it thinking men and women.

Those who say that "the religion of my father is good enough for me", will be found wanting when each individual mind takes account of its past, and weighs up all the opportunities missed. It is so much easier just to accept and not to think for oneself, just to slide down life's stream, to be a drifter and not a thinker. Some day, either here or hereafter, a rock will be struck, and the drifter will have to take stock of his surroundings and decide if drifting is to be forever his means of navigation, or, if he is to take command of himself, use his reason as his compass, and learn to steer for himself. Otherwise, when he reaches the sea, he will be either a helpless piece of wreckage, tossed to and fro with nothing to guide him, or, on the other hand, a capable navigator able and willing to use the gift of reason implanted in each one of us.

Humanity is made up of drifters and thinkers, the drifters scoffing at the thinkers, and the thinkers pitying the drifters. If there were no drifters, and only thinkers in this country, this book need never have been written. Neither would it have been written if there had been no thinkers. The information given within these pages has not been assembled by a drifter, but by a thinker. History will repeat itself, and the conclusions here reached will be criticised and derided by the drifters, who have never given an hour's thought to any of the subjects discussed.

From the time I was at the university, I have given much thought and time to the study of Comparative Religion, to the origin of the Biblical records, and the origin of Christianity, and for over thirty years I have been interested in this subject. I have been familiar all these years with the questions with which this science deals, and, until I became convinced of the reality of psychic phenomena, I was, as the result of my investigations, an agnostic, one who believed that nothing could be known of God, or the after-life, by our limited powers of comprehension. Those were questions I could not solve. I did not deny their importance, but left them aside until my knowledge increased.

I feel no bitterness towards any Church, although, when I was younger, my patience was severely tested. So far as I personally am concerned, it does not matter what the Church preaches or what the people believe; in these days everyone tolerates the opinions of others, and recognises the right of each individual to think for himself.

Why, therefore, should I trouble to write this book? Certainly it is not for profit. How can one explain the desire to share with others the knowledge possessed by a few but not by the majority? Why have some of us this desire to pass on something new, knowing that criticism will follow and nothing material will ever be gained? Why did Bruno not recant, and tell the Church and the priests of his time that he would believe anything if they would only leave him alone?

Personally I would have done that rather than be tortured. I would have told them that rather than suffer torture, misery, and, after years of imprisonment, burning at the stake, I would be silent for ever and they could remain ignorant if they wanted to. But I am not the stuff that martyrs are made of. At least, I think so now; but had I lived in those days of ignorance, my attitude might have been different. The minds of our ancestors were different from ours. There was little toleration on either side. Intolerance bred intolerance. They were not so refined in mind in those days, or otherwise they could not have inflicted and endured pain as they did. Their minds were coarser and so were their feelings.

However, in this land of the free, everyone is at liberty to express his honest and dishonest thoughts, and, as I shall not be burned by the Church, I have taken the trouble to pass on what I honestly believe is the truth. It is because I see indifference on the one hand through the folly of the Church, and ignorance on the other through the people accepting the Church's teaching, that I feel compelled to put my thoughts once more on paper. Besides that, it is only right that the general public should know the truth about Christianity and Spiritualism. The clergy frequently scoff at, and ridicule, Spiritualism and Spiritualists, but this book will show that they should put their own house in order before interfering with honest, intelligent people, in the unmannerly way they do. Their folly, I trust, I have made clear to everyone. It is because the indifferent are losing so much, and the ignorant are losing so much, that I trust this book will still further open the minds of those who are coming to believe that Spiritualism rests on reason, observation and experience, but cannot accept it because it is contrary to the Church's teaching or the Bible. To help them I have told them what I believe to be the truth about all three, and, if they still prefer to cling to a decaying institution, or an ancient book, and ignore the testimony of men and women of repute of the present day, on the facts relating to survival, then no more can be done.

Let me give the latest opinion of the Church as to its belief in survival after death. This is contained in the January 1933 issue of *Life and Work*, the official publication of the Church of Scotland, in an article by the Very Reverend Professor W.P. Paterson, D.D., LL.D., Professor of Divinity at Edinburgh University, whose opinion carries great weight in the Protestant Church. In this article he criticises Dr. Maclean's book *Death Cannot Sever,* and, while not denying some of the claims of Spiritualism, he advises Christians to keep to what he calls the "Christian certainties". Let me quote from this article of nearly four pages the only reason he can give for Christians believing in survival:

"The fundamental Christian certainty is that we shall survive death. This has been believed from of old, and many arguments were given in support of it, but the event which gave our race confidence truly to believe it was the rising of Christ from the dead."

This is a good example of clerical logic. He gives two reasons, the first being because our ancestors believed in survival. So have all races and creeds. If this is an argument we should believe that the earth is flat, and that diseases are caused by devils. According to Dr. Paterson, something that has been believed in of old is a certainty.

The second reason given is the rising of Christ from the dead, but the Church has always insisted that this was a miracle, and, if it was, it is illogical to say that, because a miracle occurred 1900 years ago, we survive death. Moreover, he does not explain the connection between what he calls the second member of the Trinity overcoming death, which power is surely an attribute of God, and a humble member of the human family likewise surviving death. God having done so, according to Christian teaching, is certainly no argument that humanity will do likewise.

Besides this, Dr. Paterson knows, just as other intelligent people know, that the so-called evidence of Christ's resurrection is based on nothing but doubtful tradition, a very flimsy basis, and, as the story was copied from earlier religions, there is no basis whatever for the belief in the physical resurrection as reported in the gospels. It was the physical body of Jesus, we are told in the gospels, that rose from the grave re-animated, and, after a short time on earth, ascended into heaven like a balloon. Whatever has this miraculous event to do with our own death and survival? Dr. Paterson is on surer grounds when he concludes his article as follows:

"Revelation was restricted in scope, and we have been left in ignorance of many things that we should have expected to know, and that we desire to know."

When, however, Spiritualists tell of their experiences, and how they are certain that they have been in communication with those who lived on earth but have died, their testimony is ignored by the institution to which Dr. Paterson belongs, and which he admits is in ignorance of many things its adherents desire to know. Instead of accepting our trustworthy evidence, it puts forward as a "certainty" of survival a non-historical event, which he says occurred some 1900 years ago, and which has no relation to the individual, as it occurred, so he asserts, to God.

Why this ignoring and denouncing of the claims of Spiritualism on the one hand, and, on the other, this doping of the people with falsehood, combined now with an admission of ignorance? Is it not that the clergy cannot now ignore the fact that the people are finding out the truth for themselves, but are still rigidly jealous of their rights? Since the adoption of Christianity as the state religion of Rome, Christian clergy have been looked on as holding a privileged position, being considered as endowed with a special authority from God to interpret what they claim as his message to humanity. They will not relinquish this privileged position without a struggle, and the comfort Spiritualism brings is a secondary matter to them when their own prestige, and that of their organisation, is concerned.

Dr. Paterson's ignorance of the after-life agrees with what a high dignitary of the Church of England said to me a few months ago:

"We do not know whether we survive death or not, and we have no means of knowing. Personally I do not believe that we do, but, if you could prove it to me, I should be for ever grateful to you."

This man was honest to me. He is the natural product of the institution to which he belongs, which never has believed in investigation, but only in faith, which so often fails, because those who rely on this easiest of all methods never give thought to the necessity for evidence on which real belief rests. He did not repeat to me worn-out phrases, which mean nothing to the thinking man and woman. He told the truth as he understood it, and did not make claims for his religion which have no basis in fact. So long, however, as the public will accept what is told them by those whose interest it is to keep alive an ancient superstition, then so long will this deluding of the people continue. The way the public accept everything that takes place, and is said, in church is pitiful. The Christian funeral service should revolt the reason of every thinking individual, and yet it is conducted hundreds of times, day after day, with never a protest.

Recently I attended a funeral service at one of our parish

churches. The man who had passed on was rich, so there were four parsons to bury his body. The service was a long one. If he had been poor it would have been short, and one parson would have been sufficient. However, their combined efforts consigned the "soul to rest till the great resurrection day", when "through the mediation of Jesus Christ he would be accounted worthy to live forever with the blessed". The various orthodox phrases were repeated from which the following extracts are taken:

"Only through Jesus Christ shall he see life eternal."
"We leave him in God's hands till the great resurrection day, when body and soul will be reunited."
"He that believeth in me, though he were dead, yet shall he live, and whosoever believeth in me shall never die."
"For since by man came death, by man also came the resurrection of the dead."
"For as in Adam all die, so in Christ shall all- be made alive."
"We shall not sleep, but we shall all be changed in a moment, in the twinkling of an eye, at the last trump, for the trumpet shall sound and the dead shall be raised incorruptible, and we shall all be changed."
"The sting of death is sin, and the strength of sin is the law."
"0 Lord most mighty, 0 holy and most merciful Saviour, deliver us not into the bitter pains of eternal death."
"Spare us, Lord most holy, 0 God most mighty, 0 holy and merciful Saviour, the most worthy judge eternal, suffer us not at our last hour for any pains of death to fall from thee."
"In the sure and certain hope of the Resurrection to eternal life through our Lord Jesus Christ, who shall change our vile body, that it may be like unto His glorious body according to the mighty working whereby He is able to subdue all things to Himself."
"They rest from their labours."
"Lord have mercy upon us, Christ have mercy upon us, Lord have mercy upon us."
"That we with all those that are departed in the true faith of Thy holy name may have our perfect consummation and bliss."
"0 merciful God, the Father of our Lord Jesus Christ who is the resurrection and the life, in whom whosoever believeth shall live though he die, and whosoever liveth and believeth in Him shall not die eternally."
"For them that sleep in Him."

"That we may rest in Him."

"And that at the general resurrection in the last day we may be found acceptable in Thy sight, and receive the blessing which Thy well beloved Son shall then pronounce to all that love and fear Thee, saying, 'Come, ye blessed children of My Father, receive the kingdom prepared for you from the beginning of the world.'"

"Grant this, we beseech thee O merciful Father, through Jesus Christ our Mediator and Redeemer."

All this is contrary to what Spiritualists know to be true, and the Church has not a scrap of evidence to support any of these extraordinary statements.

The words "Jesus Christ", or "through Jesus Christ", were repeated twenty-nine times at this service. God was asked not to lead us into temptation, which is something we should attribute to the devil, and not to infinite wisdom. God was also told many things he was to do and not to do. The following are extracts taken from the hymns sung:

>"Day of wrath! O day of mourning!'
>"When our final doom is near."
>"Leave we now thy servant sleeping."
>"He who died for their release."
>"Leaving him to sleep in trust
>Till the Resurrection day."
>"On the Resurrection morning
>Soul and body meet again."
>"Here awhile they must be parted
>And the flesh its sabbath keep."
>"For a while the tired body
>Lies, its feet towards the morn."

All this again is quite contrary to what Spiritualists know to be true. Christianity looks on death as a curse which was removed, for believing Christians only, by Christ's death. Spiritualists say this is an ancient superstition having no relation to present-day thought. Death is not a curse but a blessing, a step further on in our life of progress towards some far-off goal. It is but a change of appreciation, and comes to all for our good. The belief in Christ does not affect our destination in the least, and for Christians to go on concurring in these antiquated opinions shows mental indolence and a low conception of the power we call God, the giver to all mankind of a natural death as of a natural birth.

The foregoing is 20th-century Christianity. The Protestant Church, like the Roman Catholic, has not varied a jot in its fundamental beliefs since A.D. 325 when its creeds were manufactured by an assembly of ignorant men presided over by Constantine, a murderer.[1] Moreover, it never will make any advance until the people cease to accept what it offers them as the truth, and think for themselves.

This entire funeral service is a travesty of the truth. What the Church believes was Saint Paul's opinion is always given at length, but no mention is made of the great fact of survival contained in thousands of Spiritualist books and records, written during the past eighty years by men and women of our own time, some of whom were men and women of eminence. These testify to the return of the departed, and to their being able to communicate with us. This testimony is so overwhelming in its power that it should compel the attention of any who have any regard for facts. The facts it presents are among the best attested of those which constitute our present day knowledge.

Let it be stated once more without any equivocation that those the Church calls "dead" come back and say they are very much alive and active, and further that, in their world, no one believes that any of them will come back to take up their old bodies, even if they could find them. They also testify that Jesus Christ has nothing to do with the question of life and death, and they know nothing about "the mediation of Our Saviour Jesus Christ".

In answer to this testimony, Christians say it is devils who come back to beguile us and delude us; but, as I have shown, Christians have nothing whatever wherewith to support their beliefs. These are unscientific and unhistorical, and Christians are too ignorant, too stupid, or too lazy to change with the

---

1 Those who doubt this statement have only to read *What it means to be a Christian*, just published by Dr. Headlam, when Bishop of Gloucester, to find all the old superstitions reiterated with emphasis. Not a particle of evidence is given in support of the tremendous assertions he makes, such as "Jesus was God", "Jesus was truly God", and "Jesus was perfect God". If Jesus was God it follows that God, the creator of the seemingly infinite Universe, was Jesus. This degrading of the Infinite to the level of humanity is blasphemy, and moreover the past tense should not be applied to Infinite Intelligence. The Infinite must always be, but never was. According to present-day Christianity God is therefore Jesus, just as Jesus was God to the ignorant framers of the various Christian creeds. Christian people unfortunately use words so loosely and seldom think what they mean. Dr. Headlam admits the unreliability of the gospel narratives, and relies on Church tradition and the creeds to support his assertions.

changing times. So long as the Church continues to propound and preach flagrant lies about those who pass on, it deserves the contempt of all intelligent and honest people. I am sure there must be many enlightened Christians who will welcome the truth being told, though they may fear to tell it themselves.

What a difference between the service just referred to, and the service at the burial of the body of a Spiritualist! There it is all brightness, knowledge instead of hope, praise that the etheric body is liberated into a fuller life. Clairvoyants present see many friends on the other side who have come back, often bringing with them the one whose physical body is being buried. The knowledge of what death really is, is accepted as a matter of course, and the expectation is expressed that the departed will be back again soon through some medium to report his safe arrival on the further shore.

There is no mourning, no black, as all is understood. Death is known to be but a step round a bend in the road of life, and, this being so, there are no vain repetitions from ancient documents which mean nothing, and which are of only slight comfort to the ignorant, and of none to the intelligent.

Such is a Spiritualist's funeral. Spiritualists are guided by those who have made the change, and Christians by ignorant speculation thousands of years old. Which of the two affords the greater comfort, the true or the false? I shall leave it for each reader to judge. While Christians have been drifting, Spiritualists have been thinking.

The following is one of the most vivid pen pictures of what really happens at death, and of humanity's failure to grasp its true meaning. Who wrote it I know not, but I give it as I found it:

> As the faint dawn crept upwards, grey and dim,
> He saw her move across the past to him-
> Her eyes as they had looked in long-gone years,
> Tender with love, and soft with thoughts of tears,
> Her hands, outstretched as if in wonderment,
> Nestled in his, and rested there, content.
>
> "Dear wife," he whispered, "what glad dream is this?
> I feel your clasp - your long remembered kiss
> Touches my lips, as when you used to creep
> Into my heart; and yet, this is not sleep-
> Is it some vision, that with night will fly?"
>
> "Nay, dear," she answered; "it is really I."

"Dear heart, it is you I know,
But I knew not the dead could meet us so.
Bodied as we are, - see, how like we stand!"

"Like," she replied, "in form, and face, and hand."

Silent awhile, he held her to his breast,
As if afraid to try the further test-
Then speaking quickly, "Must you go away?"
"Husband," she murmured, "neither night nor day I"

Close to her then she drew his head,
Trembling, "I do not understand," he said.
"I thought the spirit world was far apart . . ."

"Nay," she replied, "it is not now, dear heart I
Quick, hold fast my hand, lean on me . . . so . . .
Cling to me, dear, 'tis but a step to go I"

The white-faced watchers rose beside the bed;
"Shut out the day," they sighed, "our friend is dead."

Such is a description in poetic words of what is happening thousands of times every day. Is it not time that everyone should wake up and try to grasp the true meaning of death, so that it can be looked upon as a friend and not as an enemy? Only Spiritualists can teach the lesson. Only Spiritualism can save the world from blank materialism.

Only Spiritualism will unite mankind in one religion, a religion that can be accepted by the Hindu or the Mohammedan, by the Buddhist and the Christian. Spiritualism could make the world one great family, could make all men brothers, and could make all men free. Some day all such labels as Christian, Moslem, Hindu and Buddhist will disappear, and then there will be no need for the label Spiritualist, as all will merge into one, the great natural religion of humanity.

On the platforms at my meetings throughout the country, I have had supporting me men and women of all creeds and sects, namely Mohammedans, Hindus, Jews, and all the sects of Christianity, who, now that they know the truth, realise the futility of the creeds and dogmas of the religions into which they were born.

Spiritualists do not believe in sending missionaries to try to convert those belonging to the leading eastern religions. It is futile to replace one superstition by another, and yet millions of money have been, and still are, spent in trying to convert the "heathen Chinese", the "heathen Buddhists", and others whose ancestors all had a part in laying the foundations of Christianity. This is like taking coals to Newcastle! Spiritualism will succeed, however, when other efforts have failed, as its principles lie at the back of all religions.

Meantime Spiritualist organisations grow and flourish. In every large city there are many Spiritualist churches, and at least one in the smaller towns, where those who wish to get in touch with their friends and relatives on the other side should go, as connected with them are the reliable mediums of the district. These churches hold services every Sunday, and lectures and discussion classes during the week. The Sunday schools, which go under the name of Lyceums, are well-organised and cared for. These churches advertise their meetings in the weekly Spiritualist journals and newspapers.

In those papers will also be found advertised those organisations which make a special point of helping the enquirer. They are becoming large and influential and for a small annual subscription the subscriber has the privilege of attending their lectures without further charge, enjoys the use of the library, and can have sittings with the best mediums at the minimum of expense.

I can only briefly refer to one aspect of Spiritualism which is of growing importance, namely that of Psychic Healing, through healing mediums. This is not what is termed faith healing, as faith no more enters into it than it does when we consult and are treated by medical science.

The patient attends the centre where the healing medium works in trance, and, with the help of assistants with psychic power, but not in trance, healing takes place by means of psychic rays which are passed through the medium by etheric doctors, who use him as their instrument and vehicle to make contact with the sufferer. The diagnosis of the disease is remarkable for its accuracy. In serious cases the patient has been put to sleep by the etheric doctor working through the medium, and thus no pain is felt. Thousands are being cured by means of psychic rays working on the etheric body of the patient, because it is through the etheric that the cure of the physical body is effected.

One of the best healing mediums in this country at the present time is F.J. Jones, who works under the direction of a doctor in Etheria, giving himself the name of "Medicine Man".

He claims to treat over 20,000 cases a year, and to have treated over 60,000 during the last three years. The etheric doctor just makes use of Jones as an instrument for the passage of his healing rays. No charge is made for the healing, each patient only giving something, if able. This wonderful medium who has accomplished so many cures through his etheric doctor "control" is only one of quite a number in the country today, and their great work is slowly being appreciated.

Mediums are our most precious possessions; they should be state-protected, state-aided and state-developed, until the ecclesiastical and medical professions come to realise that it is their duty to look after them as trustees for the nation. In time there will be a Chair of Psychic Science at both Oxford and Cambridge Universities, and thus the greatest of all the sciences will receive its proper recognition, and secure the attention it deserves from trained investigators.

Spiritualists do not pretend to have solved all the problems of mankind. We do not think that we can comprehend the universe. We do not believe that we have reached the bottom of the well of knowledge; but we do most emphatically believe that Spiritualism, along with the recognised sciences, will solve many problems thought to be beyond the wit of man. Spiritualism is opening up for mankind a grand panorama, and only as we increase in intelligence will we be able to grasp its full extent. Spiritualism is rounded on the sure rock of reason and experience, and on this foundation the next generation will build its religion.

Meantime, we believe it is better to work for the brotherhood of man, and his advancement, than to repeat meaningless creeds. It is better to love our fellow man than to fear a God created in man's own image. It is braver and nobler to think and investigate for yourself, than to let some institution think for you. We do not expect to accomplish out work in a few years, the prevailing opposition is too strong to enable us to do that, but we do want to do all the good we can in the holy cause of human progress.

We are not laying the foundations of a new sect, but of a noble temple in which all humanity can gather together, with the same knowledge animated by the same great ideals, and believing that our first duty is service to others. We believe that it is more important to serve our brother man, whom we can help, than to waste our time trying to placate an imaginary wrathful deity, who expects us to believe the impossible before we can enter heaven.

We are doing what we can to hasten the great day when reason will be robed, crowned and enthroned, and when those who do all the good they can will be the saints in the truest and noblest sense. We are doing all we can to relieve suffering, to comfort those who mourn, and to place the star of hope in the midnight of despair. This we consider is true holiness. We pity those who attribute to the Almighty deeds and words which would debase a savage, and we look forward to the day when all who do so will be considered blasphemers and not looked up to, honoured, and given positions of wealth and importance, as they are today.

This is the ethical side of the religion of Spiritualism. The old creeds are too narrow; they are not for our world of today. The old dogmas lack breadth and kindness; they are too cruel, too savage, too merciless. We are growing more humane in spite of them. The many who repeat them would not themselves, if they were God, enforce them.

There is only one acceptable belief, and that great creed contains all the truths that man has uttered. There is only one litany required by mankind, and that contains all the aspirations, all the noble thoughts, all the ecstasies of the soul, all dreams for nobler life, all hopes, all joy.

The real Church is built on all that man has discovered, the real edifice is adorned and beautified by all the arts, by all the beauties of nature ever depicted by colour on canvas. The real choir contains all the beautiful music of the world, and the true worshippers are all who have made the world a better and a happier place in which to live. Its priests are the true interpreters of nature. Its Bible is all the ennobling literature of the world, and its mediator betwixt earth and heaven is that gifted class of people called mediums, who can bring heaven to earth and unite the two worlds in one.

When Christians are intelligent enough to organise their worship and their churches on these lines, then will gather in them all the good and true, the learned and the simple. All together will hold communication with the wise and the good, who have passed on, and who now come back willing and anxious to help us in our search for the truth and the real meaning of existence.

This is what Spiritualism is working for, and, as the knowledge of it increases as the number of mediums increases, so will its principles become more and more widely accepted. But never will Spiritualists hand over their precious knowledge to the orthodox Churches to be compressed into creeds and dogmas, or to be embellished by ritual, pomp and circumstance. The Church, which should have been the protector of those gifted persons, our mediums, has so long persecuted and ill-treated them, that it cannot now be trusted with their care and protection. The Church, which has mistaken the blundering guesses of ignorant men for the wisdom of Infinite Intelligence, must purge itself thoroughly of its folly before it will be trusted by the Spiritualists whom it hates and despises.

The Christian Church has been weighed too often in the balance and found wanting, the ecclesiastical mind is too narrow, too closely related to that of the theologians of the past, for Spiritualists to wish to see a fusion of Spiritualism with Christianity. The time will come when the Christian Church will absorb all the teachings of Spiritualism and agree to bury and forget its creeds, its dogmas, its holy documents and holy relics, but it is not yet. Spiritualism has no need of a fusion of the past with the present. It need not go back to the days of ignorance for its beliefs. It is a religion based on the facts of today.

Meantime we work and wait, we watch the flow and ebb of life and death. We contemplate with greater knowledge what those who are ignorant call the mystery of death. Ignorance still holds the stage, and players act their part and disappear. The orthodox and the stupid play their part and vanish without the slightest knowledge of the significance of their part or the purpose of life's drama. The scene shifts, some new actors come, and disappear. The scene shifts again. To them all is mystery, mystery everywhere. They try to explain, and the explanation of one mystery contradicts another. To them, behind each veil is just another. Life is an enigma. The Church claims it has had the only revelation from the creator of heaven and earth, and yet this revelation tells us nothing. Everything of value in life man has discovered for himself. This revelation has never explained the wonder of growth, production and decay, the reason for our existence, or our destiny.

All things are of equal wonder. One drop of water should excite our imagination as all the oceans, one speck of dust as all the worlds, one butterfly with painted wings as all the things that fly, one egg as all the seeds of life. The smallest bud is as wonderful as a mighty oak, a stone as all the whirling stars.

If we now know something more of our wondrous universe than those who lived before us, it is because some have thought and reasoned for themselves, and have not been content to rely on so-called holy records as their guide. An institution relying solely on sources such as these need not look for help to Spiritualists, who have suffered too long from the abuse of the ignorant to wish to amalgamate with them. Spiritualists will work and wait until the Church discards all the old garments of ignorance. Until it does so Spiritualists will uphold the torch of truth alone. They know the strength of their position, and the weakness of their opponents. They know that their religion is built on the rock of truth, on experience, on reason, and they are content to wait until the edifice built on sand crumbles and disappears. It is only a matter of time. Truth always wins through in the end.

Meantime, we work for the great day when mankind will be mentally free, and when the truth, and the truth only, will be preached and believed.

CHAPTER XII.

LIFE'S CERTAINTIES.

AMID the confusion of beliefs in this age of the decay of faith, on what then have we to rely? So much that we were taught as certainties we find in these days of greater knowledge must be discarded as error. What now remains?

Everything there is of value remains. It is only the chaff that we must throw away. All the aspirations of the soul can now be satisfied, not by faith and hope, but by knowledge. We have seen how our ancestors, realising that here on earth both life and death are equal kings, took from natural phenomena their beliefs, arguing that as the sun sets to rise again, and as vegetation dies to come again to life, so would humanity likewise follow the course of nature, and that death was but the threshold of another life.

Around this universal instinctive belief that death is not the end of life, there developed, in many crude and often cruel ways, a ritual which, in course of time, became religion. From observing the course of nature our ancestors argued that there was a force, an intelligence, in nature outside themselves, and so, in a simple way, there developed the belief that various separate intelligences governed the world. Their gods were like men, only stronger and braver, but just as cruel as their creators. To them were given attributes drawn from natural phenomena. Later still were given to outstanding men after their death the attributes of the gods, and thus there was wound round their lives the fables and myths told about the gods.

So we come to the present time, when still by far the majority believe the truth of these stories told of these god-men. Some, however, have found by research the basis of the world's beliefs, and so have come to realise that what so many believe in as religious certainties are but ancient fables spun to please a childish world. Most people are still the slaves of habit, the followers of custom, and believers only in the wisdom of the past. Custom is like a prison locked and barred by those of long ago, the keys of which have followed them to their graves. Old beliefs thus die slowly and very few can see the light. The multitude still kneels at the shrine of antiquity, and worships what it believes are the sacred products of the past.

The educated, the thoughtful, the really intelligent person now thinks for himself, pities the mistakes and follies of the people, and tries to enlighten their minds and conscience by pointing to the future and not to the past. The thinking man and woman are the ones who help to carry forward the light of truth, and thus bring nearer the glad day when the world will be filled with intellectual light.

With all the fabled treasure of the past gone beyond belief, what have we still? Are we now without a lamp for our feet and a light for our path? Assuredly no, for have we not the knowledge now, instead of the hope which caused our ancestors to weave legend and myth, and develop ritual, much of which has come down to us in the garb of sacred and holy beliefs and rites?

What, then, are our certainties? Firstly, so far as the great mysteries of life and death are concerned, knowledge has taken the place of faith and hope. With knowledge fade away all creeds and ceremonials. During the past hundred years the mystery which has kept mankind in fear and bondage, the mystery which has kept, and still keeps, in being a mighty organisation throughout the world, has been explained and unravelled. The Sphinx has spoken.

From over the seemingly wide unending sea have come, floating on its waves, twigs and branches, to show that life exists beyond the horizon, and that the seemingly cruel sea is just a bridge, a span from life to life. Where the dead have gone reason now can go, and from the further shore the revelation has come. No need to feel now that life is but a narrow vale betwixt two bleak eternities. No longer need we strive in vain to look beyond the heights, nor cry aloud and hear only the echo of our wailing cry. No longer need we say that from the lips of the unreplying dead there comes no word to calm out fears.

Life we now know is a greater, a grander, and a nobler thing than ever our forefathers imagined. Life we now know is a great privilege. The creative mind that made it possible has wisely planned our future, and it is the duty of each one of us to live worthy of its thought and design. Nothing in nature is lost, and, as we think here, so shall we be hereafter. Our thoughts will be with us eternally to be our judge. As our thoughts are ourselves, we shall judge ourselves justly, and the place we reach will be that lot which we have fitted ourselves here.

The invisible world, which will be our eternal home, is beyond imagination, as there to think is to achieve; as we think, so we are. We must therefore give serious thought to our future, because we are building here what will be our future home. We have a great future planned out for us, but here, with our limited physical senses, we can barely imagine the wonderful civilisation which we shall join some day, to be either its good or its bad citizens, to be one of the honoured and respected, or one of the degraded, of that vast community living unsensed by us around this earth of ours.

All wish for happiness beyond this life. Immortality is a word that hope has whispered throughout the ages. In the democracy of death the rag of wretchedness and the purple robe lose distinction and only character counts. Our thoughts there condition our environment in a way they cannot do here. Consequently there is therefore nothing wiser, nothing grander than for each one of us to sow seeds of noble thoughts and virtuous deeds, and to endeavour in every possible way to help to liberate the minds of our fellow men. A noble thought, just as a noble life, enriches all the world and hastens the harvest of universal good. It climbs the heights and leaves all superstitions far below. Those who have worked for the advancement of mankind are the leaders of the human race, and, had it not been for such outstanding men and women of the past, who have led humanity upwards, we never would have risen beyond the beasts.

In every land and every clime, in every age, there have been the orthodox, the stupid and the backward on the one hand, and, on the other, the thinker, the investigator and the inventor. The former have always tried to frustrate the latter; there has been a continual warfare between them, and, fortunately for humanity, the thinker in the end has always won. The battle still continues between the two, and the thinkers are now fighting the greatest battle of all, which when won will liberate mankind from the fear of death, and make clear to all what has always been a mystery.

When our day here is over, nature returns the worn-out body to earth, and releases the psychic structure which, during earth-life, has been limited by our physical limitations. We cannot hear the words of welcome which greet the released individual, but we know that they are said. We cannot yet follow those who leave us, but we can leave them in the tender care of the friends who have gathered to give them welcome. What causes sorrow here, gives joy and gladness there.

Nothing is more touching than the death of the young and the strong, but, when we realise that to them it is not loss but gain, we need not sorrow unduly. Death comes, however, to the aged like a benediction. When the duties of life have been nobly done, when the sun touches the horizon, when our body becomes a burden, nature relaxes and relieves the weary traveller of his load. The day has been long, the road weary, and the tired wayfarer lies down to rest, to reawaken refreshed and gladdened by the change called death.

On making this change, a world beyond imagination for its delights will be the home of all who have lived here aright. The flowers, the colouring, the scenery, the beauties, the absence of care, of pain, and of fatigue, will at once become apparent, and none will ever wish to return to live again on earth.

All physical deformities will become right, because the physical was the cause, and mind there controls the etheric body in a way it cannot direct the physical. Pain and suffering here are the result of our mind being out of harmony with its physical vehicle, but in Etheria the vibrations of mind and the etheric body are more akin. Consequently pain and suffering are almost unknown, as mind by thought can conquer pain.

The next life would be naught unless we know and love again those we once loved here, and this reunion will be an added pleasure, though the grief at parting from our friends on earth will last until this reunion is complete. This sorrow in Etheria, however, is not so acute as it is with us on earth, because our friends there can still hear us and see us, and to them it is just a brief span between the parting and the meeting.

The master mind that has planned it all has decreed that for the present we on earth cannot appreciate all that life holds out for each. We are limited for the present to our earth condition, but we can gather information now from those who have made the change, and faith and hope have changed to knowledge. The more we learn the more we realise the importance of right living and right thinking, because retribution to the evil-doer is relentless and sure, but the very thoroughness of it all in time raises the mind to thoughts of higher things.

Everything that man has made or done was first a mental creation, first pictured in the mind, and then translated into its physical representation. All the wondrous creations of mankind were first mental pictures, and only thus was it possible for them to take shape. The physical can be changed primarily only by thought, and then by touch, and so we realise that mind is behind the physical wherever there is change. However, in the world of finer matter about us, though unsensed, mind is much more apparent, as there it can change its surroundings by thought without the necessity of touch. As we sow here we reap hereafter, because there we create our surroundings by our thoughts.

Our mind, like a moving film, produces and records our thoughts, which some think pass into oblivion, but this is not so. No mental creation is necessarily forgotten, and all our good and noble thoughts will be our companions for ever, and so will be our evil thoughts until they become obliterated by the good. If evil persists over good we sink lower and lower until sheer misery will make us change.

Back of everything is mind, which can only find expression in lower vibrations than its own. Out of these it constructs our conditions just as it has developed. If we keep to pure and noble thoughts, and self-denying deeds, face facts and accept only what is true, our future habitation will be in harmony with our thoughts, and our companions will be likewise. Honesty is the oak round which all the other virtues cling. Without character, without integrity, there is only poverty, an abyss.

We never finish our education, we never cease to learn, though some learn folly, and some learn wisdom. Those who have thought wisely in the past have scattered the priceless seeds of wisdom and knowledge, and we are now reaping the golden grain. Consequently our surroundings here on earth are better and happier than ever before, because on earth, just as in Etheria, our thoughts make our surroundings, but not so easily.

Not so many years ago the investigators, the thinkers, the unorthodox, were looked upon with horror, and cruel laws were made against them. Antiquity, those thinkers said, added nothing to probability, the lapse of time could never take the place of evidence, and dust can never gather fast enough upon mistakes to make them equal with the truth. They believed that the unbroken and eternal march of cause and effect had never been arrested. They were denounced and traduced, persecuted, tortured and martyred by the mob which never thinks. After their deaths the same mob returned to worship at their graves, and embellished their names as brave far-seeing courageous heroes and martyrs.

In their day they were told that God never gave us a mind to question or to doubt, and that everything we could know of life and death had already been revealed. They were told that great was the mystery of Godliness; great was the mystery of the Trinity; great was the mystery of the Godhead; great was the Mystery of Life and Death and the hereafter.

Fortunately all the opposition of a powerful organisation was unable to prevent the mystery being explored, and the more it was the quicker it vanished. Likewise it became clear that what had been preached as a special revelation from God was no revelation at all, and what was imagined to be a divine revelation was nothing more than the blundering guesses of superstitious men. Humanity is only now beginning to appreciate that this discovery has released it from a mighty thraldom.

Knowledge begins where faith ends, and faith no longer satisfies the hunger of the intelligent mind. To those with knowledge the warp and woof of the fabric of the mystery of death has been rent, and peering through it we find a more beautiful world, and a grander civilisation, than was ever dreamed of by the seers of old. In this newly discovered country we find a wondrous race which looks on us in pity for our ignorance, because so many here still limp on crutches, which they could so easily discard, and walk erect.

In the next state there is no gold, no money, and all we gain there is mental wealth, but no one can wish for more, as the mind gives us all we wish to have. To increase our possessions we must develop our mind, and this can best be done by helping others less fortunately placed than ourselves, because there we cannot live for ourselves alone. Thus and thus only is our happiness increased, just to the extent to which we impart happiness to, and increase the knowledge of others.

We need not wait; let us learn to do it here and now, and let those who know the truth tell all they can. Let those with experience and knowledge proclaim that there is no death, that what seems so is transition, a change of appreciation only. When this becomes known the happiness of the world will be increased a hundredfold. Then mankind will be knit together in the common knowledge of a common destiny. The brotherhood of marx will then be understood in its true meaning, and war should be no more.

Let us therefore cease from giving thought to ancient beliefs, developed when the world was young, and instead give consideration to the development of our characters, because character alone counts, not belief in creeds. Thus we are commencing here the refining process which will lead us to the life in the higher spheres beyond. Let us try to loose the shackles of those still bound by old beliefs, who think that by believing the impossible they are pleasing the Creator.

Unfortunately we have still many of the ignorant, the uneducated and the superstitious, amongst us, and so long as we have these so long shall we have priests and prelates, who benefit by their ignorance. Just as oil and water cannot mix, neither can priest-craft and intelligence. Spiritualists are doing all they can to spread the great news that mankind's greatest enemy, Death, is conquered, while the clergy, led by Dr. Temple, Archbishop of York, stand within the pulpit's narrow curve and decry them for their efforts. It is not desirable, say our religious leaders, for the public to know. To the leaders, public ignorance of this vital matter is better than knowledge, because so long as the mystery lasts the organisation is maintained. It is not desirable, they say, for man to have his greatest longing satisfied!

Just so long as ignorance flourishes will money be wasted keeping up an expensive organisation, whose policy has always been to keep humanity ignorant. The ignorant cannot see that it is in the interests of the priests and clergy to keep them ignorant, because, when knowledge comes, their influence ceases. Let all, therefore, who have the good of humanity at heart, oppose these purveyors of superstition, help the helpless, put the star of knowledge in the midnight of despair, and show the ignorant that all who live aright here have a bright and happy future before them.

We are not exiles here from God, which our ancestors imagined we were, because of the mystery of life and death. Consequently they created saviours and holy records. The belief in these, they thought, adjusted the difference, but now we know from those who have made the change that all this was wrong, and that what the ancients felt they needed they created out of their own imagination. Let us therefore not look back, but forward, and remember that every stream, no matter how it wanders, turns and curves, amid the hills and rocks of life, however long it lingers in the lakes and pools, will sometime reach the sea, and every one of us can eventually reach the sea of full understanding.

These views enlarge the soul and make us tolerant with wrong-doing, though ever anxious that the stagnant pool be cleared and mental indolence not last too long. Let us adopt the serene philosophy which relegates the beliefs and the needless ritual to a bygone age. They are but phases in the development of man. Remember that Infinite Mind planned our birth, our life; that we are part of this divine purpose, and, as such, must always be, and never can we cease to think.

Let us therefore spread the doctrine of the brotherhood of

man, that we are all part of the divine, and that, having a common heritage and destiny, to kill each other in war is such a crime that those responsible will suffer bitter remorse. Spread this news far and wide, until the rulers of the world, in fear of their ultimate fate, will never dare to rush their people into war.

If all will only think aright, war will cease, and disputes be justly settled, as the result of harmony between the minds of those whose duty it is to settle international differences. Let us not be either tyrants or slaves, but thinking men and women, and let us help to make the whole world free. In the democracy of the mind the peasant may be equal to the king. In the intellectual hospitality of the mind all may be equal. The domain of the mind is unbounded and none can control out thoughts.

Next best to finding the truth is to search for it, and to do so all should question and reason, as these are the guide posts scattered on the winding road that leads to truth. Truth loves discussion, and the doubting questioning mind of the investigator which creates intelligence, candour, honesty, sympathy and charity for all. Truth is the enemy of ignorance, prejudice, egotism, bigotry and hypocrisy. The one lives by day, the others by night. Let us each, therefore, be a torch-bearer of the truth and always strive for light, more light.

We now realise that all past mistakes just taught mankind to reach the road of truth. We pity the follies of the past but understand them. We admire the achievements of the past and should try to emulate them. All the past errors and mistakes of man, with their consequent sufferings and cruelties, were caused by the stones of ignorance, over which he stumbled, on the road that leads to perfection. As a result his next steps were taken with greater thought.

Let us strive to follow the religion of duty and forget the religion of mystery. Let us follow the religion of reason which will result in the civilisation and mental development of humanity. Let us preach the gospel of humanity, and that each should be noble enough to live for all. Let us teach the religion of knowledge and truth. Pure thoughts, brave words and generous deeds will never die. A noble self-denying lie increases the mental wealth of the universe, a life well spent runs like a vine for all to see, and every pure unselfish act is like a perfumed flower.

I have had impressed upon me, by those who have spoken to me from Etheria, the necessity of right thinking, because those who teach error here may after death feel themselves compelled to stand on the threshold of the after-life and meet again all those misled. What is shrouded here will be clear there, and error will unfold itself with relentless certainty. Those, therefore, relying on ancient tradition must divest themselves of prejudice and learn anew. Think straight and true, and put truth always first and foremost. Never say something is true and must be believed because it is found in an old book, unless you yourself have proved it true by definite evidence, and never attribute to God something for which you have no evidence.

Around an open grave the clergy should speak of the life beyond as something real, as something greater and grander than the one here, of the meeting again with those loved here, and proclaim that what to us is loss, is gain to them. Clergymen, tell your congregations that the next world is a real world, and that in it live real men and women, whose etheric bodies were unseen when on earth because of the physical covering. Tell the mourners of the organisations in our various cities where contact between the two worlds is made. Do not add conditions and reservations for which you have no authority. Do not talk about salvation as if some are saved and some are damned.

Try to be rational, thinking individuals, and do not make God appear irrational. If you do not know about the after-life, as very few of you do, then learn from those who do. Read and, if possible, experience for yourself. Your duty principally lies in ministering to the ignorant, and, if you are as ignorant as they are, you cannot help them much. Remember you will meet every one of your congregation again, and, when the meeting comes about, you will have to explain to each the reason for your preaching that which is false.

Your future happiness will rest on the amount of truth and error you have preached. The more this great revelation increases, the greater is your responsibility if you neglect it, and let pass opportunities of telling the people the truth. Open your pulpits to those who really know, and cease from thinking that you are a select body apart from the rest of mankind, because all thinking people now realise that you know no more, and are no better, than the rest of humanity.

My message to all who live is this. From the world, which some day will be our home, come messengers bearing words of good cheer to all who live on earth. They tell us that we need only do our best, and if we do that no more is expected.

We must, therefore, cease from wasting our time on that which is unnecessary, and apply ourselves to useful things which will develop our mind and character and make us worthy citizens of the country which will some day be our home. We are not born to live only upon this narrow strip of substance called the earth. A great and glorious country awaits us after death. Mind knows no limitation, and each one of us is mind and nothing more.

When the end of earth life comes let us not think that we have reached the twilight, or that for the last time the golden sky is fading in the west. Let us not think that night has come, but that a grander sunrise awaits us beyond the grave. We must meet death as we meet sleep, knowing that the morning follows night. Thus should we enter the dawn called death.

No one has ever seen the structure behind the man or woman, flower or tree. All we see is the outer garment that life wears and functions in during a short physical life. The real man and woman is something far beyond what the physical senses can appreciate. We all have a duplicate permanent body governed by a mind which none can see or touch. We can see only the physical expression of this mind. No physical matter has sensation, and all our feelings come from our mind.

No one has seen the seed that gives life to earth, but only the physical garment which is warmed and wooed by sun and rain, and, from a tiny speck of dust-like stuff, a violet or a rose springs forth. It was not the physical that gave the life and form, but the mind within, and when we realise that mind is all, and all is mind, we shall then begin to understand the universe.

We know now that death holds no terror for us, because it is only the name given to the door through which we enter, to reach another phase of our existence, in a world which is better, happier and easier to live in. Death is only a change in our appreciation of the vibrations which make up the universe. This being so, we now know that life on earth, with its gleams and shadows, its thrills and its pangs, its ecstasy and its tears, its wreaths and its crowns, its thorns and its roses, its glories and its failures, is but a preparation, a school, which all must pass through, and learn life's lesson, a lesson which does not end on earth, but is forever being taught.

Slowly we are learning to appreciate that wondrous stream of life, with its cataracts and pools, that rises in the world unseen, and flows through earth back to that etheric world from which it once emerged. What seems a struggling ray of light, twixt gloom and gloom, that lightens for a time this strip with verdure clad, between two great unseens, is never dimmed. What appears a dream between the shores of birth and death is a great reality, and, though we seem to stand upon the verge of crumbling time, to love, to hope and disappear, yet it is the greatest of life's many certainties that each individual life will never die, because each one of us is part of the Divine Mind which never dies.

·

EPILOGUE.

LAST year, when in Edinburgh, I stood in that wonderful cathedral, built on the pinnacle of the Castle Rock to the memory of the sons of Scotland who had passed on to a fuller life, so that freedom and justice might take the place of greed and brutal strength.

As I stood within this magnificent shrine I thought of the meaning of it all. Scotland had expressed her soul in the grandest war memorial in the world.

And just as the minds of the people of Scotland have expressed themselves, so is the Universal Mind, of which they are part, forever seeking expression throughout its boundless domain.

Just as the graceful lines of this beautiful building denote a perfect thought in stone, so is Mind forever seeking, everywhere, to reach in everything a fuller and more perfect expression.

What an advance from the Pictish dug-out I had seen in Aberdeenshire the previous day, to this noble thought in stone!

How Mind had developed in its capacity for expression! What a chasm of time between the past and the present! What a contrast was presented between the mind of the primitive savage living like an animal in the ground, and that of his descendants of today!

Mind, I realised, must be a developing, expanding, growing substance, when it is capable of such an advance as was here illustrated. It must be something apart from the physical body through which it works. The chemical ingredients of the physical are always the same. Mind has advanced, and in doing so has been able to express itself better with the material at its disposal.

What a distance between the savage and the savant, between the primitive coracle and our ocean palaces, between the crooked stick and the motor plough! Man has developed just as he has applied his mind to his surroundings, just as he has mingled his thoughts with his labour.

I thought of the countless multitude who had passed through the portal of death, and of the gathering hosts which for ages have been populating the world beyond, and I wondered at the magnitude of it all. I thought of the myriad minds out there in space, waiting for improved communication to pour out to us on earth their wisdom and experience accumulated through countless years.

At the altar of rugged rock within this great monument to

self-sacrifice, I wondered at the great unceasing purpose of the Master Architect. Developing mind in man was expressing itself in ever nobler creations. By thought nature's laws had become subject to his will and purpose. Wherever mind is there is thought, and, this being so, then above me in the unseen of space this ever increasing purpose is likewise at work, creating and transforming the substance of Etheria into conformity with its desires.

Infinite Mind counts not our years on earth when time is infinite. When our work here is done it is but continued elsewhere, and death is no more than a bend in the road on which we are forever travelling. Each one is part of one great whole, which never loses strength or power, and that which seems loss to us is never so to that which always was, is now, and ever shall be.

I thought of that unceasing Divine Mind of which we are each and all a part, always changing in form and expression.

And yet how feeble are our efforts to define it all in rigid words. How can the part define the whole? How can we, in face of our obvious limitations, hope to express in words what none on earth can ever comprehend?

How careful all should be to prove all things true, to accept only what is so, and to entertain nothing that our reason assures us is contrary to the truth.

To speculate on what is yet to come, without a basis to build upon, is mere folly and unworthy of our intelligence. Better to say we know not, than to hazard guesses without knowledge, better to be candid and honest than pretend to a knowledge we do not possess.

Our ignorant ancestors, believing that all had been revealed to them, recorded their beliefs in words on stone, on skins and parchments. Thus they produced the entire story of our origin and our destiny, and to this day their faithful followers in our midst strive in every way to justify it all.

To leave the past aside, to live in the present, and to contemplate the future from the standpoint of our present knowledge, is surely wiser. To the historians let us leave the past to be placed in its proper setting and perspective. They are the best judges as to what is true and what is false.

For us it is better far to assimilate the knowledge of the present than the ignorance of the past; better far to show our gratitude to the past by profiting by its mistakes and by avoiding their repetition.

To those of the past who by intelligent thought have laid the foundations of our present knowledge, let all praise be given, but never let us exalt the past at the expense of our present knowledge, or attribute to Infinite Intelligence its barbaric cruelties and false claims.

Let each one of us remember that our destiny lies not in the past but in the future, and that, as we lay the foundations of our characters now, so shall we erect structures that will be ours for ever.

Let each one of us make the most of the present, learning all it has to teach, as nature's revelation is greater and grander today than ever before. All the knowledge of the ancients is as nothing compared with that of the present.

We should not let the past think for us. Rather should we make full use of the treasures of nature's store-house, and avail ourselves of all it has now to offer us.

Those who do not think for themselves, who fail to use the holy gift of reason, who employ some others to think for them, are slaves to tradition.

All we have of value has been accomplished by man himself. In his upward struggles against the forces of nature, he has burdened himself too long with those who professed that they, and they only, could understand the deeper things of life and death.

Just as our countrymen fought and conquered the forces of reaction during the years of war, so will all thoughtful people in time defeat the purveyors of superstition everywhere, and thus help to carry forward the light of truth which will bring nearer the glad day when the world shall be filled with intellectual light.

When this time comes, sects and divisions will disappear, and the world's religions will be united into one which conforms with the laws of nature. Religion and science will then join together for the common good of all mankind, and war will be no more.

That this book may make clear to all the fundamental certainties of life, and also help the orthodox, belonging to all the world's different faiths, to extricate themselves from the quicksands of superstition and reach the rock of truth, is the author's earnest hope and desire.

The subjects discussed in this book are further considered in the concluding volume of this Trilogy on Spiritualism entitled "The Unfolding Universe".

THE END

ENDORSE

"What a gift. Not a quick fix, not a shallow set of trite words and phrases.

In his book, *You'll Get Through This: A Father's Letters About Suffering*, Dr. Gridley patiently guides you, the reader, through his letters to understand exactly what happens when you have suffering in your life. He slows you down with letters followed by questions that help you identify and process your thoughts and behaviors....and relates his counseling to your circumstances and life.

Dr. Gridley shares techniques and tools he uses in his successful counseling practice to help you move through your suffering, while also leaning on his extensive pastoral education, experience, and faith to help us understand the very reasons we suffer as well as the process we undertake to move through suffering.

Dr. Gridley has done all the work and refined the tools to guide you through suffering. All you have to do is follow and participate. He teaches you how to recognize your emotions and work through them to a balance of emotion, will, and mind. He helps provide the mirror so that you can better understand your behaviors and situation. He has you ask the question: 'What is my best response to this?' And he teaches the life lessons needed to manage your suffering and use it to better yourself.

Suffering does not cease as we age. We face more and more challenges. But Dr. Gridley provides the tools to understand suffering in a whole new light – that of focus, character development, joy, and yes, love.

I highly recommend this book for any reader, especially someone dealing with suffering and trauma. How wonderful it would have been to have had this years before, as I traveled through sufferings in my own life. I will be using this book. And I will be sharing it with many people. It's a guide to an engaging adventure in embracing your life.

Nicely done, Dr. Gridley. And thank you."

—**Patricia (Patty) Farley Karthauser**
Vice President of Nebraska Wesleyan University - Retired

"What are we to do when all hell breaks into our lives and threatens our trajectory? In *You'll Get Through This*, Dr. Barry Gridley gives staggering hope, perspective, and practical help. This book is more than a theological treatise; it's a lifeline for the hurting heart. It is a must-read for anyone seeking solace and strength in their faith journey amidst life's most challenging moments. This is the EXACT book you need during seasons of suffering."

—**Brook Mosser**
Executive Director of Intentional and host of "The Intentional Parents Podcast"

"You'll Get Through This: A Father's Letters about Suffering is rock-solid non-fiction disguised as a fictional one-way correspondence between a loving dad and his daughter. And it's excellent. The author, a professional counselor and Christian pastor, invites you into life's most complex and necessary adventure--finding Jesus in your suffering.

'Why?' 'What now?' If those questions about suffering give you pause, it might be because you have privately wondered if you'll ever get through your troubles. Do not lose hope. Dr. Barry Gridley wants to guide you through your harrowing adventure of suffering to illuminate Truth. His 39 letters to Bethany and subsequent personal study questions accomplish that goal. This book is the work of a master counselor and seasoned teacher in his professional prime.

Scott is the author of HEROIC DISGRACE: Order Out of Chaos. Hope Out of Fear. — A Worship Hero Story

—Scott W. Box
Pastor of Development, Shiloh Ranch Church

"When I am lost, I look for a competent guide. That's what this book is! As you journey through the practical tools, visual illustrations and spiritual directions, you will be guided by a masterful combination of counselor, pastor and friend.

Whether experiencing loss, conflict, tragedy, or betrayal, *You'll Get Through This: A Father's Letters about Suffering* will help us navigate the emotional twists and turns of our interrupted life situations. With wisdom and compassion the author leads us from the pain and anger of suffering to relief and restoration.

I highly recommend this written roadmap to the hurting, friends and family of the suffering one, as well as professional and spiritual counselors."

—**Peggy Robinson MSW**
Retired Clinical Counselor and University Professor of Trauma, Grief and Loss

YOU'LL GET THROUGH THIS

A Father's Letters About Suffering

BARRY GRIDLEY

LUCIDBOOKS

You'll Get Through This: A Father's Letters About Suffering
Copyright © 2024 by Barry Gridley

Published by Lucid Books in Houston, TX
www.LucidBooks.com

All rights reserved. No part of this publication may be reproduced, stored in a retrieval system, or transmitted in any form by any means, electronic, mechanical, photocopy, recording, or otherwise, without the prior permission of the publisher, except as provided for by USA copyright law.

Unless otherwise indicated, scripture quotations are taken from the ESV® Bible (The Holy Bible, English Standard Version®), copyright © 2001 by Crossway, a publishing ministry of Good News Publishers. Used by permission. All rights reserved..

ISBN: 978-1-63296-698-8
eISBN: 978-1-63296-706-0

Special Sales: Most Lucid Books titles are available in special quantity discounts. Custom imprinting or excerpting can also be done to fit special needs. Contact Lucid Books at Info@LucidBooks.com

TABLE OF CONTENTS

Preface	ix
Introduction: A Troubling Promise	1
Letter 1: How Suffering Distorts Perspective: Part 1	3
Letter 2: How Suffering Distorts Perspective: Part 2	9
Letter 3: Facing Suffering's Greatest Challenge	13
Letter 4: Life Outside the Emotional Good Zone: Spin Cycles	19
Letter 5: Calming Your Body When in a Spin Cycle	27
Letter 6: What You Tell Yourself in a Spin Cycle: Your Thinking Errors	31
Letter 7: When Your Self-Talk Hurts You Instead of Helps You	35
Letter 8: Replacing My Thinking Errors While I Suffer	41
Letter 9: When Calming Takes Time	47
Letter 10: Suffering and Trauma: Part 1	53
Letter 11: Suffering and Trauma: Part 2	57
Letter 12: Trauma and Shame	61
Letter 13: Self-Contempt in Suffering	65
Letter 14: Suffering and the Brain	69
Letter 15: Suffering's Triggers	75
Letter 16: Grieving in Suffering	79
Letter 17: Processing Grief Emotions	85
Letter 18: Suffering and Life in a Broken World	89
Letter 19: Suffering While Gazing at God	93
Letter 20: Suffering and Losing Hope	99
Letter 21: Growing Through Suffering	105

Letter 22: The Challenge of Responding to Suffering With Evil	111
Letter 23: Trusting God in Suffering	121
Letter 24: Worshiping God in Suffering	127
Letter 25: The Helpful Practice of Lamenting: Part 1	133
Letter 26: The Helpful Practice of Lamenting: Part 2	137
Letters 27: The Pain of Self-Inflicted Suffering	141
Letter 28: Rebuilt by Suffering	147
Letter 29: When Suffering Lasts	153
Letter 30: How to Persevere while Suffering	157
Letter 31: Finding Jesus in Your Suffering	163
Letter 32: Finding Contentment in Suffering	169
Letter 33: How Suffering Shows Us Who We Truly Are	175
Letter 34: Living Confidently in a Broken World of Suffering: Part 1	183
Letter 35: Living Confidently in a Broken World of Suffering: Part 2	189
Letter 36: Suffering and Forgiving	195
Letter 37: Suffering and Rebuilding Trust	203
Letter 38: Suffering and Boundaries	209
Letter 39: Thankfulness in Suffering	213
Afterword	217
Postscript	219
References and Resources	223
About the Author	229

PREFACE

Hi there. Will you take my hand? I'm a fellow sufferer, the real-life daughter of Dr. Gridley. Never jealous of sharing his parental attention, I feel no qualms about his adopting you, dear reader, into my cadre of "siblings" by opening these letters to you, for your healing too.

Before you ask, yes, I do recognize myself in these letters. None of us is exempt from dark days. The paradox is that those dark days often produce our greatest growth. I promise that the wisdom and compassion poured into these correspondences reflect the real deal Dad who has loved me through excruciating seasons of grief and fear and pain in my own life. It is exactly *this* wisdom, in *this* voice, that often gives me the strength to cling to faith while fighting for health. The gentle guidance written here comes as much from his own personal experience as it does from any study or counseling practice. Like Jesus, my dad understands our suffering from the inside. His journal prompts, specifically, if we let them, may cut with scalpel-like precision into our souls and psyche so our Maker can do the deepest work. None of us wanted to suffer, but here we are. The only way out is through. Let's journey together.

You'll Get Through This

I remember first coming across this Janet Chester Bly poem and recognizing my story inside it.

> I would rather
> clutch my invitation
> and wait my turn
> in party clothes
> prim, proper
> safe and clean.
> But a pulsing hand
> keeps driving me
> over peaks
> ravines
> and spidered brambles.
> So, I'll pant
> up to the pearled knocker
> tattered
> breathless
> and full of tales.

—Janet Chester Bly

Friend, we ARE going to make it through "this" treacherous peak or foggy ravine or spiny bramble, but we won't be the same. We cannot go back to the people we were before the bruising, nor would our good God want us to. We will tell better tales of courage, be safer arms for other crushed souls, demonstrate perseverance or forgiveness or hope to a cynical world. Moreover, polished by suffering that has passed through His hands, we better know and reflect our Savior who suffered it all: betrayal,

Preface

loss, rejection, false accusation, deprivation, and extreme physical pain. Because he knows it, in my own suffering, Christ has been the only place I find rest as He reveals parts of His character, reforming mine. I once wrote while journaling through a dark season, "There is a functional version of me, but I cannot figure out whether she is pretend or a different kind of real. The broken me has a vacuum that cannot be touched. God, please come fill me with only you." Jesus has remained near. So have my father's reminders to suffer well.

With deep hope that we continue learning to suffer well, please allow me to invite you into these letters with a prayer:

I pray that your Heavenly Father, the God of All Comfort, uses these letters to hold you tightly on this side of Heaven, shape your heart, and carry you through whatever suffering you have encountered and will encounter, until Revelation Chapter 21 is our reality.

Amy (Gridley) Ihde

Introduction
A TROUBLING PROMISE

I have a confession to make. There is one promise Jesus made that I wish he had not made. The promise is in John 16:33, which says, "In the world you will have tribulation." I dislike trouble. I much prefer peace, serenity, predictable routines, sunny days, a life that is more comfortable than it is inconvenient, and a life without what-now moments.

But like so many, I have experienced tribulation—trouble—in this world. I have encountered my share of unexpected but promised troubles. I am a cancer survivor. Two of my family members took their own lives, including my father who did so at Christmastime. We buried him on Christmas Eve morning. My wife, Pamela, and I were once poor enough that we qualified for food stamps and the Women, Infants & Children food support program. Pamela had two miscarriages within one calendar year. At another time of pain and disruption in our lives, friends proved untrustworthy. Other friends stayed silent or kept away. Perhaps these things tell you why I wish Jesus had not made that promise.

You'll Get Through This

I write this book to help you find courage, hope, and help when you come into your own times of Jesus's fulfillment of his promise. I write to give you courage when trouble comes knocking on your door. I write to give you hope in knowing you can move beyond the hurt of trouble to gaining the benefits trouble brings you. Yes, the benefits are there, and you can find them. I plan to show you how. I write to help you during the trouble you face, perhaps even right now.

In short, this is a book on suffering. It is shaped by my life as a pastor and licensed professional counselor. It comes from a life lived 40 years on the front lines of suffering with hurting people just like you. Writing this book from my own life means that I write from a Christian worldview shaped by biblical theology and a counselor's understanding of the impact that suffering brings to our lives.

In order to give you the courage, hope, and help you need when you suffer, I organized the book into 39 letters to Bethany, my fictitious daughter. Each letter is about suffering in its various dimensions and guises. Each letter focuses on a common struggle when trying to make sense of suffering. I divided the letters between those that address a particular challenge that suffering brings to our lives and those that focus on how to respond to suffering. To help readers with various sufferings, I don't mention Bethany's specific struggles in the book. By doing that, my hope is that as you read the book, you will insert the particular trouble you are facing right now.

At the end of the book is a list of helpful references divided into Books for the Head, Books for the Heart, and Books for Both the Head and Heart. I encourage you to use the list to learn more about the tools and techniques of dealing with suffering.

Here is my question to you: Are you ready to get through your suffering? Turn the page, and together we'll learn about suffering.

Letter 1

HOW SUFFERING DISTORTS PERSPECTIVE: PART 1

Dear Bethany,

Mom and I were sad after your phone call last night about the recent upheaval in your life. I am sad you now face sorting out its impact on you and how you are going to move past it into the future that can still be yours. This letter is my effort to help clear away the fog the upheaval brought you. I know, I know. This is a very dad thing for me to do since you grew up in our home watching Mom and me walk people through their times of heartache. Now it is your turn to walk the road of suffering.

I understand the depth of your heart hurt when you said, "Why, Dad, is this happening to me and happening to me now? Did I do something wrong?"

What you really are asking is this: How do I think about suffering? How do I make sense of it? Your heartache makes you ask that question. Your upheaval did not come with advance notice.

Instead, it ambushed you. Now, everything feels out of balance. Think of it this way. Imagine a playground seesaw.

```
( HEAD ▲ HEART )
```

On one end of the seesaw is your head—how you think about life. On the other end is your heart—how you feel about life. Most of the time, these are in balance. When they are, life is fine. When they are, life is predictable. When they are, life feels safe.

But what happened in the last 48 hours caused your seesaw to swing wildly and rapidly. It seems wildly out of control. One moment you know you will get through this (that's your head talking), and the next minute you are screaming in pain at the injustice and unfairness of it (that's your heart talking). Unexpected suffering always causes that to happen. Right now, your seesaw is wildly gyrating between the two. Bethany, please know that these gyrations are 100 percent normal and 100 percent unpleasant.

While your personal seesaw is gyrating, you must know that the past is distorting your perspective. Do you remember the time you had a toothache and the dentist had to pull it to make the pain stop? When you were in pain, you did not care about going outside to ride your bike. When you had that toothache, you did not want to think about the slumber party at Karen's that weekend. All you wanted was for the pain to stop. Similarly, this pain you are feeling makes you want the pain to stop. Pain distorts your perspective. Let me explain two of the distortions you have faced since Sunday night.

The first area of your life where pain distorts perspective is your view of yourself. Suffering makes you think, "I will never

How Suffering Distorts Perspective: Part 1

be the same after this." Suffering seems to define your life. It seems to have unpacked its bags and moved into your soul. The way you see yourself and think about yourself is the seesaw at work. The fear of never being the same is common after an event like yours.

Often when suffering comes into our lives, we feel like a victim. "I've done nothing wrong to deserve this," you say. We wonder if we are being punished for something. We feel unloved. We feel powerless. We feel small. We feel trapped in the pain.

When you called in tears the other night, I told you the experience traumatized you. Here's what I meant when I said that. A traumatic event is any event that overwhelms our ability to cope with it. A traumatic event has a before and after sense to it—I was one way before this happened, and now I am someone different. That is one way to define trauma—an experience that creates a before and after aspect to your life. Your pain will try to get you to believe this: "I will never be the same."

Such thought distortions are what you are fighting right now. Because recovery from emotional pain and trauma takes time, you will become oh so familiar with this pain-influenced thought distortion.

Pain also distorts your view of God. As long as your life was free of suffering, God seemed good and kind. You trusted his plans for you. Now, as your heart breaks and you struggle to express how much this hurts, you see God as an adversary. You wonder if he is really all you thought him to be. You wonder if he is angry with you. Trusting his will and his ways seems foolish and dangerous in ways it never did before. You wonder if you will ever feel safe enough to trust him again.

Bethany, both these distortions are normal because of

what just happened to you. While they are normal, they are unpleasant and distressing. But trust me on this; you will get past them. You will survive this. But for now, it hurts. And that's okay.

I'll write tomorrow about three other thought distortions pain brings. Right now, I need to see a client.

I love you,
Dad

How Suffering Distorts Perspective: Part 1

My Heart Response to Suffering

1. What events in your life have overwhelmed your ability to cope with them?
2. Which of the two distortions explained in this letter do you most relate to in your suffering? How is that distortion at work in your life even now?
3. Are you prepared to have your suffering last longer than you want it to? Why or why not?

Letter 2

HOW SUFFERING DISTORTS PERSPECTIVE: PART 2

Dear Bethany,

 I promised yesterday to explain three more thought distortions that pain creates. Here is what you need to know about them as you walk through this suffering.

 Pain distorts your perspective and misshapes your view of other people. Too often, the pain we feel comes from someone we know. Then when we try to talk to that person about what happened, the person blows us off. The person can do that by minimizing what took place or denying any wrongdoing. Finally, the person can blame the problem on you. That will leave you thinking, "What in the world is going on here?" and "Now what do I do?"

 Your pain makes you no longer trust people. A common first reaction—and a very common reaction—is to vow to trust no one ever again. Trusting people now makes as much sense as stepping on a land mine or taking a boat ride on a lake when there is a hole in the boat. You don't feel safe. You blame yourself for trusting the very person who is now the source of your pain. That's the first distortion at work.

The vow to trust no one is understandable because you do not want to hurt like this ever again. And yet isolating from others, not sharing your heart with a select group of friends, seems so lonely. You know you don't want to be lonely, so you feel stuck. You do not know whether to risk being hurt again by forming new friendships or if living on a deserted island for the next year would be a good idea. Bethany, all those thoughts are your seesaw at work. I promise it will get better, but just not as fast as you want it to.

Another thought distortion is that pain distorts your perspective about your future. You wonder if you will ever get back to being you. You suspect you won't. You're wondering if you'll trust others again or if you'll keep them at a distance from your thoughts, desires, and dreams. Even worse, your pain lies to you, telling you that you won't recover from this. Pain tells you that from now on, you will walk through life with a limp.

Finally, pain distorts your view of the world. Until Sunday night, the world was predictable. It had a familiar routine to it. You got up. You went to work. You ate lunch. You drove home. You did all that so often that you never thought much about it. Now, however, that predictability and its sense of safety are gone. The world now feels dangerous.

Do you remember the time I told you about the accident I had when the lady pulled out in front of me at the convenience store? I drive through that same intersection at least twice a day and four times a week on my way to the office. I was used to going through it and had no thought of it being a dangerous intersection. But after the accident, I started slowing down as I approached it.

How Suffering Distorts Perspective: Part 2

I made sure I looked both ways at least three times before going through it. That one accident distorted my memory of all the times I drove safely through that intersection. The accident made the intersection feel unsafe in a way it had not felt in 20 years of driving through it. That's an example of what I mean when I say that pain distorts our perspective of the world.

Bethany, you are right when you texted me and said, "I feel like I am in a fight with myself." The distortions pain brought you explain why you feel like that. The five distortions in these two letters are your seesaw gyrating. Your seesaw swings between knowing yourself and being unsure of who you are now. It swings from trusting and distrusting God's presence in your life. It changes from feeling safe to feeling in danger when you are around others. It's once feeling confident about your future and now cowering from it. It's being at ease in the world and now feeling wary in it. You are not losing your mind, although I know it feels that way. You will make it to the other side of all this. I promise.

Love,
Dad

My Heart Response to Suffering

1. Which of the three distortions identified in this letter do you wrestle with most often? In what way are those distortions connected to a painful event in your life?
2. How are these distortions disrupting your life? What does it make you think? How does it make you feel? What does it make you do?

Letter 3

FACING SUFFERING'S GREATEST CHALLENGE

Dear Bethany,

I want to return to the way pain distorts your view of God, something I mentioned in my first letter to you. I know how important your faith in Christ is to you, so I also know this can be one of the greatest wounds your suffering inflicts on you.

The greatest temptation you will face in your suffering is to lose sight of God because of your pain. Your pain will always try to pull your gaze from God to your circumstances. Here are three ways pain will challenge you to keep faith's eyes on God.

First, your pain will tell you that your circumstances, and not God, are in control of your life. This pain-shaped message comes to you because the suffering hurts so much. Your suffering was such a surprise, and you were blindsided by it. Being blindsided means you were unprepared for it. That makes you wonder if your suffering slipped past God's notice.

Throughout the history of the church, people have found

elaborate explanations for the so-called problem of evil. Those explanations are called theodicies. Theodocies seek to defend God against charges that he is limited in power, knowledge, or both. While those explanations may help the mind, they do not help your hurting heart. My letters will take a different approach to your suffering. I write them to help ease your heartache.

Here is what I recommend you do as you face this temptation. Go back to Square One. Think of the times we played Chutes and Ladders when you were small. Once in a while as we played that game, one of us would land on a square that sent us all the way back to the start, and we had to begin again. That is what I mean by returning to Square One.

Returning to Square One means you remind yourself what you know to be true about God's character and his names. Those are the clearest ways God makes himself known to us. An example of that is Psalm 103. David begins that psalm by reminding himself to worship God (verses 1–2). He then lists several of those benefits in verses 3–5. By doing that, David slows down the gyrations of his head-heart seesaw. While I cannot tell you what challenging circumstance David faced, the psalm shows that he returned to Square One. By doing so, he saw the bigger picture of God's work in his life rather than what his distress was showing him (verses 6–19). Seeing the big picture, David refocused on worshiping God rather than quarreling with God (verses 20–22). As he reminded himself and rehearsed what his head knew about God, his heart grew calmer, and his perspective changed.

That is what I want you to do. Use your head to help calm your heart by following David's example. Tell and retell yourself what you know to be true of God, and you will find your heart growing calmer. That is the benefit of returning to Square One.

The second pain-shaped message that challenges you to lose

sight of God is when you say, "I am forgotten and abandoned by him." Heman, the author of Psalm 88, struggled with this challenge. As he looked at his life and his circumstances, he could not make sense of what God was doing. In fact, Heman felt rejected and believed that God was hiding from him in his time of need (Ps. 88:14). The psalm shows that Heman's sense of God's hiddenness had not changed by the end of the psalm (Ps. 88:18).

But what I love about this psalm is that although Heman still felt God was playing hide-and-seek with him, he kept calling out to God. He kept telling God about the pain in his heart. Why? I believe he did that because he kept going back to Square One. Heman knew enough about God and his ways that he kept practicing his habit of prayer, even when his prayers did not make an immediate difference in his life (Ps. 88:13, 18).

The final pain-shaped message that challenges you to lose sight of God is when you say, "My circumstances won't change." I call this Multiplying Times Forever. That means pain tells me the way things are now—painful—and that is the way it will be from now on. Pain tells me it will never go away. I will always hurt in all the tomorrows to come. Pain distorts your thinking so it seems your pain is greater than God.

The best way I know to tell you how to respond to Multiplying Times Forever is to think of the difference in the lives of Christ's disciples between late afternoon on Friday and early Sunday morning. On Friday after the crucifixion, they grieved the loss of their rabbi. But all that changed when first Mary and then Peter and John confirmed that Jesus had risen from the dead (John 20:1–8). Instead of sadness and grief, they felt inexpressible joy. That mood shift in 72 hours shows that pain lies to you and me when it tells us it will never leave us.

Bethany, I am not telling you that your pain will end in the next 72 hours. I wish I could! What I am telling you is that you do not have to believe it will be with you forever. Instead of believing your pain is permanent, remind yourself what God can do in only three days.

    I'll end this letter with one final thought for you to consider. The challenge to lose sight of God by focusing on your circumstances comes down to where your gaze is and where your glance is. Either you will gaze at the circumstances and glance at God, or you will gaze at God and glance at the circumstances. Gazing at God and glancing at your circumstances will lead to peace. Gazing at your circumstances and glancing at God will lead to distress. And if you gaze too long at your circumstances, your eyes will glaze over, and you will be unable to find God anymore at all.

                                        I love you!
                                        Dad

My Heart Response to Suffering

1. In what way(s) has your suffering challenged your faith in God? If you have not been a person of faith prior to your suffering, how does your suffering challenge the possibility of your believing in God?
2. When you need to go back to Square One, what do you need to remember about God?
3. How do you take your current circumstances and Multiply Times Forever? What is the result when you do such multiplication?
4. How can you tell whether you are gazing at God in your circumstances or gazing at your circumstances? What happens to your emotions when you do either of those?

Letter 4

LIFE OUTSIDE THE EMOTIONAL GOOD ZONE: SPIN CYCLES

Dearest Daughter,

Thank you for letting me know how out of control your emotions feel. You always held them in check and let your head rule your heart. Now you can't. Let me explain to you what is going on with your mood swings. As human beings, we have three parts to what I call our soul—our innermost life. The three parts are our mind, our will, and our emotions. All three of them exist in our bodies.

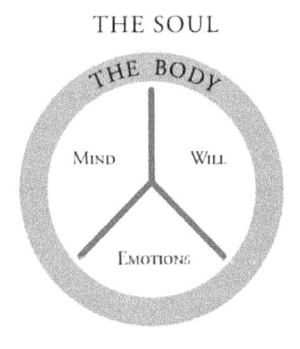

THE SOUL

THE BODY

MIND | WILL

EMOTIONS

Most of the time, the three parts of our soul work well together. When they do work together, it looks like this. Your mind leads the way, thinking about and evaluating an event or conversation. Then your mind takes input from the emotions, considering how you feel about the event or conversation. Finally, both your mind and emotions join with your will to make a choice about how to respond to the situation. All of this is what I call self-talk. Your self-talk—the conversation you have with yourself—goes on all day long in your head.

Self-talk can impact your body. Doctors tell us that many of our American health problems are stress-induced. Conditions such as high blood pressure, ulcers, and migraine headaches can exist because of how people talk to themselves about life and the world around them.

Your body can also impact your self-talk. Think of trying to cope with a headache or an upset stomach. Bethany, I find it harder to get through a day with a persistent headache. It becomes such a distraction that I think about little else except that I want it to go away.

When your mind, emotions, and body work in harmony like I have described, you stay in what I call the Emotional Good Zone.[1] It is a zone where we experience a variety of emotions during a day or week with little emotional upheaval. I get excited when friends find out they are going to be grandparents, and then later in the day I am sad at the news of a tsunami halfway around the world. In both cases, I stay in the Emotional Good Zone. A word picture

---

[1] Astute readers will recognize my Emotional Good Zone as another name for what many counselors call the Window of Tolerance. My clients uniformly tell me that Emotional Good Zone is easier for them to understand than Window of Tolerance, and hence my use of it throughout the book. For a good discussion about the Window of Tolerance, see Aundi Kolber's book *Try Softer*, Chapter Four.

may be helpful here. Think of being in the Emotional Good Zone as perfect weather conditions for sailing the sailboat of your soul.[2]

THE EMOTIONAL GOOD ZONE

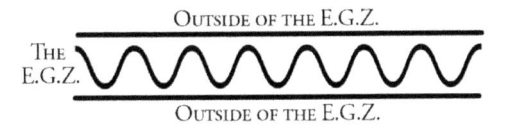

```
              Outside of the E.G.Z.
   The      _____
   E.G.Z.  \/\/\/\/\/\/\/\/\/\/\/\/\/\/
              Outside of the E.G.Z.
```

However, in relationship pain, the mind, emotions, and body do not work together. Your emotions quickly override what you think about the situation, so they sweep away your will in an emotional soul storm. When the storm hits, your emotions overrule your thoughts and will. That means you are no longer in the Emotional Good Zone. Not being in that zone means you usually go into either a state of anxiety or depression. With anxiety, you sail in stormy and tempestuous seas because you are on high alert due to the events that are happening around you, and you overreact to the surrounding events. With depression, you underreact because your sailboat is becalmed and you lose your ability to respond to the circumstances.

THE EMOTIONAL GOOD ZONE

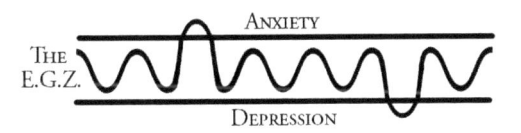

```
                  Anxiety
   The      _____
   E.G.Z.  \/\/\/\/\/\/\/\/\/\/\/\/\/\/
                  Depression
```

Once when I explained the Emotional Good Zone to a client, he declared he was tired of his emotions "bullying" him. What a

---

[2] This word picture is from *Treating Depression with EMDR Therapy: Techniques and Interventions 1st Edition* by Arne Hofmann et al., Springer Publishing, 2022.

great way to describe when our emotions are in charge of our soul! They certainly feel like a bully to our mind and our will since the emotions insist on getting their way in the moment.

So in times of upheaval and unexpected suffering like yours, it is important to know which part is in charge of your soul—which part is "driving the bus," as I like to say. It is important that you know how to make the shift from your emotions bullying you so you react to what is happening. You need to decide (with your mind) how you will respond to your pain. It is important to understand this distinction between reacting and responding to an event. Understanding what happens in both cases provides the key to reset your emotions so you can again respond rather than react to the pain.

When emotions pull you out of the Emotional Good Zone, you experience what I call a Spin Cycle. Let me explain what a Spin Cycle is since we all go into one from time to time.

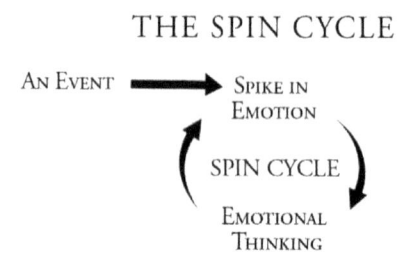

THE SPIN CYCLE

An Event → Spike in Emotion

(SPIN CYCLE)

Emotional Thinking

First, something happens that causes a spike in our emotions. For example, I feel rejected when coworkers do not invite me to join them for a Saturday morning of disc golf. The heightened sense of rejection colors my thinking, which influences what I tell myself about the event. Here is an example of an emotionally colored rejection thought: "Why don't they want me to join them? I guess they are not my friends after all." Next, the emotionally colored thought makes my sense of rejection go even higher. As the sense of rejection goes higher, it further distorts my thinking, and what I tell myself gets shaped even more by my feeling of rejection. Unless you know how to interrupt the Spin Cycle, it will keep spinning, causing you more and more emotional and mental distress.

At some point—and this point is different for each one of us—the Spin Cycle will activate your body's threat response, causing you to take action to survive whatever the perceived (emotionally distorted) threat is. When this happens, what I call your Adrenaline Alert System kicks in to get your body to take action in order to survive the perceived threat. When the Adrenaline Alert System takes over, you will respond in one of these four ways: (1) your thinking is short-circuited so you fight back against the situation, bypassing problem-solving to go into survival mode; (2) you flee the situation; (3) you freeze and become paralyzed by the situation; or (4) you fold and succumb to the situation. When the Adrenaline Alert System takes over, you will inevitably act in one of those four ways.

THE SPIN CYCLE & THE FOUR F'S

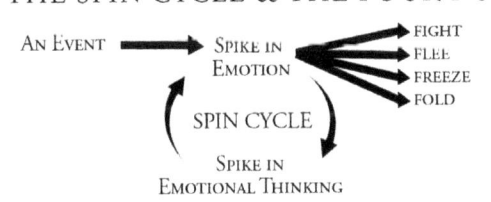

An Event → Spike in Emotion → FIGHT / FLEE / FREEZE / FOLD

SPIN CYCLE

Spike in Emotional Thinking

Bethany, you need to know that when the Adrenaline Alert System throws you into survival mode, that is a good thing. You do not want to lie in bed when the smoke detector goes off at 3:30 a.m., wondering what your 27 best options are to respond to that sound. If you do, it is likely you will be dead from smoke inhalation by the time you get to option number nine. No, you want the Adrenaline Alert System to kick in and get you out of the house. Once you are outside and safe, the Adrenaline Alert System is no longer needed, so it goes offline, allowing you to again problem-solve to consider what to do next (such as calling your insurance agent).

While our Adrenaline Alert System usually works for our good, when suffering ambushes us, it works against us because we may not need to respond to the situation with fight, flee, freeze, or fold. But when it does throw you into one of these four Fs, the first thing you need to do is calm your body so you can get out of the Adrenaline Alert System and get back to your problem-solving mode.

Bethany, I have written enough for now, so just ponder and reflect. I encourage you to think back to times when you know your Adrenaline Alert System kicked in. Look for what the perceived threat was and how the Adrenaline Alert System influenced what you did next.

I love you,
Dad

LIFE OUTSIDE THE EMOTIONAL GOOD ZONE: SPIN CYCLES

My Heart Response to Suffering

1. What kinds of pain and suffering hurled you into a Spin Cycle in the past?
2. When you were in that Spin Cycle, what emotion spiked in that situation?
3. How did the spike of emotion color your thinking?
4. Remembering that situation, which of the four Fs of survival action did you take—fight, flee, freeze, or fold?
5. Are any of those four actions your so-called default setting when you are in a Spin Cycle? If so, which one?

Letter 5

CALMING YOUR BODY WHEN IN A SPIN CYCLE

Dear Bethany,

    I want to pick up with what I said in my last letter. It is important for you to recognize the signs that you are in a Spin Cycle so you can calm your body to get out of it. Unless you know how to calm your body, you will stay in a Spin Cycle. Most of my clients find it easiest to start by paying attention to the signals their bodies are giving them so they know when they are in a Spin Cycle. They learn to recognize things such as dry mouth, rapid shallow breathing (think of a dog panting), and the urge to leave the scene of an uncomfortable conversation—all signs that their body is activated and needs calming down.

    I always teach my clients three ways to reset their bodies. The first is what I call the butterfly tap. I learned this in my Eye Movement Desensitization and Reprocessing (EMDR) training. It works like this. Cross your arms over your chest so your right hand is near your collarbone on the left side of your body.

Then cross your left hand to your collarbone on the right side of your body. The crossed arms supposedly look like the wings of a butterfly—hence the name. Then start tapping your hands, alternating back and forth between the two of them. I have my clients do this for 20 or so alternating sets of taps.

The second calming skill I teach my clients is belly breathing. As I mentioned, one sign a person is in a Spin Cycle is that their breathing gets higher in their chest, more rapid, and shallower. To do belly breathing, a client puts both their hands over their navel, one stacked on top of the other. Then they practice taking in a long, slow breath so they feel their belly move. Then they slowly exhale, noticing how their belly contracts. I tell my clients to do at least 10 of these as a way of resetting their body.

The third calming skill I teach my clients is the ability to visualize a calm place such as a beach, a mountain stream, baking cookies with Grandma in her kitchen, or anything they associate with a sense of calm. I usually use EMDR bilateral eye movements to enhance their ability to really see that calm place. To do that, I tell them to notice all the things they see as they visualize that beach. Then I have them notice all the features of the other four senses so the beach is as clear as it can be when they visualize it.

It is also possible to do all three of these calming skills at once. That is what I did each night during my nine months of cancer treatments. When I went to bed, I did the butterfly taps while focusing on my breathing and concentrating on my recording of surf sounds. Combining all three let me shift my focus from the next day's treatment so I could relax enough to go to sleep.

That is enough for you to ponder and reflect on for now. I encourage you notice what your body is telling you when you are

Calming Your Body when in a Spin Cycle

going into or are already in a Spin Cycle. I also urge you to try all three calming skills in this letter whenever you feel stressed this week.

            I love you now and always,
            Dad

My Heart Response to Suffering

1. What are your body's signs that you are going into or are already in a Spin Cycle? Where do you feel your body's stress?
2. As you practiced the three calming skills mentioned in this letter, which of them worked most efficiently to help you exit a Spin Cycle?
3. What other calming skills make sense to you? How will you practice them this week? Write your plan for doing so here.

Letter 6

WHAT YOU TELL YOURSELF IN A SPIN CYCLE: YOUR THINKING ERRORS

Dear Bethany,

    I am glad you experimented with the grounding skills I taught you in the last letter. Good for you! Keep using them, and try a few of the others to see if they might also be helpful. You can never have too many of them in your calming skills toolbox.

    In addition to calming your body when your Adrenaline Alert System is activated, there is a second way to get out of a Spin Cycle and back into the Emotional Good Zone. The second way is knowing what you say to yourself when the spiked emotion is coloring your thoughts and replacing the way of talking to yourself. By shifting your self-talk, you can escape the repetitive cycle and regain problem-solving skills.

HOW TO STOP THE SPIN CYCLE

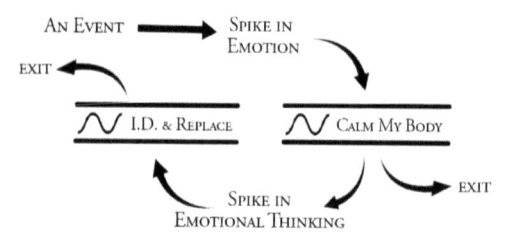

```
    An Event  ──▶  Spike in
                   Emotion
  Exit ◀─┐                    ╲
         │  ∿ I.D. & Replace   ∿ Calm My Body
         │                           │
         │                           └──▶ Exit
          ◀──  Spike in        ◀─┘
              Emotional Thinking
```

Throughout your life, you learned to talk to yourself in certain ways. Sometimes you sound exactly like me in what I would say to you. At other times, you may sound like Mr. Hanson, your eighth-grade math teacher. Sometimes you sound like Coach Debbie of the Blue Dolphin swim team. The point is that you learned to talk to yourself in certain ways and do not think about what you are saying to yourself.

Classically, counselors and pastors like me identify 10 ways you talk to yourself that lead to a Spin Cycle. We call them Thinking Errors[1]—how you learned to talk to yourself in times of stress or pain. Those Thinking Errors send you into a Spin Cycle and keep you in one. Over time, those Thinking Errors became the automatic way you talk to yourself when you are stressed or in pain. In fact, they are so automatic that you no longer notice what you tell yourself. And that, my dear daughter, is the problem.

Since one or more of the Thinking Errors are how we talk to ourselves, no one stops to ask, "Where is this thought taking me?" or "Is this a helpful thought or not?" Nor do we ask, "Is this thought true?" If we asked any of those questions, we would see how unhelpful Thinking Error self-talk is. Your Thinking Errors

---

1 My Thinking Errors handout is my personal adaptation of such a list from many sources. In its present form, it is uniquely my own design. Identifying Thinking Errors is an essential skill in Cognitive Behavioral Therapy.

throw you into a Spin Cycle and keep you in it, but knowing that allows you to change what you say to yourself.

In his book *Spiritual Depression: Its Causes and Its Cures*, the late D. Martyn Lloyd-Jones asks, "Have you realized that most of your unhappiness in life is due to the fact that you are listening to yourself instead of talking to yourself?"[2] He uses Psalm 42 and Psalm 43 as examples of how the psalm writer talked back to his emotionally colored thinking. "Why are you cast down, O my soul, and why are you in turmoil within me? Hope in God; for I shall again praise him, my salvation and my God" (Ps. 43:5).

Bethany, notice how the psalmist repeated that statement to himself until it took hold of him and he got out of his Spin Cycle and could see clearly again (see Psalm 42:8 as the example of how he regained his perspective).

Here is the point. If you learn to talk to yourself in certain ways, you can learn to replace those ways with new ways of talking to yourself. That new way of talking to yourself will either keep you from a Spin Cycle or will get you out of one. This is the second way you interrupt your Spin Cycle—change what you are telling yourself about the situation.

I'll have more to say about this in my next letter.

                Until then,
                Dad

---

[2] D. Martyn Lloyd-Jones. *Spiritual Depression: Its Causes and Its Cures*, Grand Rapids: Wm. B. Eerdmans Publishing House, 1965, p. 20.

My Heart Response to Suffering

1. What emotion most often bullies you when you are in a Spin Cycle? When it does, what does your self-talk sound like?
2. Does your self-talk help you face unexpected circumstances or throw you into or keep you in a Spin Cycle? If so, how?
3. Because you learned to talk to yourself in unhelpful ways, have you ever thought to challenge your self-talk when you are in a Spin Cycle?
4. Now that you know you can identify and replace your emotionally colored self-talk, how will you use that knowledge the next time you find yourself in a Spin Cycle?

Letter 7

WHEN YOUR SELF-TALK HURTS YOU INSTEAD OF HELPS YOU

Dear Bethany,

    I understand how upset you are with yourself right now. As you said last night, you are mad at yourself for falling apart at work after lunch yesterday. That is to be expected since you are not even a month beyond this unplanned suffering. You are learning how to use the skills I describe to slow down your head-heart seesaw. Learning how to do that means that sometimes your Spin Cycle wins, and you fall apart. That will happen for a while, but you will get better at using these skills so you will fall apart less often and less intensely. I promise.

    Let me return to what I talked about in my last letter. Here's how you change what you tell yourself when you are in a Spin Cycle. First, you need to know exactly what you tell yourself when you are in a Spin Cycle. To help you do that, I enclosed my Thinking Errors handout in this letter so you can see which of them you most often tell yourself. Use the handout to help you identify the two or three Thinking Errors you usually tell yourself. (No one I ever counseled told themselves all 10! Whew!) You then become your own detective, Bethany. You will look for what heightened emotion prompts you to tell yourself a particular Thinking Error.

To help you do that, I also included a copy of my Thought Log handout.[1] It will become your detective sheet as you look for the clues that tell you what you say to yourself when you are in a Spin Cycle. To use it, follow the order of the items at the top of the three columns. First, identify the heightened emotion. Second, list what Thinking Error you tell yourself that accompanies the spiked emotion. Third, record what happened when that emotion rose and what Thinking Error you told yourself when it did. The combination of all three is what your personal Spin Cycle looks like.

Bethany, that's what I want you to do this week. Track what gets you into a Spin Cycle so you can identify it and get out of it. Use the Thought Log to help you do that. We'll talk next time about what you learned from doing that.

I love you,
Dad

---

[1] For more insight into using a similar thought log, see McKay, Davis, and Fanning's *Thoughts and Feelings: Taking Control of Your Moods and Your Life, Third Edition,* New Harbinger, pp. 20–27.

10 COMMON THINKING ERRORS. WHICH ARE YOURS?

1. **All or Nothing Thinking.** You see things as "all or nothing," or "black and white." There is no middle ground, no gray areas in life, no room for mistakes. Things are either really great or they are really terrible.

2. **Overgeneralizing.** You see a single event as a never ending pattern You use "always" and "never" labels to describe your behavior or that of others around you.

3. **Villain-Victim Thinking.** You see other people or an external circumstance as the cause of your problem or unhappiness. Life will not get better, nor change, until the other person or circumstance changes. This keeps you feeling powerless which creates frustration and anger. Because you feel powerless, you do not take the actions you could take to make things better.

4. **Justifying.** You do not take responsibility for your own actions or feelings. This pattern of thinking often leads to outbursts of anger against those who hold you accountable for your actions, attitudes, or words. You are mad they do not see things your way. This pattern often accompanies Villain-Victim thinking.

5. **Filtering.** You see and focus on only the bad, the

disappointing, the negative about people or situations in your life. You discount and ignore the positive people and things around you.

6. **Mind reading.** You are convinced you infallibly know what other people are thinking and feeling about you. You know and are convinced you know what that raised eyebrow, or sigh means. You know all of this without bothering to ask or verify your perception of what you are sure you know.

7. **Catastrophizing.** You expect only the worst to happen. You expect disaster, despair, and defeat. If there are 100 possible outcomes, you focus on the 1 that is worst of all. You are 100% sure you are right about what is ahead.

8. **Magnifying.** You exaggerate the frequency, intensity, or duration of a problem. You focus on the bad, puffing it up until it is a monster to you. You make the negative loud, large, and overwhelming.

9. **Personalizing.** Everything people say or do reflects on you and on your flaws, shortcomings, and failures. You endlessly compare yourself to others which makes you feel worse about yourself.

10. **Shoulds and Musts.** You have a list of rules and standards that you must follow as others must do also. These rules are about how you should and must act, think, behave, feel, and treat one another. You are angry when you and other people do not keep to these rules and standards. You feel ashamed when you do not live up to your own expectations.

WHEN YOUR SELF TALK HURTS YOU INSTEAD OF HELPS YOU

THOUGHT LOG

        Emotion   +   Thought   =   Result

1.

2.

3.

4.

5.

6.

7.

8.

9.

10.

My Heart Response to Suffering

1. Who does your self-talk sound like? Does your self-talk help you face unexpected circumstances or throw you into a Spin Cycle? Which of the Thinking Errors do you usually tell yourself that sends you into a Spin Cycle.
2. What emotion most often bullies you? When it does, what do you usually do? Use your own Thought Log to help you answer those questions.

Letter 8

REPLACING MY THINKING ERRORS WHILE I SUFFER

Dear Bethany,

I am glad you found the Thought Log and Thinking Errors sheets helpful. Now you realize that you tend to catastrophize the situation by the way you talk to yourself and that you are prone to black-and-white thinking.

Here is how you take advantage of that knowledge. The next time you catch yourself in a Spin Cycle, say, "This happens when I catastrophize my pain" or "I know what is happening here; I am resorting to black-and-white thinking about this situation." Those are both examples of talking back to your unhelpful Thinking Errors.

I also appreciate your honest question when you asked, "Dad, what is another way I replace my Thinking Errors? What can I tell myself instead of what I always told myself?" For us as Christ-followers, the best way to do that is to replace the Thinking Errors with Bible verses. Doing so helps us see things from God's perspective rather than our pain-distorted view of things. Before I give you some recommended verses, let me share two helpful principles for understanding your suffering.

The first principle is that suffering is to be expected and prepared for in a broken world. You know that the first three chapters of the book of Genesis depict two different worlds. In chapters one and two, we see the original creation that is free of sin, suffering, pain, death, and Satan. However, all that changes in chapter three. The first two humans' choices to act apart from God's guidance for their lives brought sin, suffering, death, and Satan's influence on their lives. The world is no longer the perfect world God created. It is far more broken than we like to admit because of the consequences of those choices.

Once that happened in Genesis 3, God spelled out four consequences. The first consequence is the conflict between Satan and humans. There is now enmity between them (Gen. 3:15). The second consequence is a change in people's relationship with each other. Adam and Eve no longer related to each other the way they did before (Gen. 3:16). The third consequence is a change of humans' relationship to nature, which now works against human efforts to tend and care for it (Gen. 3:17–19). Then, in Genesis 5, we read about the promised consequence for their disobedience—death.

Here is what I want you to remember and remind yourself of often. Suffering is to be expected and prepared for in the broken world we live in. Suffering is the rule not the exception in this life. Everyone will suffer. We do not choose the suffering we experience, how long it stays in our lives, or how it will come. Job said that "man is born to trouble as the sparks fly upward" (Job 5:7). He knew trouble was common in this life. You and I and everyone else cannot avoid trouble and suffering in this life. So we must expect it and prepare for it.

The second principle about suffering I want you to hold onto is that my view of God determines my response to suffering. The conversation between Job and his wife at the onset of his terrible suffering illustrates this. When the second wave of suffering hit Job, his wife's advice was to "curse God and die" (Job 2:9). She was telling him to stop worshiping during his suffering, something Job did during the first wave of suffering (Job 1:20–21). She believed his suffering canceled Job's need to worship God. She let the suffering determine her view of God instead of her view of God shaping her suffering. Because Job kept himself conscious of God in his suffering, he persevered and emerged the better for it (Job 42). His wife did not share his worshiping heart, so she became embittered by what happened to her husband.

In your current suffering and recovery from it, you face the same choice. Will you be like Job or like his wife? Will you continue to worship or curse him in your heart? Your view of God determines what your response to suffering will be.

What view of God do we need in suffering? As I wrote previously, I believe Psalm 103 answers that question. Let me explain how. The psalm begins with King David, the writer, talking to himself. He exhorts himself to remember to worship the Lord (Ps. 103:1–2). Then he recites the various ways God shows up in his life (Ps. 103:3–5). Why does he do all that? Why does he need to do that?

I suggest to you, dear daughter, that David did that because he had forgotten to worship and remember God's goodness to him. When has that also been true for you and me? I think the answer is that it's true when we suffer. Remember, pain distorts our view of God. David does not tell us he is suffering, but I think that is the background to the first five verses of Psalm 103.

Are you with me in this line of thinking? If you are, then the question becomes this: What does Psalm 103 tell us about the character of God in our suffering? My answer is that it tells us three important aspects of God being God in our lives that are true even in our suffering. I want to highlight each of them for you as you pursue moving beyond your current season of suffering.

The first aspect of God's character you need to know in your suffering is that suffering does not change God's power. This is clear when the psalmist reminds himself of the acts of God's power he has experienced in his life. David mentions God's forgiveness and that God has given him new strength. He mentions the times God lifted him out of life's pits and more (Ps. 103:3–5). The focus is on God's unchanging power. Everything on this list comes from the reality that our circumstances change, but God's power never does.

Psalm 103 also teaches us that suffering does not change God's character. That is clear in Psalm 103:7–18. Notice the many qualities of God's character found in these verses. Verse 8 mentions his mercy, grace, patience, and abounding steadfast love. Verse 12 mentions his forgiveness. Verse 13 identifies him as compassionate. Verse 17 reminds us that his steadfast love is eternal, not touched or changed by our changing circumstances. We all need to remember these when we suffer. And we need to remember that suffering does not cancel God's ability to send all we need of his character into our lives.

In suffering, we must remember that God remains in control (Ps. 103:19). The what, the when, the how, and the length of our suffering does not change God's governing of our lives. His throne being established in the heavens means it is untouched by earthly events or circumstances. His kingdom rule means our suffering does not surprise him, even though suffering often surprises us. We must always remind ourselves of the three ways that suffering does not change God.

I am sure, Bethany, that as you reflect and ponder on these lessons from Psalm 103, you will find more strength for your heart. Let me close this letter by suggesting some individual verses that you can replace your distressing thoughts with.

When I was going through what I call my Cancer Road Walk, I fell asleep every night reciting Psalm 46:10: "Be still, and know that I am God. I will be exalted among the nations, I will be exalted in the earth!" That verse reminded me that God was bigger than my cancer and I could trust him to do what would grow his fame in my life.

When I felt bitter about harsh words spoken to me as a pastor, I found solace in Ephesians 4:32 that reminded me to be kind, forgiving, and tenderhearted. This verse saved me on more than one occasion when I had the opportunity to be bitter. I hope it helps you fight that battle too.

The last verse I want to recommend to you is Romans 8:18: "For I consider that the sufferings of this present time are not worth comparing with the glory that is to be revealed to us." In the hardest times of my life, this verse reminded me to look beyond the present pain to what will be. Suffering does not get to have the last word in our lives. This verse tells us that the last word is *glory*!

Reread these thoughts as often as you need to in the days ahead. I learned all of them in my school of suffering. They were life to me, and I pray they will be life for you.

Love,
Dad

My Heart Response to Suffering

1. What painful time of suffering caused you to question God's presence in your life?
2. Which of the principles or verses do you want to hold onto and recite to yourself during your season of suffering? What verse or verses do you run to in your pain?
3. How does the fact that suffering does not change God's character, his power, or his governing in our lives impart strength to your heart or challenge you to believe it is true?

Letter 9

WHEN CALMING TAKES TIME

Good day, Bethany,

How I appreciate your question from last night! "What do I do until my body responds to calming itself as I use a Grounding Skill and replace my Thinking Error?" That's a great question. I was going to tell you that in this letter anyway, so here we go.

You need to know that like any skill, learning to calm your body takes practice. The reason for that is because in this season of suffering, your body is responding as it learned to do in the past rather than as you want it to respond now. With previous past hurts, the calming down did not take as long as it seems to take now (remember the head-heart seesaw). Think of it this way. Imagine a Stress Meter that is something like a thermometer but measures the amount of stress you are experiencing.

STRESS METER
I.D. = Spin Cycle

- 10 = Spin Cycle
- 7.7 = High Stress
- 2.9 = Manageable Stress
- 0 = No Stress

Let's say the Stress Meter measures your stress from 1–10, with 1 being low and 10 being high. In the past, your stress never rose above a 4 or a 5. Because of that, it was easier for your body to reset to a 2 or a 3. (I say 2 or 3 because every day has some kind of stress in it.) But the suffering you are experiencing now is intense and is lasting longer than your previous stresses. Let's assign a 7.7 to your current suffering on the Stress Meter. That number means two things. First, it means it doesn't take much to throw you to a 10 with its resulting Spin Cycle. Second, it means that it takes your body longer to respond to your calming by using the Grounding Skills and changing your self-talk. That is not a flaw of your making. It is normal in times of high stress such as college final exam week or times of prolonged suffering, which is what you are facing now.

So do not berate yourself for these things not working as though it was your fault they aren't. It is not your fault. Your body knows how to go into a Spin Cycle. It is not as well practiced at coming out of and down from a Spin Cycle fueled by the suffering you are facing right now.

Here's what you do to help your body learn to reset itself faster than it is doing right now. While your body is resetting,

When Calming Takes Time

practice the skills of Riding the Wave and Acting Opposite[1] of what you used to do when you were in a Spin Cycle. You can find worksheets that may help you work through these skills all over the internet.

Riding the Wave means that as you use your Calming Skills, the body will respond. Until it does, you note that it hasn't yet. The fact that it hasn't responded yet doesn't mean it won't at all. Riding the Wave is what you do while you wait for your body to relax. Riding the Wave means you outwait your body's delay in calming down. Riding the Wave means you know your body will respond if you do not talk to yourself in ways that keep you in the Spin Cycle. Riding the Wave means you trust your Calming Skills to kick in and help your body calm down. Riding the Wave means you do not panic when it takes a little longer than you want it to take to achieve a calm body. Outwaiting your body's delayed response may mean that you need to use another one or two of the Calming Skills. The more you practice Ride the Wave, the sooner your body will learn to calm down.

The second action you take to help reset your body is to Act Opposite. Act Opposite of what? Act Opposite of what you often do in moments of high stress. Rather than worrying on the couch, take a walk around the block. Rather than mindlessly browsing social media, channel your energy into writing a thank-you letter to someone who encouraged you. Rather than telling someone off, make a gratitude list of all the reasons you have to be thankful today. Do you see how this works?

---

1 Both Ride the Wave and Act Opposite are skills taught by Dialectical Behavioral Therapy, commonly called DBT. DBT teaches people how to hold two contradictory realities together (e.g., a strong emotion without giving in to the emotion but considering how to respond to the situation that created the strong emotion).

You'll Get Through This

I can almost hear you say, "Dad, this sounds too simple to work." Yes, I know it does. But you and I know that simple things are not always easy to do. Riding a bicycle is simple, but most of us did not master it the first time we tried it. That was especially true for you since you learned to ride your bike on a rural washboard road. Adding numbers together is simple but not easy as evidenced by the hours we spent reviewing math flashcards until you could say that three plus five equals eight. Simple things take practice too.

Because simple things take practice, give yourself some mercy in your expectations about how quickly all this will fall into place for you. (Remember the math flashcards!) You can and will learn to help your body calm down faster than it is doing right now. Keep at it, and you will surprise yourself how quickly you can get your head, heart, and body out of a Spin Cycle.

I love you!
Dad

My Heart Response to Suffering

1. How does your impatience with your healing journey show up in your life?
2. When you are upset with yourself because your healing is taking too long, how do you need to change your self-talk?
3. Which tool—Ride the Wave or Act Opposite—will be most helpful to you when you are impatient with yourself or the use of your tools?

Letter 10

SUFFERING AND TRAUMA: PART 1

Dear Bethany,

The depth of your pain and the fact that things are not getting better as fast as you would like them to causes you to rethink what happened to you. You wonder if it really is trauma. So let's revisit what trauma is.

Here are the two easiest ways to identify an event as trauma. First, a traumatic event overwhelms your normal ability to cope with sudden and unexpected changes. Second, a traumatic event leaves you feeling that you were one person before the event and a different person after the event. From all you told me, this event was and is traumatic for you. (Note: There is a difference between traumatic and dramatic!)

Here is a simple example of a traumatic event. For the surviving family members, a relative's suicide is a traumatic event. It is overwhelming because no one can prepare in advance for such a death. It is overwhelming because it ushers into our lives a grief process that differs from a sudden death such as a heart attack or a disease-based death such as cancer. A relative's suicide leaves survivors with a distinct before-and-after feel to their lives, along with the sense that they will never be who they were before the suicide. I wish I did not know this firsthand, but I do. Your grandfather and great-grandfather both took their own lives. So I know how traumatic the event is for family members.

There are four other factors that determine the severity of a trauma. The first of these is the frequency of the event. In your case, it was a one-time event, but its impact still affects you. With childhood sexual abuse, the abuse is seldom a one-time event. Frequent and one-time events both leave their marks on our souls.

The intensity of an event also determines how traumatic the event is. You grew up hearing Mom and me tell the story of the night on December 28, 1978, when United Flight 178 crashed into our backyard in Portland, Oregon. While it was a one-time event, it was an intense event because it landed in our backyard. It took three days for crash investigators to complete the investigation. During that time, every time we looked out our apartment's kitchen window or its sliding glass door we saw where the crash tore the front end of the plane off from the rest of the fuselage. We always knew our apartment was on the flight path from Mount Hood to the airport, but after the crash, we both sucked in our breath for a couple of months, hoping the jet we heard overhead stayed in the air.

The third factor that determines the severity of a traumatic event is a person's proximity to the event. One of my friends from seminary was on Flight 178 that night, so the crash for him was even more traumatic than it was for Mom or me. Our trauma grew when we learned that 10 people on the flight lost their lives. My friend felt two contradictory emotions about the crash. First, he was grateful that he survived. He also felt profound grief for the families of those who perished. In his case, it was his proximity to the crash that increased its impact on his soul.

The last factor that shapes the severity of a traumatic event is the duration of the event. Ongoing trauma such as a child whose home never had enough food leaves more of an impact than missing one meal. Similarly, ongoing domestic violence in a marriage leaves more lasting soul damage than a single outburst. Indeed, the person in a marriage shaped by domestic violence cannot begin the healing until the violence stops or they go to a safe place. There is no place for healing when the person always has to be ready for the next outburst of violence. The healing cannot begin because that person is always in survival mode, not thriving mode. Until the abused person gets out of survival mode, there are no resources to promote their healing or the way they deal with the trauma's impact.

Bethany, I trust this explanation of trauma promotes your ability to accept that what happened is really a trauma event for you. One other thing you should know about trauma is that its impact lasts longer than you will want it to last. It takes time and practice to slow the gyrations of your head and heart seesaw. When it does slow down, you will start to feel normal again.

> I love you,
> Dad

My Heart Response to Suffering

1. Think of a recent event that overwhelmed your coping skills. In what way(s) did you get overwhelmed?
2. Using the four characteristics of a traumatic event, how many of them did your recent event involve?
3. Based on what you've learned in this letter, what might you tell the wounded part of your soul?

Letter 11

SUFFERING AND TRAUMA: PART 2

Hello, Bethany,

You asked a good question last night when we talked. You wanted to know why you—a confident person, a good leader, an open-hearted friend—feel like you are now someone else. As I mentioned in an earlier letter, trauma's pain changes how we see ourselves. In that letter, I mentioned the sense of being one way before the event and a completely different way after the event. But what you are asking now is a different question. What you are asking comes down to this: "How do I make friends with myself again?" Let me explain why that is the question beneath your question.

You need to make friends with yourself again because trauma renders us powerless. You are not used to seeing yourself without options and without the ability to make good choices to influence your own life. Trauma changes all that. Because you could not expect or stop the trauma, you felt powerless in the moment. That sense of powerlessness intensified because as you look back, you see options you did not see in the moment. You wonder why you didn't take an action that now seems so clear as a response you should have made in the moment. And now you see the perfect thing you could have said but did not.

All this is confusing to you now. Words come easily to you. You seldom stumble, trying to find the right word to say what you want to say. You have a large vocabulary, but at the moment you needed to speak up, you didn't, and that baffles you now.

Your silence is another indicator of the intensity of the trauma. Trauma renders us voiceless. Trauma takes away our ability to speak up or cry out. Our silence occurs because when we enter the survival state of fight, flee, freeze, or fold, our brain overrides the speech center, and we remain silent. Think of it this way. A woman being raped may make things worse for herself if she cries out while her rapist holds a knife to her throat. A moviegoer walking to his car may lose more than his wallet and jewelry to an armed robber if he shouts for help. In those cases, silence is a good thing—perhaps even a life-saving thing.

Bethany, I hope this letter helps you be gentler with yourself. I hope it helps you stop judging yourself for what you did not do. Stop beating yourself up with all those shoulds and musts about what you didn't do. Those shoulds and musts are another Thinking Error. Until you do let go of what should have happened (but didn't) and what you could have said (but didn't), you will be stuck in your recovery. Now that you are not in the trauma, you are thinking of a dozen things you could have said or wished you had said. You are mad at yourself for not saying at least something. You need to realize that this is you who is no longer in the trauma judging the part of you that was in the trauma. Now you are telling yourself what that part of you should have said. The problem is that now you have a bigger perspective, a bigger lens through which to look at the event than you did when you were in it. Then you were in survival mode; now you are not. That difference explains why you need to make friends with yourself for your powerlessness in the moment and also your silence.

Bethany, as you look back at what happened, it no longer feels like a life-and-death matter, but your body did not experience it that way. That is why you went into survival mode. You felt threatened, and your body took over from there. Understanding you were in survival mode explains your silence and your lack of action. In your case, the powerlessness you experienced and the silence are normal reactions to a traumatic event.

Love,

Dad

My Heart Response to Suffering

1. List the ways you are mad at yourself for how you handled the moment of your traumatic event. How many of those are because you were powerless in the situation? How many of them are because you were silent in the situation?

2. How does realizing that both powerlessness and voicelessness are normal parts of a traumatic event help you release your anger at yourself?

3. If you choose to stay angry at yourself, how long do you do plan to be angry with yourself before you can forgive yourself for your silence or powerlessness and move on to the future you can still have?

4. What is staying angry at yourself accomplishing for you?

Letter 12

TRAUMA AND SHAME

Dearest Bethany,

No, you are not weird for not wanting to tell people about what happened to you. Not everyone you know may know everything about you. Having good personal boundaries means people know what you choose to tell them on an as-needed basis. For you, that means only your closest personal friends need to know what happened to you. You decide how much to tell them. Those outside your inner circle do not need to know what happened when they say, "You don't seem to be yourself."

Beyond the matter of having good boundaries, your reluctance to talk with others about what happened keeps you from feeling ashamed. Shame is the distance between who you are and who you want to be.

IDEAL ME vs. REAL ME

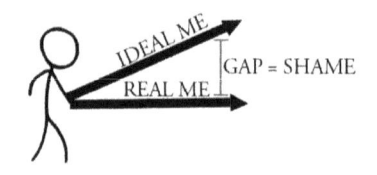

Shame is a normal but unpleasant human emotion. Getting a lower grade than expected on the final exam makes you feel ashamed. I felt shame when I forgot my line in the middle of the senior class play. And I especially feel ashamed when other people see the ideal me versus the real me gap in my life.

The reason a traumatic event produces shame is because the event exposes the gap between your current coping skills and what you need in order to cope with the new, unexpected, and overwhelming event of a trauma. When a traumatic event happens, you feel shame about yourself before you feel ashamed in front of others who saw what happened to you.

Think of it this way. With an 8 out of 10 rating, my coping skills can handle most life events. However, trauma produces a situation where I need my coping skills to be at 16. The gap between my current 8 and my need for a 16 creates my sense of shame.

In moments of shame, you can be angry at yourself for having the ideal you versus the real you gap. That anger quickly becomes contempt because you did not measure up to the standard you set for yourself. At those times, you may have the urge to punish yourself because you fell short of measuring up to the ideal you, the "I should've done this" or the "I should have done that" part of you.

This contempt shows up in our self-talk. We call ourselves unflattering names. We rehearse what we will do next time in order to not be ashamed. We berate ourselves for having the gap at all. We chastise ourselves for not seeing what was coming. We question our ability to see what others are up to in our lives.

You feel angry when there is a gap between the real Bethany and the ideal Bethany because others see that gap. You get angry at them for seeing the gap. The anger can be the start of a Spin Cycle where you lash out at them for seeing the gap (that's your Spin Cycle fight reaction kicking in). Fleeing from them is another indicator of a Spin Cycle.

Bethany, realize that your head-heart seesaw means you will swing back and forth between your sense of shame and anger at yourself. And it will swing between your sense of shame and the contempt you feel toward others. It is that swing that makes you feel weird when you are around others. You're afraid they see your shame. You do not want them to see your anger, but you fear that they do. Thus you will feel shame and contempt and bounce back and forth between the two. That is the power of shame. The swinging of your head-heart seesaw is both normal and unpleasant.

I will write tomorrow about four ways that shame can impact your life.

I love you so very much,

Dad

My Heart Response to Suffering

1. Which of the two emotions associated with the ideal me versus the real me gap do you feel most often?
2. How do you talk to yourself when you are feeling shame or contempt?
3. When you are in a shame Spin Cycle or a contempt Spin Cycle, how do you talk to yourself?
4. Considering what this letter showed, how do you need to change how you talk to yourself?

Letter 13

SELF-CONTEMPT IN SUFFERING

Dear Bethany,

I want to add to what I wrote in the last letter. It is important to understand how shame and contempt will change your outlook toward yourself and your outlook toward others. As I wrote in my first letter, those are two of the five ways that pain—and in this case, shame—distort your perspective. In order to minimize the change in outlook, it is important for you to understand the four functions of contempt when you feel ashamed.

I've adapted these four insights about contempt's relationship to shame from Dr. Dan Allender's work with sexual abuse survivors found in his book *The Wounded Heart*.[1] I know that is not your story, but the features of contempt he identified are present at any moment you or I feel shame. Since you are angry at yourself, in this letter I will explain how the contempt we feel turns on us and damages our souls.

---

1 Dan B. Allender, *The Wounded Heart*, Rev. Ed., 1995, Chapter 4.

Since contempt is such a powerful emotion in a moment of shame, contempt first works to lessen your sense of shame. Contempt energizes you to take action to reduce your sense of shame. Making a joke about your clumsiness when you trip while carrying a tray of food to your table is one way contempt lessens shame. That is contempt toward yourself. Lashing out in anger at those who laugh at your clumsiness is contempt toward others. When people laugh at your clumsiness, anger reduces the shame by making you feel contempt toward them for watching.

Contempt also dulls my sense of longing for a relationship connection. When I express contempt toward myself, I dull my longing for you to care about me since I am less-than, defective, and more as the moment of exposure shows. When I express my anger toward you because you saw me in my shame, I dull my longing to receive love, support, and connection from you. In both cases, I lie to myself because my contempt makes me believe I do not want what I need—love and connection from others—even in a moment of shame.

Because contempt energizes me to take action, I believe I can do something to correct the flaw in me that revealed the Ideal Me versus Real Me gap. I go on a search-and-destroy mission against that flaw. I do so because if I can destroy that flaw, I will not be ashamed again. When I notice a flaw in others who have seen my mistake, I take action against them to avoid future embarrassment.

Contempt challenges my dignity instead of helping me acknowledge my mistakes and seek forgiveness from God alone. You and I have dignity because we were created in the image of God (Gen. 1:26). Our depravity comes from the consequences of the Fall passed on from generation to generation until it reaches us (Rom. 5:12–14). Because of God's mercy, our dignity is not destroyed by sin, Satan, or our suffering. Likewise, God's mercy

SELF-CONTEMPT IN SUFFERING

limits our depravity, so none of us are as evil as we could be. That is why Francis Schaeffer called humans "a glorious ruin."[2] A moment of shame shows my dignity to be less than I want it to be or less than I thought it was. However, the moment of shameful exposure is an opportunity to realize I put my trust in someone unworthy of my trust, whether myself or someone else. That mistrust shows my depravity. If I allow shame to do its work of revealing my false trust, shame could act as a tool to redirect and reset my trust in God.

You know, Bethany, the entire history of Israel in the Old Testament is misplaced trust in something other than God. Whether trusting the golden calf on the Exodus journey or the political alliances with Egypt and Assyria in Jeremiah's day, Israel's continual drift to idolatry reveals the consequences of a misplaced trust in something or someone other than God. Idols are our substitute god in which we trust, so we do not have to trust God himself. As Dr. Allender says, "A false god will disappoint."[3]

Until next time,
Dad

---

2 Quoted in Dan B. Allender, *The Wounded Heart*, Colorado Springs: NavPress, 1995, p. 60.
3 Dan B. Allender, *The Wounded Heart*. Colorado Springs: NavPress, 1995, pp. 72.

My Heart Response to Suffering

1. What would your life be like if you believed you were a person of dignity? What adjustments in your life would you make if you believed that?
2. What kind of contempt—toward yourself or others—are you most prone to have? What did this letter teach you about the impact of contempt on your life and relationships?
3. Looking back at your moment of shame, what did that moment reveal you were trusting instead of God? In what way do you need to shift your focus back to God?

Letter 14

SUFFERING AND THE BRAIN

Dear Bethany,

So you are having nightmares about what happened. That is not surprising. Here's why. While we sleep, our mind reorganizes itself, connecting experiences and conversations. Our brain works to make connections among concepts, events, or people like the ones our brain previously reorganized. This work of organizing takes place when we dream.

Think of your brain's ability to reorganize itself like this. Think of the color red. When I think of red, I think of the American flag, the Nebraska Cornhuskers football uniforms, the brick house we once lived in, and so on. I organize and associate all these with the color red.

Now think of a Marine veteran of Iraq who saw his best friend's Humvee get blown up by a roadside bomb. Despite running to his friend's Humvee to rescue him, his friend lost too much blood from the explosion and died in his arms. That Marine will probably have nightmares as his brain tries to organize the image of his friend's bloody body with the color red. The nightmare is the brain's failed attempt to make good associations with that memory. When it cannot do so, the Marine will have repeated nightmares until the Iraq memory links up with his stored associations with the color red. The brain behaves differently when it can establish strong connections to known facts, people, or memories. Let me give you a personal example using some people you know.

A few months ago, Mom and I talked about where we would like to retire. We considered returning to Nebraska for its lower cost of living and our friends who live there. I mentioned Greg and Deb in South Dakota, wondering out loud how much fun it might be to retire in Mitchell where they live.

That night, my dream involved doing that. I dreamed about the entire relocation process and finding a house around the corner from Deb and Greg. I dreamed about having summer water fights with them, going camping together, having blizzard parties, and enjoying other events we did when we all lived in O'Neill, Nebraska. Since I remembered the dream when I woke up, I knew why I had that dream. Then I called Greg and told him about it. We laughed, and then he said, "What kind of house do you want? I'll start looking today."

All that was my brain taking the conversation Mom and I had, linking it to my memories of Greg and Deb, and then dreaming about them. In that case, my brain associated a small conversation with other memories of Greg and Deb.

Your nightmares show that your brain is still trying to make sense of what happened so it can link it to other events in your memory. The repeating of the nightmare shows your brain still cannot make such positive associations, but it keeps trying to do so.

But not every trauma survivor has nightmares. Many experience flashbacks of the emotionally overwhelming event. A flashback happens when our memory travels back to the original event but with such vividness that it feels like it is happening in the present, not in the past. In essence, a flashback is a daytime nightmare, a reliving in the present of a past event. For example, the Marine who lost his buddy in the convoy may hear a motorcycle backfire and be suddenly and unexpectedly taken back to the moment the Humvee exploded. He reacts as if he was still in Iraq, not in his front yard mowing his lawn.

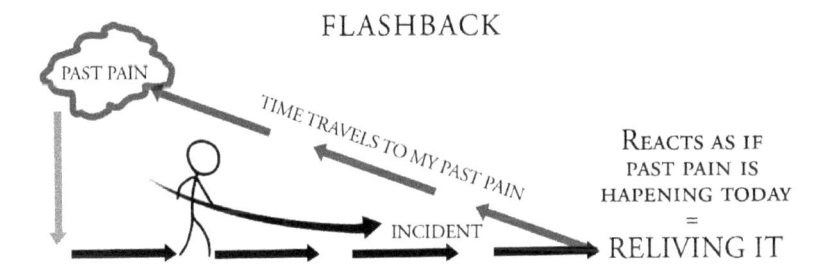

FLASHBACK

PAST PAIN

TIME TRAVELS TO MY PAST PAIN

INCIDENT

REACTS AS IF PAST PAIN IS HAPENING TODAY
=
RELIVING IT

So what do you do about that? I recommend getting some help with a therapist who uses EMDR to help your brain link the painful parts of your trauma to other memories. Indeed, all that I just wrote is the basis for EMDR's effectiveness. EMDR is based on Adaptive Information Processing.[1] The story about the Marine and the story about Greg and Deb illustrate what the Adaptive Information Process does. It links new experiences with older memories, so the new experiences connect with memories of similar experiences, conversations, and friendships. EMDR accesses and stimulates memories that are not adaptively stored with other memories and moves them into association with those other memories, so they

---

[1] See Francine Shapiro, *Eye Movement Desensitization and Reprocessing (EMDR) Therapy*, *3rd Edition*, New York: Guilford Press, 2018; Francine Shapiro, *Getting Past Your Past*, Emmaus: Rodale Books, 2013.

lose their emotional impact on us. You can read more about this in Francine Shapiro's introduction to EMDR in her book *Getting Past Your Past*. You can find a trained EMDR therapist by going to psychologytoday.com and putting "EMDR therapist near me" in the search bar. It will give you a list of therapists who use EMDR in their practice. The therapist listing will also tell you what kind of clients they work with, their fee structure, and more. You can also find an EMDR therapist by going to www.emdria.org and clicking on the "Find a Therapist" tab.

I know. I know. None of that is fresh news to you since you know I have used EMDR in my counseling practice for 10 years. You know that I see firsthand what EMDR does in helping people resolve past hurts and traumas. EMDR empowers individuals to live joyfully, leaving behind painful memories. I see how it helps people resolve past hurts and traumas. I know it can do the same for you.

I love you,
Dad

My Heart Response to Suffering

1. Do you dream about your suffering or have nightmares about it? How long have you had nightmares, if any?
2. How does the Adaptive Information Process help you understand why you are having nightmares, and what can you do about it?
3. Are you ready to work with an EMDR therapist to resolve your nightmares or flashbacks? Why or why not? What do you fear will happen if you start working on the nightmares? What will happen if you do not?

Letter 15

SUFFERING'S TRIGGERS

Dear Bethany,

    Having intrusive memories of your painful incident is not unusual. These intrusions are what many people call "getting triggered." What that means is a sight, a smell, a location, or a person's name that brings back images of their suffering. They do not want to remember it. They do not want intrusive images. Neither do you, but they come anyway.

    The reason they still come is because the brain is trying to make sense of what happened to you. Triggers can make you feel like your suffering is happening again, whether at work, while cooking, or after falling asleep. In one sense, you time travel back to the moment your suffering occurred. That is why a flashback is a daytime nightmare, a reliving of the past event.

    Yes, it is maddening, since you do not have to be thinking about the incident when the memory comes. Often, it is something out of your awareness that triggers the memory. One day after my mother died, your mom and I were shopping at a mall when a lady who walked past us was wearing my mom's favorite perfume, White Linen by Estée Lauder. Immediately, my head whipped around, looking for my mom. Why did that happen? It happened because a woman walking past me was wearing the same perfume my mom always wore. Before I could stop it from happening, that scent of Mom's perfume caused me to turn and look for her. When I turned my head, I knew it was not Mom, but the sense of smell overcame the reality of what I knew and made me look for her although she had been dead for six months.

So, too, your intrusive memories come while your attention is elsewhere. Whenever something triggers you, the memory will come up, and you won't be able to identify its cause. Such instances come because something outside your awareness stimulates part of your painful memory. The moment of suffering overshadows putting the lasagna in the oven. When you get triggered, you will feel powerless, voiceless, and violated, just like you did when the pain entered your life.

This is both normal and maddening. But as you use the tools I gave you in earlier letters, as you find some safe friends to share your hurt with and do some EMDR work, the frequency of these triggers will lessen and lose their emotional charge. In the meantime, expect them to occur. Deal with them one at a time by reorienting yourself—out loud is best—to your present setting and task. Say something like this: "I feel I am back in my pain, but I am in my kitchen getting supper ready and setting the table so we can all eat." You may need to repeat that several times before you feel 100 percent back in the present, but as you do, you will escape the pull to stay stuck in the past pain. Talking back to the trigger diminishes its power. Talking back to it will help you become trigger-resistant by keeping you in the present.

Suffering's Triggers

Each time you reorient yourself to the present, you strengthen your ability to respond to the past pain and not react to it. When you talk back to the trigger, you are building new thinking patterns so the trigger will not push you into acting to cause more pain. Talking back to the intrusive memory will bring you freedom to move on with your life, the life you can still have despite what happened. Isn't that what you seek? Of course it is. That is why I am writing you these letters. Ponder what I said in this letter, and put it to use. I'll contact you in a few days to see how you're managing your triggers.

I love you,
Dad

My Heart Response to Suffering

1. How do you react when something triggers you? Are you satisfied with your reaction? Why or why not?
2. This letter recommends talking back to your trigger and gave one example of doing so. As you ponder your reactions to getting triggered, how do you need to talk back to your trigger in order to respond to it?
3. Practicing talking back to your trigger creates a new habit. What habit would you like to come from talking back to your painful memory? What insights about that habit can facilitate personal growth in your life?

Letter 16

GRIEVING IN SUFFERING

Dear Bethany,

 Last night's talk let me know just how much you are struggling with the sadness of what happened to you. You said, "Dad, I feel I am in a black hole I cannot get out of." Yes, I am sure you feel that way. That is your head-heart seesaw gyrating. While you did not use the word, I know what you feel is grief. Let me explain why.

 Grief is the process we go through to adjust our heart-head seesaw following loss. Most of the time, people use the word grief to describe their sense of loss after a death. But grief happens anytime we experience a loss. Getting fired from a job brings grief. The closing of a favorite restaurant brings grief. Getting a promotion that requires moving across the country brings grief. In fact, Bethany, we experience any change in our lives as grief before we get excited about the new possibilities in the change.

 Reflect on what Mom and I felt when we left Wyoming. I grieved the loss of no longer going to our favorite burger place inside the downtown pharmacy. We both felt the loss of our long desert walks on the Bureau of Land Management land so near our home. Mom hated leaving Dr. Greg and the crew at the dental office. I was sad to no longer be part of the healthy pastors' Tuesday morning meetings when we laughed together, cried together, and encouraged one another. While we were both excited to return to Oregon, we keenly felt the loss of all those things.

You are grieving the loss of who you were before suffering knocked on your door and let itself in. You do not trust others as easily as you did. You are more afraid of getting hurt by others than you ever were. The fear of missing out on something that could cause you more pain keeps you on high alert. You are sad this event happened because it feels so unnecessary. Your grief creates that sadness.

Here's what to expect as you continue to grieve the losses in your suffering. While some counselors see grief with five phases, I believe it is helpful to see it in eight phases of walking on what I call the Grief Road. You are already past the first two phases—shock and denial. When all this first occurred, you couldn't believe it was happening to you. The third phase is anger. The anger you wrestle with the most is the anger at yourself, the anger I explained as contempt in a previous letter. You have yet to feel anger toward the one who caused your suffering, but eventually you must confront that anger in order to move forward. The fourth phase is guilt or shame. You have faced this phase because the suffering exposed the gap between your ideal Bethany and the real Bethany. Please refer back to my earlier letter for guidance on dealing with shame. The fifth phase is bargaining. This is either an attempt to reconcile or a plea to God for healing. In either case, the suffering remains, and so we continue to grieve.

The sixth phase is sadness—a pervasive, all-encompassing sorrow that seems to swallow you whole and not spit you out. This is the phase people associate with grief. The seventh phase is acceptance. The initial step in moving on is accepting and incorporating suffering into your life story. Suffering did its work in your soul, and you learned new lessons about who you are and how to keep moving forward in times of pain. The eighth and last phase is beginning again. You start living the life you now have, no longer mourning the life you no longer have.

Bethany, this may be the most important and annoying thing I tell you in this letter. These phases will feel more like a pinball game than a sequential process. Instead of moving through one phase and being done with it, you will bounce back and forth through all eight phases, never knowing what will send you through any stage. You'll feel like you're losing your mind because the phases do not happen in a predictable order. Such bouncing around is the head-heart seesaw trying to reset itself. You must go through these hard movements to find peace in and from your suffering.

This will take longer than you want it to take. It is customary for us to do grief work for one to three years before we feel we have finished walking the Grief Road. I wish I didn't have to say this, but I do. You can't rush the grieving process. It takes the time it takes. Some things we can grieve about within a year. Other things take longer. I cannot tell you how long it will take for you. I wish I could.

You never know what will cause a moment of grieving. That is why my favorite word to describe grieving is ambush. That is what grief does; it ambushes us. You can hear a song nine times, and the tenth time you hear it, you have to pull to the side of the road because the tears are flowing. The realization hits you while bowling that the last time you went was with someone who is no longer in your life. Grief ambushing means you cannot schedule a time, like 3 pm. Sunday afternoon, for a good cry to release your grief. It just does not work that way. Bethany, you are not crazy for feeling the profound sadness you now have. You are not losing your mind because of your grief-related mood swings. You are not abnormal when your grief ambushes you. You are doing important soul-healing work when you grieve. I promise you that your head-heart seesaw will reset itself. Be patient and kind to yourself until it happens.

Love,
Dad

My Heart Response to Suffering

1. Which phase of grief are you in today as you process your own suffering?
2. Think about when you were most recently ambushed by grief. What set the grief in motion? How did you express the grief you felt?
3. What is your response to the fact that grief can take from one to three years? How far along are you in walking your Grief Road?
4. What are you doing that is helping you keep moving through your grief?

Letter 17

PROCESSING GRIEF EMOTIONS

Dear Bethany,

In this letter I want to talk with you about a helpful way to process your strong grief emotions as you walk the Grief Road. It's called journaling. You already know that I consistently journal because writing in my journal is part of my morning spiritual habits I employ to stay spiritually and emotionally healthy. Because I am no stranger to grief, I want to pass on to you three ways that journaling helps you process grief.

Before I give you those three ways, I need to pass on some preliminary advice about journaling. First, find a notebook size that will encourage you to write in it daily. When I first began to journal, I found the standard 8.5" x11" notebooks too intimidating. I wondered how in the world I would ever fill a page. Since I found that size too intimidating, I settled on a 5" x 9" notebook. I used that size for many years until 10 or so years ago when I switched to a 7.5" x 9.75" notebook that often goes on sale during the start of the school year when parents are buying their children's supplies.

Second, decide on a time and a place to journal. Your journaling place can be anywhere in your home where you can retreat to process your inner world of thoughts and emotions. Mine is my home office, but yours can be that big plush chair in your fireplace room or the comfy sofa in your upstairs bonus room. The main thing you want for your journaling place is quiet and solitude. You need both in order to truly pay attention to your inner world's tempest of grief.

My third piece of advice is deciding what form your journal will take. Some people I know use bullet points, listing the various ideas and emotions that emerge while they sit in the quiet. Some write a record of the events of the previous day, mentioning what they felt as they moved through those events. I write a letter to God each day. My letter begins by listing the things I am thankful for. Then I ask myself and the Lord this simple question: What is inside me today that I need to talk over with you? Then I start writing whatever comes to mind. My journal is also the place I record my thoughts as I read my Bible each morning. Sometimes I take a thought from that reading and put it on a 3" x5" card so I can carry the thought with me all day and frequently remind myself of it.

Bethany, you will need to experiment to find what best prepares you to journal about your inner world. Stay with it until you find what works for you.

Now I want to tell you about three benefits of journaling while grieving. First, journaling forces you to find the words you need to use to express what is going on inside you. To do that, you have to pay attention to what emerges from your soul as you sit in your solitary and silent place. Sometimes, finding the right word is the hardest part of writing about what you are feeling during this time of loss.

The important thing about finding the right words is to not censor yourself. If you are angry, pour it out on the page. If you are deep in your sense of loss, write about how alone you feel or how hard it is to go on after your walk on the Grief Road begins. If you are grateful for someone's help along that road, write that down. If a soul-healing Bible verse stands out to you as you read, record it. Write what emerges from deep within you.

The second benefit of journaling is the physical act of writing. As someone once said, "Thoughts disentangle themselves out through the fingertips." I've found that true over and over during the years I've been journaling. As I write, I recognize when my anger grows beyond whatever triggered it and I am sliding into bitter resentment. As I write, I can see self-pity oozing out of me. As I write, I recognize I have more help along the Grief Road than I first realized when I began to write.

Bethany, as a Christ-follower, I cannot tell you the times the Holy Spirit has pointed out something as my thoughts and emotions disentangled themselves as I wrote. That is why journaling is part of my spiritual habits. It keeps me close to God from the inside out.

The third and last benefit of journaling is that it helps you make peace with the loss you experienced. As you journal your strong emotions, you will find over time that they lose their ability to bully you or ambush you as they once did. Journaling helps you sort things out so you can find peace in your soul again.

Here is one last thought about journaling. I learned how to journal from Gordon MacDonald's marvelous book *Ordering Your Private World*. I highly recommend it if you want to learn more about journaling than what I put in this letter. Go get yourself a copy.

I love you,
Dad

My Heart Response to Suffering

1. Have you tried journaling in the past? Was it helpful in sorting out your inner world? Why or why not?
2. Where and what time of day will work best for you to begin journaling?
3. What uncomfortable emotions do you think you will initially avoid when writing in your journal? Why would you exclude them from being included?
4. List three ways you think journaling will be beneficial to you in sorting out your soul's tempests.

Letter 18

SUFFERING AND LIFE IN A BROKEN WORLD

Hi, Daughter!

In this letter, I want to pass on to you three normal responses to suffering found in Romans 8, a Bible chapter I know you love. I want to do that based on what you said when you called. Your head-heart seesaw swings wildly, making you doubt your sanity. Let me assure you that the thoughts you have are normal, and you can find them in Romans 8. The three responses are in verses 19–23. Here they are.

First, suffering causes us to experience futility because of how broken the world truly is (Rom. 8:20). How do I define a broken world? Let me put it this way. The Bible has 1,189 chapters. Only four of those chapters—the first two (Genesis 1 and 2) and the last two (Revelation 21 and 22)—are free of the realities of sin, Satan, suffering, and death. That means the other 1,185 chapters include the struggles with sin, Satan, suffering, and death that we all face in this life. That tells me the world is more broken than I like to think it is. I suspect the mathematics of all this is God's way of telling us to expect suffering in this life.

According to the late Dr. Larry Crabb, we all yearn to go back to Eden, but the way is blocked, and we cannot.[1] The blocked longing creates our sense of futility in suffering. We know the world is not what it should be or could be. But no matter how we try, the world remains deeply broken. In suffering, we can either deny or numb the longing for Eden, or recognize that it will only be fulfilled at the second coming of Christ.

Second, the futility we all experience in life comes from the bondage to decay that marks this present age (Rom. 8:21). It would be bearable if the world's brokenness didn't worsen as time goes on. But it does. Diseases have secondary consequences, and one bad financial decision can affect our ability to pay our bills.

You see it in your own life in this season of suffering. What started small grew so your suffering shaped your relationship with friends, your view of the future, and the three other distortions that pain brings. As you said in your phone call, your suffering is affecting your health. You are not sleeping well. You've lost your appetite. When feeling the full sadness of your suffering, you binge eat chocolate. Those are not unique to you; they reveal the bondage to decay and suffering and your struggle to cope with it.

Third, suffering creates painful groanings (Rom. 8:23). Our response to the world's brokenness is to groan. We groan because we cannot get back to Eden. Those groanings grow when the world's brokenness enters our lives at unexpected times and in unexpected ways. We groan when things go from bad to worse. We groan because it could be so much better than it is, but it isn't.

How do we face the frustrating futility, the bondage to decay, and the painful groanings? The answer is that we face them with the power of the Holy Spirit (Rom. 8:26–27). As those verses show,

---

1 Larry Crabb, *Waiting for Heaven*, Larger Story Press, 2020.

the Holy Spirit translates all we feel in our suffering into prayer. Despite our speechlessness, the Holy Spirit persists through the pain of the broken world and our suffering. Prayer in suffering is a powerful means of facing the frustrating futility, the bondage to decay, and our heartfelt groans.

In Romans 8:19, the Holy Spirit enables us to endure suffering because he reminds us of what is ahead. Ahead lies a world free of suffering, filled with God's glory. On that day, life's futility in a broken world will vanish. When that day arrives, things will stop getting worse. When that day comes, groans will turn into praises. The Holy Spirit shifts our attention to the future.

"But what about now?" you ask. That's a good question. The answer is in Romans 8:28–39. While we suffer in this broken world, the Holy Spirit reminds us of God's love for us. We can see from these verses that God's love remains unchanged, unweakened, and present even in our sufferings. Knowing that means we live hopefully and confidently in our sufferings (Rom. 8:24, 25, 39).

I will write more about the key to doing that—keeping your gaze on God and not your circumstance—tomorrow.

I love you,
Dad

My Heart Response to Suffering

1. In your moments of suffering, which of the three normal responses to suffering do you find yourself identifying with?
2. Why do you think you identify most often with that response?
3. How do you need to open your life today to the work of the Holy Spirit in your suffering? Do you need the bigger picture of what lies ahead? Do you need the Holy Spirit's help in praying? Do you need the reminders he gives of God's love for you?

Letter 19

SUFFERING WHILE GAZING AT GOD

Good evening, Bethany,

Today was a long day at the office, so I am just now reading your text from this morning. You are right about what you said. You need more advice about how to keep your gaze on God and not on your circumstances. Let me do that now. The source of my recommended action steps comes from the Apostle Paul's letter to the Philippians. Let's think through what he says in Chapter 1 about how he handled the adversity of being in a Roman prison while he wrote to the congregation in Philippi.

The first action step is to not focus on the circumstances (Phil. 1:12). Remember the issue is where your gaze is and where your glance is. Because I already gave you some recommendations on how to not focus on the circumstances, let's move on to the next action step.

What you want to do so you don't focus on your circumstances is to look for what God is doing (Phil. 1:13–18) rather than on what he is not doing. Paul had a lot of reasons to be discouraged, to be multiplying his imprisonment times forever, but he didn't. He looked for what God was doing through others while he was in jail. Doing so kept him from giving in to the twin perils of bitterness and blaming.

When we let our circumstances fill our vision, we become bitter toward whoever we blame for our suffering. When we let our circumstances fill our vision, we blame others for the suffering. Blaming others leads to one of the Thinking Errors I previously discussed with you—Villain-Victim thinking, which means I blame someone for my suffering. That makes that person my villain. Then, as long as the villain in my story does not change, I remain a victim to my suffering. As long as I stay in Villain/Victim thinking, I am powerless to make changes. I then lose my ability to choose my response to my suffering. Paul overcame that Thinking Error by looking at what God was doing in his suffering—using other people to make Christ known (Phil. 1:13–14). That focus brought Paul joy, not bitterness or blaming.

The second action step you can take to keep from losing sight of God is to believe God will deliver you, even if he has not yet. This action step is important because, as I told you before, pain will try to get you to believe your suffering changed God's power, his character, or his sovereignty. It can only do those things if you stop believing God can still deliver you. By adding the word *yet* or the phrase *for now* to your self-talk, you remind yourself that just because the change you seek did not happen today, it does not mean it will never come. Adding those to endings to your self-talk also injects hope into your thinking. Try adding those to endings to your self-talk and see what happens.

Suffering while Gazing at God

Believing that God would deliver him was Paul's focus in Philippians 1:19. Notice what gave him that hope. He knew others were praying for him. Paul knew God's goodness continued even when his circumstances were not good. You can believe that too.

Bethany, do you remember what I wrote about shame's ability to silence us? Paul avoided being silenced by any shame associated with his imprisonment (Phil. 1:20) by asking others to pray for him, knowing they would. So my question to you, dear daughter, is who have you asked to pray for you to come out of this season of suffering? Paul shows us that his expectation of the prayers of the Philippians kept him from bitterness or blaming. He knew the Holy Spirit would move on his behalf as others prayed for him. You need that hope too.

What if those prayers are not answered immediately and your suffering does not change as fast as you want it to? I tell you that God will send sustaining grace until he sends transforming grace. Paul learned this when God denied releasing him from the messenger of Satan, as described in 2 Corinthians 12:9–10. God told him and then showed him, "My grace is sufficient for you." So will you wait for a change in your suffering and hold on to God's ability to sustain you in it?

The third action step you can take that will keep you from focusing on your circumstances and lose sight of God is to concentrate your energies on exalting Christ, not escaping your circumstances (Phil. 1:20–21). But how do you do that? Pray for courage. Pray for the courage to outlast your circumstances. Pray for courage, knowing that others are praying for you. Pray for courage so you can make Christ further known during your suffering. Pray for courage so others may better know Christ as they witness how you handle your suffering.

Finally, take this last action step to keep you from focusing on your circumstances and losing sight of God. Anticipate telling your faith story of how God worked in your life through your suffering (Phil. 1:25). Paul believed in his future release from his cell so he could minister to and with the Philippians again. In his imprisonment, Paul believed he would impact their lives because of the action steps he took while suffering. You need to believe that too. Why? You need to believe that God is giving you a faith story right now in your suffering that can bring joy to others (Phil. 1:25). Your suffering faith story can inspire and encourage others when they come into their time of suffering (Phil. 1:27–30). Remember, Bethany, there is always someone watching your life as a Christian. Following these action steps can help them find courage to persevere in their suffering like they saw you do.

I love you,

Dad

My Heart Response to Suffering

1. What can you identify that God is doing in your suffering that perhaps you did not see before reading this letter? What evidence do you see of God sending you sustaining grace until he sends your transformative grace? Make a list of what you can see now, and then refer to the list when you are tempted to give in to bitterness or blaming.
2. Who are you going to ask for prayer support while you suffer? In what ways do you need courage to hold on while you suffer?
3. How will knowing that people are praying for you change your outlook on your suffering?
4. What can you do to exalt Christ in your current circumstance? What can you tell others that God is doing for you while you wait for the suffering to end?

Letter 20

SUFFERING AND LOSING HOPE

Dear Bethany,

I am so glad you went to a concert last night. That is practicing good self-care by doing things that bring you joy. I look forward to hearing all about it when you call tomorrow night.

You asked a good question in your morning text to me. You wonder what will happen if you gaze at your circumstances instead of at God. You asked that because your head-heart seesaw pulls you to gaze at God one minute and then gaze at your circumstances the next.

Bethany, that is a normal head versus heart battle when you are walking through suffering. It is unpleasant but normal. You are likely noticing the abundance of head-heart battles you encounter. You are noticing them because they happen more frequently than you want them to. That will be the way it is for a while.

When you gaze at your circumstances and thus lose sight of God, you give way to despair and hopelessness. That will be especially true during the three times your emotions are prone to despair instead of hope. Here they are.

First, we are prone to hopelessness when we feel forsaken by God. As I mentioned in a previous letter, this is what Heman battled as he wrote Psalm 88. You can see it in verse 5 where he says of himself, "[I am] like one set loose among the dead, like the slain that lie in the grave, like those you remember no more, for they are cut off from your hand." From there it gets worse: "O Lord why do you cast my soul away? Why do you hide your face from me?" He is feeling abandoned. He feels perplexed. All this is because he felt forsaken by God.

Second, we are prone to hopelessness when we cannot understand God's ways of dealing with us. This is especially true when God takes longer to answer our prayers or change our circumstance than we think he should. I find the perfect example of that predicament in Isaiah 50:10–11[1]. Verse 10 says, "Who among you fears the Lord and obeys the voice of his servant? Let him who walks in darkness and has no light trust in the name of the Lord and rely on his God." Isaiah tells whoever feels they are in the dark about God and his ways to "trust in the name of the Lord." He redirects his reader's attention from his circumstance of being in the dark to what the reader knows about who God is. Isaiah's point is that knowing the *who* eliminates the need to know the *what*.

What's the alternative to doing that? The alternative is trying to fix our circumstances by ourselves. But note the warning Isaiah gives about doing that in Isaiah 50:11. "Behold, all you who kindle a fire, who equip yourselves with burning torches! Walk by the light of your fire, and by the torches that you have kindled! This

---

1 These two insights about Isaiah 50:10–11 are adaptations of what Dr. Crabb says about this passage in his book *Connecting*. (Larry Crabb, *Connecting*, Dallas: Word Publishing, 1997).

Suffering and Losing Hope

you have from my hand: you shall lie down in torment." If we try to get out of the darkness of our circumstance by our own means, by our own lit torches, it will make the situation worse. We will lie down as a result of trying to fix our situation on our own. The choice is ours—trust or torment.

Third, we experience helplessness when we feel overwhelmed. David described the state of his soul, which depicts what our emotions are like when we feel that way. Notice Psalm 31:9–10 and the keywords he uses. "Be gracious to me, O Lord, for I am in distress; my eye is wasted from grief; my soul and my body also. For my life is spent with sorrow, and my years with sighing; my strength fails because of my iniquity, and my bones waste away." Distress and anguish come into our lives when we feel overwhelmed.

What causes us to feel overwhelmed in our suffering? After years of living with myself, I learned I am most prone to feel overwhelmed when I run at too many RPMs for too long. I must monitor the pace of my life and the number of things I am trying to accomplish. I look out for the twins of being overwhelmed—hurry (running too fast) and flurry (trying to do too many things).[2] When both hurry and flurry are in my life, I feel overwhelmed and lower my gaze from God and onto my circumstances. Reversing where I place my gaze makes my circumstances seem larger than God is rather than the truth—that God is bigger than our circumstances.

How do we know God is bigger than our circumstances? The Bible often uses three word pictures to help us understand how big God is and how great his power is. One frequent

---

[2] I learned about the evil of hurry and flurry from Eugene Peterson in his book *The Contemplative Pastor*, Grand Rapids: Wm. B Eerdmans Publishing Company, 1989, p. 25.

reference is to God as the Creator of all things. Psalm 121:1–2 is an obvious example of this: "I lift up my eyes to the hills. From where does my help come? My help comes from the Lord, who made heaven and earth." All creation tells the story of God's almighty power.

The God of the Exodus illustrates that God is greater than our circumstances. "Then Moses and the Israelites sang this song to the Lord: 'I will sing to the Lord, for he has triumphed gloriously; the horse and his rider he has thrown into the sea'" (Exod. 15:1). The song goes on. "Pharaoh's chariots and his host he cast into the sea, and his chosen officers were sunk in the Red Sea. The floods covered them; they went down into the depths like a stone. Your right hand, O Lord, glorious in power, your right hand, O Lord, shatters the enemy" (Exod. 15:4–6).

The third word picture the Bible uses to show us God is greater than our circumstances is the resurrection of Christ from the dead. Paul encourages the readers of his letter to the Ephesians to contemplate that the same power of God that raised Christ from the dead is available to them when they pray and know "what is the immeasurable greatness of his power toward us who believe, according to the working of his great might that he worked in Christ when he raised him from the dead and seated him at his right hand in the heavenly places" (Eph. 1:19–20). In Peter's first letter, he stresses the same thing—"who through him are believers in God, who raised him from the dead and gave him glory, so that your faith and hope are in God" (1 Pet. 1:21).

Bethany, think about what Peter says. He tells you that your faith in God means you believe in the God of the resurrection. You trust in a God who can do the impossible, including raising the dead.

Suffering and Losing Hope

My dear daughter, whenever you believe your circumstances are bigger than your God, you will feel hopeless. In such moments, remind yourself that you believe in the God who created everything you see. Speak to your fainting heart these words: "I believe in the God of the Exodus from Egypt." When discouraged, say this as often as you need to: "I believe in the God who raised Christ from the dead." By speaking these truths about the power of God that is available to you, you will not give way to discouragement and hopelessness.

I love you,
Dad

My Heart Response to Suffering

1. Which of the three times we are most likely to feel hopeless shows up most frequently in your life? What changes must you make to protect yourself from its message of hopelessness?
2. What happens in your life when you have too much hurry and flurry? How can you adjust your pace to avoid feeling overwhelmed by those two things?
3. Which of the three recommended word pictures fits you best? Remind yourself of it whenever you feel hopeless. How can you carry that word picture with you? Perhaps you can put it on your phone's home page or carry a 3" x 5" card with it written on it so you can read it when you need to push back against hopelessness.

Letter 21

GROWING THROUGH SUFFERING

My Dear Firstborn,

    I see that the head-heart seesaw still upsets your confidence and your peace. Today I want to address what sounds like more of a head question but is also a question of the heart. "Why is this suffering happening to me, Lord?" The one question I get asked most by my clients is "Why?"

    To help answer that question, I want you to think of the trip we took to the Joslyn Art Museum in Omaha, Nebraska. You may remember that when we first walked into the main gallery we all said, "Wow!" We were awestruck by the many pieces of art before us. It was hard for our eyes to take it all in. Then one-by-one we walked to the unique pieces that caught our eyes.

    That is what I want to do in this letter. I want to present the big picture of why suffering comes into our lives. Then I want to move on to tell you about specific ways suffering achieves the specific purposes of God in our lives. Are you ready? Let's go.

Bethany, no matter what type of suffering we face, Romans 8:28–29 tell us that suffering comes into our lives to make us like Christ. To be conformed to his image is how Paul expresses it. Romans 8:28 is a verse you memorized in Sunday school. It tells us that God is at work in all our circumstances whether they involve joy or suffering. But it is a mistake to view verse 28 apart from verse 29. Look at them together: "And we know that for those who love God all things work together for good, for those who are called according to his purpose. For those whom he foreknew, he also predestined to be conformed to the image of his Son, in order that he might be the firstborn among many brothers" (Rom. 8:28–29). Do you see the link between God's work in our lives in all things and how that makes us like Christ? God is so committed to making you, my dear daughter, more like Christ that he uses even suffering to achieve that in you.

And that is the big picture view of suffering. Like entering an art museum, the view is too staggering to comprehend all at once. However, it is an answer when our head asks, "Why this?" and "Why now?" That part of the head-heart seesaw has what it needs to slow down, but what about the heart side of the seesaw?

Head answers do not satisfy our hearts. Think of a mom who sees her five-year-old boy chase his red bouncy ball into the street just as a car turns the corner. As she sees the car hit her son, she screams out, "Why Johnny?" Bethany, at that moment, will it be helpful to her if I as her neighbor walk up to her and explain the laws of physics at work when the car hit her son? Of course not! Her cry of "Why?" sounds like a head question, but it is a heart question. What she wants to know is if anyone else cares that the car hit her son. She wants to know if anyone else loves her son enough to hurt with her too. She wants to know if anyone will compassionately walk with her through the days of Johnny's recovery. How can we support her during this painful and challenging time?

The initial response is to recognize when to provide logical answers and when to allow the heart to grieve. That is what Romans 12:15 tells us in instructing us to "rejoice with those who rejoice and weep with those who weep." In suffering, weeping has to come first. Weeping lets the heart make room for the work suffering can do to make us more like Christ. Just like grief helps us let go of what will make room for what still can be, so weeping lets the heart get ready for head answers. But until it weeps, the heart will not be ready to understand the physics of a car accident.

Doing the grief work I mentioned in a different letter is so important in our suffering. Grieving what you lost in your suffering prepares you to learn what God wants to teach you. What does God want to teach you? Let's look at four life lessons suffering teaches us after we weep. These lessons are in 2 Corinthians 1:3–11.

Life lesson number one is that suffering teaches us who God is. We see this in 2 Corinthians 1:3. In suffering, we learn that God is the Father of mercies (note the plural) and the God of all comfort (note the word all). We need mercy in suffering. And then we need comfort. Bethany, I will go further and say the only time we learn what mercy and comfort are is when we suffer. We do not learn what they are in times of prosperity when life is pain-free. But in our suffering, God shows us who he is if we turn to him rather than away from him. Turning away from him makes sense if we let our pain continue to distort our view of who he is.

Life lesson number two is that suffering comes to give us a ministry marked by love. This is the lesson of 2 Corinthians 1:4–6. Here is how that works. When I turn to God in my pain, I learn how he comforts me. I learn how he cares for me in real and practical ways. As I learn how God is at work in my affliction, I learn from him what I need to know so I can comfort others when they have a similar affliction.

Let me give you a personal example of this. After my dad's suicide at Christmastime in 1979, I learned that not only could God comfort me in my excruciating pain but that he did comfort me. At another Christmas five years later, one of the older adult men in our church took his life after his wife of 60 years died earlier in the year of a slow death from cancer. When I walked into his daughter's home, she exclaimed, "Oh, Barry's here. He knows what we are going through." And I did. In their pain, I could offer comfort and love because of what I learned God did for me when my father died.

God has a plan for your pain and suffering, Bethany. He can use it if you keep setting your gaze on him, just like he did with me that Christmastime in 1984.

Please notice 2 Corinthians 1:6. Not only can God comfort us in our suffering but he does comfort us. Paul says God's ability to comfort us is always greater than the pain we feel in the suffering. No suffering exceeds God's ability to comfort us. But remember, pain will try to distort this in our thinking and in our heart, as I mentioned in the first letter. Will you listen to your pain or to what you see in this passage?

Life lesson number three is that suffering teaches us is to rely on God and not on ourselves. Look at 2 Corinthians 8–9: "For we do not want you to be unaware, brothers, of the affliction we experienced in Asia. For we were so utterly burdened beyond our strength that we despaired of life itself. Indeed, we felt that we had received the sentence of death. But that was to make us rely not on ourselves but on God who raises the dead." Paul says the afflictions he endured in Asia made him feel like he was going to die. That is what he means when he says he "despaired of life itself." The intensity of those sufferings made him feel he would not survive them.

However, Paul learned that God had other plans for him—plans to teach him not to be self-reliant when the pain he felt exceeded what he thought he could endure. Paul in and of himself could not endure the suffering he faced, but God could enable him to endure it if Paul turned to him in it. Paul learned that feeling overwhelmed did not mean being overwhelmed when he invited God into his sufferings.

How did he do that? That is the fourth life lesson that suffering teaches us—that we need the prayers of others. Paul says, "You must also help us by prayer" (2 Cor. 1:11). Asking for prayer support from others defeats shame's ability to keep us silent and feeling powerless. Asking for prayer support from others causes many to rejoice when God answers those prayers.

Bethany, these are the most important life lessons I've learned from suffering.

I'll be praying that you learn these lessons too.

Love,

Dad

P.S. One more thing. I've learned that rather than ask why something is happening (I live in a broken world), I should ask, "What is my best response to this?" That keeps me focused on doing what I can in the situation while trusting God to use the situation in the ways I described in this letter.

My Heart Response to Suffering

1. Can you think of a time in your suffering when someone offered you a head answer when all you needed was a shoulder to cry on or someone to cry with? How did that make you feel?
2. As you review the life lessons suffering can teach, which one of them stands out to you? How do you see your suffering teaching you that lesson?
3. What qualities of character is your suffering producing in you that will make you more like Christ? How does knowing God want to make you like Christ relieve you of the fear that your suffering is meaningless?
4. As you look around you, what and who is God using to teach you that he is the Father of mercies and the God of all comfort?

Letter 22

THE CHALLENGE OF RESPONDING TO SUFFERING WITH EVIL

Dear Bethany,

You are not unusual for fighting thoughts of revenge. Getting back at someone we blame for our hurt is as old as the Bible. The desire to respond to suffering with evil is another challenge you will face as you heal your heart. The desire for revenge is the outgrowth of the other challenges we've looked at in other letters.

Think of it as a progression. First, we lose sight of God by focusing on our circumstances rather than on him. Then we lose hope. After we lose hope that our circumstances are going to change, we ask God, "Why?" If we don't understand what God can do in our suffering to make us more like Christ, then we face the challenge of responding to suffering with evil.

I mentioned that this challenge is as old as the Bible. In fact, Genesis gives us a clear example of what happens when we give in to responding to suffering with evil. We find the story in Genesis 34. The chapter tells the story of Shechem raping Dinah. Shechem was a resident of the area where Dinah and her family lived. Dinah's brothers were enraged because in their family, "such a thing must not be done" (Gen. 34:7). Their anger opens the door of their lives to the challenge of responding to suffering with evil. The chapter tells how they gave in to that challenge and what the consequences were. The brothers provide us with four life lessons so we can avoid responding to suffering with evil.

The first life lesson is the challenge to respond to suffering with evil that happens when we mishandle our emotions (Gen. 34:7). That means we are in a Spin Cycle. Bethany, your suffering brings you to a decision. You can either handle your anger, your Spin Cycle, or your anger will handle you.

One common way your anger will try to handle you is by stuffing it. When you stuff your anger, you merely delay dealing with it. If you try to bury the anger, it will show up again because what we bury, we bury alive. That means if you choose to stuff your anger, it will leak out from time to time. It will surface in your soul as a temptation to become embittered toward the one you blame. Or it will spill over to someone else because your anger cup is so full.

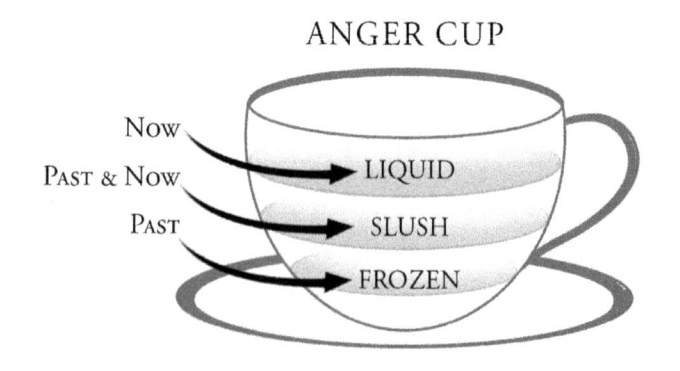

ANGER CUP

Now → LIQUID
Past & Now → SLUSH
Past → FROZEN

The Challenge of Responding to Suffering with Evil

What do I mean by an anger cup? Think of a coffee cup. Imagine that the cup has three layers. The first layer—the frozen layer—is at the bottom of the cup. The middle layer is the slush layer—part liquid and part ice. The top layer is all liquid.

Here is the significance of each layer. The frozen layer is the anger and hurt we stuff and do not deal with in the moment. The slush layer is part past anger and the anger you feel right now. The top layer is just the anger you feel when you first become angry.

No matter the size of your cup, how much room each layer takes up in the cup determines how well you respond to anger-producing situations or people. The larger the frozen and slush layers of anger, the less room you have for dealing with today's irritations and frustrations.

The anger cup explains why you will either deal with your anger now or later. If you want freedom from anger or your desire for revenge, you must identify what is in each layer of your anger cup and manage those layers. But there is no escaping the fact that you will have to deal with them.

Your cup might be a sadness cup, a fear cup, or something else. The emotion in the cup is not the important thing. What is important is whether you handle it or not.

In Ephesians 4:26, Paul shows you how to handle your anger. He offers you an alternative to allowing your anger to handle you. He simply says, "Be angry and do not sin." Handling your anger means you acknowledge how you feel, but then you choose how you will express it. Rather than becoming angry because you cannot understand the reason you suffer and rather than inwardly rebelling at the shape your suffering takes or focusing on who to blame for your suffering, ask yourself, "How can I best respond to this suffering?" That is what Paul stresses. You and I will become angry, but what is important is if the anger is handling us or we are handling the anger.

Jesus illustrates being angry but not sinning. One day after walking through the temple, he saw those who were selling animals for sacrifices and those who were exchanging local currency for the temple's currency (John 2:14). Jesus recognized that both the sellers and the money changers were taking advantage of those who traveled to Jerusalem for Passover. The next verse says, "And making a whip of cords, he drove them all out of the temple" (John 2:15). Don't miss this: he made the whip himself. What he saw made him angry, but he considered the best way to handle his anger. Thus, he made the whip.

Another way of managing anger is using a time-out when you are angry but are not sure why you are or how best to handle it. At those times, you can say to yourself, "I am not sure why I am so angry right now. I need to take some time to think about this to find out why I am so angry." Then take the time you need to sort out what is making you so angry. If you are around others, say, "Right now, I am too upset to talk about what just happened. So please give me 30 minutes to cool down and think about my reaction. Then we can talk about what made me so angry."

Returning to Genesis 34, we see that the brothers faced a choice. Whether the rape should or should not have happened—and you and I agree that it should not have happened—they still needed to decide how they were going to handle their anger. They chose to respond to one evil with another evil.

Hamor, Shechem's father, tried to make the situation right by explaining that Shechem wants to marry Dinah. Hamor hoped their marriage would resolve the situation. Note, however, the response of the offended brothers. "The sons of Jacob answered Shechem and his father Hamor deceitfully, because he had defiled

The Challenge of Responding to Suffering with Evil

their sister Dinah" (Gen. 34:13). The key word in that verse is *deceitfully* since it shows you the second life lesson about the challenge of responding to suffering with evil.

The second lesson is—responding to suffering with anger—can be hidden for a time. Other people may not recognize your anger. They may even comment on how well you seem to deal with your adversity. Sadly, Shechem and Hamor did not see the deceit of the brothers when they agreed to the marriage. The brothers hid their anger well.

The brothers said, "We cannot do this thing to give our sister to one who is uncircumcised, for that would be a disgrace to us. Only in this condition will we agree with you—that you will become as we are by every male among you being circumcised. Then we will give our daughters to you, and we will take your daughters to ourselves, and we will dwell with you and become one people" (Gen. 34:14–16). The deceit was in apparently agreeing to the marriage while they had something else in mind. They disguised their anger in a reasonable, alternative solution.

Because they were in a Spin Cycle, they did not think clearly. Remember, if your Spin Cycle goes on too long, you cannot problem-solve your situation because you will be in the survival mode of fight, flee, freeze, or fold. All four of those get you out of the problem-solving mode. Getting revenge on Shechem and the townspeople made sense to the brothers because they were in a Spin Cycle. They could not ask themselves, "What is the best response to what happened to Dinah?" They reacted instead of responding to the rape.

Not knowing the brothers' deceit, Shechem and his father agreed to the marriage, asking the brothers to name the bride's price. According to the brothers, every male in the town had to be circumcised as the bride's price. Shechem and his father took this matter to the city council that met at the town's gate. After listening to them, the city council agreed, and all the men became circumcised (Gen. 34:18–24).

What happens next shows that the brothers gave in to the challenge of responding to suffering with evil. "On the third day, when they were sore, two of the sons of Jacob, Simeon and Levi, Dinah's brothers, took their swords and came against the city while it felt secure and killed all the males" (Gen. 34:25).

Lesson three is that anger's response to suffering has a wider reach than blaming the person we blame for our suffering. Shechem was the one who raped Dinah, but the brothers enacted their revenge on everyone in the town, not just Shechem. When you or I respond to suffering with evil, it will affect more than the one we blame for our suffering.

Bethany, I know you are not contemplating murder, but let me show you what this might look like for you. You are hurting, and you will tell all your friends about your hurt. That's venting, the second way anger will try to handle you. Venting your anger means you verbally vomit your pain onto others. It is an indiscriminate pouring out of your anger. Rather than finding one or two friends you can speak to honestly about your hurt, you tell many others how badly you feel. You vent to people who cannot help you move beyond your hurt. It provides brief comfort but conceals a dangerous trap. Listeners are confronted with the challenge of responding to your suffering with evil actions.

Your friends now may become angry too. They may contemplate revenge. They may even have to decide whose side they are on if they know the person you are blaming for your suffering. In all these ways, the challenge of responding to suffering with evil impacts more than the person you blame for your suffering.

The Challenge of Responding to Suffering with Evil

The last life lesson about the challenge of responding to suffering with evil is that anger creates trouble we cannot control. Again, ponder what is happening here. The original source of the problem was Shechem. But the brothers did not limit their act of revenge to Shechem. They took action against the whole town.

Their father, Jacob, knew this was a significant problem. In Genesis 34:30, he declares, "Then Jacob said to Simeon and Levi, 'You have brought trouble on me by making me stink to the inhabitants of the land, the Canaanites and the Perizzites. My numbers are few, and if they gather themselves against me and attack me, I shall be destroyed, both I and my household'" (Gen. 34:30). The brothers did not see this aspect of the consequence of their taking revenge, but Jacob did.

We won't see it either.

When I attended Grace University, I resided in the Duplex, a house that was the men's residence. One man who also lived at the Duplex was Clare. One winter night, a group of girls who lived in a college residence near ours intercepted Clare as he returned to the Duplex. Clare came bursting through our front door just ahead of six snowballs the girls threw.

Jim, a senior in the Duplex, yelled his famous battle cry. "Ah, now they shouldn't of, oughtn't of gone and done that! Not to one of our guys." Taking up an offense for Clare, we filled up three trash cans with water.

You know where this is going, right?

We could hear the girls on the front porch calling, "We want Clare! We want Clare!" We, of course, would not give them Clare. But we were going to give them three trash cans full of water. We counted down from three and then opened the door. We dumped several gallons of water on the girls on our front porch. (It is important for you to know that Clare threw the first snowball, a little detail he omitted.)

Surprisingly, the dean of men deemed our response to the snowballs inappropriate. I suspect that since it was 20 degrees outside, all the girls on the front porch got a thorough soaking with water that quickly froze. Clare's starting the whole thing was one factor in the dean's lively talk with us about our wrongdoing.

My point in telling you this story is the same as Jacob's. Since Clare did not tell us he threw the first snowball, it caused trouble he could not control. When we respond to suffering with evil, that always happens.

Dearest Bethany, I urge you to follow Paul's directive for handling your anger and your desire for revenge. Recognize the anger, hurt, and urge for revenge, and then determine your response. Just do not make it an emotional one. By doing so, you will save yourself and possibly others a lot of unnecessary trouble.

I love you,
Dad

The Challenge of Responding to Suffering with Evil

My Heart Response to Suffering

1. Who do you blame for your suffering? Which of the two ways that anger can handle us—stuffing it or venting it—marks how you customarily let anger handle you?
2. What would it look like for you to "be angry but do not sin"? How would your response to your suffering have to change?
3. In your current suffering, which of the four life lessons are you facing as you pursue healing your heart from the suffering? How can you effectively remind yourself of that lesson so you will avoid giving in to it?

Letter 23

TRUSTING GOD IN SUFFERING

Dear Bethany,

You are right, Bethany, it takes a lot of emotional energy to stay mad at God (or anyone). Indeed, when we spend emotional energy being angry, the usual result is emotional exhaustion, which leads to depression. I want to spare you any unneeded battle with sadness, so in this letter I will teach you what I've learned about trusting God amid suffering. It is easy to trust God after the suffering is over. How to do it in the midst of suffering is the challenge you are facing.

The passage I will use to guide you in trusting God while you suffer is Romans 11:33–12:2. Here's what you need to know about the setting of the verses. Romans 1–8 are Paul's explanation of all that salvation from sin through faith in Christ involves. Then in Romans 9–11, he explains what God is doing with the nation of Israel while continuing to bring Gentiles to faith in Christ. In Romans 11:28–32, Paul declares that both Jews and Gentiles receive God's mercy. That is the setting of Romans 11:33–12:2.

Paul's awareness that salvation is available to all people everywhere leads him to worship (Rom. 11:33–36). That worship concludes the first section of the book (chapters 1–11). Beginning with chapter 12, Paul tells us how we live out that salvation in our day-to-day lives (chapters 12–16).

In your suffering, Bethany, you can rely on God's supply of mercy (Rom. 11:32, 12:1). Mercy is synonymous with all Paul said about salvation in chapters 1–11. His point is that if he were to use one word to describe all he presented in those chapters, that word would be mercy. Then, Paul calls us to an appreciation and apprehension of God's mercy for daily Christian living in his exhortation in Romans 12:1–2. By highlighting mercy's role in our past and our future, Paul reminds us that God's mercy flows into our lives all the time. Not even our suffering is greater than the mercy God sends into our lives. In other words, we continually live under God's mercy toward us.

While we want relief from suffering, God sends us his mercy as our refuge in suffering. Let me say that again because it is important to understand. In our suffering, we want relief, but God gives us the refuge of his mercy in the suffering. (You can see that in many psalms.)

If you know God's mercy is ever flowing into your life in your suffering, then you can trust God's character despite the mysteries of your suffering. This is the focus of Romans 11:33 that says, "Oh, the depth of the riches and wisdom and knowledge of God! How unsearchable are his judgments and how inscrutable his ways!" Because both his judgments (why he does what he does) and his ways (what he does) are beyond our ability to know, we struggle to understand the mysteries involved in our suffering.

If you know that an unending supply of mercy is yours, then when you cannot make sense of your suffering, you can trust

God because he is doing more than you know. And because his ways are both unsearchable and inscrutable, unless he reveals to you what he is doing, you will misunderstand what he is doing. In your suffering, you need to remind yourself that God sees the big picture of your suffering while you see only the part of it that happens to you day by day. His perspective is always bigger than yours (Rom. 11:33).

But we hate not knowing why we are suffering. Because we want to understand why we are suffering—we think understanding why we suffer will make the suffering easier to bear, but it doesn't—we fall into two errors, both addressed in Romans 11:34–35. The first error is to tell God what he ought to be doing in our suffering rather than trust him in it (Rom. 11:34). The second error is to rebel against God in our suffering rather than trust him in it (Rom. 11:35). Thus, verse 35 addresses the challenge of responding to suffering with evil. Trust God instead of dictating to him what he should do with your suffering. You need to trust God rather than demand relief from him. You can trust God in your suffering because he will supply you with all the mercy you need in the suffering. You can also trust that he knows what he is doing in your suffering.

Let me say this again, Bethany. In your suffering, God continually gives you his all-sufficient mercy. Look for it because it is there. The outpouring of his mercy will guard you against questioning him and keep you from rebelling against him.

If you know that all his mercy is flowing into all your suffering, you will trust him for who he is and what he does that is consistent with his character (i.e., showing mercy). No matter what your circumstances are, you can trust him. Trust is possible when you recognize his involvement in everything. Trust frees you to keep your focus on him rather than on the circumstances of your suffering. Trust keeps you from blaming others for your suffering. Focusing on the circumstances of your suffering and blaming others for your suffering are two of the biggest challenges you will face. Trusting God for who he is and what he does in your life, even in your suffering, will keep you adjusting to your suffering rather than give way to anger or despair.

Here is a mistake many people make. When suffering comes into someone's life, they often will try to satisfy the head part of the gyrating seesaw by reasoning from the suffering to God. That means they will let suffering shape what they believe about God.

What I encourage you to do is the opposite of that. In your suffering, start by reminding yourself of what you know about God, and then let that view of God shape your response to the suffering. That is the pattern of Romans 11:33–12:2 that I describe in this letter.

As I said before, in your suffering, one of the most important decisions you will make is your answer to this question: "Where is my gaze, and where is my glance?" If you gaze at God and glance at your suffering, you will outlast your suffering by moving on through it. If you glance at God and gaze at your suffering, your suffering will overwhelm you. Your ability to identify where your gaze is and where your glance is during your suffering will determine how your suffering affects you.

Whatever form your suffering has taken, whatever form it takes now, and whatever form it might take tomorrow, you can trust God because he can lead you through what you are facing. In your suffering, you can trust God because he governs all you face. God and his mercy are always greater than the suffering we experience in life.

I know this is true because Romans 11:33–36 prepared me for it and sustained me in walking the Cancer Road in 2006 and 2007. Because you were already out of our home during that time, you may not know this story.

Following a week at a post-doctoral seminar at Denver Seminary in January 2006, I came home convinced that I needed to add meditating on a Bible passage to my spiritual habits. I meditated on Romans 11:33–12:2. I read it every morning for six months, journaling about what I saw in the passage each day.

On July 27, 2006, when I woke up from a colonoscopy to learn I had colon cancer, this thought came to me: "This is what Romans 11:33–12:2 was all about, wasn't it, Lord?" Through all the treatments during the next nine months, my six months of meditating on the passage kept me from anger and kept me from asking God why. It kept me from second-guessing what God was doing in my life while I walked the Cancer Road.

Bethany, I suggest that you do the same. Spend the next month reading and rereading this passage in Romans. See what you learn from it about trusting God in your suffering. I promise that you will see things you've never seen before as you meditate on these verses.

I love you,
Dad

My Heart Response to Suffering

1. What new thought about God emerged for you as you read this letter?
2. Which of the challenges of suffering is your challenge right now?
3. Today, where is your gaze and where is your glance?
4. What action step can you take to remind yourself to trust God as you go through your suffering right now?

Letter 24

WORSHIPING GOD IN SUFFERING

Dear Bethany,

No, I did not forget to include my thoughts about Romans 12:1–2 in my last letter. I gave you enough to think about in that letter, so today I am writing this letter to explain how Romans 12:1–2 helps you worship God in your suffering. Are you ready? Here we go.

As I mentioned last time, Romans 11:33–12:2 are the transitional verses between all Paul said about God providing salvation (chapters 1–11) and all he said about living a Christian life (chapters 12–16). Paul uses the phrase "the mercies of God" in Romans 12:1 to summarize all he wrote in chapters 1–11. Understanding that God's mercy flows unendingly into your life serves as corrective lenses for your vision of who he is and what he is doing when you suffer.

How does knowing God's mercy flows to you in your suffering help you choose what you do in your suffering? According to Romans 12:1, the answer to that question is that the knowledge of God's ever-flowing mercy leads you to worship him. Worshiping while suffering means you make God, not your circumstances, the focus of your gaze. Worshiping while suffering means you remind yourself of who God is, knowing he is fully aware of what you are facing (this is the "wisdom" of Romans 11:33). Worshiping while suffering means you know his ways are fully trustworthy, even when you cannot understand them (the "inscrutable ways" of Roman 11:33). Worshiping while suffering means you believe God is fully sovereign over what you are facing (Rom. 11:36). Worshiping while suffering means you give yourself up and over to God each day the suffering lasts (the "present your bodies as a living sacrifice" of Romans 12:1).

Worshiping while suffering means you change your thinking about what God is doing in your suffering. Look for the mercy he is sending instead of focusing on how he doesn't relieve your suffering quickly or in the way you want. Worshiping while suffering means you change your mind about God's leading in your life by adjusting to your circumstances. In all these ways, worship becomes the fuel for walking through suffering.

My favorite Puritan writer, William Gurnall, put it this way: "My Father is wiser than I am. His wisdom will prompt him what and when to send and his fatherly affections for me will neither permit him to deny anything that is good, nor miss the time that is fitting."[1] Adjusting your thinking about God will be the biggest challenge you face in your suffering. But according

---

1 William Gurnall, *The Christian in Complete Armour*. Peabody: Hendrickson Publishing House, 1:42.

to Romans 12:2, when I pursue personal transformation through the renewing of my mind, I discover how good God's will truly is. How can that be?

Suffering teaches me that what I really want in my suffering is God himself. Our society tries to persuade us that in order to have a meaningful life, we need three things. First, our society continually tells us what we need in order to have a meaningful life. For example, society tells us what we need is a certain amount of annual income. Second, our society tells us that what we need for a meaningful life is to be someone important such as a good public speaker. Third, our society tells us that what we need for a meaningful life is to have something like a new car. However, suffering exposes the lie behind all these messages because doing what I think needs done may not change my suffering. Suffering shows me that becoming something I am not does not relieve my suffering today. Suffering also shows me that what I have does not relieve the suffering I face. Suffering strips all those misbeliefs from me so I can discover that what I really want in my suffering is God.

Suffering reveals my preference for God's will over mine. Suffering teaches me this lesson, Bethany, when all my efforts to change, escape, or stop my suffering fail. When nothing I do ends the suffering, I find that what I want is God's will to be done in my life.

Bethany, the hard thing about learning these lessons from suffering is that we learn them only when our suffering lasts. Suffering must last in order to strip away our demands for relief and show us the futility of our own efforts to make the suffering stop. Only when our suffering lasts do we discover that what we really want is God himself. Only when suffering lasts do we learn that what we really want is God's will, not ours. We simply do not learn those lessons when suffering comes and goes quickly from our lives.

Let me close this letter with this thought from another of my favorite Puritans, Jeremiah Burroughs. He wrote, "There can be no afflictions in this world as great as the mercies I have."[2] That, dear Bethany, is exactly what I believe Romans 11:33–12:2 can teach us.

I love you,
Dad

---

2 Jeremiah Burroughs, *The Rare Jewel of Christian Contentment*, Carlisle: The Banner of Truth Trust, p. 201.

My Heart Response to Suffering

1. What is the toughest challenge to worshiping God in your suffering that you face today?
2. Which of the benefits of worshiping God in suffering helps you meet that challenge?
3. What aids to worship can you use to strengthen your ability to worship God in your suffering? Some examples are keeping a thankfulness journal, keeping worship music on as you go through your day, reading the Psalms, and more.
4. Which of the two lessons we learn when suffering lasts is the primary lesson you are learning in your suffering?

Letter 25

THE HELPFUL PRACTICE OF LAMENTING: PART 1

Dearest Bethany,

I knew after you read my last letter that you would want to know what to do if you can't give in to your hurt and anger. What does that mean? Lament is the ancient practice of telling God all about your hurt and your anger. It is the biblical way of being angry but not giving way to the anger by sinning.

Did you know that almost half of the psalms are laments? That's true.[1] When you read the psalms, you find there are two kinds of laments. First, you discover the laments of the people, the community of faith (Ps. 80). Second, you find the laments of the individual (Ps. 142). For both kinds, there are three key elements to a lament.[2]

First, a lament expresses the pain of hurting. I know I do not need to convince you that suffering brings pain. Indeed, I write

---

[1] I first learned this in Dr. Ronald B. Allen's Hebrew language class on the Psalms in the fall of 1981 at Western Seminary, Portland, Oregon. You can learn about it in his book *Praise! A Matter of Life and Breath*, Nashville: Thomas Nelson. 1980.
[2] Ronald B. Allen's Hebrew language class on the Psalms, fall 1981, at Western Seminary, Portland, Oregon.

these letters to help you know how to deal with the pain of your suffering. The second element of a lament is that the hurting person feels like God does not care. In one of my early letters I told you that pain distorts your view of God. This aspect of lament tells God how confused you are about what is going on in your life and the spiritual struggle involved in finding his goodness in your pain. The third element of a lament is the complaint that your foe, or your circumstance, seems to win the battle for your continued faith in God.

In the Psalms, these elements of a lament turn into prayer. A prayer of lament found in a psalm asks God to act in three ways. First, the psalmist asks God to hear his prayer. Second, the hurting person asks God to save him from his current predicament. Finally, the person asks God to deal with those who cause him to suffer.

These factors are the reason I tell you to read and reread the psalms. Why? When you read the psalms you will find language for your hurt, your pain, your desires, and your faith in God in suffering. The psalms will teach you how to pray when you hurt. In allowing the psalms to shape your prayers, you avoid the problems that come with stuffing your anger rather than expressing it. The laments show you how to express it so you are angry but do not sin.

Reading the psalms will also teach you to remember God's goodness in your pain. Remember that half of the psalms are laments, and the rest are praises. When you hurt, especially on the bad days, you need reminding even in your pain that God remains good. The psalms will teach you that too.

Okay, I can hear you asking, "Yes, but how?" I recommend that you read the psalms using one of two plans. You can read two psalms a day, which will get you through all 150 psalms in 75 days, or about two and a half months. Or you can read five psalms a day, which will get you through all 150 psalms in 30 days.

The Helpful Practice of Lamenting: Part 1

If you choose to read two psalms a day, I suggest you read them from the outside in or the inside out. Reading them from the outside in means you start with Psalm 1 and Psalm 150 the first day. The next day you read Psalm 2 and Psalm 149. You continue that pattern until you read all 150 psalms. Reading them from the inside out means you start with Psalm 75 and 76 and then read Psalm 74 and 77, continuing the pattern until you read all 150 psalms.

If you choose to read five psalms a day, use the day of the month for the number of the first psalm you read. Then add 30 to that first psalm's number. After you read the second psalm, add 30 again to get to the third psalm. Using this method looks like this: Psalm 23, 53, 83, 113, and 143 are the psalms you will read on the 23rd day of the month. On the 24th, you will read Psalm 24, 54, 84, 114, and 144. Get the idea? You do not have to read all five psalms at once. You can read two in the morning, one at lunchtime, and two that night, or whatever suits the rhythm of your life. When one month has passed, you will start all over again. Since you will not be at the same emotional place on June 1st as you were on May 1st, you will notice different truths as you read all 150 again. I used the five-a-day method for years to keep myself emotionally healthy. By the way, if you use the 5 psalms a day method, skip reading Ps. 119, the longest chapter in the Bible, and read it when a month has 31 days.

Bethany, I also suggest that you keep using your journal as you read through the psalms. Use it to capture what you see as you read. Use it to record your heart's responses to what you read. Use it to write out your own prayers of lament. Then when a new season of suffering comes, you can refer to your journal to remind you of all God taught you as you walked with him through the psalms.

I love you, Bethany,
Dad

My Heart Response to Suffering

1. Were you surprised to learn that almost half of the psalms are laments? Why or why not?
2. Which element of the lamenting fits your current suffering the most? What about that element caused you to identify with it today?
3. Which suggested method of reading the psalms while you hurt will work for you? Once you select your method of reading the psalms, determine when you will read through them. Are you a morning person or a night owl? Use your knowledge of when you are most alert during the day to guide you in determining when you will read the psalms.
4. How do you plan to record what you find in the psalms? Do you do better with a written record in a journal or capturing it on your phone or laptop? Use whatever works best for you.

Letter 26

THE HELPFUL PRACTICE OF LAMENTING: PART 2

Dear Bethany,

This is my second letter about the helpful practice of lamenting. One question I didn't answer was this: "Why bother with lamenting at all?" Here's my answer in four parts.

First, lamenting purifies our hearts from a love of the world. This insight comes from 1 John 2:15–16, which says, . Those verses state: "Do not love the world or the things in the world. If anyone loves the world, the love of the Father is not in him. For all that is in the world - the desires of the flesh and the desires of the eyes and pride of life - is not from the Father but is from the world."

John contrasts "the world" with God's desired way of thinking and living. John is not telling you and me to not love a walk in the woods, to spend a weekend at Bandon, Oregon's beach, or a fine summer at the park concert. John argues that those things are in competition for the love we should exclusively have for God. We learn from the suffering we endure that relying on the lust of the flesh, the lust of the eyes, or pride for the source of our life or significance is futile, as they cannot fix it. God purifies our hearts in times of suffering to prioritize our love for him.

Second, lamenting teaches us contentment comes from subtraction, not addition. I learned this truth from Jeremiah Burroughs, my favorite Puritan, in his book, *The Rare Jewel of Christian Contentment*.[1] Americans associate having more with being happier. Suffering, however, shows us what I tell my clients, "Externals cannot fix internals." When we come into suffering, the desires of the flesh, the desires of the eyes, or our pride cannot relieve our heart's pain. In our suffering, we need something to lessen that pain. Whatever we have, whatever we plan to have someday, or whatever we take pride in simply cannot reach the deep inner ache in our soul. Through suffering, we learn to be content even in loss. Bethany, I plan to say more about that in another letter, but let's go on and look at another benefit of lamenting.

Third, lamenting teaches us to reset our affections on things above. This benefit matches what Paul writes in Colossians 3:1–4. "If then you have been raised with Christ, seek the things that are above, where Christ is, seated at the right hand of God. Set your minds on things that are above, not on things that are on earth. For you have died, and your life is hidden with Christ in God. When Christ who is your life appears, then you also will appear with him in glory."

Each day we choose what we pay attention to. Will I be preoccupied with my circumstances or with Christ's past and present actions on my behalf? This goes back to what I wrote in an earlier letter. Where is my gaze, and where is my glance?

---

[1] Jeremiah Burroughs, *The Rare Jewel of Christian Contentment*, Carlisle: Banner of Truth Trust, p. 36ff.

Suffering trains me to keep my gaze on Christ, not my painful circumstances.

Finally, lamenting reminds us of the brevity of life and the lastingness of eternity. That is Paul's point in 2 Corinthians 4:17–18. "For this light momentary affliction is preparing for us an eternal weight of glory beyond all comparison, as we look not to the things that are seen but to the things that are unseen. For the things that are seen are transient, but the things that are unseen are eternal."

Notice the contrast Paul sets up. The lightness of our current suffering—and yes, I know suffering rarely feels light—is in contrast to the weightiness of what is coming in eternity. Paul also contrasts the momentary nature of suffering with the eternal glory that is on its way to us. Finally, he contrasts the visible things with the invisible things. Therefore, ask yourself, "Am I focusing on my pain or am I focusing on the future that awaits me?" That is the gaze-versus-glance focus we must choose every day. Pain will always pull our perspective to our suffering because it seems unending (remember the five distortions of pain I mentioned in an earlier letter). We have the power to reject pain's distortion and trust in Christ.

Bethany, in addition to these four benefits of lamenting our pain in our suffering, remember that Job, David, Jeremiah, and Jesus all lamented at one painful point or another in their lives. If they needed to lament, don't you also need to lament?

Keep pressing on through this!

I love you, Bethany,

Dad

P.S. We know that learning how to lament is important when one entire book of the Bible is called Lamentations!

My Heart Response to Suffering

1. What causes you to lament in your suffering today?
2. How does that knowing Job, David, Jeremiah, and Jesus lamented help you give yourself permission to lament your suffering?
3. What aspect of the four ways lament helps us connect with God is most meaningful to you today? Why is that so?

Letters 27

THE PAIN OF SELF-INFLICTED SUFFERING

Dear Bethany,

    You ask a good question when you ask, "How do I move beyond all this when I know I caused part of it myself?" What a great question! Sadly, all of us know what it is like to create our own suffering. Whether it is speaking a harsh word that wounds a friend or underestimating how much our employer should withhold in taxes and we suddenly owe a lot of money to the IRS, we all know what it is like to live with self-inflicted suffering.

    In this letter, I want to think with you about the pain of self-inflicted suffering by studying the life of a man who, for all his successes in life, failed miserably in the first third of his life because of self-inflicted suffering. This man was Moses. Before God used him to lead Israel out of Egypt, Moses created unnecessary suffering for himself. I want to point out the process that led to Moses's self-inflicted suffering. So, Bethany, think with me about all the words that explain his downfall before God used him mightily in the Exodus.

In self-inflicted suffering, the starting point is always talent. Acts 7:22 tells us, "Moses was educated in all the wisdom of the Egyptians and he was proficient in speaking and in action." Thus, on many levels, he was a man of talents.

After talent comes privilege. All of Moses's education and training made him a good fit for a government leader. He was an up and comer, a man who would go somewhere in life because of all the privileges afforded him by being part of the royal household (Acts 7:21).

After privilege comes pride. The evidence of Moses's pride was what he did when he saw the Egyptian slave master cruelly beating an Israelite. After checking to see if anyone was looking, Moses killed the slave master and then buried him in the sand. Moses's pride told him, "I know what to do about this injustice," so he did what his proud heart told him to do. His pride made him self-reliant. Instead of reporting the slave master to his superior, Moses took the matter into his own hands. Self-reliance flows out of pride and makes us think, "I've got this."

The problem is that when I am proud and self-reliant, I act impulsively. For Moses, the impulsive action was murdering the Egyptian and then hiding his body. In his impulsiveness, Moses did not consider the possibility that someone saw the whole thing. But someone did.

Our impulsive action always leads to a crisis. The next day, Moses saw two Hebrews fighting. When he tried to intervene, one of them asked if he was going to kill them like he had killed the Egyptian (Exod. 2:13–14). The crisis for Moses was what he would do next. He thought he literally got away with murder, only to discover that it was public knowledge. Now what would he do?

You see, Bethany, a crisis born out of our talent, privilege, pride, self-reliance, and impulsiveness always exposes where we

The Pain of Self-Inflicted Suffering

placed our trust in ourselves. The pain of self-inflicted suffering carries with it the knowledge that it did not have to be that way. Our self-reliance exposes our failure, just like it did for Moses.

That's the next word: failure. Moses knew his failure would soon be known to the entire royal household, placing his life at risk. That is exactly what happened when Pharaoh heard about it (Exod. 2:14–15). He knew he would experience the wrath of the Pharaoh with the loss of his privileged position as a member of the royal household.

The next word that describes the pain of self-inflicted suffering is shame. As I wrote about in an earlier letter, shame is the gap between the ideal me that I carry in my head and the real me that I truly am. Misplaced trust in ourselves always leads to shame. When shame hits, you will want to run and find a place to hide. That is the flee response of a Spin Cycle. For Moses, that place was 40 years in the desert in the land of Midian. Your encounter with shame will move you to despair. It will make you think you will never put your life back together.

Your shame leads you to demand that God put an end to your suffering. While the Bible does not give an example of Moses doing this, hours in the counseling office with deeply hurting people taught me that this is the next word that describes our anguish in self-inflicted suffering. We demand that God put an end to the suffering now! Where does being demanding take us?

The next word is surrender. When God does not act to end the suffering, we learn to surrender our anger, our hurt, and our pride because he is not listening to our demands.

And then God steps in.

How will you know when God steps into the middle of your self-inflicted suffering? You will know it because you will give up fleeing from your suffering and shame. You will stop blaming other people for the mess you know you created (that's the fight response). Know, however, Bethany, that in your effort to find relief from your suffering and shame, often by using something to numb the pain, this blaming of others differs from lamenting your suffering. Why? When you lament, you tell God you are hurting and why, but you leave it to God how he moves into your suffering to lessen it, lift you out of it, and shape your character by it.

Silence—that's the next word. When you are done with your screaming at God to fix it, when you no longer use your words to blame others, when all your reasons for what you did are exhausted, God meets you with his silence. In his silence, he teaches you that he, not you, is in charge of your life. When you are silent, you know you are truly broken and ready for God to remake you.

You are ready for God to show up and remake you because you are humbled. You no longer trust in your talent, your privileges, or yourself. You've become humbled to the point of depending on God, not yourself.

How will you know when you've given up relying on yourself and are depending on God? The next word—acceptance—explains that. When your self-inflicted suffering accomplishes God's work in your life, you will accept where you are because of your suffering. You will accept that your life won't be what you thought it would be before the self-inflicted suffering occurred. Moses, after 40 years of being a shepherd, likely accepted that as his life, not the life of an heir to the throne of Egypt.

When you move through this process, the last word is broken—broken of your pride in your talents and privileges in life; broken of your prideful self-reliance that makes you think you do not need the help of other people; broken of your impulsiveness

The Pain of Self-Inflicted Suffering

because you saw the havoc it created; broken of your paralyzing sense of failure and your crippling sense of shame; broken of your demand that life go your way and at your pace; broken by God's silence so you are humbled and you accept your life as is rather than the way you wanted it to be.

Here is the path to self-inflicted suffering. Talent leads to privilege. Privilege leads to pride. Pride leads to self-reliance. Self-reliance leads to impulsiveness. Impulsiveness leads to crisis. Crisis leads to failure. Failure leads to shame. Shame leads to being demanding. Being demanding leads to God's silence. God's silence leads to humility. Humility leads to acceptance. And all this leads to brokenness.

What happens next? That's what I will show you in my next letter.

I love you,
Dad

My Heart Response to Suffering

1. Is your current suffering the result of self-inflicted pain? If it is, what did you do to create the suffering you now face?
2. What word describes where you are in your self-inflicted suffering? How does that word fit the challenge of what you are facing now? What emotions go with that word?
3. What evidence of your silence and being humbled because of your suffering is appearing in your life? Or are you demanding an end to your suffering?
4. If you are silent and humbled, what does brokenness look like in your life?

Letter 28

REBUILT BY SUFFERING

Dear Bethany,

I am glad to know you see yourself emerging from the pain you've felt for the last year. I am glad you are seeing God take the humility that suffering produced in you. Most of all, I am thrilled you are identifying the ways God makes himself known to you.

I promised to tell you what happens next after your self-inflicted suffering breaks you. Moses is again our teacher about what comes next. You can find what happened in his life in Exodus 3:1–4:17.

When we are broken by our suffering, God can get our attention in ways he could not before. For Moses, this was the burning bush (Exod. 3:1–4). The unique feature of the burning bush was not its burning. In the heat of the desert, small bushes could spontaneously combust, but it was God speaking to Moses from the bush that was unusual. Moses was shepherding when this remarkable event happened on an ordinary day. Once we break, no day remains ordinary. Any day is an opportunity for God to appear.

As God reveals himself to Moses, God tells him three things he needs to know (Exod. 3:4–10). First, God is holy (Exod. 3:5). God is unlike us in his ways and in what he does (Isa. 55:8–9). God sees suffering differently than we do. He sees how he can work in our lives through suffering in ways we cannot imagine. Moses was about to learn how true that is.

Second, Moses learns that God is a promise-keeper (Exod. 3:6). God tells Moses he is the God of Abraham (Gen. 15:13–14), Isaac (Gen. 28:13–15), and Jacob (Gen. 48:4, 15–16). To each of these three ancestors, God made the same promise—their descendants would occupy the land God would give them. In the promise to Abraham, God declares he will bring the Hebrews back to the land of promise after they have suffered in Egypt. God's invoking his relationship to each of the three patriarchs shows us that not even our suffering stops God from keeping his promises.

Finally, God reveals to Moses that he is the man who will accomplish the return to the Promised Land. However, for that to occur, Moses needs to go back to Pharaoh, the man he once escaped from. Since the pain of self-inflicted suffering broke Moses, he was now available for the work God wanted to do through him. Available is the first word in God's work of rebuilding us.

Although brokenness makes us available to God, our normal response to becoming available for what is next in our lives is fear. Moses fears being available when he says in Exodus 3:11, "Who am I that I should go to Pharaoh and bring the children of Israel out of Egypt?" This is what Moses is really saying: "God, you know my past disqualifies me from usefulness."

Why does Moses believe that? Perhaps he believes that because his gaze is on his spectacular failure instead of what is ahead of him. Remember, that is the way pain distorts our view of the future. Once we fail, we believe we are no longer qualified to be useful to God.

God reassures Moses by saying, "I will be with you" (Exod. 3:12). God would achieve this through Moses. Our past failures and self-inflicted suffering do not disqualify us from being available for what God wants to do next in our lives. God is not limited by our past or our pain.

Although God strives to redirect Moses's focus from himself to God, Moses remains governed by his fear. He objects to being available by telling God that he doesn't know what he will say to the people of Israel so they will believe that God called him to do this. He fears that he does not have the answers to the problems that will arise when he leads the people out of their bondage. Like Moses, we doubt our problem-solving abilities due to our self-inflicted suffering. After all, we say, it was our attempted solution to a problem that led to our brokenness. We don't want to experience that pain again. We want to avoid facing people such as Pharaoh who witnessed our failure. We don't want to experience the shame of being exposed again.

God answers this fear by telling Moses to tell them who he is (Exod. 3:14–17). Specifically, God told Moses to tell the nation that God remains the promise-keeper and that he would keep his promise to their ancestors. That, God assures Moses, will be enough for them to believe that he sent Moses to them. What Moses did not yet believe was that he knew enough about God right then to help his people. That is true for us too. Because we were unwise in the past, we think we will be unwise in the future. Although broken, we remain afraid. We are afraid because our gaze is on ourselves, not on God.

That fear continues in Moses's heart. His next objection to being available to God is that the people will ignore him (Exod. 4:1). Knowing the pain of failure, he does not want to fail again. He does not belief he can survive being rejected. The temptation in our brokenness is to equate brokenness with insignificance. Being ignored is one kind of pain, but being rejected is what we dread. Moses feared both.

This objection didn't deter God. He patiently and thoroughly explained to Moses all the ways his divine power will work through him (Exod. 4:2–10). Moses mistakenly thinks the Exodus is his responsibility. God tells him that it isn't. We need to learn the lesson that our brokenness prepares us to learn—that God can use us when we leave the results to him.

God's answers to Moses's three fears did not release Moses from two deeper and darker fears. Now, Moses expresses his belief that he does not have what it takes to do the job. "I am not eloquent . . . I am slow of speech" (Exod. 4:10). Moses tells God that he doesn't have the skills he needs for this to happen. Moses's focus is still on himself, not on God. So once again, God redirects Moses and says, "Who has made man's mouth?" (Exod. 4:11). God knows what skills Moses has, so this objection does not dissuade God from his plan to use Moses. God can use Moses as he is now, not someday. We need to learn the same lesson. In our brokenness, we tend to tell God "not yet" when he shows us the next step in our lives. When he does so, God will use you as you are, not what you will be on some far-off someday.

One last fear lurks within Moses. It is a fear of comparing himself to others. Moses pleads for God to send someone else—anyone else (Exod. 4:13). His fear stems from the belief that he is not as qualified as others for this task. He believes he is less than other people.

When we compare ourselves to other people, we either see ourselves as superior to them or less than they are. Bethany, in all my years of being a pastor and counselor, I have yet to meet someone who compares themselves to others and thinks they have equal skills, knowledge, and talents. Moses falls into the trap of seeing himself as less than those he compares himself with. That is a counterfeit of genuine humility.

Humility knows we have strengths and weaknesses. We have expertise in some areas and are inexperienced in others. Humility is understanding our limitations. Only brokenness teaches us both.

In his exasperation with this last objection, God gives Moses a teammate—his brother, Aaron (Exod. 4:14). Aaron, not Moses, will do the speaking that is needed to complete the Exodus. What Moses needed to learn was that God supplies those he uses with the companions they need. God knows what we need to learn in our self-inflicted suffering. We need others to help us do what we can't.

Now, at last, with all his fearful objections answered, Moses is rebuilt from his self-inflicted pain. He has moved from prideful self-reliance to God-dependence. Our lives can only be rebuilt if the same thing happens to us. The rebuilding process looks like this: attention, fear, rebuilding. Our ability to move through the rebuilding process means we need to shift our gaze from what we fear to God. That is what our self-inflicted suffering is meant to do in our lives.

Bethany, if God did this for Moses, never doubt that he can and will do it for you.

I love you,
Dad

My Heart Response to Suffering

1. How is God trying to get your attention today? How is he getting your attention for what he has in store for you?
2. Which of Moses's five fearful objections do you find arising in your heart? In what way do you connect with the fear Moses faced?
3. How are you learning to take your eyes off yourself and your suffering and put them on God? Why is that an essential next step for you?
4. Who has God already strategically placed in your life who can help you walk into the future God has for you? How can you express gratitude for their presence in your life?

Letter 29

WHEN SUFFERING LASTS

Dear Bethany,

I fully understand your frustration at how long it is taking you to feel better, to feel like the old you. As I stated in a previous letter, when you suffer, you want relief—the end of the suffering as soon as possible—but God gives you refuge. God's refuge comes to you as you cling to his promises and as you keep your gaze on him rather than your suffering.

As you are discovering, suffering often lasts longer than you or I want it to. In this letter, I want to pass on to you what I learned God does when our suffering lasts. These lessons are from Romans 5:1–5, so it will be good if you have a Bible handy and open to that passage.

When suffering lasts, God uses the suffering to transform your character (Rom. 5:3–5). This perspective protects you from the mistaken thinking that you are suffering because God is mad at you. That is a mistake in thinking because Romans 5:1 tells you that you have peace with God through your faith in

Jesus Christ. You have that peace because through your faith in Christ, God has declared you not guilty of your sins. That is what justification means. So your suffering is not in your life because God is angry at you.

Furthermore, God does not send suffering into your life because you are not measuring up to his commands or his will. We find that truth in Romans 5:2, which declares that we stand in grace. Standing in God's grace means we are not under a system of performance-based acceptance or measuring up. Our justification is based on what Christ did, not what we do. When suffering enters your life, it is not because God is mad at you or because you failed to measure up. It comes to transform your character.

How does suffering transform your character? The suffering needs to be long-lasting for that to happen. Why? When suffering lasts, it causes you to hang onto God and believe his promises. Romans 5:3 says that happens because when suffering lasts, it produces endurance—perseverance—in you. When suffering lasts, you learn just how much you need God. Knowing how much you need him sends you to the Bible to discover more about him and find his heart-strengthening promises (see 2 Peter 1:3–4 for how his promises provide heart-strength). As I wrote before, God is always working to make you more like Christ, as Romans 8:29 declares. Suffering is one tool he uses to sculpt you into a greater likeness of your Lord.

When suffering lasts, it changes your expectations about how life works. Suffering shows you that your way of handling life does not work. Since it doesn't work, you need to seek a different way of living. Romans 5:3–5 reveals that other way of living, which is described as hope. So suffering shifts your hope away from expecting your way of living to bring you a fulfilling life. Instead, biblical hope means you believe you can be a different person because God works in your life through suffering. Paul tells you that a transformed character, or the hope of being a different person after the suffering than you were before it, means you learn how to love. As you go through the process of character transformation by your suffering, you will grow in your ability to love God and love people. And the end of suffering's character transformation process is joy (Rom. 5:3). You will have joy because you discovered God is at work in your life in the suffering.

In my next letter, dearest daughter, I will explain how we persevere in suffering.

I love you,

Dad

My Heart Response to Suffering

1. What is your response to learning that God does not send suffering into your life because he is mad at you? Describe how that fear may have been showing up in your life before you read this letter. How does that knowledge impact your self-image?

2. What is your response to learning that God does not send suffering into your life because you did not measure up to some standard? How has your suffering made you feel ashamed? How does this lesson about suffering release you to no longer judge yourself?

3. In your suffering, God transforms your character. What aspect of your character do you think God is trying to change by your current suffering? Why do you think your suffering is working to change that character quality in you?

4. From your suffering, how do you hope to love better? How would loving better look in your life?

Letter 30

HOW TO PERSEVERE WHILE SUFFERING

Dear Bethany,

In this letter, I will answer your question: "How do I persevere while I suffer?" Based on our phone call last night, I know you are there. Your suffering has lasted far longer than you thought it would. Your head-heart seesaw still gyrates, although not as wildly as it did at the beginning of your suffering. You told me during our phone call that since the suffering continues, you want to learn what you need to learn from it. One lesson suffering teaches is our need to persevere. Here is what I know about persevering in suffering, as promised in my last letter. All I will tell you in this letter comes from the Apostle Paul's suffering. He describes the impact his suffering had on him in 2 Corinthians 1:1–11.

Bethany, you learn to persevere in suffering by not letting your suffering define your life. Paul begins 2 Corinthians by stating who he is—an apostle of Jesus Christ—and that he is an apostle by the will of God (2 Cor. 1:1–2). He refrains from identifying himself as Paul who suffered much for you or as Paul the apostle who was traumatized by what happened to him in Philippi. Instead, he aligns himself with his identity in his relationship with Christ and God the Father. You need to do the same. He knew his relationship with Christ was greater than any suffering he endured.

Persevering in suffering comes from reminding yourself that your suffering does not define who you are. God does that for you. You are his child by faith in Christ (John 1:12–13). And your suffering does not define what you can do. Although Paul suffered in Philippi, he kept on with his ministry of making Christ known. Suffering also does not define where you are stuck in your pain. We can feel stuck in the pain, but we aren't. Paul tells us why that is so.

If you don't let suffering define who you are, then what do you do? You worship. That is what Paul does in 2 Corinthians 1:3–4. He learned that worship is the fuel for persevering. Worship frees you from feeling stuck in your pain. The most important thing in your suffering, Bethany, is your view of God. If your view is clear, you will worship. If your suffering changes your view of God, then you cannot worship. Once again, the real question in your suffering is this: where is your gaze, and where is your glance? If you keep your gaze on God, you will worship amidst your pain. If your gaze is on the suffering, you will not worship. The key is to keep your gaze on God and only glance at your suffering.

Notice what Paul says your view of God can be. In 2 Corinthians 1:3, he tells you three ways God is present with you in your suffering. God is your father; therefore, your suffering does not change his relationship with you. God is merciful; therefore, your suffering does not change his love for you. God is the God of all comfort; therefore, your suffering does not change his care for you.

Why do I say suffering does not change God's care for you? Notice how verse 3 ends and how verse 4 begins. Paul contrasts God as the "God of all comfort" with "in all our affliction." The contrast means there is no suffering that is greater than God's ability to comfort you when you hurt. There are simply no exceptions to God's ability to comfort you in your suffering. Look around for the evidence of God's comforting love for you, and you will find it.

One factor you need to consider as you look for God's comfort is that comfort comes from anticipating what God can do in your suffering. If you focus on what he did not do, you will not find his comfort. Instead, you will face the challenge of losing sight of him because of disappointment or bitterness. (If you are looking at what he did not do, go back and read Letters #3 and #18 on losing sight of God because you suffer.)

Bethany, another habit that promotes perseverance is aligning with God's purpose in your suffering. Paul discovered that no suffering is ever wasted by God. He is not capricious in handing out pain to us. Rather, as Paul explains in 2 Corinthians 1:4 and 6, God intends to use suffering in our lives to give us a future ministry of comfort for others. God does not comfort you to make you comfortable but to make you useful. Paul's logic is this: when I find God's comfort in my suffering, I learn lessons about what God is really like and what he can do in my life. Then, when a friend, a coworker, or a family member comes into a time of similar suffering, I can pass what I learned on to them.

Remember the story I told you in a previous letter about the elderly husband who took his life at Christmastime? That story exemplified what I just wrote. God never wastes any pain he brings into our lives. He can always redeem the pain we feel now to help someone else down life's road.

Bethany, that is the situation Paul has in mind when he says we can comfort others with the comfort we received from God in our pain and suffering. How do you learn that? You look for God's abundant supply in your suffering. That is Paul's big idea in 2 Corinthians 1:5. As abundant as your suffering is or feels like, God's abundant supply to us through Christ's presence is far more than your suffering. When I know God's supply of comfort is not limited by the suffering I face or how long it stays in my life, its duration in my life gives me hope to persevere through it. God is almighty; your suffering is not.

Bethany, I'll close this letter by briefly mentioning two other perspectives that create perseverance in suffering in your life. You persevere through suffering by knowing that feeling overwhelmed does not mean being overwhelmed. Paul's suffering in Asia (2 Cor. 1:8–9) was severe enough to make him think he would not survive it. That is an example of feeling overwhelmed. But Paul found a benefit in feeling overwhelmed. It sent him to Christ for Christ's strength and abundant supply of what he needed.

When suffering lasts a long time, we can gradually believe the suffering is more powerful than God. We might believe that because God hasn't removed it as fast as we want him to. Does that sound familiar? But not being overwhelmed means we believe God's release from our suffering is on its way. That's what it means to live with hope, the hope Paul had despite what happened in Asia.

How to Persevere while Suffering

What created Paul's hope and perseverance? It was the prayers of other people (2 Cor. 1:10–11). You, Bethany, can persevere through your suffering when you ask others to pray for you. Your willingness to ask others for prayer shows that you aren't trying to handle suffering by yourself. Knowing others are praying for you helps you hold onto God's provision. When others pray for you and God answers their prayers, you will have a new story to tell others of God's faithfulness to you in your suffering.

I love you,
Dad

My Heart Response to Suffering

1. What challenge makes you want to give up and give in rather than persevere?
2. What would persevering through suffering look like in your life? What habits, skills, and more can you use to help you persevere?
3. Living one day at a time is a prescription from Jesus (Matt. 6:34). What action will help you persevere just for today?

Letter 31

FINDING JESUS IN YOUR SUFFERING

Dear Bethany,

One of the most important books I've ever read on the topic of suffering is Diane Langberg's *Suffering and the Heart of God*.[1] As an experienced trauma counselor, she writes from 40 years of sitting in the presence of deeply hurting and deeply wounded people. I mention all this because I want to pass on to you an adaptation of her insights about how Jesus enters our suffering. While the main ideas I pass on to you are hers, I am telling you how I apply those thoughts to the suffering that walks into my office every day. I pray they will be heart-strengthening for you.

---

1 Diane Langberg, *Suffering and the Heart of God*, Greensboro: New Growth Press, 2015, pp. 112–116.

As background to what I am going to say, let's look at the following passage from Philippians 2:5–11:

> Have this mind among yourselves, which is yours in Christ Jesus, who, though he was in the form of God, did not count equality with God a thing to be grasped, but emptied himself, by taking the form of a servant, being born in the likeness of men. And being found in human form, he humbled himself by becoming obedient to the point of death, even death on a cross. Therefore, God has highly exalted him and bestowed on him the name that is above every name, so that at the name of Jesus every knee should bow, in heaven and on earth and under the earth, and every tongue confess that Jesus Christ is Lord, to the glory of God the Father.

Bethany, this is the classic New Testament passage on the incarnation of Christ. Its application to our suffering is in the following six truths.

We find Jesus in our suffering when we remember he left glory to enter our broken world. That is what Paul says in Philippians 2:7 as he describes Christ entering this world, the event we celebrate every Christmas. Please realize, Bethany, that he did not come to an unbroken world, a world where there is no frustrating futility, no bondage to decay, and no painful groanings, but to a world deeply marked with all three of those evidences of the world's brokenness. In other words, he came into our world to meet us in our suffering.

We find Jesus in our suffering when we remember that he became little. Read Philippians 2:7–8 to catch the impact of that statement. In order to meet us in our suffering, Christ laid aside all he knew and had in heaven. He voluntarily did that. He was not ignorant of how deeply broken the world is, not the amount of evil he would find in it. He became little in order to meet us in our litteleness when we suffer.

We find Jesus in our suffering when we remember he entered the darkness of this world. John, one of Jesus's followers, consistently uses the contrast between light and dark to depict the twin realities of sin in this world along with its brokenness in contrast to the light, the holiness of God (read 1 John for an explanation of that contrast). Jesus did not let the evil he knew he would meet in becoming a man stop him from becoming a servant who suffered because he entered the darkness (see Philippians 2:7–8 again).

We find Jesus in our suffering when we remember that Jesus did not get lost in the darkness. In our suffering, we often feel we've lost our way. We wonder how we got to our place of pain. We no longer see things as we did before we entered our suffering. It is normal at such times to be afraid. (Think of those childhood fears of monsters in the bedroom closet I had to lock in when it was time for bed so you would go to sleep without fear they would escape and bother you!)

The point I am making is that in order to meet us in our suffering, Jesus had to enter the darkness of this world without getting lost, without becoming afraid—without refusing to enter the darkness of our suffering at all. Because he did not shrink back from entering the darkness and did not hold himself back from what we fear—our suffering—we can find him in our suffering, not merely outside of it.

We find Jesus in our suffering when we remember he did not abandon us. Instead of abandoning us, he walked through this broken world all the way to the cross—the ultimate experience of suffering (see verse 8 again). Realizing Jesus experienced the great agony of the cross means he can comfort us in all our sufferings. "For we do not have a high priest who is unable to sympathize with our weaknesses, but one who in every respect has been tempted as we are, yet without sin. Let us then with confidence draw near to the throne of grace, that we may receive mercy and find grace to help in time of need (Heb. 4:15–16). Notice what verse 16 says we can receive his mercy and grace to help us in any kind of suffering. No suffering leaves us bereft of Christ's aid. None. Not ever.

Finally, we find Jesus in our suffering when we remember he is Lord of even our suffering. That is the point of Philippians 2:9–10. We can break all the groans, the cries, the pleas for the removal of our suffering because he is Lord of all things. Note what happens when we remind ourselves of these truths. We worship (Phil. 2:11). Some of us will worship now, even in our suffering, and others will admit who Jesus is on that day when he returns.

Bethany, what you need to remember is that you are never alone in your suffering. You can feel, will feel, and have felt alone in your suffering, but there is no pain or heartache you experience now or will face in the future where Jesus cannot meet you.

That feeling of being alone and isolated in your suffering was a theme of many books by the Puritans because even in their day, Christ-followers felt that aloneness and isolation. They described the feeling of being alone and isolated in suffering as spiritual desertion, which meant they could not find God in their suffering. An example of that is Joseph Symonds' good book *The Case and Cure of a Deserted Soul*.[2]

---

[2] Joseph Symonnds, *The Case and Cure of a Deserted Soul*, Morgan: Soli Deo Gloria Publications. 1996.

But as I hope I've shown you, that is never the case with you. If you look for him, you can find Christ in your suffering. Look for his presence in your suffering, not outside of it. He is there, I promise. You just have to know how to look for him.

May God bless your looking.

> I love you,
> Dad

My Heart Response to Suffering

1. What dimension of your suffering makes it hard to find Christ? How is your pain blinding you to his presence?
2. Which of the dimensions of Christ being with you in your suffering have benefitted you as you read this letter? How will you record that dimension so you remember it as you go into your day today?
3. Read Hebrews 2:14–18 and 4:14–16. What new thoughts about Jesus's presence with you in your suffering do these two passages emphasize for you?
4. Which of the five Christian virtues of faith, hope, love, joy, or peace did this letter stir up within you?

Letter 32

FINDING CONTENTMENT IN SUFFERING

Dear Bethany,

    I know too well the feeling of making progress toward accepting suffering only to relapse into anger at having to suffer at all. Remember, anger is part of the grief journey we all experience when we lose something or someone we value. In all our phone calls, you tell me that the hardest loss for you is your loss of trust in people. Yes, that is often the most painful part of suffering—finding those who walk into your life while you suffer and finding those who walk away from your life because you are suffering. That is genuine grief indeed. When that happens, we lose our trust in others.

    In our suffering, some people will walk out of our lives, and others will walk into our lives. The challenge is adjusting our hearts to that. It subverts our ability to find God's peace in the suffering. When that happens, we feel rejected and abandoned. We feel ashamed, wondering if we caused people to walk out. We also feel anger at them and anger at ourselves for our misplaced trust in our friendship. All these emotions become the challenge of walking through the suffering with a contented heart.

I can hear you ask, "Dad, did you really mean a contented heart?" Yes, Bethany, I did. I want to pass on to you three ways I learned to find contentment in my suffering. I learned these lessons from Paul in his letter to the Philippians, chapter 4. Let me walk you through what he taught me in a previous time of my suffering.

In Philippians 4:11–13, Paul's logic about contentment runs like this. Contentment is possible in all circumstances (verse 11). Since contentment is possible in all circumstances, contentment must be possible in suffering. Paul declares that is what he has learned (verse 12). A rereading of chapter 1 shows that Paul is content even while he is in a Roman jail. So this is no theory for Paul. It is something he is living while he writes to the Philippians.

A good place to start in understanding the lessons Paul has for us about contentment is to first define what contentment means. Contentment is finding more delight in my relationship with Jesus Christ than I do in my circumstances. Too often we live that backward, thinking that contentment means my circumstance is pleasing to me and that until it is, I will be miserable. Verse 13 shows that is not true. Paul learned contentment in suffering from Christ who gives him the strength to find contentment in every circumstance.

But notice this. Contentment does not mean you deny that your circumstance is painful and causes your suffering. Contentment does not mean you minimize how much you hurt. Contentment means facing the facts of your circumstances and the emotions that arise in your circumstances. That is what Paul means when he tells us he knows how "to be brought low" and "how to abound" (Phil. 4:12). The rest of verse 12 gives examples of the kinds of difficult circumstances Paul experienced. He learned that his contentment did not come from the pleasantness of his circumstances. Instead, it came from his relationship with Christ.

So the hard truth that suffering exposes in you and me is that suffering shows me where I do not know Christ well enough to delight in him in all my circumstances. Let me say that again. Suffering shows me where I do not know Christ well enough for him to be enough to get me through my suffering.

Yes, you can see Paul's logic in those words. This question arises: "Yes, Paul, but how?" Here is what I learned that answered that question in my heart during my sufferings.

Life Lesson #1: Develop the habit of rejoicing in Christ, not in your circumstances. That lesson is the heart of Philippians 4:4. The time to learn to rejoice in Christ is before suffering comes, not when it comes. If you do not have the habit of rejoicing in Christ before the suffering comes, the suffering will overwhelm you so you cannot rejoice. Rejoicing in Christ, not circumstances, is another way of saying that worship is the fuel for perseverance and contentment.

Notice that Paul calls you to rejoice in Christ always. That always includes rejoicing in times of suffering. Yes, but how? Rejoicing in Christ in suffering requires us to remember that the Lord is near (Phil. 4:5). In what sense is Christ near to you when you suffer? He is near to you because he is Immanuel—God with us (Matt. 1:23, 28:20). Immanuel means he never leaves us or forsakes us (Heb. 13:6). Immanuel means Christ is right next to you (Ps. 16:8) while you suffer.

Remembering Christ is near also means he is coming. That is how James thinks of the nearness of Christ. He says of Christ, "for the coming of the Lord is at hand" (James 5:8) and "the Judge [Christ] is standing at the door" (James 5:9) ready to open it and come.

Remembering the coming of Christ fits what Martin Luther once wrote in his writings. He wrote, "There are two 2 days in my calendar: "This day [today] and that Day"[1] [the second coming]. Living today by that day enables you to persevere through suffering, for today may be the day that becomes that day when your suffering ends.

When you learn to rejoice in Christ and not your circumstances, your mood does not change. Paul says, "Let your reasonableness be known to everyone" (Phil. 4:5). In suffering, that means we do not give way to anger, petulance, despondency, or bitterness. Suffering does not change how we treat people. When I go through hard things, I can still treat people well because I learned to rejoice in Christ, not my circumstances. Got it? Let's move on to life lesson number 2.

Life Lesson #2: In my suffering, I increase my prayer times. This lesson comes from Philippians 4:6–7. Notice how Paul directs us to pray in every situation, which includes suffering. How do you do that? Turn your groans into prayers (Rom. 8:25–26). Suffering will cause you to groan. When it does, turn those groans into prayers. And no, groaning does not mean you lose your reasonableness or gentleness toward others. Groaning means you are honest with yourself and with God about your suffering. Suffering hurts. Turning your groans into prayers brings that hurt to God, even when you cannot put what you feel into words. Said differently, this life lesson means that when your circumstances trouble you, you trouble them with your prayers.

Increasing your prayer time as you suffer requires faith. Faith in Christ in your suffering means you believe Jesus can do something about this, so you pray. Having faith in Christ during suffering

---

[1] This quote is commonly attributed to Martin Luther.

means trusting that it won't last forever. Faith in Christ in your suffering means you gaze at him and glance at your suffering. One way to do that is to see that the qualities of Philippians 4:8–9 are all found in Christ. So when your circumstances pull your gaze off of Christ, rehearse those qualities to yourself as being true of Christ. Then, whenever you notice your suffering more than you notice Christ, pray.

Life Lesson #3: In your suffering, look what Jesus is doing (Phil. 4:10–19). To be content in suffering means shifting your focus from what Jesus isn't doing to what he is doing. Contentment is focusing on what you have in your relationship with Christ, not on what you lack in your circumstances. Contentment is embracing what Christ gives you instead of being bitter about what he withholds. Although Paul was in a Roman jail, he noticed the good Christ was doing in the Philippian church and in those who were still free to preach Christ (Phil. 1:14–18).

Bethany, I know these are difficult lessons to learn, especially when your suffering continues. But I know you can apply them to your life now, and you will find that Christ is greater than your suffering. Knowing that, you will find contentment. I promise.

> I love you,
> Dad

My Heart Response to Suffering

1. Which of the three life lessons means the most to you today? Why?
2. What can you do today to work that life lesson into your life while you suffer? What part of your life will be affected the most by your working that lesson into your life?
3. Since Life Lesson #2 speaks of increasing your prayers, compose a prayer you can use when your suffering threatens to overwhelm you. Then carry it with you and pray it when your suffering presses in hard against you.

Letter 33

HOW SUFFERING SHOWS US WHO WE TRULY ARE

Dear Bethany,

You are not weird for wondering who you are anymore. Wondering that is a normal part of the disorientation and distortion that pain brings you. You saw yourself one way before the suffering came. Now you wonder if you'll ever be the same after the suffering. What I want to show you in this letter is how suffering teaches us who we are. It does so by exposing the false view of ourselves. It is only when the false view we all hold of ourselves is torn from us that we discover who we truly are.

Those who study how we think of ourselves—our so-called self-esteem—tell us that how we think of ourselves comes from these three dimensions of our lives: our sense of belonging, our sense of worth, and our sense of performance. The three dimensions blend together in our thinking, so each plays a vital role in how we think about what it means to be us. In this letter, I'll discuss features of each of the three dimensions and demonstrate how suffering reveals their inadequacy for our self-esteem.

SELF-ESTEEM vs. CHRIST-ESTEEM

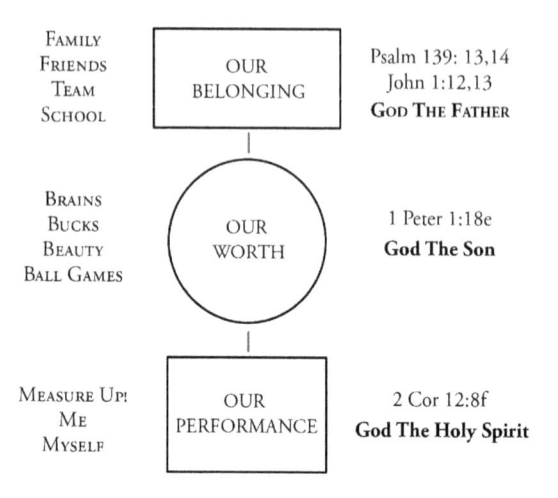

Family Friends Team School	OUR BELONGING	Psalm 139: 13,14 John 1:12,13 **God The Father**
Brains Bucks Beauty Ball Games	OUR WORTH	1 Peter 1:18e **God The Son**
Measure Up! Me Myself	OUR PERFORMANCE	2 Cor 12:8f **God The Holy Spirit**

First, let's look at our sense of belonging. It comes from our connection to other people. Adam's solitary state was the first thing God deemed "not good" in Genesis 2:18. If the pandemic taught us anything, it taught us how much we deeply need connection with other people. Zoom meetings did not meet that need. We need personal interactions with other people.

We get our sense of belonging from being in relationships with other people. For some, that means they connect because they went to school together. For some, it means they cheer for the same team. For some, it means they work at the same company in the same department. For others, it means an affiliation with a faith community. For even others, it means playing on the same team on a recreation league volleyball team. Our families also give us a sense of belonging, whether positive or negative.

The problem with basing part of our view of ourselves from our relationships is that relationships can change. People move away. People die. People decide to end their friendship. Work transfers can mean moving to a different department or even a different state. In all these ways, part of our self-esteem equals basing it on relationships that shift, change, and can be lost.

The second dimension of self-esteem is our sense of worth. In our American life, the message we get about our individual worth comes down to what I call the 4 Bs—bucks, brains, beauty, and ballgames. If we have wealth, we have status. If we have brains, we are respected. If we have beauty, we are admired. If we have athletic abilities, we become heroes to our fans. However, each of these can change. We can lose wealth in the stock market or by a poor business decision. Father Time brings forgetfulness to even the sharpest of minds. Beauty fades as wrinkles appear and bellies get larger. Even gifted athletes such as Derek Jeter or Michael Jordan retire because they cannot do what they once did or the younger players play harder, faster, and better than the aging athlete. So trusting bucks, brains, beauty, or ballgames for self-worth is doing so on shaky ground.

Depending on the third dimension—our sense of performance—as the basis for self-worth comes down to these three people I am sure you know well: me, myself, and I. To perform well enough in order for performance to be a source of my self-esteem means that in all ways and at all times I must measure up. I must measure up to what my boss expects of me. I must meet the job requirements to get hired. I must measure up to my wife's expectation of time together if I want a happy marriage. I must measure up to what I expect of myself if I am to have a composed mind and quiet emotions. I'll be ashamed if I don't measure up. As someone wittier than I once wrote, shame stands for "should have already mastered everything." Thus, basing how we view ourselves on our performance is also to base it on something that can be lost or decay.

In short, to base my self-worth on my sense of belonging, worth, or performance means that my self-worth will go up and down like riding a roller coaster or climbing up and down a ladder. I will fluctuate between peace and distress due to changes in my self-worth.

Our sense of self and inner serenity is uniquely exposed when suffering reveals our misplaced reliance on these three unrealistic foundations for self-esteem. When we depend too heavily on any of these three dimensions, it can turn into idol worship. If I rely too much on belonging, I might not address the things that annoy me in a relationship so I can maintain a connection. If my sense of worth comes from my stock portfolio, I will experience anxiety when the market is up one week but down the next. If my sense of performance is a source of how well I like myself, I may become a workaholic, sacrificing time with my wife and loved ones for the sake of measuring up at work.

How can you replace these things in order to establish a stable sense of self? You move from basing your identity on self-esteem to what I call Christ-esteem. Here's how. Moving from self-esteem to Christ-esteem in belonging means you see yourself belonging to God in two ways. First, you belong to him because he made you. Psalm 139:13–14 says, "For you formed my inward parts; you knitted me together in my mother's womb. I praise you, for I am fearfully and wonderfully made. Wonderful are your works; my soul knows it very well."

Since you are God's handiwork, you belong to him. You also belong to God through your faith in Christ. John 1:12–13 declares, "To all who did receive him, who believed in his name, he gave the right to become children of God, who were born, not of blood nor of the will of the flesh nor of the will of man, but of God."

How Suffering Shows Us Who We Truly Are

By placing my faith in Christ's death on the cross as payment for my sins, my relationship with God changed from sinner—which defined who I was in my relationship to God when I chose to sin over following him—to that of a son or a daughter. When he adopted me into his family, my relationship changed with him forever (Gal. 3:25–29, 4:5–6). It changed forever because God does not die but lives forever. It changed forever because he gave me his kind of life—eternal life—when I believed in Christ. So I now have an unwavering relationship of belonging because I am God's child.

My sense of worth also changes when I pursue Christ-esteem. Just like a car is worth what we pay for it (hopefully), you are worth what Christ paid for you, "knowing that you were ransomed from the futile ways inherited from your forefathers, not with perishable things such as silver or gold, but with the precious blood of Christ, like that of a lamb without blemish or spot." (1 Peter 1:18-19)

Christ paid to ransom me from sin. So his death determines my worth. Let me remind you not to confuse your worth with being worthy of Christ's death. Because of the great love with which he loved us (Eph. 2:4), Christ died for us. That establishes our worth. But Christ did not die for us because we were worthy of his doing so. Romans 5:8 tells us that while we were yet sinners, Christ died for us. Being sinners means we could not do anything and did nothing to deserve Christ's death for us. Instead of our being worthy of Christ's death, his death was the ultimate demonstration of God's grace toward us. And grace means getting what we do not deserve. So in a Christ-esteem view of myself, my worth is determined by the price paid for me—the death of Christ.

A Christ-esteem focus also gives me a new source for my sense of performance. In his weakness, Paul learned that God's grace reaches its full extent (2 Corinthians 12:9,10).

You'll Get Through This

Dearest Bethany, what I want you to notice about what I just wrote is this. In your pursuit of a stable and unchangeable source of self, the Holy Trinity provides all you need. The Father provides you with your sense of belonging. The Son of God provides you with your sense of worth. And the Holy Spirit empowers your performance. Thus, one function that suffering provides is the exposure of our faulty ways of looking at ourselves so we are driven outside our self-reliance to our faith in God. Only God as Father, Son, and Holy Spirit provides us with a stable basis for self-esteem.

I know this is a lot to grasp in one letter. Please go back and reread this letter until you base your esteem more on what the Bible says is true of you and less on what the world says is true of you. You'll be amazed at what happens in your life when you do that.

I love you,
Dad

My Heart Response to Suffering

1. Which of the three sources of self-esteem did you rely on the most in the past? What did that source of self-esteem require you to do in order to find stability in your view of yourself?
2. What was the emotional cost to your efforts to belong, establish your worth, or measure up?
3. Knowing God provides a lasting and stable source of self-esteem, what can you do?

Letter 34

LIVING CONFIDENTLY IN A BROKEN WORLD OF SUFFERING: PART 1

Dear Bethany,

    I loved reading that you feel like spring is coming back into your soul. It reflects your determination to surpass your suffering. Few understand the hard work needed to tend to your soul in suffering. As you found out, it taxes your mental, social, spiritual, and physical resources and resiliency. So I am glad to respond to your question: "Dad, how do I go on living confidently now that I know suffering can be around the next corner of my life?" I will answer that by directing you to Romans 8 with its marvelous insights.

    Let's begin by explaining the phrase broken world. I use it to describe human life on the wrong side of Genesis 3. That chapter is the turning point of the Bible. In Genesis 1–2, all is as it should be after God finished his work of creation. But in chapter 3, the first couple chose disobedience over obedience to God's first command. After that, nothing is as it should be. Life is not as God intended, making it a broken world. In the brokenness of this wrong side of Genesis 3, life includes suffering.

In Romans 8:18, Paul acknowledges the reality of suffering in "this present time." Then he moves on to describe three features of broken-world living that are inescapable. Bethany, as you have figured out by now from my other letters, we live in that "present time."

The first feature of living in a broken world is futility (Rom. 8:20). This is a feature I know you are familiar with because you know what it is like when your brother Timothy got sick in the middle of our summer camping vacation and we spent time finding a doctor who would prescribe an antibiotic for his ear infection. You know how frustrating futility is when you are running late for work in the winter and discover that the battery in your car is dead. Picture dealing with a broken septic system before a weekend with out-of-town family as happened to one of our church families several years ago. Sometimes things are frustratingly futile in this broken world.

The second feature of life in a broken world is its "bondage to corruption" (Rom. 8:21). Your eighth grade science teacher taught you this in the second law of thermodynamics—things decay from a state of order to disorder. In our lives, that means things wear out. Think of it this way. We recently went shopping for a new washer and dryer because ours are as old as your brother. The salesperson we talked to declared, "Nothing I sell you now will last that long. Nowadays, things last 10 years, tops." That is bondage to corruption (decay) at work.

I also discover this feature every time I look at myself in a mirror. My wavy brown hair is gone and now looks like a beach. And yes, nephew Isaiah was right when he observed, "Must be low tide." You remember how hard we all laughed at his interpretation of my baldness.

The third feature of life in a broken world is inward groanings (Rom. 8:23). The groanings come from the first two features. Groaning happens when life doesn't go as planned. It is inevitable that we will groan when life does not go as we thought it would.

In a broken world, you must decide how to live despite future suffering. You have three options regarding how you are going to live. First, you can live afraid and allow Future Events to Appear Real (F.E.A.R.) to your mind and heart. Fear comes from focusing on externals such as the economy, the election, and so on.

You can live anxiously, wondering how to survive this broken world with fewer heart scars. Anxiety comes from focusing within, wondering if you have what it takes to meet the suffering you face. Then you conclude that you probably don't.

Finally, you can live confidently knowing God will handle your future. Your focus should be on God, not your circumstances or resources. When you focus on God, nine realities from this passage will support you. I will tell you about four of them in this letter and the last five in the next letter.

The first reality about God that will help you live confidently in a broken world is that God gives you his Spirit to aid you in your prayers while suffering. What I find interesting in Romans 8:26 is that while we groan in life on the wrong side of Genesis 3, the Holy Spirit helps us pray with his own groanings. His groanings translate our groanings so he can present them to God the Father. By praying through the Spirit of God, I can confidently live in the aftermath of Genesis 3.

The second reality that helps you live confidently in a broken world is that God is at work for your good in your present circumstance, even when that circumstance is suffering. Romans

8:28 is the classic verse on God's sovereignty over and in our circumstances. Because it is so familiar, you can overlook its amazing truths. Verse 28 declares that God is at work in all things that pertain to your circumstance. All things mean there are no exceptions to God's working in your life. No circumstance is bigger than God is. No circumstance is greater than his power. No circumstance stumps his wisdom. No circumstance can hurt more than God's comfort can flow into your life. Bethany, God is at work in your life even when you suffer.

Verse 28 goes on to tell you that he works in your circumstance for your good. As I wrote to you previously, pain distorts your perspective, including your view of God. This verse provides an antidote for that distortion. It is an antidote because when you consider the word *know*, you discover that the truth of God working in your circumstance is an absolute truth.

Think of it this way. Understanding God's character means knowing he never works against it. God is always almighty, not sometimes. If you are familiar with the other aspects of verse 28, then you can be certain that God is working for your good, regardless of your specific situation.

The third reality that enables you to live confidently in a broken world is that God has his purpose for your present circumstance—to make you like Christ (Rom. 8:29). In suffering, you want comfort, but in your suffering, God wants to increase your conformity to Christ. In our suffering, God focuses more on your character development than on your comfort. That means any circumstance can make you more like Christ if you focus on the forming of your character rather than finding the comfort of release from your suffering. Verse 29 means God intends so intensely to make you like Christ that he will sacrifice your comfort by bringing suffering to you in order to make you like him.

Living Confidently in a Broken World of Suffering: Part 1

The fourth reality that enables you to live confidently in a broken world is that God has already solved your present circumstance (Rom. 8:30). How do I reach that conclusion from this verse? My confidence that God has already solved my present circumstance comes from the fact that all the verbs (predestined, called, justified, glorified) are in the past tense. Thus, from God's perspective, every aspect of our salvation in Christ has already been accomplished.

Glorification is the one thing we don't accomplish in our everyday lives. Second Corinthians 3:18 explains that we are still in the process of growing into all we will be. Paul says in that verse that "we are being transformed," a phrase that denotes the process we all grow through in becoming like Christ. This is ongoing in this life. Living confidently in a broken world means being confident that the suffering you face now is part of the process that is making you more of what you will be one day.

Bethany, please think carefully about these four realities of life in a broken world. Think through the parts of your current suffering that these realities make a little lighter. Think about how they apply to this particular moment on your journey through your suffering. It may be helpful for you to journal your thoughts about what I said in this letter. You'll get through this. I promise.

I love you,
Dad

My Heart Response to Suffering

1. Which of the four realities of Romans 8 explained in this letter caught your attention? Why did it do that?
2. How can you review the lessons of Romans 8 so they gradually become part of your outlook on life and suffering?
3. Which of these lessons can you turn into a prayer for your growth and make it a lifestyle?

Letter 35

LIVING CONFIDENTLY IN A BROKEN WORLD OF SUFFERING: PART 2

Dear Bethany,

I will help you walk through your suffering and to the other side of it by giving you the other five realities of Romans 8 about living in a broken world. Before I do, I want to pass on something I heard Alistar Begg say in one of his sermons. He said our lives are lived between the no condemnation of Romans 8:1 and the no separation of verses 35–39. Please keep that in mind as I explain the other realities found in this chapter that will help you walk out of and beyond your current suffering and its pain.

The fifth reality that enables you to live confidently in a broken world is that God actively opposes all who oppose you. Look at Romans 8:31. "If God is for us, who can be against us?" Paul uses the if at the start of that sentence to mean "since." Think of that. Since God is for us, who can be against us? Who can oppose his power? Who can oppose his wisdom? Who can oppose his Spirit who always indwells us? Obviously, the answer to those questions is no one. Since God is for you, no one—nothing—can be against you. Even in your suffering, you can live confidently in a broken world.

The sixth reality that enables you to live confidently in a broken world is that God freely gives you what you need in your present circumstance. Romans 8:32 declares, "He who did not spare his own Son but gave him up for us all, how will he not also with him graciously give us all things?" The key word to notice is graciously. You could translate that word "giftly," but that doesn't sound right in English. But the principle is that God freely gives you what you need in your present circumstance. You don't and cannot earn all God wants to give you to equip you to suffer. It is God's daily gift to you to supply you with what you need for that day, one day at a time.

The seventh reality that enables you to live confidently in a broken world is that Jesus is your defense attorney in your present suffering (Rom. 8:33–34). This is important because one of Satan's favorite tactics in the painful moments of our suffering is to tell us that we are in a painful moment because of what we said, did, or didn't say or do. When he does that, he is acting as the accuser (the prosecuting attorney) that Revelation 12:9–10 says that he is. Notice how verse 10 declares that he does this "day and night."

How do we withstand his incessant accusations? We withstand them because we know that Jesus is our advocate, our defense attorney, in God's presence. First John 2:1 tells us, "But if anyone does sin, we have an advocate with the Father, Jesus Christ the righteous." Where do you need a defense attorney? You need him in the right courtroom at the right time. If your trial is in Portland, Oregon, it will not do you any good if your defense attorney is in Omaha, Nebraska. But we have the right defense attorney, Jesus

Christ, in the right courtroom in God's presence. You can live confidently in a broken world because Jesus Christ is your defense attorney in the right courtroom when Satan comes to accuse you and blame you for your present suffering.

The eighth reality that enables you to live confidently in a broken world is that Jesus is praying for you in your circumstance. That is what Romans 8:34 tells us when Paul uses the word interceding. The word intercession is used in Hebrews 7:25. "Consequently, he is able to save to the uttermost those who draw near to God through him, since he always lives to make intercession for them." The word consequently points you to Jesus Christ, your fully qualified High Priest. The high priest represented the people of Israel before God. That is what Jesus does for you in suffering; he prays for you. That enables you to live confidently in a broken world. Remember that before Jesus raised Lazarus from the grave, he gave thanks to God when he announced, "Father, I thank you that you have heard me. I knew that you always hear me, but I said this on account of the people standing around, that they may believe that you sent me" (John 11:41–42). If God always hears Jesus's prayers and if Jesus is praying for you in your suffering, then you can live confidently in a broken world.

The ninth and final reality that empowers you to live confidently in a broken world is that God's love for you is greater than any circumstance you face. Read these next verses slowly, and let them penetrate your heart.

> Who shall separate us from the love of Christ? Shall tribulation, or distress, or persecution, or famine, or nakedness, or danger, or sword? As it is written, "For your sake, we are being killed all the day long; we are regarded as sheep to be slaughtered. No, in all

these things we are more than conquerors through him who loved us. For I am sure that neither death nor life, nor angels nor rulers, nor things present nor things to come, nor powers, nor height nor depth, nor anything else in all creation, will be able to separate us from the love of God in Christ Jesus our Lord.

—Rom. 8:35–39

Let me summarize these verses from Romans 8 with this final thought. In Christ, you are a conqueror, not a victim, so you can live confidently in a broken world.

Bethany, I have given you a lot to think about. My hope is that you will read and reread these two letters until you are absolutely certain you can live confidently in this broken world. When that happens, you will be the conqueror in Christ that Paul wrote about.

I love you,
Dad

My Heart Response to Suffering

1. Which of the five realities mentioned in this letter offers you soul strength today?
2. It can be a staggering thought to think that Jesus is right now at this moment praying for you. How will that knowledge strengthen your walk today through your suffering? List all the ways Jesus's prayers for you can give you the power to walk on.
3. Which of the nine realities in the last two letters do you need to remind yourself of most often? Once you identify that reality, write it down so you can reread it throughout today.

Letter 36

SUFFERING AND FORGIVING

Dear Bethany,

I am not surprised to learn that the farther you feel from the suffering, the more you battle forgiving the person who caused it. As you said last night, "Dad, I thought I was getting better, but I am so angry. What do I do with all this anger?"

Bethany, you have only two choices with your anger, especially when it pops up unexpectedly. Choice number one is letting the anger slip into your thoughts like a thief who wants to steal the most valuable thing you have—your serenity. Choice number two is to practice forgiving each time you remember the person through whom your suffering began. There is no middle-ground choice between these two choices.

Choice number one happens easily. You do not have to practice getting angry at the hurt you've carried these past few months. Forgiving, however, is something you have to practice and practice and practice again whenever your anger pops up. Here's how to do that. (I knew that "Dad, how do I do that?" was your next question.)

You begin by realizing that the essence of forgiveness is giving up your right to hate a person for hurting you. The temptation to be angry because of your hurt will grow into hate if you do not deal with it each time it intrudes your thoughts. Yes, I said each time. Forgiving someone every time you feel the pain or the memory of how all this started is exhausting, but getting stuck in bitterness or resentment is not just exhausting but can poison your heart if you let it.

In order to give up your right to hate, you must not keep score. You can't compare what happened to you versus the pain you've caused others. The thing about comparison is that no one concludes they are as good as the one they are comparing themselves to. If you envision comparing yourself to who hurt you, you will either feel superior to that person and hold onto the anger you feel, or you will feel less than that person, and shame will be your companion. That is why Paul says we are not wise when we compare ourselves to others (2 Cor. 10:12).

Here is a question to ask yourself. Do I want to be foolish when my pop-up anger happens? If you want to be wise at such times, you must give up comparing the hurt the person caused you to the hurt you think you've caused others.

Forgiveness grows within you as you realize that forgiveness is treating the person with grace just like God did in forgiving you. I know that long ago you memorized Ephesians 2:8–9 in AWANA. Let me remind you that verse 8 states we are forgiven. "For by grace you have been saved through faith. And this is not your own doing; it is the gift of God." Bethany, you did not earn God's forgiveness. Instead, he forgave you because of your faith in what Christ accomplished on the cross—a full and complete payment for your sins. You forgive someone because you choose not to make others earn your forgiveness. That's why forgiveness is an act of grace.

SUFFERING AND FORGIVING

You grant forgiveness to a person because you see what they could be if they lived with your forgiveness. Pause for a moment, Bethany, and remember the joy of a clear conscience you gained when God forgave you. Forgiving a person offers them a small taste of that same joy when they understand that you forgive them for all the pain they have brought into your life.

All this is preliminary to the actual work of forgiving. How do you do that?

First, you must remove the three barriers to forgiving. You must deal with any pride that says, "You can't do that to me and get away with it." Such an attitude looks for an opportunity to take revenge. Revenge is thinking you can make the person hurt as badly as you hurt when they wronged you. That is impossible, Bethany. It is impossible because that person does not have the same personality or personal history that you do. You simply cannot make them hurt the same way or to the same extent that you hurt. Forgiveness means you give up any hurt-shaped desire for revenge. That is the first barrier to forgiving. You must remove it from your life.

How?

You turn your anger and impulse to hate over to God, knowing his promise that "vengeance is mine, I will repay" (Rom. 12:19). Believe me, Bethany, God knows when and how to get that person's attention better than you do. The battle with forgiveness is a battle to trust that verse 19 is true.

You must also remove hurt as an excuse not to forgive. You might be holding onto hurt as a reason not to forgive. You may be thinking, "I hurt too much to forgive this person." You hurt too much? I don't mean to diminish your pain, Bethany, but the pain you feel is not comparable to what Christ felt on the cross as payment for your sins. Do not focus on the hurt; instead, focus on your forgiveness. That focus frees you to release your anger by forgiving.

The last barrier to forgiving someone is waiting for them to go first. Sadly, there are some people in our lives who will never ask for our forgiveness. I do not know if your person is one of those people, but if they are, waiting for them to go first means you will be in a battle with anger until they do. What if they never do? Think of that.

Because you know about Christ's forgiveness, you have a pattern of what forgiveness looks like. Christ was ready to forgive you before you ever thought of asking him for it. You face the same choice. Can you prepare your heart to forgive someone whether they ever ask for your forgiveness?

Once you decide to offer forgiveness, you are ready to forgive. Here is how you do that. You decide to live a life of forgiveness. That means no matter what happens to you in life, nothing will be too big for you to forgive. Obviously, Bethany, you make that decision before you even need to forgive. Why would you decide to live a life of forgiveness? You decide that because you are a Christ follower, you will do what he does—offer others forgiveness. Doing so brings your life in alignment with Ephesians 4:32 that says, "Be kind to one another, tenderhearted, forgiving one another, as God in Christ forgave you."

Bethany, once you make that decision, you then pray for the power to forgive. You already know you cannot forgive this person on your own; otherwise, you would not have the anger you are experiencing. Being a counselor and a pastor taught me this one truth: people do not have the power to forgive without God's help. Let me repeat that, Bethany. You do not have the power to forgive without God's help. Therefore, you pray for the power to forgive. You could pray like this: "Holy Father, I need to forgive someone who hurt me deeply, but I do not have the ability to forgive on my own. I ask you to give me the power to truly forgive this person as you forgave me. In Jesus's name, amen."

The next step in forgiving this person is to make a list of all the ways they hurt you. It does not matter how long or short your list is. Here's a good way to make that list. At the top of a sheet of paper write, "Lord, I forgive this person, but. . . ." Then list all the things that bubble up from inside you. Those are your barriers to forgiveness. Once you have finished that list, then by an act of your will declare, "Holy Father, I forgive this person for . . ." and name each item. When you are done, you will know you genuinely forgave them. If all this seems too hard, then take a baby step to forgiving by praying, "Lord God, I need to forgive. But Lord, I can't, so make me willing to forgive." Pray that until you are able to grant this person forgiveness.

When I worked at the treatment center, sometimes I sent clients to the chapel. I asked them to stay in the chapel until they could pray for the willingness to forgive. I did that because the willingness to forgive is the essential first step to being able to forgive. I asked them to pray for that willingness as a first step because granting forgiveness to someone who hurt us is that important!

There is one last step in forgiving. When you remember the hurt, you need to let go of the rope. Here's what I mean.

I learned to water ski at on a mountain lake on my friend Jay's family ranch in Wyoming. The water in Torrey Lake came from mountain snow melt. It was so cold that even the wetsuit I wore did little to dull the frigid temperature of the water. One of the basic instructions I received on my first day of learning to ski was, "If you fall, let go of the rope. You need to let go of the rope or the boat will drag you through the water."

One time I fell as I was crossing the boat's small wake. I fell so quickly that I did not have time to let go of the rope as I fell face first into the water. It seemed like forever before my head and chest popped out of the water and I could let go of the rope. It was not fun getting pulled under the water. I did not think I was ever going to break the surface. Finally, I came up and threw the rope as far as I could.

Bethany, if you do not let go of the rope by choosing to forgive each time the hurt or memory of an incident pops up, you will be dragged through the waters of bitterness and resentment until you do. So when you remember the hurt, let go of the rope.

I love you,
Dad

Suffering and Forgiving

My Heart Response to Suffering

1. Who in your life do you need to forgive?
2. Which of the three barriers to forgiving do you face? How do you plan to deal with that barrier?
3. If you need to re-forgive, how will you remember to let go of the rope?
4. In your suffering, you may need to forgive someone who is already dead or someone who will likely never ask for your forgiveness. (I've faced both of those situations myself, so I know what you face in doing so.) Forgive them anyway by using the method presented in this letter. Doing so will set your heart free from lingering bitterness or resentment toward that person.

Letter 37

SUFFERING AND REBUILDING TRUST

Dear Bethany,

You ask an important question when you say, "How do I begin to trust people again, Dad?" Although your pain is not as great as it was when all this first happened, you realize your view of people is different now. Remember, I told you that pain changes your view of other people. Now, even though your head and heart seesaw is no longer wildly gyrating, you are still suspicious of others. So your question is an important one. Let's think through this together.

Bethany, you need to realize the difference between forgiving someone and trusting someone. They are not the same, although many people think they are. Here's the difference. Forgiveness is always a gift we give to someone who hurt us. It is a choice we make when we are hurt or when we remember the hurt. Forgiveness releases the person from our anger. Forgiveness releases us from bitterness and resentment. I wrote about all this in my last letter.

But forgiving is not the same as trusting. While forgiveness is a gift we give to others, trust must be earned. How? Trust grows when a person who hurt you proves by their actions that they really did change their behavior. When that happens, the person who felt dangerous now feels safe. That means trust cannot be rushed. Enough time has to pass in order to show real change has taken place in the life of the offender.

The biblical word for that change is *repentance*. Repentance involves a change of mind that results in a change of direction. A few months back, our pastor said in a sermon that repentance was the word used by the ancient Greek army to command that they reverse the direction of their march. That captures what I am talking about. Repentance is recognizing I cannot go on hurting someone in the way I have in the past, so I modify my behavior to not do that anymore. As I modify my behavior, the person will feel safer and safer when they are around me.

Repentance shows itself when a person confesses the wrong and the impact their action had on me. A true confession is like this: "I was wrong for hurting you when I called you a petty and angry woman the other night at the party. Will you forgive me?"

Yes, Bethany, that is how Mom and I taught you, your sister, and your brother to ask each other for forgiveness. That form of asking for forgiveness acknowledges the wrong behavior, identifies the hurt caused, and seeks forgiveness from the person hurt by your action.

A common form of asking for forgiveness is, "I am sorry I hurt you. Will you forgive me?" The reason we did not teach you and your siblings to ask forgiveness like that is because it leaves out the aspect of repentance. At best, it acknowledges regret but does not acknowledge the need for repentance.

Suffering and Rebuilding Trust

Think of it this way. Imagine me as a five-year-old me asking your grandmother if I can have one of her chocolate chip cookies before supper. Of course, she told me, "No, you may not" because everything was almost ready to eat. So she leaves to put the plate of roast beef on the table. Then picture me crawling up to the counter and putting my hand in the cookie jar just as she walks back into the kitchen. Suppose I immediately start crying, "Don't spank! Don't spank!" How will my mom know if I repented or not? She will know I repented the moment my hand is no longer in the cookie jar (a change of mind resulting in a change of direction). But as long as I leave my hand in the cookie jar while asking not to get spanked for my disobedience, she knows I am only sorry about the unpleasant consequence about to come. Do you see the difference? My regret at the coming discipline is not the same as my honest confession of disobedience.

Bethany, repentance is also necessary because forgiveness sought and granted leads to reconciliation. Reconciliation ends the hostility wrongdoing creates in a relationship. Reconciliation, based on repentance, repairs the relationship. Indeed, without repentance, reconciliation is not possible because if there is no repentance, there is no reconciliation.

So the first step in rebuilding trust is an honest confession of wrongdoing and an honest granting of forgiveness so the relationship can be repaired.

Here is what most folks do not understand. Honest confession and honest forgiveness remove the barriers to repairing the relationship but do not immediately restore trust. As I said earlier, trust must be earned. That means the change of behavior must be sustained. Sustaining the changed behavior shows the repentance was deep and thorough.

The biblical example of this is in 2 Corinthians 7:8–11. The setting of these verses is 1 Corinthians chapter five in which Paul addressed the church's tolerance of sexual sin. Now Paul commends them for their response to his rebuke.

> For even if I made you grieve with my letter, I do not regret it—though I did regret it, for I see that that letter grieved you, though only for a while. As it is, I rejoice, not because you were grieved, but because you were grieved into repenting. For you felt a godly grief, so that you suffered no loss through us. For godly grief produces a repentance that leads to salvation without regret, whereas worldly grief produces death. For see what earnestness this godly grief has produced in you, but also what eagerness to clear yourselves, what indignation, what fear, what longing, what zeal, what punishment! At every point you have proved yourselves innocent in the matter.
>
> —2 Cor. 7:8–11

Notice what Paul says in verse 9. The Corinthians experienced true repentance when they read Paul's rebuke. He calls it "godly grief."

How do we know they truly repented? Look at what Paul says in verse 11. He mentions their earnestness to clear themselves, their indignation at what they did, a godly fear because of their wrongdoing, their longing to follow Paul's instructions, and the zeal they displayed in carrying out the punishment Paul called them to administer in 1 Corinthians 5. Verse 11 demonstrates true repentance in action. Their actions showed they really did change.

Suffering and Rebuilding Trust

The same will happen in our lives when someone genuinely repents of the harm they caused. But—and do not overlook this—all of that takes time to see and believe that the person truly changed. That is why granting forgiveness can be immediate upon a person's confession, but trust takes time to rebuild.

Very simply, a person shows they truly repent by replacing the hurtful behaviors with behaviors that repair the relationship. Remember, repentance is a change of mind that leads to a change of direction. Repentance does not necessarily require tears—think of five-year-old me with my hand still in the cookie jar—but it does require a change of direction.

All of this is why your honest response to someone asking for your forgiveness could look like this: "I fully and freely forgive you for what you did to hurt me, but it is going to take some time before I know if I can trust you not to hurt me that way again." That is an honest admission that you can give forgiveness in the moment but regaining your trust will take time.

Sadly, and I surely wish I did not have to write this, some who ask for forgiveness will by their behavior over time show that they are not to be trusted. Some will go on hurting us in the same way they did before; therefore, they are not to be trusted as a safe person in our lives. Remember, there is no reconciliation without repentance. And without reconciliation, there is no repair to the relationship. Forgiveness is an essential first step in repairing a relationship, but it must be matched by the change of behavior for the relationship to truly be repaired. That is what happened between Paul and the Corinthians, but it does not always happen. You must be prepared for that.

I love you,
Dad

My Heart Response to Suffering

1. A key thought in this letter is that without repentance, there cannot be reconciliation. Who in your life showed repentance for what happened between the two of you? Who showed by their subsequent behavior that they did not genuinely repent, thereby earning your trust?
2. In your life, what is the difference between regret and repentance? How do you tell the difference between the two?
3. Rebuilding trust and repairing the relationship does not happen quickly. To whom do you need to give more time to show they can be trusted before you write them off as unsafe?
4. Someone may not prove trustworthy now, but are you prepared to grant forgiveness to that person when they come to you and you see they have really changed? What barriers in your heart arise at the thought of doing that? How do you need to deal with those barriers based on these last two letters?

Letter 38

SUFFERING AND BOUNDARIES

Dear Bethany,

You ask such good questions! This last one shows you are far from the initial hurt and pain of your trauma. You said, "All of this sounds like I need good boundaries in my life. How do I set good boundaries so I do not set myself up for future hurt?" Let's think about that together in this letter.

The boundaries we set in our lives are all about respect. I respect myself by having boundaries. I ask and expect others to respect my boundaries by observing them and acting in accord with them. Hence, they are all about respect.

The function of a boundary is to let trustworthy people into my life and keep untrustworthy people out of my life. Not everyone deserves access to my life. Let me illustrate that thought by telling you a story from when I was first a pastor.

In 1985, a couple in the small town where we lived were going through a nasty, nasty divorce. Because the town was small, both partners in the marriage were well-known, as were the families from which they came. Because of the stress Sam (not his real name) felt, he was not eating well. He was, however, drinking more than a dozen Mountain Dews each day.

You can imagine what drinking that many Mountain Dews did for his sleep. Right—he wasn't sleeping. Because he was not sleeping, things were always bigger and scarier at 3:00 a.m. than they were at 3:00 p.m.

Guess who he would call at 3:00 a.m.

Yep, me. This happened a couple of times in the same week, so I needed to set a boundary with Sam about waking me up in the middle of the night. That was my boundary. I told him something like this: "Look, Sam, you are not getting the best version of me when you call me at 3:00 a.m., so my advice is likely not to be as helpful as it would be if you came by to talk with me at 3:00 p.m. I am glad to talk to you anytime you come by, but I cannot talk with you at 3:00 a.m. because neither you nor I are thinking well at that time of day."

I am thankful to report that Sam followed the boundary I set. He stopped calling me at 3:00 a.m. and began coming by in the afternoon. (He also stopped drinking so many Mountain Dews.)

That is an example of what setting a good boundary looks like. I respected myself enough to not allow Sam to keep calling me at 3:00 a.m., and he respected my boundary by adjusting when he talked to me.

But boundaries do not always work that way. There are three possible problems with setting a good boundary. The first problem is that I can set my boundary too tight so no one can enter my life when they need to do so. Think what would happen if I told the people of that church they could not call me at all after midnight. By setting a boundary that rigid, I would be shutting them out from receiving pastoral care when they may really need it.

When I think of a boundary that is too tight, I think of what would have happened if I did not go with the State Patrol officer to tell a family that a family member was killed that night in a car accident. Because that accident and home visit occurred after midnight, that family would have missed out on pastoral support during one of the worst times of their lives if I had set a boundary that was too tight.

Not only can boundaries be too tight; they can also be too loose. A boundary that is too loose is the same as not having a boundary at all. That would mean everyone would have access to my life for any reason at any time. A loose boundary would allow people who should not have access to my life into my day. The result of a too loose boundary is that people who need to be kept out of my life or have limited access to it are not kept out.

Again, the issue with boundaries is respect. With good boundaries, people who really do need access in my life can have it. With too loose boundaries, many people have too much access to my life. With too tight boundaries, people who really need to be in my life are kept out.

When I have been hurt and am waiting to see if the one who hurt me really did repent, I need to have just right boundaries to afford both of us opportunities to repair the relationship. If all goes well in repairing the relationship, I can open the boundary wider so I can enjoy a relationship with that person again. If the repair goes badly, I can tighten the boundary to limit the amount of future damage they may bring to my life. If I have too tight of a boundary because of my heart hurt, the person my never have the opportunity to demonstrate repentance and their desire to rebuild the relationship.

There is so much I could say about boundaries, but I can't say it all in one letter. If you have more questions about boundaries, give me a call, and read Cloud and Townsend's marvelous book *Boundaries*, a book about how to set good boundaries.

I love you,
Dad

My Heart Response to Suffering

1. As you think back over your recent hurt, did your lack of boundaries or a too tight boundary contribute to how the hurt happened? Why or why not?
2. After reading this letter, what boundary style do you typically have in your life? Too tight? Too loose? Just right? What is an example of a boundary in your life that shaped your answer to the question?
3. What adjustments do you need to make to the boundaries currently in place in your life? How will making those adjustments help your relationships with other people?
4. How does having a just right boundary allow for repentance and repairing a relationship to occur? With whom do you need to have a just right boundary? How will making that adjustment benefit your relationship with that person?

Letter 39

THANKFULNESS IN SUFFERING

Dear Bethany,

There is one last lesson about suffering I want to pass on to you. It's the lesson of being thankful in suffering. (I can see you rolling your eyes even as I type!) I know that suffering and thankfulness are strange bedfellows. And I know you are likely thinking, "Dad, that's impossible. Don't be silly thinking they go together." I suspect that is what you are thinking, so let me explain myself.

Remember in middle school youth group when we challenged the senior high youth group to a Bible Bowl quiz on 1 Thessalonians? As part of that challenge, I taught you and your friends 1 Thessalonians for five weeks before quiz day. In preparation for the last lesson, I faced a verse I always found difficult to apply. "Give thanks in all circumstances; for this is the will of God in Christ Jesus for you" (1 Thess. 5:18). In all circumstances? Seriously? Really? Yes, that is what the verse says. "In all circumstances" means just what it says, that in suffering we need to learn to give thanks. How do we do that? Let me pass on what I learned by studying that verse.

So how do you give thanks in your suffering? Here are three actions you can take to make that possible. First, begin each day with thanksgiving for your relationship with Christ. I will not say much about this because I already discussed it when I wrote about Romans 5:1. You have peace with God because Jesus died for you, and you placed your faith in him. The result of your faith is that you are declared not guilty (the meaning of justified), and that courtroom verdict came through your faith, not working for it or earning it.

Second, even in suffering, be thankful for what you know is coming—the return of Christ. In Romans 5:2, Paul writes of our hope of the glory of God. Hope carries the idea of anticipation, not wishful thinking. An example of this is Titus 2:13—"waiting for our blessed hope, the appearing of the glory of our great God and Saviour Jesus Christ." There is no suffering you experience that prevents the second coming of Christ from happening. Thus, you can be thankful, even in your suffering.

Third, in suffering, be thankful that God is always at work in your life. Romans 5:3–4 tells us that in suffering, God is not letting you stay the same as you are. Instead, God uses suffering to produce three effects in your life. He uses suffering to teach you perseverance. Perseverance is learning to hold onto him no matter what. Instead of letting the suffering turn you away from God, the great temptation of suffering I wrote about in an earlier letter, you hold onto him all the more.

God uses suffering to produce in you a changed character. Suffering forces you to decide what kind of person you are going to be. We usually do not think about that much. But suffering makes us face ourselves, our emotions, our thoughts, and our motives in ways that prosperity does not. God uses suffering to purge our character defects. He uses suffering to show us where our faith is weak in places where it needs to be strong.

He also uses suffering to give us hope. The hope is being a different person when the suffering is over. That is seen in Romans 5:5 where Paul declares that our hope of developing perseverance and growing our hope is not disappointed because the Holy Spirit is poured into our lives. We do not face suffering alone. With the presence and aid of the Holy Spirit, we can become more loving because we suffered.

This is the way to be thankful even in suffering, Bethany. As impossible as that may seem now, it is possible as you focus on removing the two thinking errors and practice the three action steps I just described.

I promise this is possible,

Dad

My Heart Response to Suffering

1. To which of the two thinking errors presented in this letter are you vulnerable? How does this letter help you challenge and replace that thinking error?
2. Which of the three action steps to being thankful in suffering do you most need to build into your life? What is your plan for doing so? (Hint: memorizing Romans 5:1–5 might be a good way to do that.)
3. What character qualities might God want to become part of your character because of the suffering you are presently going through? How can understanding that make you thankful that your suffering is neither random nor purposeless?

AFTERWORD

Dear Reader,

I began this book by telling you I have a problem with Jesus promising us that "in this world you will have tribulation [suffering]" (John 16:33). So it is only fitting that I show you the remedy to my problem with that verse by closing this book with an even greater promise from Revelation 21:1–7.

> Then I saw a new heaven and a new earth, for the first heaven and the first earth had passed away, and the sea was no more. And I saw the holy city, new Jerusalem, coming down out of heaven from God, prepared as a bride adorned for her husband. And I heard a loud voice from the throne saying, "Behold, the dwelling place of God is with man. He will dwell with them, and they will be his people, and God himself will be with them as their God. He will wipe away every tear from their eyes, and death shall be no more, neither shall there be mourning, nor crying, nor pain anymore, for the former things have passed away."

And he who was seated on the throne said, "Behold, I am making all things new." Also he said, "Write this down, for these words are trustworthy and true." And he said to me, "It is done! I am the Alpha and the Omega, the beginning and the end. To the thirsty I will give from the spring of the water of life without payment. The one who conquers will have this heritage, and I will be his God and he will be my son."

The end of all suffering is coming, dear reader. It is coming.

Amen.

Postscript

HOW TO TRUST CHRIST AS YOUR SAVIOUR

Dear Reader,

As you read, *You'll Get through This*, you realized that much of what I told my daughter came from our shared faith in Jesus Christ. It is the foundation of our lives. But it may not be the foundation of your life.

But if these letters stirred something new in your life and you realize your foundation for living does not meet the challenges suffering brings, you may now consider your need for Jesus Christ as your Saviour. But you may not know how to make that happen. To help you trust Jesus as your Saviour, here is what you need to know and do.

First, you need to know that whatever form your suffering takes in your life, your bigger problem is your sins. I know that sin and sins are old-fashioned words and even out of favor, but what they mean is that you have broken God's laws, his commands (think of the Ten Commandments with their statements of do not lie or do not covet what other people have). Breaking God's laws and commands makes us sinners. Sinner does not define you compared to other people, but it describes your standing before the holy God. You are truly guilty before him. So the first step to trusting Christ as your Saviour is to admit you are a sinner.

Second, you need to know you cannot fix the problem of being a sinner before a holy God on your own. Paul explains why. "For all have sinned and fall short of the glory of God" (Rom. 3:23). Because you have sinned, you miss the mark of attaining the same moral character as God. The Bible says that "by works of the law no one will be justified" (Gal. 2:16). Not being justified by works of the law means we cannot measure up to God's holiness by our efforts to keep his law or commands. We simply cannot be as good as he is. All your hopes to be good enough to get into heaven or to measure up to his holiness are in vain. You cannot do it.

Third, because you cannot measure up, Christ died for you as your substitute. Romans 5:8 says, "But God shows his love for us in that while we were still sinners, Christ died for us." The word *for* in that verse means on your behalf, or as your substitute. Christ died on the cross to take your place so you would not have to face God's anger and judgment for your sins. Instead, Christ is "the propitiation [a sacrifice that satisfies God's anger] for our sins, and not for ours only but also for the sins of the whole world" (1 John 2:2). Wherever you are at, Christ died to be the sacrifice that lifts God's anger at your sins from you.

Fourth, your response to these first three realities is to believe and receive Christ as your Saviour. John, the follower of Christ, said, "But to all who did receive him, who believed in his name, he gave the right to become the children of God, who were born, not of blood nor of the will of the flesh nor of the will of man, but of God" (John 1:12–13). To believe in his name means you understand who Jesus is—your substitute—and what he did for you—he died for your sins—so you receive him as your Saviour. Receiving him as your Saviour means you reach out and take him as the one who takes your sins away and gives you God's forgiveness for all of them.

How do you do that? You can do that by saying to God, "I realize I am a sinner and guilty before you as a holy God. I realize I can never be good enough not to be a sinner. But I believe that Jesus Christ died for me to take away my sins and to bring your forgiveness into my life. So, I welcome him into my life as my Saviour. Because of what Jesus did for me, forgive me my sins, and give me all you have for me as your child."

When you pray that from your heart in the simple faith all of that is true, you pass from being a sinner to God's child, you pass from death to eternal life, you pass from guilt into forgiveness. Welcome to the family, dear reader. Welcome.

If you believed in Christ as your Saviour through reading this book, please contact me at drbarrygridley@gmail.com and I will send you some information to help you get started in your new life as a Christ follower.

REFERENCES AND RESOURCES

All the diagrams in this book are replicas of diagrams I draw on the whiteboard in my office as I explain them to my clients. I hope you find them as helpful as my clients tell me they are for them.

Books for the Head

Alcorn, Randy. *If God Is Good*. Colorado Springs: Multnomah Books, 2009.

Cloud, Henry, and John Townsend. *Boundaries*. Grand Rapids: Zondervan Publishing House, 1992.

Feinberg, John S. *Theologies and Evil*. Lanham: University of America Press, 1979.

Howard, Deborah. *Where Is God in All of This?* Phillipsburg: P & R, 2009.

Keller, Timothy. *Walking with God through Pain and Suffering*. New York: Penguin Books, 2013.

Kreeft, Peter. *Making Sense Out of Suffering*. Ann Arbor: Servant Books, 1986.

Langberg, Diane. *Redeeming Power: Understanding Authority and Abuse in the Church*. Grand Rapids, MI: Brazos Press, 2020.

Lewis, C. S. *The Problem of Pain.* New York: Macmillan, 1962.

Piper, John, and Justin Taylor. *Suffering and the Sovereignty of God.* Wheaton: Crossway Books, 2006.

Shapiro, Francine. *Eye Movement Desensitization and Reprocessing (EMDR) Therapy, 3rd Edition.* New York: Guilford Press, 2018.

Shapiro, Francine. *Getting Past Your Past.* New York: Rodale Books, 2013.

van der Kolk, Bessell. *The Body Keeps the Score.* New York: Penguin Books, 2015.

Yancey, Philip. *Where Is God when It Hurts?* Grand Rapids: Zondervan Publishing House, 1977.

Yancey, Philip. *Disappointment with God.* Grand Rapids: Zondervan Publishing House, 1988.

Books for the Heart

Card, Michael: *Sacred Sorrow.* Colorado Springs: NavPress, 2005.

Cairns, Scott. *The End of Suffering.* Brewster: Paraclete Press, 2009.

Elliott, Elizabeth. *A Path through Suffering.* Grand Rapids: Revell, 1990.

Eswine, Zach. *Spurgeon's Sorrows.* Ross-Shire: Christian Focus, 2014.

Feinberg, John S. *When There Are No Easy Answers.* Grand Rapids: Kregel, 2016.

Lloyd-Jones, D. Martyn. *Spiritual Depression: Its Causes and Cures.* Grand Rapids: Wm. B. Eerdmans, 1965.

Swinton, John: *Raging with Compassion.* Grand Rapids: Wm. B. Eerdmans, 2007.

Vroegop, Mark, and Joni Eareckson Tada. *Dark Clouds, Deep Mercy.* Grand Rapids: Crossway, 2019.

Books for Both the Head and Heart

Allen, Ronald B. *Praise! A Matter of Life and Breath*. Nashville: Thomas Nelson. 1980.

Allender, Dan B. *The Wounded Heart*. Colorado Springs: NavPress, 1990.

Allender, Dan B., and Traci Mullins. *Healing the Wounded Heart*. Grand Rapids: Baker Books, 2016.

Allender, Dan B., and Cathy Loerzel. *Redeeming Heartache*. Grand Rapids: Zondervan, 2021.

Allender, Dan B., and Tremper Longman III. *Cry of the Soul*. Colorado Springs: NavPress, 1994.

Brand, Paul, and Philip Yancey. *Pain: The Gift Nobody Wants*. New York: Harper Collins, 1993.

Crab, Larry. *Shattered Dreams*. Colorado Springs: Waterbrook Press, 2001.

Crabb, Larry. *A Different Kind of Happiness*. Grand Rapids: Baker Books, 2016.

Crabb, Larry. *When God's Ways Make No Sense*. Grand Rapids: Baker Books, 2018.

Crabb, Larry. *Waiting for Heaven*. Denver: Larger Story Press, 2020.

Crabb, Larry, and Dan B. Allender. *Hope when You're Hurting*. Grand Rapids: Zondervan Publishing House, 1996.

Johnson, David, and Jeff van Vonderen. *The Subtle Power of Spiritual Abuse*. Bloomington: Bethany House Publishers, 1991.

Kapic, Kelly. *Embodied Hope*. Downers Grove: IVP Academic, 2017.

Kolber, Aundi. *Try Softer*. Carol Stream: Tyndale, 2020.

Kolber, Aundi. *Strong Like Water*. Carol Stream: Tyndale, 2023.

Langberg, Diane. *Suffering and the Heart of God*. Greensboro: New Growth Press, 2015.

MacDonald, G. *Ordering Your Private World*. Nashville: Thomas Nelson Publishers, 1984.

McKay, Matthew, Martha Davis, and Patrick Fanning. *Thoughts and Feelings, Third Edition*. Oakland: New Harbinger Publications, 2007.

Ramsey, K. J. *This Too Shall Last*. Grand Rapids: Zondervan Reflective, 2020.

Ramsey, K. J. *The LORD Is My Courage*. Grand Rapids: Zondervan Reflective, 2022.

Savary, Louis M., and Patricia H. Berne. *Seven Stages of Suffering: A Spiritual Path for Transformation*. Mawah: Paulist Press, 2015.

Schaeffer, Edith. *Affliction*. Grand Rapids: Baker Book House, 1993.

Tchividjian, Tullian. *Glorious Ruin: How Suffering Sets You Free*. Colorado Springs: David C. Cook, 2012.

Thompson, Curt. *Anatomy of the Soul of Desire*. Carol Stream: Tyndale Momentum, 2010.

Thompson, Curt. *The Soul of Shame*. Downers Grove: IVP Press, 2015.

Thompson, Curt. *The Soul of Desire*. Downers Grove: IVP Press, 2021.

Thompson, Curt. *The Deepest Place*. Grand Rapids: Zondervan Reflective, 2023.

Tripp, Paul David. *Suffering*. Wheaton: Crossway Books, 2018.

Wilson, Sandra D. *Released from Shame*. Downers Grove: IVP Press, 1990.

The Puritans

Bridge, William. *A Lifting Up for the Downcast*. Carlisle: The Banner of Truth Trust, 1979.

Brooks, Thomas. *An Ark for All God's Noahs*. Carlisle: The Banner of Truth Trust, 2020.

Brooks, Thomas. *The Mute Christian under the Smarting Rod*. Hail & Fire, 2011.

Burroughs, Jeremiah. *Hope*. Orlando: Soli Deo Gloria Publications, 2005.

Burroughs, Jeremiah. *The Rare Jewel of Christian Contentment*. Carlisle: The Banner of Truth, Trust, 2022.

Cosby, Brian H. *Suffering and Sovereignty: John Flavel and the Puritans on Afflictive Sovereignty*. Grand Rapids. Reformation Heritage Books, 2012.

Flavel, John. *Facing Grief*. Carlisle: The Banner of Truth Trust, 2010.

Flavel, John. *Keeping the Heart*. Morgan: Soli Deo Gloria Publications, 2005.

Flavel, John. *Preparations for Sufferings*. Carlisle: The Banner of Truth Trust, 2021.

Gurnall, William. *The Christian in Complete Armour*. Peabody: Hendrickson Publishers Marketing, 2010. (Note this is also available in an edited three-volume edition from Banner of Truth Trust or in a daily reading devotional from Moody Press.)

Sibbes, Richard. *The Bruised Reed*. Carlisle: The Banner of Truth Trust, 2021.

Sibbes, Richard. *The Saints' Comforts in the Works of Richard Sibbes, Vol. 6*. Carlisle: The Banner of Truth Trust, 1983.

Symonds, Joseph. *The Case and Cure of a Deserted Soul*. Morgan: Soli Deo Gloria Publications, 1996.

Watson, Thomas. *A Divine Cordial*. Grand Rapids: Christian Classics Ethereal Library, n.d.

Watson, Thomas. *Art of Divine Contentment*. Grand Rapids: Christian Classics Ethereal Library, n.d.

ABOUT THE AUTHOR

Author Barry Gridley is a native of Omaha, Nebraska, but has lived in Oregon for 23 years with Pamela, his wife of 50 years. He is the father of Amy and Tim, father-in-law to Adam, and granddad to Elijah, Isaiah, and Emma. Barry holds a Master of Theology from Western Seminary in Portland, Oregon and a Doctor of Ministry in Marriage and Family Therapy from Denver Seminary in Littleton, Colorado.

Dr. Gridley wrote, *You'll Get through This*, from his own experience with suffering and from 20 years as the pastor of three churches and another 20 years as a professional counselor who daily sits across from hurting people. His 40 years of helping people "get through this" is the foundation for this book that provides the foundation you need when you enter a season of suffering in your life.